T5-AGC-714

8th Edition

BUSINESS PRINCIPLES & MANAGEMENT

Kenneth E. Everard
Professor of Business
Trenton State College
Trenton, New Jersey

Jim Burrow
Associate Professor of Marketing
University of Northern Iowa
Cedar Falls, Iowa

G29

Published by
SOUTH-WESTERN PUBLISHING CO.

CINCINNATI WEST CHICAGO, ILL. DALLAS PELHAM MANOR, N.Y. PALO ALTO, CALIF.

ISBN: 0-538-07290-3

Library of Congress Catalog Card Number: 83-50491

5 6 D 9 8 7

Printed in the United States of America

This book has been reviewed and awarded the exclusive endorsement of Professional Secretaries International® for the PSI Office Opportunities Model Curriculum for Secondary Business Education.

PREFACE

For long-standing success in the business world as either an employee or an owner, it is essential for one to have a deep interest in business affairs and a basic knowledge of business operations. The broad purpose of *Business Principles & Management*, Eighth Edition, is to present the student with a solid foundation about what business is, how it operates, and how it is managed. The materials presented are designed to facilitate the accomplishment of the following basic goals:

- Aid students in acquiring a vocabulary of business terms.
- Provide students with an understanding of the many activities, problems, and decisions involved in operating a business successfully.
- Give students an appreciation of the importance of business in our economy.
- Assist students in deciding on specific career objectives from among the great number of employment opportunities in the business world.
- Provide students with facts, procedures, and concepts that will aid them in becoming effective members of the business community.

A basic understanding of business principles and management is needed by everyone who plans a career in business. For this reason, this book is written especially for students who:

- Will enter business as beginning employees.
- Will return to the classroom after having gained some business experience.
- Will eventually have an opportunity to manage a business for others.
- Will eventually own and operate their own businesses.
- Are exploring the possibility of a career in business.

Those who are familiar with the Seventh Edition will see that some organizational changes have been made in this Eighth Edition. Its organization has been somewhat modified by the addition of several new chapters, the combination of some chapters, and the reorganization of other chapters. The basic general organization of the Seventh Edition has been retained, however. There are still 25 chapters organized around 7 major units that stress principal themes or functions of business.

All of the units have been updated in terms of facts and figures. In addition, new concepts and ideas have been introduced where appropriate. One of the major changes in this Eighth Edition appears in Unit 3, Production and Marketing. The unit was greatly reorganized. A new introductory chapter, Product Planning and Production, reveals the critical relationships between the producer, distributor, and consumer in the world of business.

A second major change in this edition occurs within Unit 5, Communications. Chapter 19, The Automated Office, covers both data processing and word processing. The automated office is examined carefully, especially as it contributes to improved office productivity.

Valuable learning aids are presented throughout the text to capture and retain student interest. Each unit begins with an overview and a biographical profile of a successful business person. The seven business leaders selected for the profiles serve as role models from the various fields of business that the text covers. This edition also introduces specialized Career Capsules. Each Career Capsule provides an in-depth description of a specific business occupation. The capsules are enclosed in a box at the end of each chapter.

Valuable learning aids also appear in every chapter. At the beginning of each chapter, several clear-cut objectives are listed to guide students as they read. To further aid the learning process, carefully designed exercises are presented at the end of each chapter. These exercises begin with easy review questions and proceed gradually to realistic application problems and cases, many of which generate interesting and lively discussions. Because the case problems have successfully stimulated a high degree of student participation, many chapters now include three case problems. In addition, Achievement Tests and Study Guides and Problems are available as additional supplementary learning aids for users of this text.

We are deeply indebted to the dedicated teachers and business people whose helpful suggestions over the years have contributed much to the evolution of this book and wish that space would permit recognizing each by name.

Kenneth E. Everard

Jim Burrow

CONTENTS

UNIT 1 BUSINESS AND ITS ENVIRONMENT

UNIT 2 BUSINESS OWNERSHIP

PRODUCTION AND MARKETING

UNIT 3

FINANCE

UNIT 4

ACKNOWLEDGMENTS

For permission to reproduce the photographs on the pages indicated, acknowledgment is made to the following:

Cover	Satellite dish— © Cheryl Rossum, 1981; trucks—Consolidated Freightways, Inc.; laser—photo by Arnold Zann; Federal Reserve building— © Bob Llewellyn; Penzoil Plaza— © Bill Farrell; chip—photo courtesy of TRW Inc.
2	Courtesy of Newsweek
37	CADAM®
47	Margin photo—U.S. Postal Service
52	Merck & Co., Inc.
65	Photo courtesy of American Airlines
86	Courtesy of the Famous Amos Chocolate Chip Cookie Corporation
123	Courtesy of Exxon Corporation
124	Courtesy of Proctor & Gardner Advertising, Inc.
132	Photo courtesy of Unimation Inc.
149	NCR Corporation
167	Association of American Railroads
170	Photo courtesy of Interlake, Inc.
193	First Interstate Bancorp
203	HUD photo
220	Courtesy of American Express Company
230	Photo courtesy of Marine Midland Bank, N.A.
256	© Chris Cross/UNIPHOTO
264	Reproduced with permission of A.T.&T. Co.
331	American Red Cross photo
348	Courtesy of Advanced Office Concepts Corporation
372	Burroughs Corporation
373	Upper left photo—Verbatim Corporation; all other photos—Photographs courtesy of BASF Systems Corporation
383	Photo courtesy of All-Steel
389	Kerr-McGee Corporation
390	Courtesy of Wang Laboratories, Inc.
439	Photo courtesy of Bonne Bell
443	Library of Congress photo
454	United States Department of Agriculture
456	United Auto Workers photo
468	Courtesy of Apple Computer, Inc.
471	Courtesy of Kentucky Fried Chicken

UNIT 1

Business and Its Environment

Each of us must learn to live with others—with our families, friends, and neighbors. We learn to adjust to the world around us—to our schools, our government, and our work environment. Like people, business firms must learn to cooperate with others—with customers, employees, and other business firms. Each business must also operate within an environment that includes a social system, a legal system, and an economic system.

Unit 1 explains some of the highlights of our business system and its surrounding environment. Included is a study of how business contributes to our well-being as individual consumers and as a nation. In addition, social, economic, and legal principles that affect business operations are included along with some of the problems with which a business must deal.

One of the social concerns of business is to educate everyone about the business world. Jane Bryant Quinn, whose biographical profile appears on the next page, is one person on the business scene today who has contributed significantly to improving everyone's knowledge about economic matters affecting businesses and consumers.

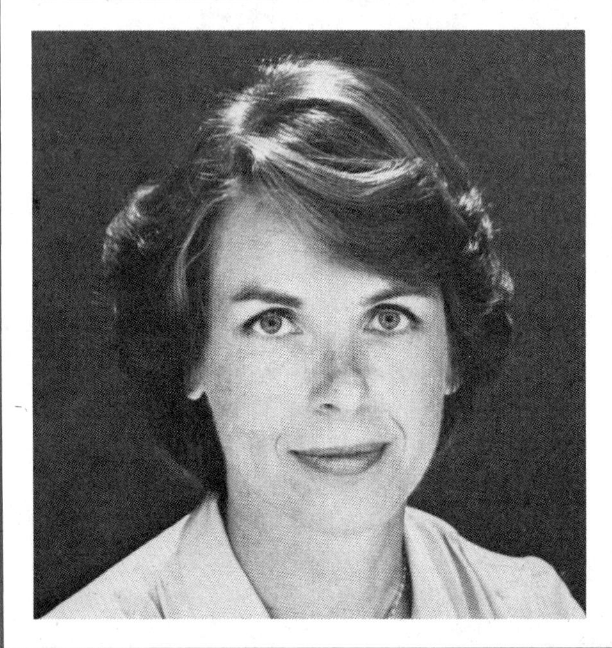

JANE BRYANT QUINN

It is difficult to write about complicated money matters in an interesting, straightforward, and understandable style; but Jane Bryant Quinn has become a household name by doing just that. She regularly discusses current business events on a popular television network. In addition, she explores financial topics in her regular columns that appear in *Newsweek* and *Woman's Day* magazines and in columns distributed nationally to over 130 newspapers through the *Washington Post*.

Perhaps Ms. Quinn is most widely known for her highly informative *Everyone's Money Book*, which is a complete guide to personal finance. She is a nationally recognized expert on how to manage one's personal money matters during difficult financial times. She is as comfortable discussing financial and economic problems with business people as she is with consumers.

Jane Bryant Quinn launched her professional career by writing about money matters. Soon after graduating from Middlebury College with honors, she became co-editor of a consumer newsletter. Later, she built her reputation as editor of a sophisticated financial-planning newsletter that was widely distributed to executives. For her clear and easy-to-read reporting of consumer and business news, Ms. Quinn received numerous awards and is listed in *Who's Who in America*.

While maintaining an extremely busy writing and speaking schedule, Ms. Quinn also has a family. She is married to an attorney and is the mother of two sons. She continually fulfills her ambition, educating people about business through writing and speaking about money management to today's generation.

1

CHARACTERISTICS OF BUSINESS

After studying this chapter you will be able to:

- Explain the changing nature of business.
- Show how business has improved the economic well-being of people.
- Discuss the role of small businesses in relation to large businesses.
- List some of the reasons why businesses fail.
- Explain the importance of studying business principles and management.

Over 15 million businesses exist in the United States today. They vary in size from one employee to more than 700,000 employees, and in assets from a few dollars to over $60 billion. Some of these businesses have only a few customers, while others have millions of customers located throughout the world.

These vast differences make the story of American business fascinating. Small businesses operate successfully alongside giant corporations. Products found in most homes come from countless producers. The flowering plant in the window could have been purchased from a greenhouse operated by a single person. The electric light bulbs could have been made by a business with 200,000 employees, a carpet from a business with 500 employees, and a loaf of bread from a bakery with only 10 workers. These and scores of other items found in homes, offices, stores, and factories are produced by various kinds of businesses.

NATURE OF BUSINESS

An organization that produces or distributes a good or service is called a **business**. Every business engages in at least three major activities. The first activity, **production**, involves making a product or providing a service. The second activity is marketing. **Marketing** deals with how a good or service gets from the producer to the user. The third activity, **finance**, deals with all money matters related to running a business. Whether a business has one worker or one million workers, it is involved with production, marketing, and finance.

This book focuses on the various activities that lead to business success. But before examining those activities in detail, it is necessary to study the general nature of business.

Types of Businesses

Generally speaking, there are two major kinds of businesses—industrial and commercial. **Industrial businesses** are businesses that produce things. Mining, manufacturing, and construction are types of industrial businesses. **Commercial businesses** are engaged in marketing (wholesalers and retailers), in finance (banks and investment companies), and in furnishing services (transportation, electric power, motels, theaters, and the like).

An indication of the importance of the major types of businesses is shown in Illus. 1–1. The graph shows the number of persons employed in each of seven types of businesses. Not included are farmers, military personnel, and government workers.

Changing Nature of Business

An important characteristic of business is that it is dynamic, or constantly changing. Businesses react quickly to the changing nature of society. For instance, the principal means of transportation for centuries had been by horse until steam power was invented and created change. By 1869 the first cross-country railroad was completed. For about 50 years, goods and people traveled mainly by rail. Then the gasoline engine arrived. Travel patterns shifted from train to car, bus, and truck. Shortly thereafter, the airplane was invented. The slow 100-mile-an-hour planes were quickly replaced by jets which cross the country carrying people and goods in a matter of a few hours.

Similar changes are visible in other industries. For many centuries only natural fibers such as wool and cotton were used for making clothing and assorted products. As a result of chemical research, synthetic fibers—rayon, nylon, dacron, orlon, and polyester—were developed and are now used to make clothing, carpets, and many other products.

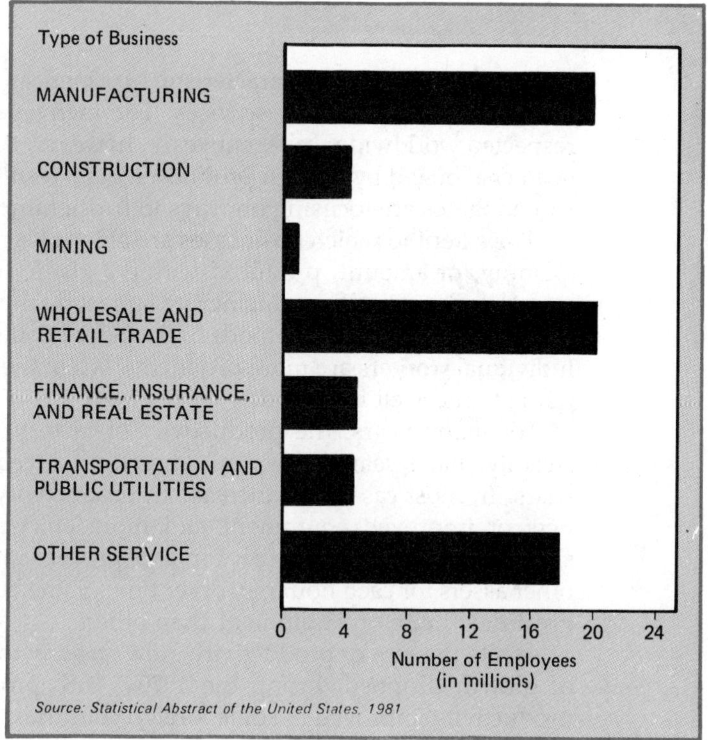

ILLUS. 1–1
Employment in major types of businesses.

Not only have changes occurred in the products made and the services offered, but changes have also taken place in the way businesses operate. Marketing methods involving buying, selling, advertising, and shipping goods, for example, have changed in recent decades and will continue to change.

The dynamic nature of business is also indicated by the major changes that have taken place in selected categories of businesses over the years. As shown in Illus. 1–2, the number of businesses in each of the four categories has increased since 1950. However, some increased at faster rates than others. In particular, service-type businesses have multiplied so swiftly that they now far outnumber manufacturing and trading (wholesale and retail) businesses.

ILLUS. 1–2
Growth in number of selected types of businesses.

Type of Business	1950	1960	1970	1977
Manufacturing	321,000	406,000	409,000	483,000
Wholesale Trade	266,000	464,000	470,000	574,000
Retail Trade	1,816,000	1,907,000	2,210,000	2,459,000
Services	736,000	2,246,000	2,964,000	4,046,000

Source: Statistical Abstract of the United States, 1973, 1977, and 1981.

Business Efficiency

Another important characteristic of American business is its efficiency in producing goods and services. For many years, that efficiency was respected worldwide. In recent years, however, American businesses have been challenged by foreign producers. As a result, business leaders in the United States are focusing on ways to further improve business efficiency.

The extent to which businesses are efficient is measured by **output**—the quantity, or amount, produced within a given time. **Productivity**, on the other hand, refers to producing the largest quantity in the least amount of time by using efficient methods and modern equipment at the lowest cost. Individual workers are more productive when they are well equipped, well trained, and well managed.

For many years, the productivity of factory and office workers grew steadily. Each year the typical worker produced more than in previous years. In most cases, the increase in productivity was the result of using new or improved equipment and more efficient techniques. Illus. 1–3 shows how selected industries in a given year invested in machinery and other assets for each hour of worker time. Some businesses need to spend a great deal more on equipment than others.

While the rate of productivity grew steadily for many decades, the rate of growth dropped during the 1970s. U.S. productivity declined while productivity improved in some foreign countries, particularly Japan. When

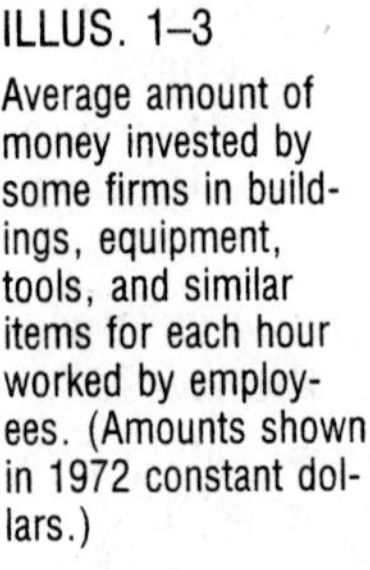

ILLUS. 1–3

Average amount of money invested by some firms in buildings, equipment, tools, and similar items for each hour worked by employees. (Amounts shown in 1972 constant dollars.)

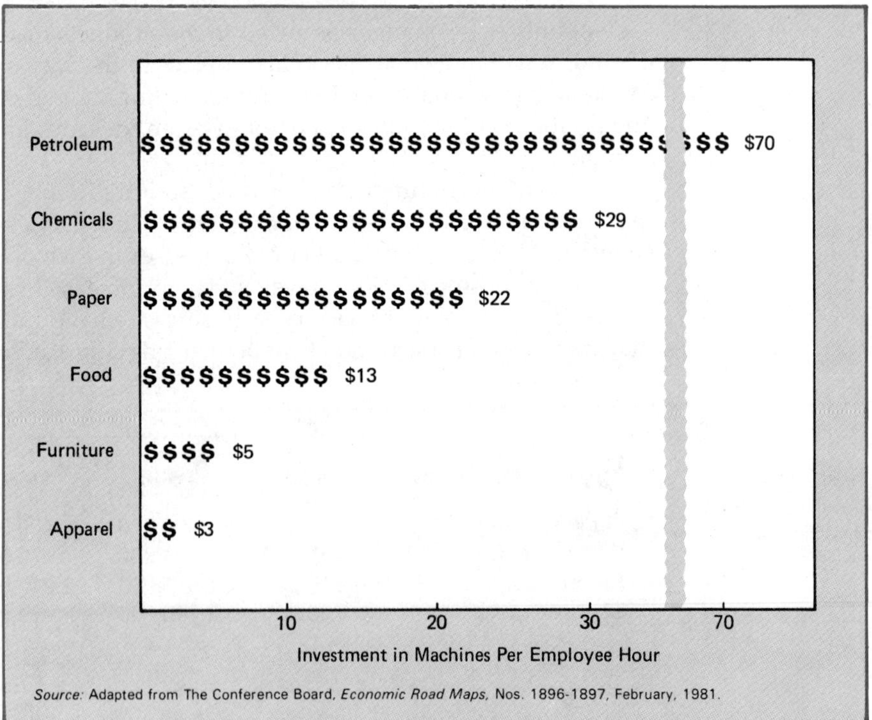

Source: Adapted from The Conference Board, *Economic Road Maps,* Nos. 1896-1897, February, 1981.

foreign firms began selling goods, such as cars and computers, in the United States at lower prices than similar goods made in this country, American businesses began reviewing ways to further improve output. As a result of this review, productivity rates for the early 1980s rose somewhat. Productivity can generally be improved in one of two ways—specialization and mass production.

Specialization. In any business with more than a few employees, it is desirable to have workers become specialists. For example, not all workers are general mechanics in a large automobile repair shop. Rather, some workers will specialize in body repair work while others will specialize in repairing transmissions or engines. When workers specialize, they become more expert at what they do. As a result, specialization can improve quality while increasing the amount produced. Because specialization improves efficiency, it is no wonder that businesses hire or train employees for many specialized jobs.

ILLUS. 1–4
Specialization improves worker efficiency.

Mass Production. Productivity can also be improved through mass production. **Mass production** is the use of up-to-date equipment and assembly line methods to produce large quantities of identical goods. Through mass production, the cost of goods manufactured decreases because it is possible to produce more items in less time. Today, the use of electronically driven equipment, including computers and robots, makes it possible to mass-produce large numbers of items with fewer workers.

Business Growth and Prosperity

Much of America's prosperity has been due to business growth. Around the world, people have admired and envied this country's economic strength. Let us look at two ways in which a nation measures its economic wealth and its benefits to citizens.

Gross National Product. The first measure of a nation's economic wealth is the gross national product. The **gross national product (GNP)** is the total market value of all goods produced and services provided in a year. Whenever a product or service is purchased, the dollar amount is recorded by the federal government. The GNP of the United States is compared from year to year, and is compared with the GNP of other countries. In this way it provides a measure of economic growth.

Certain types of transactions, however, are never included in the GNP. These transactions are not recorded because they are unlawful or do not occur as part of normal business operations. For example, when a youngster is hired to mow lawns, formal business records are not normally prepared and the income is usually unrecorded. When drugs are sold illegally, such transactions are not recorded. Income that escapes being recorded in the GNP is referred to as the **underground economy**. Business transactions that occur in the underground economy are relatively small in relation to the total GNP. However, they are large enough to concern government officials.

In a recent year, the total known and recorded GNP for the United States exceeded the staggering figure of $2.6 trillion. As can be seen from Illus. 1–5, the GNP increased by over $1.5 trillion between 1970 and 1980. And in a recent year, the GNP of the United States nearly equaled the total GNP of four major countries combined—Japan, Germany, the United Kingdom, and Italy. The rate of growth and the current size of the GNP indicate, in a rather striking way, the economic growth of the United States.

Individual Well-Being. A second measure of a nation's wealth is the individual well-being of its citizens. While GNP figures are helpful in judging the overall growth of a nation, such figures by themselves tell little about the economic worth of individuals. However, the U.S. Department of Commerce has gathered information that reveals the financial well-being of U.S. citizens.

Family income has increased steadily, with the average yearly family income currently over $21,000—much more than it was a decade ago. With increased income, the average family has improved its level of living. Today nearly two thirds of all families live in homes they own. As shown in Illus. 1–6 on page 10, items that were once considered luxuries are now owned by many families. Three out of four households have one or more cars, and almost all households have televisions and refrigerators. In

ILLUS. 1–5
Growth in GNP since 1900.

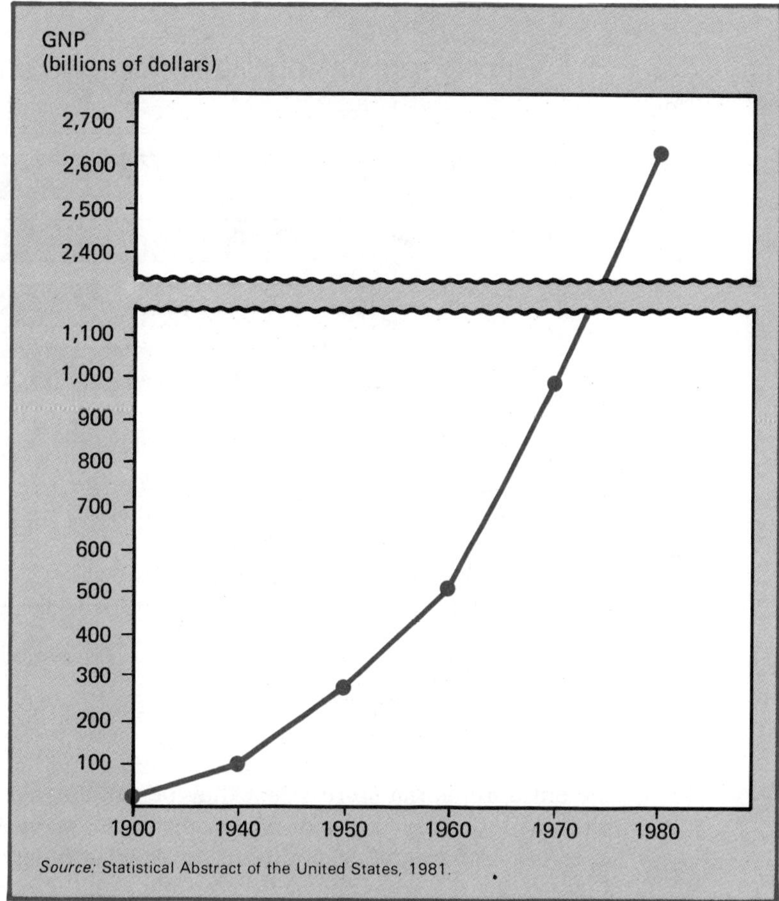

Source: Statistical Abstract of the United States, 1981.

addition, Americans have invested large sums of money in education, with many adults having some education beyond high school. Further, individuals have invested in life-enrichment activities by traveling in this country and abroad. Despite these large expenditures on material goods and services, Americans saved over $100 billion in a recent year.

ENTREPRENEURSHIP

The successful growth of business in the United States happened as a result of many factors. The strong desire by many individuals to own their own businesses and the ease with which one can start a business are two reasons for business growth. One who organizes, manages, and assumes the risks of a business is called an **entrepreneur.**

Thousands of people decide each year to become entrepreneurs by starting their own small firms. However, large businesses also encourage

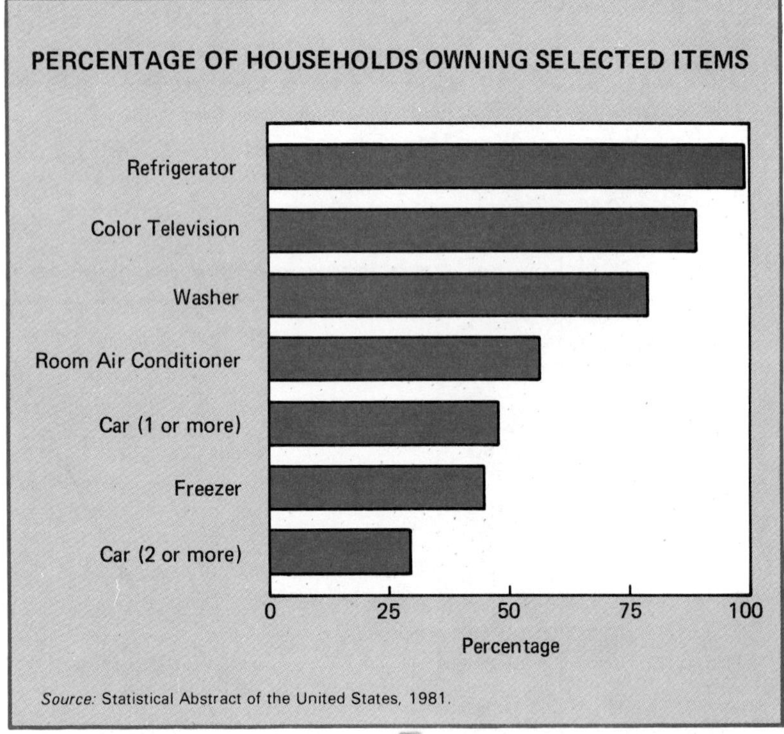

ILLUS. 1–6
Families buy cars and appliances with their income.

the entrepreneurial spirit when they permit creative employees to experiment with the development of new products, services, or ideas that might later become profitable additions to regular business operations. Small successful companies that wish to grow rapidly by expanding operations may also form new companies to do so. While these types of ventures by existing companies contribute to the growth of American business, the large majority of new ventures start as small, independently owned businesses.

Popularity of Small Business

It has been the tradition of this country to encourage individuals to become entrepreneurs. Government controls, for example, are rather limited in order to promote the formation of new businesses. Almost anyone who wishes may start a business. Therefore, a large number of new firms are organized yearly.

Small business is the term applied to any type of business that is operated by one or a few individuals. Small businesses are most commonly found in the service and retail trade fields. Because it is costly to start a manufacturing business, only a low percentage of small firms produce goods. Most small businesses employ less than 100 people, as shown in

Illus. 1–7. However, over half the total number of workers in this country are employed by small businesses. In addition, the revenue generated from all small businesses accounts for about 40 percent of the GNP.

Many of the small businesses are one-person or family operations with no additional employees. Examples include gift, tailor, florist, and beauty shops. Many businesses are also operated on a part-time or seasonal basis. Some examples include hot dog stands and souvenir shops found at popular lake and ocean vacation areas. According to the U. S. Department of Commerce, a large majority of all businesses earn less than $100,000 in yearly revenue, with many of the very small shops earning far less.

ILLUS. 1–7
More than half of the private-sector work force is employed by businesses with fewer than 100 employees.

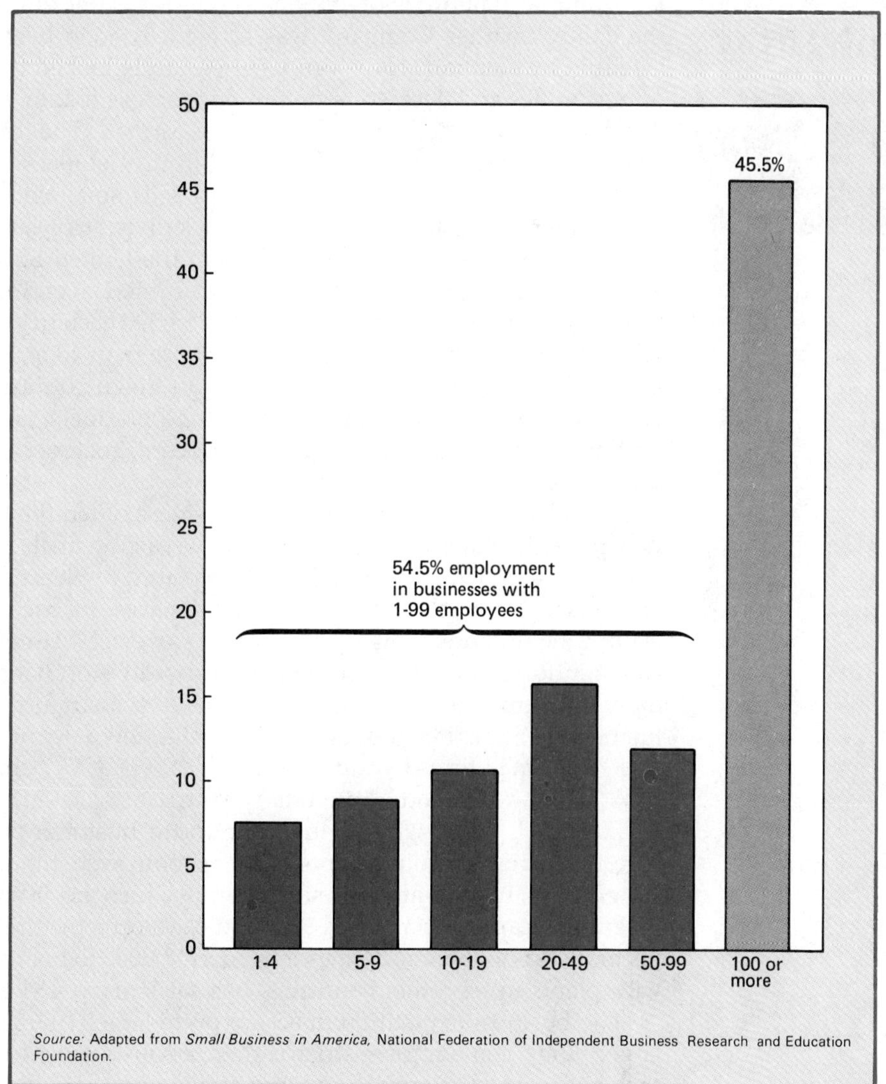

Source: Adapted from *Small Business in America,* National Federation of Independent Business Research and Education Foundation.

Growth of Small Business

Most large businesses today began as very small firms. Because they supplied products and services desired by the public and because they were well managed, they became larger and larger. A few examples include Tandy, Procter and Gamble, Sears, and Polaroid.

David L. Tandy and Norton Hinckley formed the Hinckley-Tandy Leather Company in 1923 and specialized in leather and shoe repair supplies. Mr. Tandy's son, Charles, joined the already successful company in 1948 on a full-time basis and recommended opening retail shops and launching a mail-order operation. When Mr. Hinckley left the business, the Tandy Leather Company was formed. It soon became a nationwide leader in leathercraft. However, Charles Tandy looked for other expansion opportunities and decided upon the electronics field. In 1963 the first Radio Shack electronics mail-order venture was formed. The rest is history. Since 1963, Radio Shack has grown quickly from 9 stores to more than 7,000 outlets. It operates in six countries and sells small computers as well as many other items. Today, the Radio Shack division of Tandy Corporation is one of the most successful companies in the United States.

William Procter and James Gamble formed a partnership in 1837 in Cincinnati, Ohio, with an investment of $3,500 each to start a soap-making business. Today Procter & Gamble has more than 40 manufacturing plants in the United States and 31 plants in 13 foreign countries. The company makes laundry and cleaning products, food products, and paper products. As the leading soap and detergent producer, Procter & Gamble's sales in a recent year totaled over $11 billion.

In 1886 Richard W. Sears began a business called the R. W. Sears Watch Company. Watches were sold on a small scale by mail. A short while later Alvah C. Roebuck answered a want ad placed by Sears for a watchmaker, and Sears, Roebuck and Co. was on its way to becoming the world's leading retail store. This retail giant has over 850 stores nationally, plus stores in foreign countries. The mail-order division handles thousands of different items. In addition, Sears operates insurance, real estate, and financial service businesses. Other well-known retail stores were also started as small firms by capable young leaders: J. C. Penney, S. S. Kresge, F. W. Woolworth, and Montgomery Ward.

Edwin H. Land was an inventor and a business person. In 1937 he organized the Polaroid Corporation on borrowed money and produced sunglasses and a glare-free study lamp which he invented. In 1947 he invented a camera that could take and develop a picture in 60 seconds. In his first year of operation, sales totaled $142,000. Today this large company, with plants in ten other countries, has sales of over $1.4 billion yearly.

The businesses just described are quite large. As business firms grow larger, they sometimes restrict certain small businesses; but more often they encourage the growth of other small businesses. For example, in 1960 there were only a few large companies producing computers. Today, hundreds of companies make various types of computers and thousands of small businesses sell and service computers. Even though computers have replaced some workers, many new businesses and new jobs have been created. Small retail firms now sell personal computers and provide supplies and parts. And many computer repair shops are operated by small businesses. Moreover, many businesses now exist that create new ways to use computers, such as developing instructions for various financial records and games. Video game establishments have also been created, which fulfill an entertainment need. Very often a major invention, such as the computer, creates many business opportunities.

ILLUS. 1–8
The U.S. government encourages the growth of small businesses.

Growth of Franchise Businesses

For the person with limited funds, but an entrepreneurial spirit, a popular way to launch a small business is through a franchise. A **franchise** is a legal agreement between a parent company and a distributor to sell a product or service under special conditions. Century 21 real estate offices and Burger King restaurants are operated by small business owners under such agreements. The two parties to a franchise agreement are the **franchisor**, the parent company of a franchise agreement that provides the product or service, and the **franchisee**, the distributor of a franchised product or service.

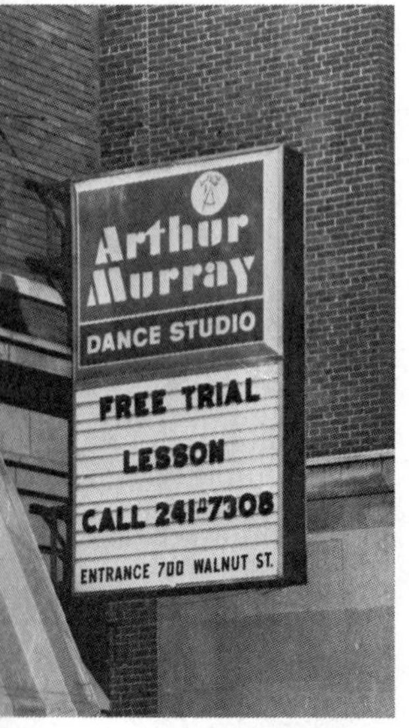

In a typical franchise agreement, the franchisee pays an initial fee and a percentage—usually 5 to 10 percent—of each month's sales to the franchisor. In return, the franchisee gets help in selecting a store site and exclusive rights to sell the franchised product or service in a specified geographical area. These services, which help to assure the success of the business, are particularly valuable to inexperienced entrepreneurs.

The franchisor also provides special training and advice in how to operate the franchise most efficiently. Therefore, a franchise business has a far greater chance of success than a firm starting on its own. While some franchises do fail, the chance of failure is much less than with a totally independent firm.

The number of franchises has grown steadily in recent years, especially in the retail area. About one third of all retail sales are made by franchise businesses, such as those listed in Illus. 1–9. The two areas in which the greatest number of franchises are found are auto and truck dealerships and gasoline service stations. However, fast-food restaurants and convenience shops such as Seven-Eleven food stores are quite popular. In recent years, franchises for service-type businesses that do not require large sums of money to get started have steadily increased in number.

ILLUS. 1–9
Many business firms are franchise operations.

The Athlete's Foot	Karmelkorn Shoppes, Inc.
Baskin-Robbins, Inc.	Kentucky Fried Chicken
Budget Rent-A-Car Systems	Key Korner Systems, Inc.
Chicken Delight	Knapp Shoe Company
Collex, Inc.	Kwik-Kopy Printing
Doctor Pet Centers, Inc.	Lawn Doctor, Inc.
Dunkin Donuts of America, Inc.	Manpower, Inc.
Edie Adams Cut & Curl	Medicine Shoppes
Empress Travel Franchise Corp.	Muzak Corp.
Firestone Tire & Rubber Co.	National Car Rental System
Go-Cart Track Systems	Ramada Inns, Inc.
Heel'N Toe, Inc.	Snap-On Tools Corp.
Howard Johnson Co.	Tidy Car
Jellystone Campgrounds, Ltd.	United Rent-All
The Jeweler's Emporium	Wendy's Old Fashioned Hamburgers

Risks of Ownership

The success of a business depends greatly on managerial effectiveness. If a business is well managed, an adequate income will likely be earned. From an adequate income, it is possible to pay all expenses and to earn a profit as well. Should a business not earn a profit, it cannot continue for long. Remember that we defined entrepreneur as one willing to assume the risks of a business. The risks and obligations of owning or managing a business are many.

Risk—the possibility of failure—is one of the characteristics of business that all entrepreneurs must face. Risk involves competition, changes in prices, changes in style, competition from new products, and changes that arise from economic conditions. Whenever risks are high, the chance of failure is also high.

Businesses close for a number of reasons. A large percentage do so because of financial failure. On the average, about 10,000 businesses fail yearly for financial reasons, as shown in Illus. 1–10. One quarter of all businesses that fail do so within three years, and over half within five years. Retail businesses usually have the highest failure rate. The causes of financial failure are shown in Illus. 1–11 on page 16. Most often businesses fail due to a lack of managerial knowledge or ability and lack of business experience.

ILLUS. 1–10
Yearly financial failures of business firms.

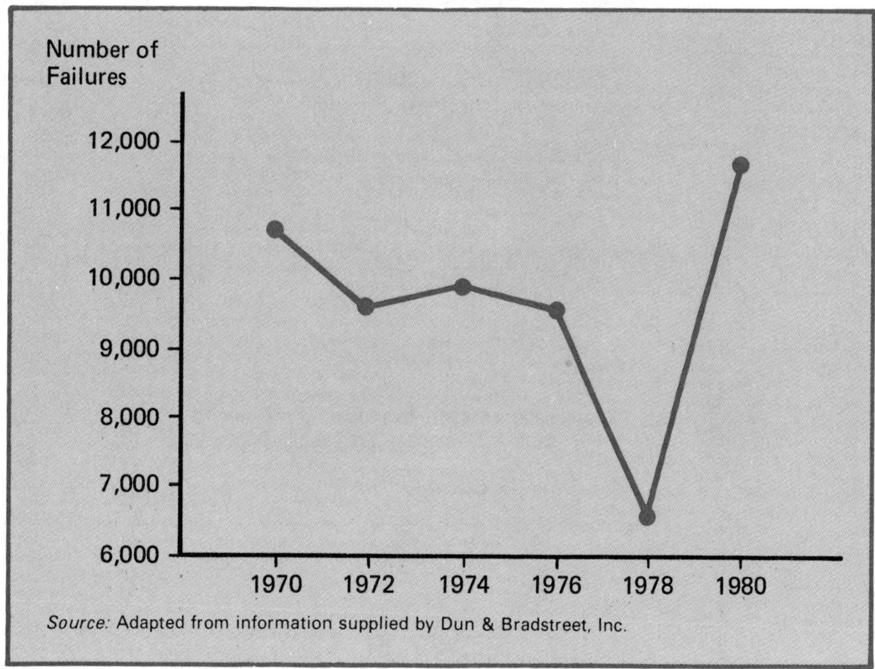

Obligations of Ownership

Anyone who starts a business has a responsibility to the entire community in which the business operates. Customers, employees, suppliers, and even competitors are affected by a single business. Therefore, a business that fails creates an economic loss that must be shared by others in society. For example, an unsuccessful business probably owes money to other firms that will also suffer a loss because they cannot collect. In fact, a business that cannot collect from several other businesses may be placed in a weakened financial condition and it, too, may fail.

ILLUS. 1–11
Causes of business failures.

Apparent Causes	Percentage of Failures	
Inadequate Sales	59.6	These failures result from lack of managerial ability, lack of experience, and lack of competence.
Competitive Weakness	23.3	
Heavy Operating Expenses	28.9	
Accounts Receivable Difficulties	9.4	
Inventory Difficulties	9.3	
Excessive Fixed Assets	3.1	
Poor Location	2.0	
Disaster: fire, flood, burglary, employees' fraud, and the like	0.5	Protection against some of these could have been provided by insurance.
Neglect due to poor health, bad habits, family difficulties, and the like	0.8	
Fraud: false financial statements, irregular disposal of assets, etc.	0.4	
Other	1.3	

Note: Because some failures are attributed to more than one cause, the total of the various percentages exceeds 100 percent.

Source: Dun & Bradstreet, Inc.

One of the executives of a major business association pointed out the following obligations of business owners:

1. TO CUSTOMERS: That they may have the best at the lowest cost, consistent with fairness to all those engaged in production and distribution.
2. TO WORKERS: That their welfare will not be sacrificed for the benefit of others, and that in their employment relations their rights will be respected.

3. TO MANAGEMENT: That it may be recognized in proportion to its demonstrated ability, considering always the interest of others.
4. TO COMPETITORS: That there will be avoidance of every form of unfair competition.
5. TO INVESTORS: That their rights will be safeguarded, and that they will be kept so informed that they can exercise their own judgment respecting their interests.
6. TO THE PUBLIC: That the business will strive in all its operations and relations to promote the general welfare and to observe faithfully the laws of the land.

Just as every business has an obligation to the community, the community has an obligation to each business. Society should be aware that business owners face many risks while trying to earn a fair profit on the investment made in the business. Consumers should realize that the prices of goods and services are affected by expenses that arise from operating a business. Employees should realize that a business cannot operate successfully, and thereby provide jobs, unless each worker is properly trained and willing to work. The economic health of a community is improved when groups in the community are aware of each other's obligations.

IMPORTANCE OF STUDYING BUSINESS PRINCIPLES AND MANAGEMENT

Whether you plan to operate a business of your own or to be an employee who expects to rise to responsible positions, you must be well informed about the production, marketing, and finance activities of a business. As an owner of a business, you must have a complete understanding of all phases of business operations, including employee relations and government regulations. In a similar manner, such understandings are also necessary if you are to be a competent employee in a specialized job or department. And, if you expect to become a department head or an executive of a company, you must fully understand how the various activities of all departments are coordinated in a smoothly operating business.

A study of business will also give you an excellent picture of the many types of jobs available and the possible path for promotions. For this reason, to assist you in your career choice, information about specific careers will be highlighted at the end of every chapter. The career capsule for this chapter is entitled, "Have You Thought About Becoming an Entrepreneur?".

NEW TERMS AND CONCEPTS

Define the following terms and concepts, which may be found in boldface type on the page shown in parentheses.

business (4)
production (4)
marketing (4)
finance (4)
industrial businesses (4)
commercial businesses (4)
output (6)
productivity (6)
mass production (7)
gross national product, or GNP (8)
underground economy (8)
entrepreneur (9)
small business (10)
franchise (13)
franchisor (13)
franchisee (13)
risk (15)

CHAPTER REVIEW

1. About how many businesses of all kinds are there in the United States?
2. What three activities do all businesses perform?
3. Which two types of businesses, shown in Illus. 1–1, employ the most workers?
4. Which type of business has grown so rapidly that it now outnumbers both manufacturing and trading businesses?
5. Name two techniques that have improved American business efficiency.
6. Why is the gross national product important?
7. What proof is there that the average American family is financially well off?
8. Are opportunities for going into business today many or few?
9. Give an example of how a very large business can encourage entrepreneurship.
10. How much do small businesses contribute (a) to the GNP yearly and (b) to total employment?
11. Give four examples of very large businesses that started as very small one- or two-person businesses.
12. In a typical franchise arrangement, what are the advantages to the franchisee?
13. Are franchise businesses more popular in the manufacturing or retailing area?
14. As shown in Illus. 1–11, if a business fails because of inadequate sales

and heavy operating expenses, what are the three reasons for these failures?

15. State some values to a prospective employee that should result from a study of business principles and management.

QUESTIONS FOR CLASS DISCUSSION

1. Discuss the dynamic, changing behavior of business as it applies to a product such as a wristwatch, a radio, or a television.
2. Explain what happened when U.S. productivity rates began to drop during the 1970s.
3. Discuss a plan of worker specialization for a company that makes motorcycles.
4. How might it be possible for the GNP to be larger than the amount actually reported in a given year?
5. What are two reasons for the growth of businesses in the United States?
6. What types of business firms could probably be operated by just one employee?
7. Why might a person who wishes to go into business not want to consider a franchise arrangement?
8. Give examples of risks that the owner of a gasoline service station might have.
9. A main cause of business failure is a lack of managerial ability. What steps can be taken to overcome this weakness?
10. Not only does the owner of a business have an obligation to employees, but each employee has an obligation to the employer. Mention some specific obligations that each has.

PROBLEMS AND PROJECTS

1. Compare the total of industrial types of businesses in Illus. 1–1 (manufacturing, construction, and mining) with the total of the remaining types of commercial businesses shown.
   a. What is the total employment for the industrial firms and for the commercial firms?
   b. By what percentage is the one group larger than the other?
2. Using Illus. 1–2, calculate the percentage increase in each of the types of businesses shown between 1950 and 1977. Label in your answers which of the types of business grew by the greatest and smallest percentages.
3. Estimate how much money you made from all sources during the last year (before deducting any expenses). Now estimate the amount you earned (before deducting expenses) that was probably not reported in the GNP by your employers or by you on your income taxes. Determine what percent of your total income for the last year was included in the GNP and in the underground economy.

4. Talk to the owner of a franchise business about the advantages and disadvantages of having a franchise. Also discuss the general advantages and disadvantages of being an entrepreneur. Report your findings to the class.
5. With the help of a librarian, find a recent article on productivity or on problems a U.S. company or industry may have competing with foreign countries. Read the article and make a report following the instructions of your teacher.

CASE 1–1

This is a true story about a large U.S. business. The company has been in business for over 100 years providing families with photographic equipment and supplies. By offering high-quality products and introducing timely new products, it has managed to keep its leadership position. The company has been so successful that, unlike most other firms, it does not need to borrow when it wishes to build new factories or to undertake new research efforts. Even though the company has not always been first with new products, over the years it has managed to compete successfully with other firms. In fact, the company controls most of the photographic market.

The U.S. company is facing a new period ahead, however. Foreign firms are successfully attracting some of the U.S. company's customers by offering their high-quality cameras and film at lower prices. Further, these foreign companies are also introducing new types of cameras and supplies. For example, electronic cameras that use tape and disks to replace film will be offered to customers. As if this were not enough, the future market opportunities for cameras and photographic supplies are relatively small. Growth opportunities are somewhat limited since most families already have cameras. The top managers are carefully studying the company's future.

Required:

1. What business is this story about? What foreign country, in particular is providing the most competition?
2. Is this company facing the same type of situation that the automobile producers have faced in recent years? Explain.
3. If this business is to maintain its leadership position in the years ahead, what might it consider doing?

CASE 1–2

Several weeks ago two close friends lost their jobs as a result of a slow period with the company for which they both work. They expect to be called back any day. In the meantime, they often spend their afternoons together jogging, playing tennis, or going to the nearby YMCA to play basketball. Often they just chat about different things, including how difficult it is to be without work and not making a steady income. One afternoon the following conversation took place.

Dirk: I have payments to make on my house and car. Fortunately, I paid cash for my new console TV. I hope the company calls us back to work soon.

Ken: I know what you mean, but just think. While we are out of work, we still have a pretty good deal. You have your own home and car. Lots of people in other countries have almost nothing.

Dirk: If we made a list of things that most of the workers at the factory own, how long would it be? Two cars each maybe? Two TVs, a lawnmower, . . .

Ken: Throw in radios, stereos, electric razors, and hairdryers. Everyone has furniture, clothes, telephones, washers, . . . We could go on forever.

Dirk: Don't forget the items in closets and drawers. Most people have at least one camera, a watch, a ring, . . .

Ken: You gave me an idea, Dirk. If we are not called back to work by next weekend, let's have a garage sale so we can get rid of some of the extra things we have lying around in our attics and basements. We can each raise enough money to buy new tennis racquets. We sure need them.

Dirk: Better yet, we could buy tickets to see the pros play in the big tournament coming up next month. That would be a great weekend for both of us.

Required:

1. If a garage sale is held, is it likely that the money earned would be included in the GNP? Explain.
2. Are the benefits of the U.S. business system revealed in this conversation? Explain.
3. Do you believe that most U.S. families would have the items mentioned in the conversation? Explain.
4. What items that Americans often buy were not mentioned by Dirk and Ken that show the economic well-being of Americans?

CASE 1–3

Ten years ago Paul and Chrissie Washington started a small restaurant that sold mostly seafood. The high quality of the food, fair prices, and an attractive dining room caused the business to become very successful. Two years after the first restaurant was opened they opened an identical restaurant in a nearby community, which also was successful. Today the Washingtons have five restaurants, and each is doing well.

They would like to continue opening restaurants in other communities and in other states. However, they know they cannot operate any more restaurants because even now their time is much too limited. For that reason they have been thinking about operating other restaurants under franchise agreements. Both are concerned about franchisees who might not run their restaurants exactly the way the Washingtons do.

Required:

1. Do you think operating under a franchise arrangment will work for the Washingtons? Explain.
2. Is there any way the Washingtons can control the way franchisees will run their restaurants? Explain.
3. What added responsibilities will the Washingtons have in helping the franchisees run their restaurants?

Have You Thought About Becoming . . .

. . . AN ENTREPRENEUR?

Some people would rather work for others, while others would rather be self-employed. Those who prefer self-employment enjoy the freedom and independence that comes from being their own boss and from making their own decisions. While successful entrepreneurs are all uniquely different, they also have some common characteristics. Perhaps you have the traits, knowledge, and skills that will enable you to have your own successful business.

Entrepreneurs are self-starters who have plenty of energy and like working on their own. They like to take charge of situations and usually work hard and for long periods in order to meet their goals. Entrepreneurs are also good thinkers, often coming up with new ideas and new ways to solve problems. Most successful small business owners like people and people like them. As a result, they are often community leaders.

Successful entrepreneurs have other common characteristics. Generally, they obtain work experience in the types of businesses they launch. The person who starts a computer store, for example, will usually have taken some computer courses and will have worked for a business that makes, sells, or services computers. As important as obtaining related work experience is, successful business owners are also well informed about legal, financial, marketing, and record-keeping matters.

Owners must also know a great deal about business operations if they are to avoid common mistakes that lead to failure. That is why a person with limited experience, who wants to start a business, often prefers a franchise. The franchisor provides training and sets policies and procedures that are known to be effective.

Persons of all ages start businesses. Some may have college degrees while others may have graduated recently from high school. To start your own business, you need adequate funds, a general knowledge about business, some work experience, and a business opportunity. Begin now to uncover opportunities that exist in your community.

2

SOCIAL ENVIRONMENT OF BUSINESS

After studying this chapter you will be able to:

- List some of the major social problems that affect business.
- Explain the changing nature of the population of the United States.
- Describe why business is concerned about energy and pollution problems.
- Offer examples of how the values of people have influenced business and government.
- Tell how business firms are likely to handle social problems.

In its relatively short history, the United States has attained remarkable achievements. It has moved from an agricultural community to the world's leading industrial society. Horse-drawn wagons have been replaced by diesel-engine trains, supersonic jet transport planes, and missile-powered vehicles for outer space. Technology has provided telephones, television, and telecommunications. Problems that once took teams of mathematicians months to calculate are now solved in minutes by small portable computers. And while our ancestors had few choices among goods, millions of consumers now purchase thousands of products in hundreds of varieties.

One must marvel at the accomplishments of this nation during the twentieth century alone, regardless of personal philosophy. The combination of hard-working people, a democratic form of government, and a business system that includes basic rights has produced a prosperous, business-oriented society. However, problems such as unemployment, poverty, and discrimination exist within the United States.

As a result, the business system must be seen in light of the total society in which it operates. As a major element of society, business affects people in material ways. Society, in turn, influences the conduct of business. Political, economic, and social forces help shape the general nature of the country and frequently affect business decisions within individual firms. Thus, one cannot study business organization and management without also having an awareness of the social forces that shape business.

SOCIAL PROBLEMS AND BUSINESS

Since business does not operate in a vacuum, it cannot isolate itself from society. Often the problems experienced by business are closely interwoven with those experienced by society. In particular, such problems as those caused by changes in population and life styles, have a direct bearing on business operations and on the well-being of the nation.

Population

The gross national product (GNP) cannot increase unless there are enough people to provide the necessary labor and to purchase the goods and services produced. Population statistics enable businesses to plan how much and what kinds of goods and services to offer. However, the GNP of a country must grow at a faster rate than its population in order to improve living conditions. Not only is the size of the population important in business planning, but so is the nature of the population.

Growing Population. The population of the United States has grown steadily over the years, as can be seen in Illus. 2–1 on page 26. However, the rate of growth has been dropping. The birth rate has basically reached the level of **zero population growth (ZPG),** the point at which births and deaths balance. With ZPG, the population will, nevertheless, grow because people continue to immigrate from other countries and because people will live longer due to improved health care.

Changing Population. Not only is the total size of the population important to business, but so is the age makeup of the population. Changes in the birth rate cause shifts in the number of people in different age groups. For example, because of the low birth rate during 1920–1945, there are fewer people today aged 40–65. However, there are more people today aged 20–40 because of the high birth rate during 1945–1965. This period is sometimes called the **baby boom.** Because of this baby boom, the number of people aged 65 and over will increase by the year 2000. On the other hand, there will be fewer teenagers by the year 2000 due to the current low birth rate.

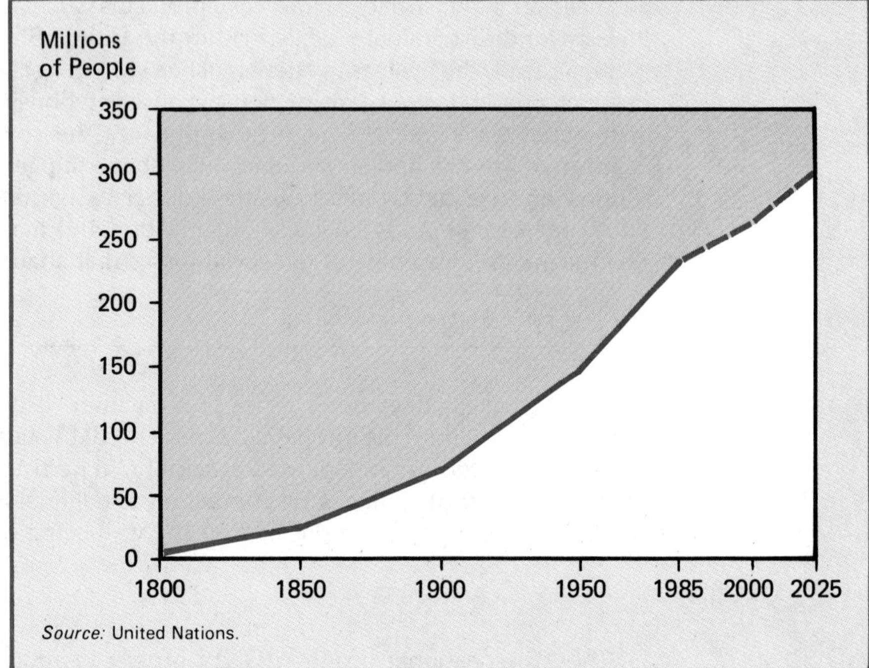

ILLUS. 2–1
The population continues to grow but at a somewhat slower pace.

Because the kinds of goods and services used by people at different age levels change somewhat, businesses must prepare for these shifts. A business that sells specialized goods for a particular age group will be affected if the number of people in that age group changes greatly. During high birth rate periods, for example, a business that sells baby foods must grow to meet customer demand. With a dropping birth rate, however, sales will decline. To offset the decline, the business might find it profitable to also sell special foods to people in the age group that is growing in number, such as those aged 65 or over.

Moving Population. Another feature of the U.S. population is that people move often. Each year millions of people change their addresses. In the past, 20 percent of the population moved yearly. Recently, however, the rate has dropped somewhat, due primarily to high interest rates on home mortgages. Of those people who move, most move short distances—within the same town, county, or state. Those who move long distances have tended to move somewhat westward and southward—from the **frostbelt,** the colder northern half of the country, to the **sunbelt,** the warmer southern half of the nation. Some businesses affected by this movement have relocated.

Prior to the 1970s, people generally moved from rural to urban areas. Since that time, people have moved away from cities and heavily populated urban areas. However, nearly three out of four people still live in a city or suburb.

These population shifts have created a variety of problems. Making wise use of limited land for farms, homes, and businesses is one. Another problem is that of transportation. How to move people and goods efficiently in heavily populated areas has received much attention by business and government. Other social problems, such as providing adequate medical, recreational, and educational facilities develop in densely populated areas. Dealing with unemployment, poverty, and crime in declining areas also represents a major social problem.

Employment and Education

As the population grows, the labor force also grows. The **labor force** is defined generally as most people aged 16 or over who are available for work, whether employed or unemployed. Of course, many of the people in the labor force may be available for work but are not actively seeking employment, such as students and homemakers. The growth rate in the labor force is shown in Illus. 2–2.

The relationship between the population and the labor force is called the **labor participation rate**—the percentage of the labor force either employed or actively seeking employment. In the last two decades, the labor participation rate has increased mainly because more women have become employed outside the home. In 1970, slightly more than 50 percent of the women aged 16–24 years were either employed or were seeking

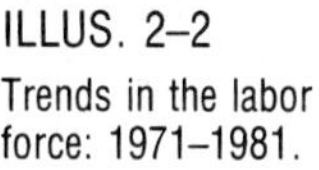

ILLUS. 2–2
Trends in the labor force: 1971–1981.

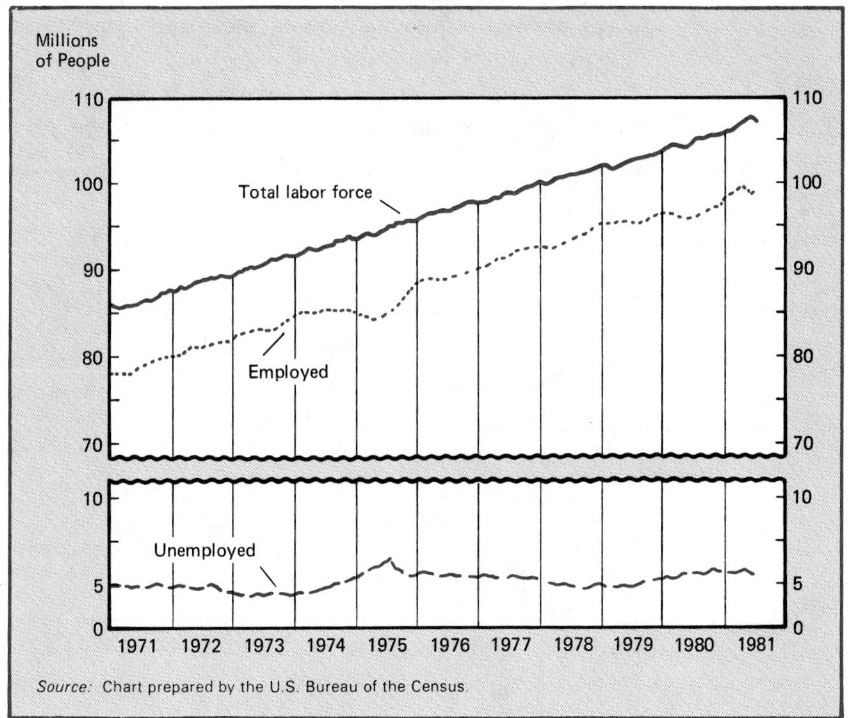

Source: Chart prepared by the U.S. Bureau of the Census.

employment. By 1990, this rate is expected to swell to nearly 75 percent as shown in Illus. 2–3. By 1990, the labor participation rate for women will be nearly equal to that of men in the same age group.

Variety exists in the types of jobs that are available. With the increased use of technology, however, the employment need is greatest for skilled employees. Accountants, secretaries, managers, and computer operators, for example, have never been in greater demand. To become skilled usually means that workers need to be educated. As a result, people are going to school longer than ever before and are being trained in specialized jobs. As new technology comes along, it becomes necessary to retrain workers.

While the demand for skilled workers has been rising, the need for unskilled workers has been falling. Finding adequately trained employees presents a problem for most businesses. Education and specialized training, therefore, must be readily available in a highly industrialized society.

Equality for All

Equality for all is one of the basic principles on which the United States was founded. Yet equality has not been a reality for all groups of people, particularly for minorities and women. While corrective steps have been taken in recent years, problems still exist. Women and blacks, for example, are still not proportionally represented in certain occupational areas. Also, the differences in average income between women and men and between blacks and whites are still large, although corrective forces are at work to eliminate these injustices. The passage of federal and state laws and the improvement of educational opportunities have provided partial solutions. Many factors within society affect equality, and business as a social institution must play an important role in arriving at solutions.

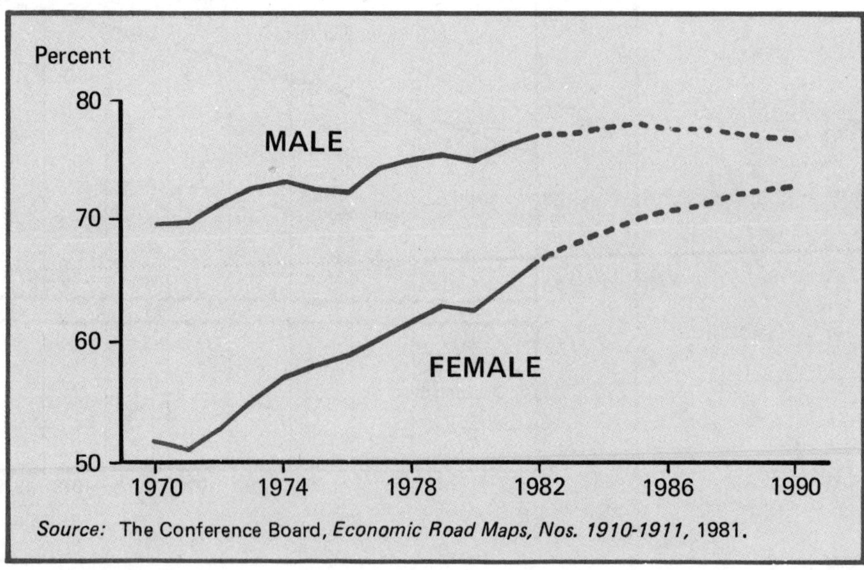

ILLUS. 2–3
The labor participation rate for women aged 16–24 has been increasing steadily.

ILLUS. 2–4
Government agencies often help unemployed people find jobs. Many people, however, lack special skills and training necessary for available jobs.

Poverty

Closely related to the problems of unemployment and inequality is the problem of poverty. Despite the United States' wealth and prosperity, many persons live in poverty. According to the United States Bureau of the Census, between 11 and 13 percent of the population in any given year fall within the poverty level. This means that millions of families are receiving little in annual income. The poverty income level, which is not the same for all, is based on family size, age of members, and location. Families within this level are usually poorly housed, poorly clothed, and poorly fed.

The majority of people living in poverty are unemployed. Many are unskilled and lack sufficient education or training to obtain or keep jobs. By training unemployed workers, many corporations have gained badly needed skilled workers while helping to reduce the number of people unemployed and on welfare. Businesses have also worked with schools and government training programs to help prepare unemployed and unskilled workers for the work force.

One way that businesses have successfully reduced poverty occurred with the creation of the National Alliance of Business. This voluntary organization of thousands of businesses created a partnership with the federal government to help hire, train, and retrain targeted groups, such as poverty-stricken and handicapped people, including disabled veterans. It has labeled its special program JOBS for Job Opportunities in the Business Sector. Since it started in 1968, JOBS has trained many previously unemployed persons.

Shortage of Natural Resources

The Arab oil embargo in 1973 alarmed U.S. citizens. People waiting in long lines to refuel their cars highlighted another severe problem for the United States: a shortage of natural resources. Many businesses rely on

resources that cannot be replaced. Examples of such resources include oil, natural gas, coal, bauxite (aluminum), iron, lead, copper, and tin. Except for only a few resources, such as coal, the total world supply could be completely used during the next century unless better planning is practiced throughout the world.

Some natural resources are used to produce energy. **Energy** is the power needed to run machines and to provide conveniences such as light. It often takes such forms as electricity and gasoline. Energy is provided by various sources such as those listed in Illus. 2–5. Certain energy sources, such as oil and natural gas, are in limited supply and are being used at a rapid rate. The limited supply of those sources has created an energy crisis. For example, oil that is used for many purposes, including the making of gasoline for running cars and trucks, is rapidly being consumed.

ILLUS. 2–5
Some sources of energy could disappear in the future.

	Generally Limited Supply	Generally Unlimited Supply
Coal	X	
Oil	X	
Natural Gas	X	
Nuclear		X
Water (electricity)		X
Sun (heat)		X

No matter how natural resources are used, it is essential to conserve those resources that are not renewable, such as natural gas and iron ore. Natural resources can be conserved in a number of ways. One way is to use less. Fortunately, oil consumption has been significantly reduced by individuals and businesses since the late 1970s. Lighter and more fuel-efficient cars and engines have been built. Factories and homes are now better insulated and thermostats have been adjusted to save fuel.

Still another way to extend the supply of nonrenewable energy resources is to use renewable energy resources instead, such as water to produce electricity and sun to heat water and buildings. A search is also under way for new ways to produce energy. **Recycling**—the reuse of products—is a practical way to conserve natural resources. Many communities, schools, and offices have assisted in recycling paper, bottles, and metal products.

Pollution

During the last decade, U.S. citizens became concerned about a dangerous problem threatening their physical environment: pollution. They were awakened to the fact that the nation cannot continue to produce goods and then carelessly discard waste without upsetting the balance of nature. Pollution affects the land we use, the water we drink, and the air we breathe. Our survival depends on how well society controls its natural environment.

Pollution did not show its damaging effect on the land, water, and air when the country was young. Few goods were produced and the population was small. Now that there are more than 227 million people, and goods are produced in abundance, the environment is seriously affected. One does not have to go far to detect pollution.

Although corrective measures have been taken in recent years to reduce pollution, the problem is still unsolved. In many cities the air is filled with harmful fumes from factories and cars. Many rivers and lakes have been filled with waste to the point of killing fish or making the water dangerous to drink. Even the land has been misused in various ways, such as the wasteful removal of natural resources, the burial of harmful substances, and the use of chemicals to destroy insects and weeds.

The condition of the environment has reached a critical stage. Local and state governments have passed laws which require businesses to install pollution control equipment or to take other measures to decrease pollution. The federal government created the U. S. Environmental Protection Agency (EPA) in 1970 to help control and reduce pollution in the basic areas of air, water, solid waste, pesticides, noise, and radiation. The EPA enforces such laws as the Clean Air Act, Clean Water Act, Resource Recovery Act, Federal Water Pollution Control Act, Federal Environmental Pesticide Control Act, Noise Control Act, and Resource Conservation and Recovery Act.

Because of various state and federal regulations and voluntary actions by many businesses, millions of dollars have been spent on pollution-related items. For some firms, the cost of products or services has increased as a result. Generally, producers and consumers realize that everyone must contribute to a cleaner and safer environment.

At times pollution control goals, such as improvement of air quality, may be at odds with energy conservation goals. For example, the use of coal, which is currently in great supply, generally pollutes the air more than natural gas, which is in short supply. A business changing from the use of coal to natural gas may meet environmental goals but violate conservation goals. On the other hand, a business changing from natural gas to coal is conserving natural gas but polluting the air more with coal. In time scientists may discover ways to use coal without creating a great deal of pollution. Until that time comes, U.S. citizens must decide how best to conserve natural resources and protect the environment.

Changing Values

Society's values generally remain rather stable for long periods. There are times, however, when values undergo change. Evidence suggests that during the last half of the twentieth century values have been shifting. The change in values is in part caused by some of the social problems already discussed.

Traditional values are changing. Dated customs and practices are being challenged. More and more adults are deciding to postpone marriage, to end unsuccessful marriages earlier, or to not marry at all. As a result, the number of U.S. citizens now living alone as heads of households has jumped dramatically since 1970.

Many women have moved into the business world on a full-time basis while raising families. The typical family now consists of a husband and wife both working outside the home. Increased numbers of young couples are postponing parenthood in order to advance their careers and to improve their financial positions. By careful planning, many families are earning more so that they can improve their levels of living and lifestyles.

The people of the United States want more time to enjoy life and to obtain personal satisfaction from their working and nonworking lives. For example, shorter or more flexible work weeks are desired, along with longer vacations. Absenteeism on Mondays and Fridays has become a major problem for managers and union officials. Absenteeism is seen by many as a symptom of the changing values of people toward work and life's fulfillment.

The wish for a better, more enriched life has affected all Americans. The increase in recreational activities and education suggest the desire by people for enriched lives. Increased recreational expenditures in recent years are revealed in Illus. 2–6. Today the majority of people not only want and have more services, but they also possess goods their parents and grandparents did not dream of owning.

EFFECT OF SOCIAL PROBLEMS ON BUSINESS

Solutions to social problems are not readily available, but many groups of people continue to search for solutions. The business world has dealt with social problems in many ways, some of which have already been discussed. Other areas where businesses have responded to social problems are in the development of goals and in the treatment of workers and consumers.

Development of Goals

Businesses have established two basic goals: profit and social responsibility. Profit has always been the basic goal. Because profit is a vital element in our economic system, it is discussed more fully in the next chapter. Businesses hope to earn a fair profit by providing customers with goods and services. While profit is the main goal, businesses in recent

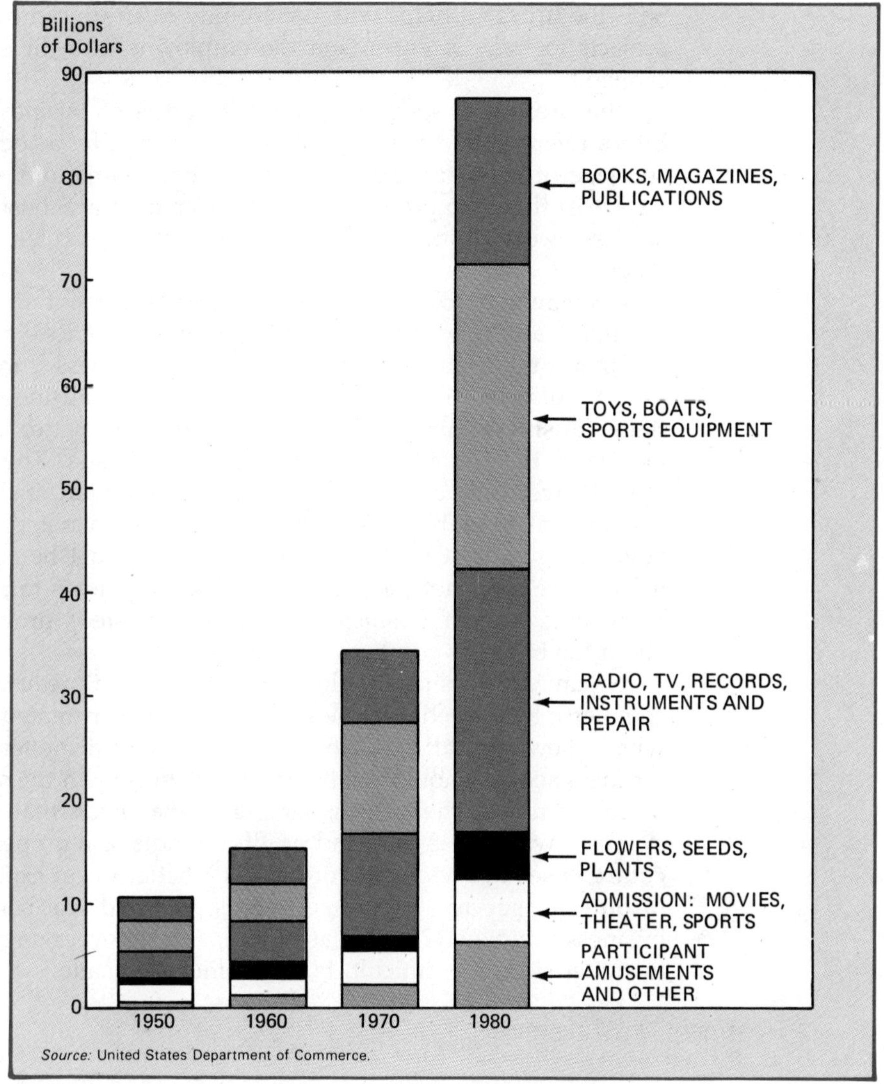

ILLUS. 2–6
Value changes are reflected in increased recreational expenditures.

years have focused a great deal of attention on the goal of social responsibility.

Social responsibility is the duty of business to contribute to the well-being of society. In a narrow sense, a firm is socially responsible when it hires workers and pays taxes. Under the broader meaning, social responsibility extends beyond that which is simply necessary. It includes voluntary actions that contribute to *improving* the quality of life.

Forms of social responsibility vary a great deal. The firm that donates a large gift to a college or builds a park for a city is being socially responsible.

So is the firm that helps with community clean-up campaigns or provides projects to train or encourage the employment of the physically handicapped.

The profit and social responsibility goals of business involve ethics. **Ethics** refer to the rules of conduct established by a society. There is no shortage of rules for fair business practice. Numerous state and federal laws exist that help protect the public from unethical business people. The business world, however, has developed its own rules for businesses to follow.

Chambers of commerce, associations representing the interests of business, are concerned about the ethical practices of all businesses. Another organization supported by the business community for the purpose of protecting consumers from unethical business operators is the **Better Business Bureau** (BBB). There are many Better Business Bureaus located in the United States, Mexico, and Canada. The BBB encourages ethical advertising and selling practices. In addition, it checks advertising and brings pressure against businesses that do not properly follow its advertising code. Generally, advertisements must be accurate, truthful, informative, and not deceptive. The BBB also helps to resolve consumer complaints against businesses and, if requested, provides information about the business practices of companies.

Organizations such as the Better Business Bureau and chambers of commerce help weed out unethical operators. Fortunately business people who follow ethical practices far outnumber dishonest ones. Though business actions should not be harmful to society in the short or long run, there are times when an owner must take action that *seems* unfair. For example, when sales drop and profits dwindle, is it proper for the owner to cut expenses by laying off workers? Is it better to cut expenses in this way in order to survive, or to keep employees and risk being forced out of business completely? In the latter case, all employees might lose their jobs. Such decisions are difficult, but they must be made.

Treatment of Workers

In addition to affecting the goals of business, social problems have influenced the action of owners and managers toward workers. Business managers have become greatly concerned about how to treat workers since values toward work have changed. Employees often complain about boredom, and are no longer content with dull jobs. They want more variety in their work and more opportunity to participate in decisions that directly affect their working lives.

The human factor in business is becoming vitally important. What motivates and satisfies workers, for example, is being studied with renewed vigor. Large businesses, especially, are offering new ways for making employment more satisfying. When possible, firms are helping workers meet personal goals while satisfying business goals. Businesses are experimenting with programs that will help improve the **quality of work life (QWL),** a term that describes organized efforts to improve jobs by involving workers in decision-making. Some firms, for example, organize workers into teams that make decisions about the work being done. By improving the QWL, many firms have found that worker morale and output have increased while absenteeism and worker complaints have decreased.

Other efforts to improve work life are also being tried. Choice of working hours, job training, and job development programs are now offered by many firms. Counseling is also available in some businesses for

ILLUS. 2–7
Many businesses let employees choose their own work hours, which allows them to spend more time with their families.

employees with personal problems. Financial and legal counseling and day care centers are now available to many workers. These and other services are being offered by more and more firms to meet the desires of workers. A discussion of job satisfaction is presented in Chapter 20.

Treatment of Consumers

The third area of change by business has been brought about by consumers. In the past, consumers expressed themselves by either buying or not buying a firm's goods or services. Today the consumer uses other means to communicate interests and desires. Special consumer groups and societies have been formed and vocal consumer advocates have assisted consumers in achieving goals.

In addition to direct contact with businesses about poor quality and high prices, consumers have worked through politicians to obtain protection from undesirable business practices and conditions. In 1962 President John F. Kennedy delivered to Congress a special message on consumer protection that included his famous **Rights of Consumers** shown in Illus. 2–8. This message was the first of its kind by a U.S. President. Later Presidents have also given support to the consumer.

ILLUS. 2–8
President John F. Kennedy's *Special Message on Protecting the Consumer Interest.*

1. **The right to safety**—to be protected against the marketing of goods which are hazardous to health or life.
2. **The right to be informed**—to be protected against fraudulent, deceitful, or grossly misleading information, advertising, labeling, or other practices, and to be given the facts needed to make an informed choice.
3. **The right to choose**—to be assured, wherever possible, access to a variety of products and services at competitive prices, and, in those industries in which competition is not workable and government regulation is substituted, to be assured satisfactory quality and service at fair prices.
4. **The right to be heard**—to be assured that consumer interests will receive full and sympathetic consideration in the formulation of government policy, and fair and expeditious treatment in its administrative tribunals.

Source: Consumer Advisory Council, Executive Office of the President.

An Office of Consumer Affairs (OCA) now exists in Washington, D.C., with its director serving as special assistant to the President. The OCA suggests legislation to protect consumers and also offers help to business firms. Consumer laws have become numerous, with many emphasizing credit, advertising, product quality and safety, and protection of confidential records. (Federal laws and regulations that affect business and the public are treated in Chapter 4.) In addition to federal legislation, many states have also adopted special consumer laws and have created consumer affairs departments to enforce the laws.

Even though most firms entered the consumer era under pressure, they now recognize the value of consumer input. As a result, consumer affairs departments are now found in many corporations. Consumer complaints and suggestions can lead the way to improved products and services, and to greater social responsibility. Some firms even allow individuals representing the public interest to serve on the major decision-making board of their organizations. In this way, consumers provide valuable input when businesses make important product decisions.

THE FUTURE

The problems and challenges of tomorrow's world will be different from those of today. While some of the current problems will continue to exist in the decades ahead, there will be new concerns and new demands on society—and on the business world.

As we move toward the twenty-first century, we will find that the work world has been greatly affected by electronic equipment which is already partially in use today. Computers can now be used to design blue jeans, cars, or houses. Intelligent robots will not only be able to custom-design products, they will also assemble, inspect, and accept or reject finished products on the assembly line. Also, office work will be affected by electronic equipment. Electronic means for recording and storing information, for example, will nearly eliminate certain paperwork tasks.

The new technology, of course, will have an impact on people. They will work fewer hours. The typical 40-hour work week will be reduced substantially. People will have more leisure time, but they will also have greater need for specialized training to stay employed. Recreational and cultural activities together with education will consume much of everyone's leisure time.

The future will have an effect on families too. Today's automobile may become an antique by the next century. New means for moving people and goods may arrive as new energy forms are created. There may also be less need for people to leave home to work or play. With computers, many employees can perform tasks at home and send the results to employers over telephone lines. Personal computers hooked to telephones will enable individuals and businesses to order merchandise and to pay bills automatically. The need for carrying cash may almost disappear because nearly all transactions will be processed through credit card devices electronically connected to businesses and banks. Of course, traveling to stores to shop can be replaced by pressing computer keys at home which display merchandise on television screens.

There is no doubt that new technology will have a major influence on jobs, on people, and on society. But one of the biggest concerns of future business leaders is how to operate effectively during a period when change occurs rapidly. Businesses must organize so that they can react very quickly to yet unknown discoveries and inventions. Workers will shift jobs many times through their work lives as new skills are suddenly needed to replace dated skills. Of necessity, workers will need to accept change more readily than they do today. Schools and businesses will jointly educate and train people throughout their working lives.

NEW TERMS AND CONCEPTS

Define the following terms and concepts, which may be found in boldface type on the page shown in parentheses.

zero population growth, or ZPG (25)
baby boom (25)
frostbelt (26)
sunbelt (26)
labor force (27)
labor participation rate (27)
energy (30)
recycling (30)
social responsibility (33)
ethics (34)
chambers of commerce (34)
Better Business Bureau, or BBB (34)
quality of work life, or QWL (35)
rights of consumers (36)

CHAPTER REVIEW

1. List three social problems that exist in the United States.
2. What two factors must exist for the gross national product to increase?
3. With ZPG, why is it likely that the population will continue to grow?
4. Will there be an increase or a decrease by the year 2000 of (a) people aged 65 or older and (b) teenagers?
5. Why is the age makeup of the population important to business?
6. Do people who move long distances tend to go to the frostbelt or to the sunbelt?
7. Would a student or a homemaker who is available for work but not actively seeking employment be included in the labor force?
8. Has the labor participation rate for women increased or decreased in the last two decades?
9. Is the employment need greatest for skilled or unskilled employees?
10. What is the role of the U.S. Environmental Protection Agency (EPA)?
11. Name the two basic goals of business.
12. Name two associations representing business that are concerned about the ethical practices of business operators.
13. Give an example of how the profit goal can conflict with the social responsibility goal of business.
14. What specific ways are being tried to improve the quality of work life?
15. List the four rights of consumers spelled out by the late President John F. Kennedy.

QUESTIONS FOR CLASS DISCUSSION

1. Why should one who studies American business principles and management also study the social problems of the United States?
2. What types of businesses will be most affected by the population mix that will exist around the year 2000?
3. List three problems primarily due to population shifts.
4. Why will the labor participation rates for males and females, shown in Illus. 2–3, be nearly the same by 1990?
5. Discuss the following social problems and how they affect each other: unemployment, lack of education, and poverty.
6. What has the National Alliance of Business done to reduce poverty?
7. Why is there an energy problem if there are several sources of energy with an unlimited supply, as shown in Illus. 2–5?
8. Give two examples of how environmental goals, such as improvement of air quality, may be at odds with energy conservation goals.
9. What evidence is there that people have a desire for improved, more enriching lives?
10. Give three examples showing how business firms demonstrate social responsibility beyond that which is required or expected of all businesses.

PROBLEMS AND PROJECTS

1. Refer to Illus. 2–2, which provides information about the labor force, and answer these questions:
   a. In what year did unemployment hit its highest point?
   b. Could it be said that as the total number of people in the labor force rises, unemployment also rises?
   c. Between what two years did unemployment increase most rapidly?
   d. If there were 109 million people in the labor force at the start of 1981, and 97 million people were either working or actively looking for work, what was the labor participation rate?
2. The following questions are related to population and employment statistics in a recent year:
   a. If there were 86 million employed white workers and 11 million black and other workers, what percent of the workers were white?
   b. If there were 56 million male and 41 million female white-collar workers, what percent of the workers were male?
3. It is estimated that the following countries and regions of the world have these oil reserves (in billions of barrels): Middle East, 440; Russia, 70; Mexico, 30; Western Europe, 25; China, 20; United States, 30; and the rest of the world, 40.
   a. How many billion barrels are estimated to exist in the world?

b. While Mexico has about the same amount of oil as the United States, why is it estimated that U.S. oil will run out in about 9 years and Mexican oil in about 59 years?
c. What percent more oil does the United States have over China?
d. How much more oil does the Middle East have over the rest of the world?

4. Visit your school library for assistance in preparing a list of inventions and scientific discoveries that have occurred since 1950. From the list write a paragraph or two on the effect you think the group of items has had on business and on the individual well-being of people.

5. Prepare an oral or written report on any one of the following social problems as it applies to your state or area: pollution, unemployment, or poverty. In your report, be sure to indicate what business firms have been doing to help solve the problem.

CASE 2–1

Fred and Irene Hamel had two high school-aged children, Marsha and Ira. Fred was an engineer who worked with Stacy, Inc., a large national firm. Irene was an office manager for the Pace Farm Cooperative. Both enjoyed their work. Marsha and Ira were excellent high school students while being actively involved in sports and other teenage activities. The entire family enjoyed the small-town atmosphere even though they had lived in a large city most of their lives.

On this particular day, however, there was a long silence when Mr. Hamel announced at the dinner table that his boss asked him to move to the new Milford Plant located about 1,000 miles away. The following conversation occurred:

Fred: The move could be good for us. I will get a nice raise, and my boss said moving was the thing to do if I wanted to grow with the company. Besides, we could leave this frostbelt for the sunbelt.

Marsha: But Dad, I only have one more year to go in high school, and I like it here. All my friends are here.

Ira: I made the first team here, Dad. I could never make first squad at Milford. Besides, look how well Marsha and I are doing with our grades . . . a lot better than at the last school we attended.

Irene: Ira is right, Fred. It is your decision and your career. But please keep in mind that I enjoy my job at the Co-op; no doubt the big city will not have a similar job waiting for me.

Marsha: You have a career too, Mom. Would Dad leave his job to follow you to the Co-op's national headquarters in Huntington if you were offered a fat raise and a bigger title? Mom makes almost as much as you now, Dad. And she would if she were a man! At least that's what Ms. Gibson at school tells us every semester in our Careers course.

Ira: Marsha has a point, Dad. What are you going to do?

Irene: Leave Dad alone. He has a big decision to make.

Fred: Since we like it here, we will stay. I don't need to be rich or get a big promotion. I like my job, and I would not trade this town for any place.

Required:

1. What did Mr. Hamel mean by moving from the frostbelt to the sunbelt?
2. How typical is it for a family like the Hamels to move? Discuss.
3. Marsha says that female workers generally make less than male workers for similar jobs. Is that true? Explain.
4. What shift or shifts in life style are revealed in this case situation?

Case 2–2

Curtis Mittler has been operating a small manufacturing business for about a year. The company makes a special type of heavy-duty paint which is used by many kinds of businesses. While Curtis made a profit of $10,000 the first year, he thought that it was small based on all the money he had invested and all the time he had put into building the business.

A few of the local citizens have complained to Curtis that some of the waste from his paint is getting into the nearby river. An engineer checked this and found that while some waste was seeping into the water it was not enough to be in violation of any laws. The engineer also mentioned that Curtis could install a special piece of equipment for about $15,000 that would solve the problem. Curtis was not sure, however, whether his new business was going to be successful enough during the next few years to justify such an expenditure.

Required:

1. What is the problem facing the community?
2. What is the problem facing Curtis Mittler?
3. Should Curtis install the equipment?

Case 2–3

For years the Gumshoe Company has been doing rather well making house slippers for distribution by a large department store chain. Its 200 workers come from the small city of 75,000 in which the plant is located.

Over 150 of the workers are women, most of whom work in the plant's cutting, sewing, and packaging departments. About 25 men work in the receiving and shipping department. There are about ten supervisors and managers, all of whom are males. The rest of the employees are office, maintenance, and design people. Last week the plant manager, Barry Danziger, received the following typewritten message:

> Sir: For too long this company has been run by men who keep women in their place. Sexist comments are heard frequently and, worst of all, not a single woman holds a management position. None of us is ever considered for a supervisory position when an opening occurs. Someone from the shipping and receiving department always gets it. We expect the next supervisory position that opens to be filled by a woman, or you will immediately see that we mean business.
>
> Women's Rights Committee

Mr. Danziger asked the present supervisors what they knew about the matter. None had heard anything. Some of the more outspoken women workers were also contacted. All remained silent. Barry Danziger was puzzled. All management openings are announced through a newsletter and posted on plant bulletin boards. When the last opening occurred, not a single woman had applied.

Required:

1. What action could the women take to show management that "we mean business"?
2. Give possible reasons why no woman applied for the last supervisory position.
3. If no women from the plant apply for the next position, what should the plant manager do?
4. Would you place a woman as supervisor in the receiving and shipping department if that were the next supervisory position available? Explain.

Have You Thought About Becoming . . .
. . . A CONSUMER SPECIALIST?

A consumer specialist is someone who works on behalf of consumers. The consumer specialist may be the consumer affairs officer in a corporation, a consumer advocate for a local or state government, a family financial counselor, or a consumer education teacher right at your school. These are only some of the employment possibilities open to someone interested in representing consumers.

Of course, many people work on a volunteer basis for consumer organizations. And this is one way of getting experience in the consumer field. It is also a way of learning whether you would like this type of work.

The education requirements vary because of the many different tasks performed by consumer specialists. However, a high school diploma and some college education are generally needed if you are interested in working in a consumer affairs office of a business, in a Better Business Bureau, or in a government agency. Your educational background will determine whether you are hired to perform clerical duties, handle customer complaints, counsel people, prepare informative pamphlets, conduct surveys, or design consumer research studies.

Regardless of the type of specialist one becomes, some knowledge of business is desirable. For some positions, such as running a legal aid society or representing citizens as a consumer advocate, a study of law is needed. Communication skills—oral and written—are a must. Listening skills, of course, are quite essential. Patience is also needed along with tact. Being unbiased is another important trait, since one must often listen to complaints from two opposing parties. Fair treatment must be given in order to make fair decisions.

While no record exists as to the total number of consumer specialists employed in the United States, the need in recent years for such specialists has grown.

3

ECONOMIC ENVIRONMENT OF BUSINESS

After studying this chapter you will be able to:

- Describe the economic system of the United States.
- Explain the role of private property and profit in our economic system.
- Describe how supply and demand affect the prices of goods and services.
- Explain the importance of economic growth.
- Compare capitalism, socialism, and communism.

All societies face the problem of trying to satisfy the wants of their citizens for goods and services. Although all societies have this problem in common, many different systems have been developed for producing and using goods and services. The body of knowledge which relates to producing and using goods and services which satisfy human wants is called **economics.**

Concepts that are essential to the understanding of any economic system are discussed first in this chapter. The economic system which exists in the United States is then described. Finally, brief attention is given to other economic systems.

BASIC ECONOMIC CONCEPTS

Business helps to make the economic system work by producing and distributing those particular goods and services that people wish to have.

Since business is a central part of economic activity, having economic knowledge is particularly important for those who are engaged in business or who are preparing themselves for careers in business. A good point at which to begin the study of economics would be to consider the two types of wants found in an economic system.

Economic Wants

People have many kinds of wants. The economic system, however, is concerned only with **economic wants**—the desire for material goods and services that are scarce. People want material goods, such as food, clothing, shelter, and automobiles. They also want services, such as hair care, medical attention, and bus transportation. Items such as these are scarce because the economic system cannot satisfy all the wants of all people for these material goods and services.

People have another kind of want known as a noneconomic want. Noneconomic wants are those wants for which there is no scarcity of that which is desired. Another characteristic of noneconomic wants is that they are nonmaterial wants. Some examples of noneconomic wants would include air, sunshine, friendship, and a happy marriage.

The goods and services that people want have to be produced. Clothes must be made. Homes must be built. Personal services must be supplied. In other words, there is creation of a utility.

Utility. **Utility** is the ability of a good or a service to satisfy a want. In other words, a good or a service which has utility is a useful good or service. The most common types of utility are form utility, place utility, time utility, and possession utility.

ILLUS. 3–1
Fresh air, sunshine and friendship are examples of noneconomic wants.

Form Utility. Changes in the form or shape of a product which make the product more useful create **form utility.** Form utility is added to cotton, for example, when a swimsuit is made from cotton. Form utility can be added only to products, but the other types of utility can be added to services as well as to products.

Place Utility. **Place utility** is created by having a good or service at the place where it is needed or wanted. If a person is vacationing in Florida and wants to buy a swimsuit, a swimsuit at a factory in California is useless. To be useful, that swimsuit must be where it is needed or wanted, namely Florida.

Time Utility. **Time utility** is created when a product or a service is available when it is needed or wanted. A swimsuit that cannot be delivered before one month is of no use to the person who is about to start a two-week vacation in Florida. In addition to being at the place where it is wanted, a useful good or service must be at that place at the time it is needed or wanted.

Possession Utility. **Possession utility** is created when the ownership of a good or service is transferred from one person to another. This transfer of ownership is usually accomplished when a person buys a good or service. A swimsuit in the display window of a department store is not useful to the person who is vacationing in Florida. The swimsuit is useful only when the person possesses it after buying it from the store.

Anyone who aids in creating a utility is a **producer** and is entitled to a reward for the usefulness which is added to the good or service. Hair stylists are entitled to a reward for the usefulness of the services they provide. The price paid for the swimsuit includes a reward for the manufacturer who made the swimsuit, the shipping companies that brought it to Florida, the merchants who made it possible to buy the suit in Florida at the time it was wanted, and the salesperson who sold the suit to the vacationer.

Factors of Production. In creating useful goods and services, a producer will use four basic resources. These resources, which are called **factors of production,** are natural resources or land, labor, capital goods, and management.

Natural Resources. The extent to which a country is able to produce goods and services is, in part, determined by its natural resources. The productive ability of the United States, for example, is related to its fertile soil, minerals in the soil, water and timber resources, and a mild climate.

Labor. Labor is the human effort, either physical or mental, which goes into the production of goods and services. Goods and services would be in short supply without labor.

Capital Goods. Before producing goods that people want, it is necessary to have capital goods. **Capital goods** are buildings, tools, machines, and other equipment used to produce other goods. Capital goods do not directly satisfy human wants. However, capital goods contribute to production because they permit production of large quantities of goods. This

ILLUS. 3–2
Labor, one of the factors of production, is necessary for the production of goods and services.

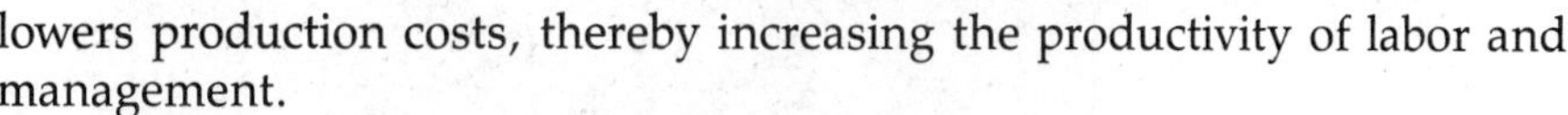

lowers production costs, thereby increasing the productivity of labor and management.

Management. For the production of goods, more is needed than the mere availability of natural resources, labor, and capital goods. Someone, or some group, must bring these factors together to plan and organize the production of the final product. Management is the fourth factor of production which brings together the other three factors. The many aspects of management are treated in Unit 7.

Because government provides many services that are essential to the operation of business, it is often listed as a fifth factor of production by some economists. Some of the essential services provided by government are streets and highways, police and fire protection, courts that settle disputes, and a postal system that provides mail service.

Capital Formation

Capital formation is the production of capital goods. Capital goods, such as buildings and equipment, are needed to produce consumer goods and services. Unlike capital goods, **consumer goods and services** are those goods and services that satisfy people's economic wants directly.

A country can produce just so many goods and services at any one time. As a result, total production is divided between capital goods and consumer goods and services. If the production of consumer goods is increased, the production of capital goods and services is decreased. New capital goods must be made—capital formation—in order to add to the total supply and to replace worn-out capital goods. Capital formation takes place, for example, when steel is used to produce the tools and machinery (capital goods) that make the automobiles rather than to produce the automobiles (consumer goods) themselves.

When productive resources are used for capital formation, it becomes possible to produce more consumer goods. For example, when tools and machinery are produced for making automobiles, it is then possible to make more automobiles.

However, using steel, labor, and management to produce tools and machinery (capital goods), means that these resources cannot be used for automobiles (consumer goods), and the immediate result is that consumers have fewer automobiles to buy. But, because the tools and machinery were made, consumers will have more automobiles to buy in the future. The scarcity of consumer goods in the Soviet Union is, in part, the result of that country using a large portion of its productive resources in capital formation.

ILLUS. 3–3
Sweaters and umbrellas are examples of consumer goods.

Economic Systems

As has been mentioned, no country has enough resources to enable it to satisfy all the wants of all people for material goods and services. Because productive resources are scarce, difficult decisions must be made as to how to use these limited resources. For example, a means is needed for deciding which is better—more capital goods and fewer consumer goods or more consumer goods and fewer capital goods.

Each country must have an **economic system**—an organized way for deciding how to use its productive resources. Decisions must be made as to what to produce, as well as to how the goods will be divided among the people in the country. Different countries have developed different economic systems. There are three very different kinds of economic systems in the world today. They are capitalism, socialism, and communism.

OUR ECONOMIC SYSTEM—CAPITALISM

The importance of the individual has always been emphasized in the United States. Because of this belief, we have designed political and economic systems which permit the individual much freedom. History tells us that there is a relationship between political and economic freedom; that is, political freedom usually is found in countries in which individuals have economic freedom.

Our economic system is called capitalism, or the free enterprise system. **Capitalism** is an economic system in which private citizens are free to go into business for themselves, to produce whatever they choose to produce, and to distribute what they produce as they please.

The definition of capitalism would have accurately described our economic system during much of the nineteenth century and the early part of the twentieth century. In the past few decades, however, government has assumed an important economic role in the United States. As our economy developed without controls by government, certain abuses took place. For example, some people began to interfere with the economic freedom of others. Some large businesses began to exploit small businesses. And some employers did not pay fair wages. To correct such abuses, it was necessary to pass laws. Further attention to the regulation of business by government is given in Chapter 4. Whether capitalism is controlled or uncontrolled, it has a number of specific features.

Private Property

The principle of private property is essential to our capitalistic system. **Private property** consists of items of value that individuals have the right to own, use, or sell. Thus, individuals can control productive resources. They can own land, hire labor, and own capital goods. They can use these resources to produce goods and services. Also, individuals own the products made from their use of land, labor, and capital goods. Thus, the company that produces furniture owns the furniture it makes. The furniture company may sell its furniture, and it owns the money received from the buyer.

Profit

In a capitalistic system the incentive, as well as the reward, for producing goods and services is **profit.** The company making furniture has costs for land, labor, capital goods, and materials. Profit is what the furniture company has left after subtracting these costs from the amount received from selling its furniture.

The profit earned by a business is often overestimated by society. The average profit is about 5 percent of total receipts while the remainder, 95 percent, represents costs. Consider a motel with yearly receipts of $300,000. If the profit amounts to 5 percent, then the owner earns $15,000; that is, $300,000 times .05. Costs for the year are .95 times $300,000, or $285,000. Some types of businesses have higher average profit percentages, but many have lower ones. Owners, of course, try to earn a profit percentage that is better than average.

Being in business does not, of itself, guarantee that a company will make a profit. Among other things, to be successful a company must produce goods or services that people want at a price they are willing to pay.

Price Determination

Demand for a product is the number of products that will be bought at a given time at a given price. Thus, demand is not the same as want. Wanting an expensive luxury car without having the money to buy one does not represent demand. Demand for a luxury car is represented by the person who wants it, has the money to buy it, and is willing to spend the money for it.

There is a relationship between price and demand. With increased demand, prices generally rise. When demand decreases, prices generally fall. For example, if a new product such as a video game suddenly becomes popular, its price may rise. However, when the video game is no longer in demand, its price may drop.

The supply of a product also influences its price. **Supply** of a product is the number of like products that will be offered for sale at a particular time at a certain price. If there is a current shortage in the supply of a product, its price will usually rise as consumers bid against one another to obtain the product. For example, if bad weather has damaged the apple crop and apples are in short supply, the price of apples will go up. When apples become more abundant in supply, their price will go down. Thus, changes in prices of products are the result of changes in both the demand for and the supply of a product.

Generally changes in prices determine what is produced and how much is produced in our economy. Price changes indicate to businesses what is profitable or not profitable to produce. If consumers want more shoes than are being produced, they will bid up the price of shoes. The increase in the price of shoes makes it more profitable to make shoes and provides the incentive for manufacturers to increase the production of shoes. As the supply of shoes increases to satisfy the demand for more shoes, the price of shoes will fall. Since it is now less profitable to make shoes, manufacturers decrease their production of shoes.

Prices, then, are determined by the forces of supply and demand; that is, prices are the result of the decisions of individual consumers to buy products and of individual producers to make and sell products. Therefore, the consumers help decide what will be produced and how much will be produced.

Competition

In our free enterprise system, sellers are trying to make a profit and buyers are trying to buy the best quality goods at the lowest possible prices. This conflict of interests between buyers and sellers is settled to the benefit of society by competition. **Competition** is the rivalry among sellers for consumers' dollars.

Competition in a free enterprise system benefits society in many ways. To attract customers away from other sellers, a business must try to improve the quality of its products, develop new products, and operate efficiently in order to keep its prices down. Thus, competition serves to insure that consumers will get the quality products they want at fair prices.

In addition to benefiting consumers, competition benefits the country in that it tends to make all businesses use our scarce productive resources efficiently. If a business firm does not operate efficiently, it will fail because customers will buy lower priced or higher quality products from a firm that is operating efficiently. Competition in our economic system also provides the chance for people to go into business for themselves and share in the profits being made by those already in business.

One aspect of competition is price competition. Price competition is when a firm takes business away from its competitors by lowering prices. Today, though, more and more competition takes the form of nonprice competition. For example, a company attracts customers away from other sellers by providing products that have better quality or by adding something to the product which competitors do not have. Or a company may attract customers away from competitors by unusual and colorful packaging of a product. Another company may conduct an extensive advertising campaign to convince the public that its product is better than all other brands. All these are effective devices used in nonprice competition.

Competition is the opposite of monopoly. **Monopoly** is the existence of only one seller who is able to avoid most of the elements of effective competition. For example, if a seller does not have to compete with other sellers for consumer dollars, profit can usually be increased by raising the price of a product. As you will learn in Chapter 4, legislation exists that encourages competition and discourages monopolistic practices.

Distribution of Income

Not only must all countries decide how scarce productive resources are to be used, but they must also decide how the goods produced will be divided among the people in the society. In a free enterprise economy, the share of goods produced which an individual receives is determined by the amount of money that person has to purchase goods and services.

People receive money—wages and salaries—by contributing their labor to the production of goods and services. Money is also received by people as interest on money that they lend to others, as rent for land or buildings that they own, and as profits if they are owners of businesses.

The amount of money which an individual receives in wages or salary is determined by many factors, including personal traits and abilities. The same factors that determine the prices of goods are also important factors in determining wages and salaries; that is, the amount of wages paid for a particular kind of labor is affected by the supply of and demand for that kind of labor. The demand is low and the supply is high for unskilled workers. Thus, the price (income) of unskilled workers is low. On the other hand, the demand for brain surgeons is high in terms of the supply of brain surgeons and the services they provide; therefore, their price (income) is high.

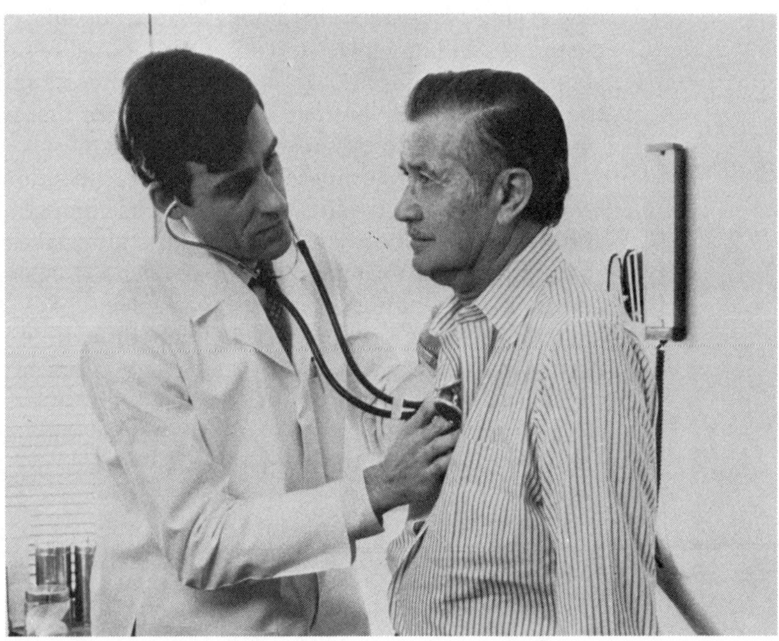

ILLUS. 3–4
Skilled workers have specialized education and training. Therefore, they usually have larger incomes than do unskilled workers.

ECONOMIC GROWTH

The strength of a nation depends upon its economic growth. Economic growth is measured by an annual increase in the gross national product, increased employment opportunities, and the continuous development of new and improved goods and services. However, growth cannot always be at the most desired rate. When the economy grows too fast or too slow, businesses and consumers suffer. Of concern to everyone is the promotion and measurement of such growth along with the identification and control of growth problems.

Promoting Economic Growth

Economic growth occurs when a country's output exceeds its population growth. As a result, more goods and services are available for each person. Growth has occurred and must continue if the nation is to remain economically strong.

The following are basic ways to increase the production of goods and services in order to encourage needed economic growth:

- Increase the number of people in the work force.
- Increase the productivity of the work force by means of education and job training.
- Increase the supply of capital goods, such as more tools and machines, in order to increase the productivity of labor and management.
- Improve technology by inventing new and better machines and better methods for producing goods and services.

For economic growth, more is required than just increasing the production of goods and services. More goods and services must also be consumed. The incentive for producing goods and services in a free enterprise economy is profit. If the goods and services produced are in demand and are profitable, business has the incentive to increase production.

Economic growth is basic to a healthy economy. Through such growth more and better products become available, such as video recorders and fuel-efficient cars. And more and better services also become available, such as those provided by hospitals and travel agencies. But more important, economic growth is needed to provide jobs for those who wish to work.

Measuring Economic Growth

To know whether the economy is growing at a desirable rate, statistics must be gathered. The federal government collects much information and uses a variety of figures to keep track of the economy. The gross national product (GNP) that was discussed in Chapter 1 is an extremely valuable statistic. Another is the Consumer Price Index.

The **Consumer Price Index (CPI)** indicates what is happening in general to prices in the country. It is a measure of the average change in prices of consumer goods and services typically purchased by people living in urban areas. The hundreds of items in the CPI include prices for food, gasoline, and housing payments. With the CPI, comparisons can be made in the cost of living from month to month or from year to year, as shown in Illus. 3–5.

When the CPI, GNP, and other statistics are examined each month by government economists, the condition of the economy can be evaluated. If the growth rate appears to be undesirable, corrective action can be taken.

Identifying Economic Problems

Problems occur with the economy when the growth rate is either too fast or too slow. One problem that occurs is a **recession,** which is a

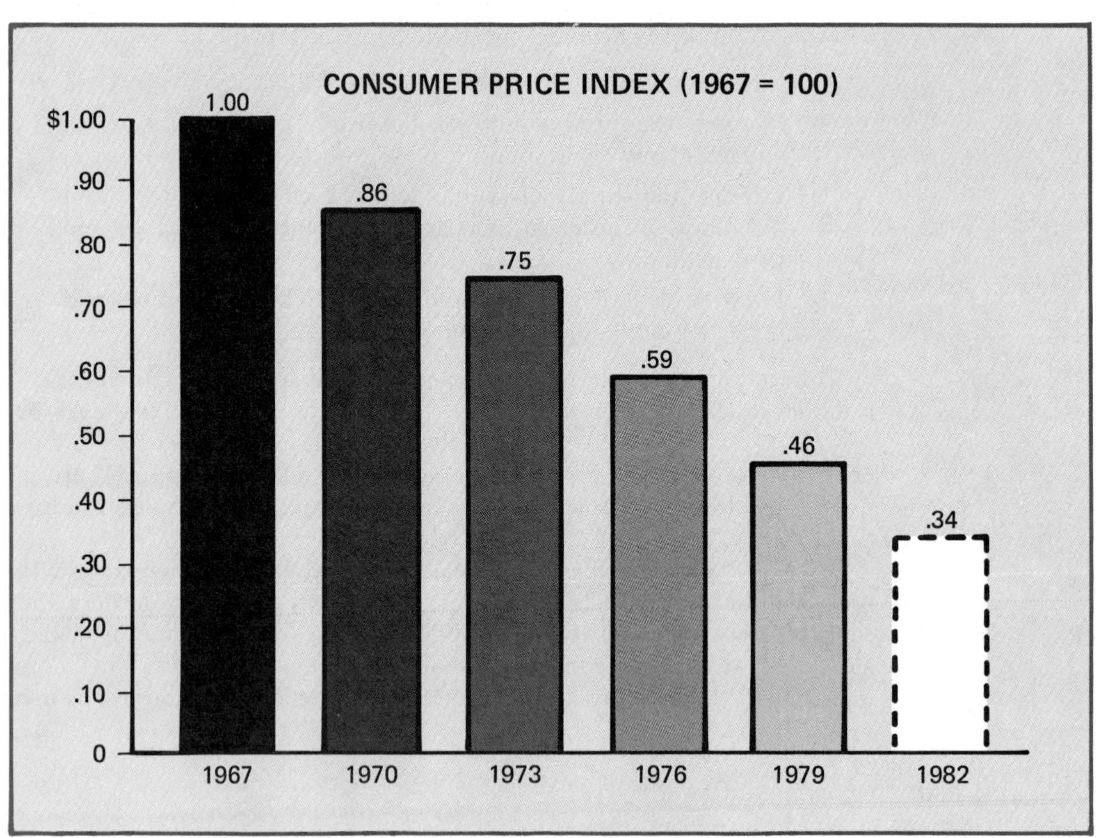

ILLUS. 3–5

The purchasing power of the dollar has declined steadily in recent years.

slowdown or a decline in the GNP that continues for six months or more. A recession is created when demand for the total goods and services available is less than the supply. Decreased production and increased unemployment occur during recessions. In most recessions the rate of increase in prices is reduced greatly and in some cases prices may actually decline slightly.

Another problem arises when consumers want to buy goods and services that are not readily available. This increased demand causes prices for existing goods and services to rise, as revealed in the Consumer Price Index. **Inflation** is the rapid rise in prices caused by an inadequate supply of goods and services. In other words, total demand exceeds supply. Inflation results in a decline in purchasing power of money; that is, a dollar does not buy as much as it did before inflation. Retired people and those with fixed incomes are financially hurt the most because their incomes buy less. The effect of inflation on the purchasing power of the dollar is shown in Illus. 3–6.

ILLUS. 3–6
Inflation has reduced the purchasing power of the dollar.

Dollars Needed to Buy an Item Costing $100 in 1967
(1967–1982)

If the item was bought in	It cost
1967	$ 100
1970	114
1973	125
1976	141
1979	154
1982	166 (est'd)

Source: United States Department of Labor.

Occasionally, economic conditions arise that are not normal. For example, during a recession it is normal for inflation to be nearly eliminated or greatly reduced within a reasonable time. However, sometimes this does not happen. **Stagflation** exists when inflation continues into a recession for an extended time. Such abnormal conditions are studied carefully by economists for possible future benefit.

Controlling Economic Growth

When the economic statistics show that the economy may be about to enter a recessionary or inflationary period, certain actions can be taken by the government. Several specific devices used include controlling taxes, government expenditures, and interest rates.

One way to control economic growth is to raise or lower taxes. Taxes are raised to slow growth and lowered to encourage growth. When taxes are raised, there is less money to spend, which discourages growth. And when taxes are lowered, people and businesses have more money to spend, which encourages economic growth.

Government expenditures also influence economic growth. The federal government operates by spending billions of dollars each year, such as to pay salaries and to buy equipment. Government can increase its spending to stimulate a slow economy or reduce spending to slow economic growth.

In addition, economic growth is regulated through interest rates, the money paid to borrow money. Borrowing generates spending. Spending stimulates economic growth. When interest rates are lowered, businesses are encouraged to borrow. This stimulates business activity and, in turn, the economy. When interest rates are raised to discourage borrowing, a slowdown occurs.

Through interest rates, government spending, taxes, and other devices, the rate of economic growth can be controlled somewhat. Control, however, is usually kept to a minimum in a free enterprise system. Further, in a complex economic system the results of such controls are not always clearly visible in the short run. Economists do not know exactly when control devices should be used or how effective they are. While the nature of controls can be debated, some control is needed to prevent a destructive runaway inflationary period or a **depression**—a long and severe drop in the GNP. Not only do such conditions affect U.S. citizens, but the economic climate of foreign countries is usually affected as well.

OTHER ECONOMIC SYSTEMS

Large companies do a great deal of business in other countries. Many small firms also do business in other nations. Those who work in firms that do business in foreign countries face special problems. Speaking the native language is only one such problem. Others include adjusting this country's customs and business practices to the foreign country's social, economic, legal, and political systems. Each country is quite different. An understanding of other economic systems allows us to gain a better understanding of our own system. Those systems that are most different from capitalism are socialism and communism.

Socialism

Socialism is an economic system in which the government controls and regulates the means of production. How scarce resources are to be used to satisfy the many wants of people is decided, at least in part, by the government.

Socialists do not agree as to how much of the productive resources the government should own. The most extreme socialists want the government to own all natural resources and capital goods. Middle-of-the-road socialists believe that planning production for the whole economy can be achieved if the government owns certain key industries, but they also believe that other productive resources should be owned by individuals and businesses.

Socialism is generally disliked in the United States because it limits the right of the individual to own property for productive purposes. Private property is basic to capitalism. Private property, however, exists in socialistic economies in different degrees, depending on the amount of government ownership and control. Socialism in its different forms exists in many countries, particularly in the Western European countries of Sweden, Italy, and Great Britain.

Communism

Communism is forced socialism; that is, all or almost all the productive resources of a nation are owned by the government. Decisions regarding what is to be produced, how much is to be produced, and how the results of production are to be divided among the citizens are made by government agencies on the basis of a plan that has been drawn up by the government. Government measures how well producers perform on the basis of volume of goods and services produced without much regard for the quality of or demand for the goods or services. Consumer goods are usually in short supply in communist countries, such as Cuba and the Soviet Union, because heavy emphasis is placed on capital formation. Even Soviet leaders have recognized the shortcomings of the system when it comes to meeting the needs of consumers. As a result, some adjustments are being made that introduce some capitalistic principles of supply and demand. Two such adjustments include judging the performance of producers by the demand for their products, and permitting control of production in terms of consumer demand.

Workers in a communist system cannot move easily from one job to another. And managers of businesses do not decide what is to be produced. A communist country's central planning agency makes most such decisions. Capitalism relies, instead, on consumers and managers to make these decisions. People in a communist society do not have private property. All economic decisions are made by governmental leaders. These leaders decide how scarce resources will be used. The members of a communist country have few of the freedoms that Americans believe are important.

NEW TERMS AND CONCEPTS

Define the following terms and concepts, which may be found in boldface type on the page shown in parentheses.

economics (44)
economic wants (45)
utility (45)
form utility (46)
place utility (46)
time utility (46)
possession utility (46)
producer (46)
factors of production (46)
natural resources (46)
labor (46)
capital goods (46)
management (47)
capital formation (47)
consumer goods and services (47)
economic system (49)
capitalism (49)
private property (49)
profit (50)
demand (50)
supply (50)
competition (51)
monopoly (51)
economic growth (53)
Consumer Price Index, or CPI (54)
recession (54)
inflation (55)
stagflation (55)
depression (56)
socialism (56)
communism (57)

CHAPTER REVIEW

1. How does an economic want differ from a noneconomic want? Give an example of each.
2. List the four most common types of utility and the four basic factors of production.
3. What is the difference between consumer goods and capital goods?
4. In relation to capital formation, what is one cause for the scarcity of consumer goods in the Soviet Union?
5. Are productive resources scarce or available in unlimited quantity?
6. Is the profit earned by a business usually overestimated or underestimated?
7. What special feature of a free enterprise system helps keep the prices of goods and services down?
8. How might a business attract customers from other sellers?
9. List three examples of nonprice competition.
10. Is the demand high and the supply low for unskilled workers?
11. Other than increasing the production of goods and services, what other element is required for economic growth?
12. List two ways used by government to measure economic growth.

13. List four problems that can occur within an economy when the growth rate is too fast or too slow.
14. List three devices used by the government to control economic growth.
15. Compare capitalism, socialism, and communism as to (a) how each allocates scarce resources among alternative wants and (b) the existence of private property.

QUESTIONS FOR CLASS DISCUSSION

1. Discuss form, place, and time utility as they might apply to a small fast-food pizza business that just opened in your community.
2. How is capital formation important to the creation of consumer goods?
3. Explain the immediate and long-range effects which the production of capital goods has on consumer goods.
4. A person who works for a local business firm made the following statement: "The company took in $500,000 last year. It is doing great." Is the firm necessarily doing great? If it were an average firm, estimate its profit.
5. Explain how supply and demand help determine the price for goods and services.
6. How do business firms know what product to make and how many to produce?
7. Your friend said: "The company I work for had a 10 percent increase in demand for its goods but the supply went up by 15 percent. Management should have raised prices if it wanted to make a bigger profit." Is your friend correct? Explain.
8. Discuss how economic growth that is too fast can cause people who are retired to be hurt financially.
9. If you were an economist working for the federal government, what would you do if you discovered the GNP and CPI were dropping too fast? Explain.
10. Discuss how you might agree with the following statement: "Economic decisions in a capitalistic country are influenced by the federal government about 10 percent of the time; in a socialist country, 50 percent of the time; and in a communistic country, 90 percent of the time."

PROBLEMS AND PROJECTS

1. Use the Consumer Price Index information provided in Illus. 3–5 to determine the following:
   a. By what percent did the CPI change between 1967 and 1982?
   b. If the CPI dropped by 10 percent between 1973 and 1974, what would the CPI be in 1974?
2. Use the following yearly gross national product figures to determine answers to the questions below:

   1970 $1.0 billion 1975 $1.5 billion 1980 $2.6 billion

a. What was the percentage of increase between 1970 and 1975?
b. What was the percentage of increase between 1975 and 1980?
c. If the percentage of increase between 1970 and 1980 remains the same between 1980 and 1990, what will the GNP be in 1990?

3. Between 1975 and 1980, average yearly consumer price rises for selected countries were: United States, 8.9 percent; Australia, 10.6 percent; Portugal, 21.2 percent; and Switzerland, 2.3 percent.
a. If you were on a fixed income, in which country would you fare the best? the worst?
b. Over the five-year period, by what percent did prices rise in the United States?
c. Which country was probably suffering from the greatest amount of inflation? Explain.
d. During the five-year period, by what percent did Australia exceed the United States in the total increase in consumer prices?

4. Select three different types of businesses (dry cleaners, supermarkets, beauty salons, furniture stores, etc.) and from the yellow pages of the telephone directory for your area find out how many firms are in each type of business. Explain why one line of business may have more or fewer competitors than the others.

CASE 3–1

Tim O'Rourke, an airline pilot who flies commercial jets to many European countries, was in the employee's lounge one day browsing through a magazine. He was in the middle of an article when Marsha Munshein, an airport traffic controller, walked in.

"Are you reading anything interesting, Tim?" asked Marsha.

"As a matter of fact I am," said Tim. "This article says Americans do not save enough money to help businesses."

Marsha looked a little surprised. "People save to help themselves, not to help business."

"In addition," said Tim, "the article says that if we saved more and spent less, we would be helping to get rid of some of this inflation."

"Either that author must have been paid by some business organization to write that article, or I don't understand what he is trying to say," Marsha responded. "Besides, I thought businesses wanted us to spend our money."

Tim was still skimming the article when something caught his eye. "Here is some information you are going to like. The author says that one of the countries I fly to weekly encourages people to save by allowing children to earn tax-free interest on savings accounts up to $10,000.

Another country exempts nearly all its citizens from having to pay taxes on interest earned on any type of savings or investment plans. I wish our government would do that."

"Those really are good ideas," said Marsha. "It is difficult to get my two children to save any money from their part-time jobs. Tim, when you are done with that magazine, could I see it?"

Required:

1. Explain how the failure of people to save can be harmful to business.
2. Do you agree that if people saved more during an inflationary period they would help reduce inflation? Explain.
3. If this country decided not to tax people on the interest they earn in savings accounts, what effect would that have on savings?

CASE 3–2

A group of workers in a small corporation were having an informal meeting one lunch hour to discuss wages in the company. One of the workers brought along the following chart, which was passed around.

AVERAGE WEEKLY EARNINGS OF FULL-TIME WORKERS	
Managers	$380
Sales workers	279
Clerical workers	215
Skilled laborers	328
Unskilled laborers	225

Some of the workers believed that the wages of all clerical and unskilled workers should be increased to match the amount earned by sales workers. Other workers believed that the clerical workers should be paid as much as the unskilled workers. Still a third group of workers believed that wages of each group of workers should be increased by the same fixed percentage. Very shortly, a heated discussion broke out.

One of the workers present, Marion, had taken several economics courses while in school. As yet, Marion had not said a word, but now was ready to give her opinion.

Required:

1. If you were Marion, what would you say to the group about how wages are set in this country?

2. Would the suggestion of raising the wages of the clerical and unskilled workers to the level of wages earned by sales workers be more acceptable under capitalism or communism? Explain.
3. Which worker suggestion would probably least violate any economic principles dealing with supply and demand? Explain your answer.
4. If wages were to be increased by a fixed percentage for all workers as suggested by the third worker, how might the rate of increase be determined? Explain.

CASE 3–3

Doris and Ed Stanley run the Appliance Center, which specializes in brand-name color television sets, refrigerators, and freezers. Their nearest competitor is at least two miles away. The Appliance Center has been doing rather well, especially during the last six months. Only a few items of each appliance are left in stock. People seem to be replacing their appliances even though the trade-in models are not very old and are in fairly good condition. Doris and Ed realize that people expect future price increases and are buying new models before prices go higher.

Today Doris pointed out to Ed two articles from the local newspaper. In one a government official announced that the CPI went up steeply again for the fourth straight month. In the second article, another government official stated that over the next several months there were plans to (a) raise the income tax, (b) decrease government spending, and (c) raise interest rates to borrowers.

Doris and Ed are now planning how many appliances to order from their suppliers for their inventory. With the increased demand for appliances, orders must be in six months before the items are likely to arrive. They are not certain whether to increase the order size, keep it the same, or decrease it.

Required:

1. Does the evidence suggest that the present economic growth of the country is too fast, too slow, or about right? Explain.
2. If they keep the order size the same, what will or could happen if demand (a) declines, or (b) increases even more?
3. If the government officials state that their measures will have a strong, immediate impact on the economy, should this influence the size of the order for the Appliance Center? Why?

Have You Thought About Becoming . . .

. . . AN ECONOMIST?

Economists are concerned about matters related to scarce resources and unlimited wants. In particular, they deal with how to use such things as land, raw materials, and human resources to provide goods and services for society. Economists also study pricing goods, capital formation, taxes, and population changes since all affect the economic system.

Most large corporations hire economists. In fact, business employs approximately 75 percent of all economists. Positions are also available with federal and state governments. Moreover, many teaching positions are available in high schools, two-year colleges, and universities.

A good general education is highly desirable because economists deal with information that applies to the entire country and to foreign countries as well. As a minimum, a four-year college degree in economics is required. Studies should include economic theory, mathematics, statistics, and computer courses. Corporate senior economists and university professors need a master's or doctor's degree in economics. Of necessity, economists often specialize in some particular area, such as international trade, labor, investments, or government policy projections.

Economists need certain skills and characteristics. Analytical ability is required to deal with the many facts and figures that are collected. Accuracy and a desire to work with detailed information, of course, are extremely important. These and other traits are needed to gather, examine, and communicate economic information.

While jobs for economists are available, competition is keen. Those who do extremely well in their college course work, however, will probably experience little difficulty in obtaining employment in the areas of business, government, or education.

4

LEGAL ENVIRONMENT OF BUSINESS

After studying this chapter you will be able to:

- Explain some of the major federal laws that promote fair competition.
- Tell how patents, copyrights, and trademarks are beneficial to business.
- Offer examples of how the government protects the public from products that may be harmful or dangerous.
- Identify methods used by state and local governments to regulate business.
- Describe the most common kinds of taxes which affect business.

American business is regulated by laws passed by local and state governments and by the federal government. These laws cover a variety of topics and govern relationships of business with competitors, consumers, and employees. Legislation exists that affects products, prices, wages, working conditions, taxes, and other matters of importance to business.

Some of the specialized laws affecting business are discussed in other chapters. For example, legislation dealing with the environment may be found in Chapter 2 and legislation dealing with labor laws may be found in Chapter 23. Laws affecting credit and other consumer matters may be found in a number of chapters.

In this chapter, attention is given to the general ways in which federal, local, and state governments regulate business activity. In particular, you will learn how government helps to maintain a free enterprise system by controlling monopolies and promoting competition. You will also learn how government protects business as well as the public. Finally, you will learn about taxes and how taxes help to regulate business activity.

REGULATIONS MAINTAINING COMPETITION

As discussed in Chapter 3, competition is the rivalry among companies for the customer's dollar. Competition, however, does not always operate smoothly by itself. To provide for fair competition, government has passed laws and created regulations to enforce the laws. These laws and regulations grow out of a need to preserve competition which is done, in part, by controlling monopolies and unfair business practices.

ILLUS. 4–1

The federal government regulates businesses engaged in interstate commerce.

Controlling Monopolies

A monopoly exists when competition is lacking for a product or service, or when producers are in a position to control the supply of goods or services. By controlling the supply of an item, a single producer can set a price that will generate the greatest profit. In business situations where a monopoly exists, prices are generally higher than where competition exists.

In actual practice, however, there are few business monopolies because of the effectiveness of competition. To illustrate, assume a business offers a new product that no other business has. The product suddenly becomes quite popular. Other companies now enter the market to help meet the demand. A temporary monopoly will exist until those competitors can produce and sell similar products. Usually, through competitive pricing, the more efficient companies will attract the greatest number of purchasers while the less efficient may struggle for survival or go out of business. Even if some competitors fail to survive, however, a monopoly will not exist as long as there are at least two or more producers.

There are situations, however, where monopolies may be preferred over competition. These situations usually involve providing public services, which have a fairly stable demand and which are costly to create, such as public utilities. A natural gas company, for example, must build many hundreds of miles of pipeline along streets and roads in order to deliver gas to homes and industries to fuel furnaces, stoves, and equipment. If two or three gas companies incurred these same costs to sell gas to a relatively fixed number of customers, the price of gas would be higher than if only one company existed. Also, installing and maintaining so many pipelines would create nuisance problems along crowded streets and highways. In these types of situations, therefore, a monopoly is more desirable than competition. When the government grants a monopoly to a company, it usually controls the prices that can be charged and influences other company policies.

The government has approved and regulated various monopolies, such as the postal system, power companies, railroads, and communication firms. While the federal government controls airlines and other industries, it has begun to reduce or eliminate controls in recent years. Information has been gathered that shows that too many federal controls can harm competition, such as with airlines. As a result, the Airlines Deregulation

ILLUS. 4–2
Power companies and transportation firms are regulated by government.

Act of 1978 was passed, loosening controls over airline routes and rates. This first major deregulation law allows airlines to operate as relatively free competitors for the benefit of society.

Promoting Fair Competition

One way to promote competition is to limit the number of monopolies. The federal government attempts to control the number of monopolies by passing laws and creating agencies to enforce the laws.

Federal Laws. Several major laws have been passed within the last hundred years to encourage competition and to discourage monopolies. A few of the more important federal laws are discussed here.

Sherman Act. The first major law promoting competition was the Sherman Antitrust Act of 1890. Though somewhat dated now, the law is still very much alive and enforced. One of its primary purposes is to discourage monopolies by outlawing business agreements among competitors that might tend to promote monopolies. Agreements among competitors, for example, to set selling prices on goods are unlawful. If three sellers met and agreed to set the same selling price on the same product each sold, they would all be violating the Sherman Act.

Clayton Act. Like the Sherman Act, the Clayton Act of 1914 was in part also aimed at discouraging monopolies. The Clayton Act contains several important features. One part of the law forbids corporations from acquiring ownership rights in other corporations if the purpose is to create a monopoly or to discourage competition. Corporation A cannot, for example, buy over half the ownership rights of its main competitor, Corporation B, if the aim is to reduce or eliminate competition.

Another section of the Clayton Act forbids business contracts that specify goods that a buyer must purchase in order to get other goods. For example, a business that produces computers cannot require a buyer to also purchase supplies, such as paper and tapes which are needed to run the computer.

Robinson-Patman Act. A portion of the Clayton Act dealing with pricing of goods was amended by the Robinson-Patman Act of 1936. The main purpose of both provisions in these laws is to prevent **price discrimination**—setting different prices for different customers. For example, a seller cannot offer a price of $5 a unit to Buyer A and sell the same goods to Buyer B at $6 a unit. Different prices can be set, however, if the goods sold are different in quality or quantity. Buyer A is entitled to the $5 price if the quantity purchased is significantly greater or if the quality is lower. The same discounts must then be offered to all buyers purchasing the same quantity or quality as Buyer A.

Wheeler-Lea Act. In 1938 the Wheeler-Lea Act was passed to strengthen earlier laws outlawing unfair methods of competition. Unfair or deceptive acts or practices, including false advertising, were made unlawful. **False advertising** is defined as advertising that is "misleading in a material respect,'' including the failure to reveal facts as to possible results from using the advertised products. Under the Wheeler-Lea Act, it is unlawful for an advertiser to circulate false advertising that can lead to the purchase of foods, drugs, medical devices, or cosmetics, or to participate in any other unfair methods of competition.

Federal Trade Commission. The Federal Trade Commission (FTC) was created as the result of many businesses demanding protection from unfair methods of competition. The FTC administers most of the federal laws dealing with fair competition. Some of the unfair practices that the FTC protects business firms from are shown in Illus. 4–3.

ILLUS. 4–3
Types of practices prohibited by the Federal Trade Commission

1. Any act that restrains trade.
2. Any monopolies except those specifically authorized by law, such as public utilities.
3. Price fixing, such as agreements among competitors.
4. Agreements among competitors to divide territory, earnings, or profits.
5. Gaining control over the supply of any commodity in order to create an artificial scarcity.
6. False or misleading advertising.
7. Imitation of trademark or trade name.
8. Discrimination through prices or special deals.
9. Pretending to sell at a discount when actually there is no reduction in price.
10. Offering so-called free merchandise with a purchase when actually the price of the article sold has been raised to compensate for the free merchandise.
11. Misrepresentation as to the quality, the composition, or the place of origin of a product.
12. Selling secondhand or reclaimed merchandise as new merchandise.

Other Federal Agencies. In addition to the FTC, other federal agencies have been created to administer laws that regulate specialized areas of business, such as transportation and communication. Some of the more important agencies are listed in Illus. 4-4.

REGULATIONS PROTECTING BUSINESS AND THE PUBLIC

Government regulations may be examined in terms of what the laws stress. One set of regulations stresses the manner in which competition is conducted while another set of regulations is concerned with the actual goods and services the business system produces. The previous section of this chapter dealt mostly with regulations that help to make the economic system work more effectively. The next part of the chapter deals with

ILLUS. 4–4

Laws promoting fair practices that benefit business firms and consumers are enforced by governmental agencies.

Some Federal Agencies That Regulate Business

AGENCY	REGULATION
Federal Communications Commission	Radio, television, telephone, telegraph, and satellite communications
Federal Power Commission	Electric power and natural gas services
Food and Drug Administration	Foods, drugs, medical devices, cosmetics, and veterinary products
Nuclear Regulatory Commission	Nuclear power plants
Securities and Exchange Commission	Stocks and bonds

regulations protecting those who create goods and services and those who use them.

Protecting Business

The federal government has passed laws to protect the rights of everyone who creates new products and new ideas. Specifically, property rights are granted to inventors, authors, and creators of distinct symbols and names for goods and services.

Patent. A **patent** is an agreement in which the federal government gives an inventor the sole right for 17 years to make, use, and sell an invention. No one is permitted to copy or use the invention without permission. This protection is a reward for the time and money invested to create the new product.

In a sense, through the Patent and Trademark Office, the government gives the inventor a monopoly on newly invented products. This encourages manufacturers to establish research departments to invent new products. These research departments have produced many inventions. For example, Polaroid and Kodak have created and patented cameras that take and develop pictures within seconds. International Business Machines (IBM) has many patents on computers, the telephone company on telephone equipment, and so on.

Copyright. A **copyright** is similar to a patent in that the federal government gives an author the sole right to reproduce, publish, and sell literary or artistic work for the life of the author plus 50 years. Under certain conditions, teachers are allowed to make copies of copyrighted material for classroom use. However, no one may publish or reproduce copyrighted work without permission of the author or publisher.

Copyrights are regulated by the federal Copyright Office. Like a patent, a copyright is a special type of monopoly given to authors and publishers. An example of a copyright can be seen on the back of the title page in the front of this book.

Trademark. Trademarks are like patents in that they are special types of monopolies. A **trademark** is a distinguishing name, symbol, or special mark placed on a good or service that is legally reserved for the sole use of the owner. Many nationally known products have trademarks which most people recognize, such as the games of Monopoly and Scrabble.

Trademarks represent a way for the government to protect the rights of a business that has spent much time and money building a product's reputation. If more than one person or business is allowed to use the same name, symbol, or mark, the original owner may suffer damage. Trademarks, like patents, are regulated by the Patent and Trademark Office.

ILLUS. 4–5
Special property rights are granted by federal, state, and local governments.

Protecting the Public

While the federal government protects the legal rights of those who create new products and ideas, it also protects those who consume goods and services. A major emphasis of consumer legislation is on product safety.

Food and Drugs. Products related to the human body are closely regulated. The Food and Drug Administration administers the Federal Food, Drug, and Cosmetic Act and other similar laws. These laws prohibit the sale of impure, improperly labeled, falsely guaranteed, and unhealthful foods, drugs, and cosmetics. Producers of cosmetics, for example, must show that products will not be harmful when used. Should a product cause harm, the Food and Drug Administration may require the producer to stop its sale or to notify the public of its possible danger.

Nonfood Products. Legislative activity dealing with the safety of nonfood products has increased in recent years. Labels are now required on many products if possible danger exists from using the product. A health-warning message, for example, must appear on cigarette packages. For the purpose of reducing death and injury, auto and highway safety laws have been passed. Other federal safety laws also have been proposed and passed.

The Consumer Product Safety Act of 1972 sets safety standards on many items. When it is found that products already sold have a defect that is or could be dangerous, businesses are legally required to recall, repair, or stop selling the products. Dangerous toys, for example, have been removed from the market. And massive recalls have occurred with such products as cars and television sets. A federal Warranty Act that took effect in 1976 requires sellers to specify carefully what will or will not be done when a product is defective. Many product safety laws also exist at the state level.

STATE AND LOCAL REGULATIONS

The federal government regulates interstate commerce while the individual states regulate intrastate commerce. **Interstate commerce** is defined as business operations and transactions that cross over state lines, such as products that are produced in one state and sold in other states. **Intrastate commerce,** on the other hand, is defined as business transacted within a state. Most small retail companies are involved mainly in intrastate commerce, for example, since they usually sell to customers located within the same state. Because most large companies are likely to be involved in both interstate and intrastate commerce, they are subject to state and federal regulations.

Moreover, each state has a constitution that allows it to create other governing units, such as cities, towns, and counties. These units also regulate business transacted within them. Large business firms especially are subject to local, state, and federal laws.

Many state and local laws are related to federal laws. Most states, for instance, have laws that promote competition, protect consumers and the environment, safeguard the public's health, and improve employment conditions. In addition, however, state and local governments regulate business by issuing licenses, franchises, and building codes, and by passing zoning regulations.

Licensing

State and local governments have used **licensing** as a way to limit and control those who plan to enter certain types of businesses. In order to start a business that requires a license, an application must be filed. If the government believes there is a sufficient number of these kinds of businesses, the application can be refused.

Business is regulated not only by the granting of licenses but also by regular inspections by government officials to see that the company is operated according to the law. If it is not being properly operated, it can lose its license. For example, a licensed restaurant is inspected from time to time for cleanliness. Failure to pass inspection may mean the license is withdrawn and the restaurant must close.

Licensing laws vary from place to place. In some cities, business firms of all types must obtain licenses while in other communities only certain types need licenses. It is particularly common to license restaurants, beauty shops, barber shops, and other types of service firms that may affect the health of customers. In most states and in many cities, licensing laws regulate the sale of such items as liquor and tobacco.

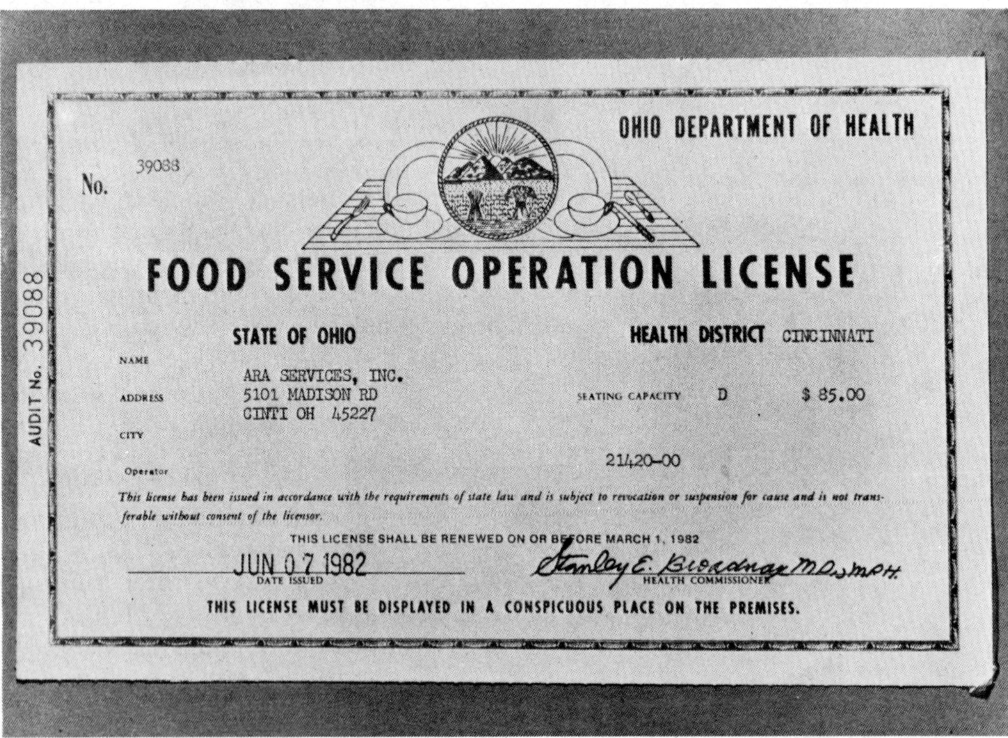

AUDIT No. 39088

OHIO DEPARTMENT OF HEALTH

No. 39088

FOOD SERVICE OPERATION LICENSE

STATE OF OHIO

HEALTH DISTRICT CINCINNATI

NAME ARA SERVICES, INC.

ADDRESS 5101 MADISON RD
CINTI OH 45227

SEATING CAPACITY D $ 85.00

CITY

Operator 21420-00

This license has been issued in accordance with the requirements of state law and is subject to revocation or suspension for cause and is not transferable without consent of the licensor.

THIS LICENSE SHALL BE RENEWED ON OR BEFORE MARCH 1, 1982

JUN 07 1982
DATE ISSUED

Stanley E. Broadnax M.D., M.P.H.
HEALTH COMMISSIONER

THIS LICENSE MUST BE DISPLAYED IN A CONSPICUOUS PLACE ON THE PREMISES.

ILLUS. 4–6
Restaurants and cafeterias must be licensed and inspected regularly.

Public Franchising

Another way for state and local governments to control business is through public franchises. A **public franchise** is a contract that permits a person or organization to use public property for private profit. No individual member of society, however, has a right to use public property for profit except through a special grant by society. Cities often grant public franchises to companies to operate bus lines or to install electric power lines.

Building Codes and Zoning

Local governments may regulate business through **building codes,** which regulate physical features of structures. Building codes may specify such things as the maximum height, minimum square feet of space, and the types of materials that may be used. To construct a new building, a permit must be obtained. While the building is being constructed, inspectors check to make certain that the building codes are followed.

Not only do local governments regulate the types of buildings permitted but they also regulate where they may be built. **Zoning** regulations specify which land areas may be used for homes and which areas may be used for different types of businesses. In most cities, for example, a factory cannot be built in an area zoned for homes. A business must obey all local regulations relating to zoning and construction.

BUSINESS TAXES

While government uses many different ways to regulate business, no way is more important than taxes. The types and amounts of taxes levied influence business decisions which in turn can influence the total amount of business activity for a region and for the nation.

Both business firms and individuals pay many kinds of taxes to local, state, and federal governments. Taxes collected by the federal government account for almost 60 percent of all taxes collected, while the various state and local taxes account for the remaining 40 percent. Most corporations pay nearly one half of their profits in various kinds of taxes.

General Nature of Taxes

Taxes are levied for different purposes, and when government decides to levy a particular type of tax, the question of fairness to taxpayers must be considered. Some types of taxes have been used for many years, while new taxes are being considered by the federal government.

Reasons for Taxes. Taxes are used by government for a number of reasons. Governments use taxes mainly to raise revenue (receipts) to fund new and ongoing programs. Governments also use taxes to regulate business activity.

Governments set goals that must be reached in order to provide the various services desired by the public. Examples of these services range from law enforcement and road building to providing for the military defense of the country. It is costly for government to provide the many services required. To pay for these services, therefore, revenue is raised by levying taxes.

ILLUS. 4–7
Taxes take a large percentage of the income of many businesses.

Taxes are also used to control business activity. Economic growth can be quickened by lowering taxes and slowed by raising taxes. The federal government also taxes certain foreign goods that enter this country in order to encourage consumers to purchase American-made rather than foreign-made products. Governments at the state and local levels also control business activity through taxation. For example, taxes are often high on alcoholic beverages and tobacco, in part to discourage customers from purchasing these products.

Fairness of Taxation. It is difficult for government to find methods of levying taxes fairly and in sufficient amount to meet government expenses. The question of fairness has always caused much debate. One problem is the determination of who will, in fact, pay a tax which is levied by government. For example, a firm may have to pay taxes on the goods it manufactures. But, since the tax is part of the cost of producing the product, this cost may be passed on to the customer. Another problem of fairness is one of whether those with the most assets or most income pay at a higher rate than those who own or earn the least.

Different solutions to the fairness problem are represented by whether a government adopts a proportional, progressive, or regressive tax policy.

Proportional Taxation. A **proportional tax**—sometimes called a **flat tax**—is one in which a single tax rate is charged regardless of who must pay. For example, the tax rate on real estate per $1,000 of property value is always the same regardless of the amount of real estate owned by the taxpayer. The total dollar amount of the tax paid by someone with a $200,000 home will be different from that paid by the person with a $125,000 home in the same area, but the rate of the tax is the same for both. A flat state tax of 6 percent on income is also proportional. Those with higher incomes pay more dollars than those with lower incomes. But the tax rate of 6 percent stays the same.

Progressive Taxation. A **progressive tax** is one based on ability to pay. The policy of progressive taxation is followed in federal and many state income tax systems. As one's income increases, the tax rate is increased. As a result, a lower income person is taxed at a lower rate than a higher income person.

Some local and state governments have combined the policies of proportional and progressive taxes. For example, a flat tax of 5 percent may be levied on incomes up to $20,000, and 6 percent on all incomes above $20,000. The federal government has also considered a flat tax, such as a 14 percent rate for everyone up to a stated amount and a higher rate for those over that amount. With some of the proposed federal flat tax plans, many of the special exemptions or deductions from total income would be eliminated, resulting in a much simpler tax system.

Regressive Taxation. The third type of tax policy is represented by a **regressive tax,** in which the actual tax rate becomes lower as the amount on which the taxes are levied is increased. While general sales taxes are often thought to be proportional, they are actually regressive because persons with low incomes pay a larger proportion of their incomes in taxes than those earning high incomes. Suppose, for example, that A and B live in a state that levies a 5 percent general sales tax. Person A has an annual take-home pay of $15,000, all of which is spent. The tax, $750 ($15,000 x .05), represents 5 percent of A's take-home pay. On the other hand, Person B spent $23,000 and saved $7,000 from an annual take-home pay of $30,000. The taxes amounted to $1,150 ($23,000 x .05). B's tax on take-home pay, as a result, was only 3.8 percent ($1,150 ÷ $30,000) compared to 5 percent for A. Because the sales tax applies to purchases rather than to income, the general sales tax is regressive. To make the sales tax less regressive, some states exclude certain types of purchases from taxation. The exclusions are usually items on which low-income families spend a high percentage of their money, such as food.

Kinds of Taxes

Taxation has become so complicated that the average business person spends a great deal of time in filling out tax forms, computing taxes, and making various reports. In many business firms the various taxes take a great percentage of the income. Illus. 4-8 gives examples of the types of taxes that a business operating in only one state may be required to pay.

ILLUS. 4–8
The most common business taxes.

Federal income tax	Property tax—intangible property
State income tax	Sales tax
Local income tax	Federal excise tax
Payroll taxes	Franchise tax
Federal social security tax	Gasoline tax
State unemployment tax	Corporation taxes
State workers' insurance tax	Severance tax
Property tax—real estate	Licenses
Property tax—personal	Motortruck licenses and taxes
Property tax—merchandise	Assessments

The three most common types of taxes affecting business firms and individuals are income taxes, sales taxes, and property taxes.

Income Tax. The federal government and most state governments use the income tax to raise revenues. An **income tax** is a tax that is levied against the profits of business firms and against money earned by individuals. For individuals, the tax is based on salaries and other income earned after certain deductions are allowed. For business firms, an income tax is usually levied on net profits (receipts less expenses). Chapter 6 provides information about income taxes that corporations pay.

The income tax is the largest source of revenue for the federal government. While individuals pay about three quarters of the total federal income taxes collected, businesses pay the remaining one quarter. The cost of collecting the individual income taxes is, in part, shared by business. Every business is required to withhold income taxes from the earnings of employees and pay this money to the government. Thus, business performs an important tax service for government.

Sales Tax. A **sales tax** is one that is levied on the retail price of goods or services at the time they are sold. A general sales tax usually applies to all goods or services sold by retailers. However, when a sales tax applies only to selected goods or services, such as gasoline, it is called an **excise tax.**

Sales taxes are the main source of revenue for most states and some cities. Although state governments do not administer sales taxes in a like manner, in most cases the retail business collects the tax from customers and turns this tax over to the state government. A business must be familiar with the sales tax law of the state in which it operates so that it can collect and report the tax properly.

Property Tax. A **property tax** is a levy on material goods owned. While the sales tax is the primary source of revenue for most state governments, the property tax is the main source of revenue for local governments. There may be a real property tax and a personal property tax. A **real property tax** is a tax levied on land and buildings. A **personal property tax** is a tax on such items as furniture, machinery, and equipment. In many states there is a special property tax on raw materials used to make goods and on finished goods available for sale.

A tax on property—whether it is real property or personal property—is stated in terms of dollars per hundred of assessed valuation. **Assessed valuation** is the value of property determined by tax officials. Thus, a tax rate of $2.80 on property with an assessed valuation of $60,000 is $1,680.

Proposed Tax Laws

Whenever governments need to raise additional revenues, tax policy is carefully reviewed. Some taxes that have been tried successfully by state governments and foreign countries are under consideration by the federal government. Two such taxes are the national sales tax and the value-added tax.

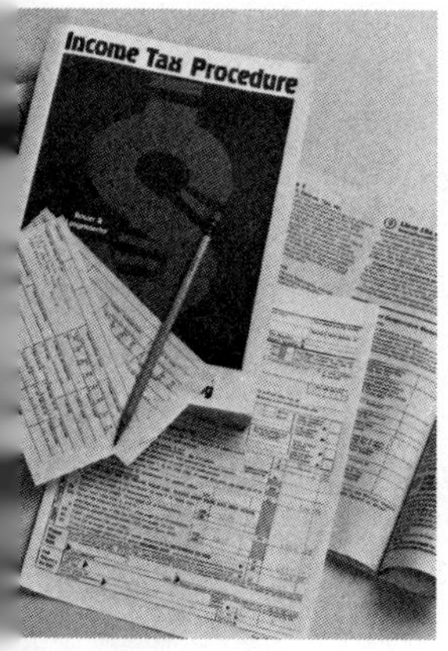

National Sales Tax. Many states have resorted to raising additional revenues in recent decades through sales taxes. Since this has been an effective means for raising revenues at the state level, a national sales tax has been recommended by some tax experts. A **national sales tax** would be levied by the federal government on most goods and services purchased. Those who favor a national sales tax suggest that it should replace the federal income tax. This tax would be relatively easy to collect, since the well-established procedure for collecting state sales taxes could be followed.

Critics of a national sales tax believe that both a state and a national sales tax might be burdensome. A further objection is that a sales tax is regressive; that is, as a percentage of income, those with higher incomes would be taxed less than lower income people. For these reasons, a national sales tax has not yet been passed even though politicians have given it serious consideration.

Value-Added Tax. Another proposed tax, which has gained popularity in Europe and is currently receiving a great deal of attention in the United States is the value-added tax. The **value-added tax (VAT)** would be a fixed tax rate levied at each processing stage on all goods and services produced.

Here is an example of how a 5 percent value-added tax would apply to a butcher-block table. Picture the table first as a tree and finally as a piece of furniture in someone's home. One company chopped the tree and processed the lumber, while another manufactured the table. The manufacturer then sold the table to a furniture store, and the store sold the table to a customer. Each business involved added to the value of the table. Therefore, each business would pay a tax, but a tax based only on the value it added to the table, as shown in Illus. 4-9.

ILLUS. 4–9
A value-added tax would be levied at each stage of processing goods from raw materials to sale to customers.

Processor	(1) Cost	(2) Selling Price	(3) Value Added (2)−(1)	(4) Tax Rate	(5) Tax (3)×(4)
Lumber Firm	—	$200	$200	.05	$10.00
Manufacturer	$200	550	350	.05	17.50
Retailer	550	650	100	.05	5.00

The lumber company added $200 to the value of the table; therefore, its tax would be $10 ($200 x .05). Since the manufacturer added $350 to the table's value ($550-$200), its tax would be $17.50; whereas the furniture store's tax would amount to $5.00 as shown. The value added by each business would allow the government to collect a total tax of $32.50.

Those who favor VAT argue that it is fairer than a national sales tax because VAT is shared by all businesses involved in providing goods and services. There is disagreement, however, as to which of the two proposed taxes would produce more income and which tax would be easier to collect. A major disadvantage to the national sales tax and the VAT is that both are considered to be regressive taxes. In spite of this disadvantage, federal authorities will consider both taxes in the years ahead as the need to raise added revenues increases.

Effect of Taxes on Business Decisions

Many major decisions that affect business firms are in one way or another related to taxes. Taxes may influence the accounting methods a business selects to calculate profits and the method used to pay managers. Often taxes are used as a basis for deciding where to locate a new business or whether to move a business from one location to another.

For example, assume that a producer of garden tools is trying to decide in which of two cities to locate a new factory. City A is located in a state that has a low state income tax and low property taxes. City B is located in a state that has no state income tax but has high property taxes. After weighing all the factors, the producer has decided to locate in City A. City A, which has both an income tax and a property tax, has been selected mainly because the total tax cost each year is less than in City B. Decisions of this nature are made every year by many businesses.

NEW TERMS AND CONCEPTS

Define the following terms and concepts, which may be found in bold face type on the page shown in parentheses.

- price discrimination (67)
- false advertising (67)
- patent (69)
- copyright (69)
- trademark (70)
- interstate commerce (71)
- intrastate commerce (71)
- licensing (72)
- public franchise (73)
- building codes (73)
- zoning (73)
- proportional tax, or flat tax (75)
- progressive tax (75)
- regressive tax (75)
- income tax (76)
- sales tax (76)
- excise tax (76)
- property tax (77)
- real property tax (77)
- personal property tax (77)
- assessed valuation (77)
- national sales tax (77)
- value-added tax, or VAT (77)

CHAPTER REVIEW

1. When does a monopoly exist?
2. What is the name of the first major law promoting competition and in what year was it passed?
3. Which federal law forbids corporations from acquiring ownership rights in other corporations if the purpose is to create a monopoly or to discourage competition?
4. What is the main purpose of the Robinson-Patman Act of 1936?
5. Which Act makes it unlawful for an advertiser to circulate false advertising that can lead to the purchase of foods, drugs, medical devices, or cosmetics, or to participate in any other unfair methods of competition?
6. Name five federal agencies that regulate business activities.
7. What type of agreement gives an inventor the sole right for 17 years to make, use, and sell an invention?
8. How are trademarks and patents alike?
9. Name the federal agency that protects the consumer from dangerous food and nonfood products.
10. Give two reasons why taxes are levied.
11. Does the federal government have a flat income tax?
12. In which tax policy does the actual rate of taxation lower as the taxable amount increases?
13. What are the three most common types of business taxes?

14. Name two proposed federal taxes.
15. Who would pay the value-added tax?

QUESTIONS FOR CLASS DISCUSSION

1. Discuss how a business that has a monopoly on a good or service can keep its prices unreasonably high.
2. Why is it necessary for the federal government to pass laws promoting fair competition?
3. Determine whether the following situation violates one of the antitrust laws and, if it does, which law: Pinter, Inc., makes one type of flashlight and sells it to retail stores. Most of its flashlights are sold to large retail stores. For Stores A, B, and C it sells in about the same quantity at the same price. It also sells to Store D in about the same quantity but at a much lower price because it has been doing business with Store D longer.
4. Name at least three different kinds of practices that are prohibited under the laws administered by the Federal Trade Commission.
5. Sundial Products placed an advertisement in the local newspaper stating that its latest suntan lotion would give a deep suntan in 24 hours, without any danger to one's health. Within a week, ten persons were badly burned by the product. Discuss how the federal government might control this company and its new product.
6. Discuss the need for patents, copyrights, and trademarks.
7. Discuss the need for state and local governments to establish licensing regulations.
8. Monica Lopez wants to start a sewing shop business in her home where she can alter clothes and sell sewing supplies. Discuss whether the local zoning law that forbids her from doing this is fair or unfair.
9. Which do you think is the fairest kind of tax—a proportional tax, a progressive tax, or a regressive tax? Provide reasons to support your answer.
10. Discuss how a local community can attract or discourage new businesses through local taxes and other controls.

PROBLEMS AND PROJECTS

1. You live in a state that has the following tax schedule:

Taxable Income	Rate
$ 0 – $ $3,999	no tax
4,000 – 11,999	5%
12,000 – 19,999	6%
20,000 and over	7%

Your state permits everyone to have $2,000 of exemptions from total income to arrive at taxable income. Your income this year is only $6,000 because of lost work due to illness. Your friend's income is $19,000.

   a. What is your tax this year? What is your friend's tax?
   b. What is the actual tax rate you and your friend paid this year based on your total incomes?

2. If the real estate tax rate is $3.40 per $100 of assessed valuation:
   a. What is the tax per $1,000 of valuation?
   b. What is the tax on real estate valued at $25,000?
   c. Using your local tax rate, compute the real estate tax on the real estate valued at $25,000.
3. Use your library and prepare a report on one of the federal regulatory agencies shown in Illus. 4-4. As part of your report, be sure to find out (a) which laws the agency administers, (b) how it enforces the laws, and (c) examples of companies that have violated the laws.
4. Three manufacturers that sell nationally discuss prices of a product that they all manufacture but which has become unprofitable to each. They believe that it is foolish to sell at a loss. They all agree to raise prices, but they do not agree on how much each will charge. Do you consider this action illegal? Explain.
5. Find ten trademark symbols or designs, such as a picture of a greyhound for Greyhound Bus Lines. Draw two columns on a sheet of paper. Place the name of the company on the left and the symbol on the right. Then cover the left column and ask five persons to tell you which company each symbol represents. Keep score of the results and give a report to your class making certain to tell which trademark symbols were most and least known.

CASE 4–1

Jason Romulus owns and operates a hardware store in a community of 50,000 people. The nearest town is at least 25 miles away but there are two competitors in the area who often run weekly advertisements.

Today, a customer he had never seen before came into the store. "I certainly hope you carry Weaver tools," the customer said. "The other stores in town don't carry the Weaver brand."

"Sure, we carry Weaver's," answered Jason. "It is one of my best lines."

The customer looked happy and relieved, and went to his truck to get the old tool he wanted to replace. While the customer was outside, Jason had a chance to think about what the customer had said. Now Jason knew why the Weaver brand was so popular in his store. As a result, he decided to raise prices on Weaver tools by tomorrow morning. Also, he could promote Weaver tools in next week's advertisements. A smile crossed Jason's face as the customer returned.

"Here is the tool," said the customer. "I hope you can replace it. As you can see, it is quite different from the other brands."

"I can see that it is different," Jason responded. "You are lucky to get it at this low price. The price will be going up in the very near future."

Required:

1. Does Jason have a monopoly on Weaver tools in his community?
2. If Jason raises his price by very much, what might happen?
3. Is raising the price suddenly and for the reason given an unfair business practice? Discuss.

Case 4–2

The Excello Company is in the food products business. It has been selling nationally to hundreds of small grocery stores that order in rather small quantities. The managers are now in the process of discussing the pricing for their canned vegetables.

One of the managers has suggested the following pricing system: selling vegetables to all customers in quantities of 1-5 cases at $6.00 a case; in quantities of 6-10 cases at $5.00 a case; and in quantities of 11-15 cases at $4.00 a case. Most stores never buy more than 15 cases.

Required:

1. Is this pricing system in violation of any of the antitrust laws? Explain.
2. The marketing manager has reported that a large chain grocery store is interested in buying in quantities of 1,000 cases. Excello can make a fair profit if it sells to the large chain store at $3.00 a case. Will this be legal?

Case 4–3

Drive-R Company and U-Drive Company are two large auto rental firms that operate nationally. Most of their branch offices are at train stations, airports, and hotels. There are other small competitors, but Drive-R and U-Drive make well over half the total auto rentals yearly.

In order to save on some of their advertising and other operating costs, the top executives of the two firms got together and agreed to share some of the market on a fair basis. A list of all the big railroad stations and airports was made, put in alphabetical order, and numbered accordingly. It was agreed that Drive-R would operate rental offices at the odd-numbered locations. And U-Drive would operate offices at the even-numbered locations. They further agreed to set the same rental prices at the large railroad stations and airports but not at the small places or at the hotels.

Required:

1. Do these auto rental companies operate in interstate or intrastate commerce?
2. If you worked for the Federal Trade Commission and fairly administered the laws promoting competition, would you find the action of these firms illegal? Explain.
3. If you were the top executive for the U-Drive Company and the FTC said that it planned to bring a court action against you, would you fight the case? Explain.

Have You Thought About Becoming . . .
. . . A LAWYER?

Lawyers—also called attorneys—are necessary to help people to understand the laws and their legal rights. But laws also affect businesses, and lawyers are needed to help executives interpret laws, rulings, and regulations that affect their businesses. Lawyers often specialize in certain types of law, such as labor, patent, tax, or contract law. Some attorneys are employed in managerial positions in large corporations, while others seek positions where legal knowledge is especially valuable, such as credit investigators and insurance claims adjusters. Regardless of their specialty, all lawyers spend a great deal of time studying and interpreting laws as they apply to varied situations.

To become a lawyer, special skills and abilities are needed, many of which can be partially developed in high school. Included are communication skills—writing, reading, speaking, and listening. Human relations skills are needed to work with others. And especially important is one's ability to analyze information and to give opinions about how laws apply to special situations.

Lawyers usually complete about seven years of schooling beyond high school. Suitable major areas of study in college include social sciences, natural sciences, and humanities. Attorneys need a good general education, so they should also have courses in government, history, economics, and mathematics. If you are interested in specializing in a particular field of law, you should take some courses in that specialized field while in college. For example, if you plan to become a tax lawyer, take some accounting courses, and perhaps even obtain an accounting degree before or after completing law school.

To be admitted to law school, you must make excellent grades throughout your educational career. A good educational background should also help you to obtain a high score on a special test required for admission to law school (Law School Admissions Test). And, after you complete law school, an extremely difficult examination called the Bar Exam must be passed in order to practice law in most courts.

While the need for attorneys has grown and will continue to grow, the number of law school graduates is now greater than the number of jobs available. As a result, employers will be very selective in hiring new lawyers. Students who rank high in their classes should find positions in law firms, on the legal staffs of corporations and government agencies, or as law clerks for judges. Lower ranking graduates often find jobs where legal training is an asset but is not necessarily required. Many positions are available in real estate firms, banks, insurance firms, and government agencies. In general, a law degree is particularly valuable for many administrative and managerial positions in government and business.

UNIT 2

Business Ownership

Look up or down the main street in your community and you will see many businesses—large and small. A few of those business firms started within the last 12 months. The excitement and challenge of owning and operating a business leads thousands of individuals into business ownership each year. A decision to start your own business is an important one because it presents many challenges and responsibilities.

You will discover some of the challenges and responsibilities of business ownership in Unit 2. In addition, the most common forms of ownership—proprietorship, partnership, corporation, and cooperative—are discussed along with the advantages and disadvantages of each.

At one point in his life, Wally Amos decided to become self-employed by starting his own business. His career in business ownership, which is included in the biographical profile on the next page, is representative of the success experienced by many people who have become business owners.

WALLY AMOS

Wally Amos opened a cookie shop in Los Angeles on March 9, 1975, selling his popular "Famous Amos" chocolate chip cookies. The Famous Amos Chocolate Chip Cookie Corporation now prepares over six tons of handmade, high-quality cookies every day and distributes them to fine stores throughout the country.

Wally Amos has not always been a cookie entrepreneur. He first attended cooking school, then served as a radio repair person for four years while in the Air Force, and then worked as a stock clerk and supply manager for Saks Fifth Avenue after learning secretarial skills in a business school.

He then took a job with the William Morris Agency, where he worked first as a mailroom clerk and then as a secretary to the company's vice-president. Because of his ability to identify potential entertainers successfully, Wally Amos became a talent agent for the agency. He later formed his own talent agency and operated it for a brief period. During his career as a talent agent, Mr. Amos experimented with making cookies and sharing them with others.

Combining his hobby of baking chocolate chip cookies, his promotional skills as a talent agent, and his recent entrepreneurial experience, Wally Amos followed the advice of his friends. He convinced a few entertainers to invest $25,000 in his first retail outlet where he made and sold cookies. The rest is history. His business became an instant success.

Wally Amos is now recognized nationally as a model black entrepreneur. As a successful business owner, Famous Amos has made his mark "managing the cookie," as he is fond of saying. But he has also successfully managed his basic personal beliefs—a strong belief in quality, in truth and honesty, and in helping others. He has demonstrated his desire to help others by hiring handicapped employees, serving as national spokesperson for the Literacy Volunteers of America, and spending much of his time working with young people and promoting the goals of charitable groups.

5

PROPRIETORSHIPS AND PARTNERSHIPS

After studying this chapter you will be able to:

- Outline some of the responsibilities of owning your own business.
- List advantages and disadvantages of proprietorships.
- List advantages and disadvantages of partnerships.
- Identify kinds of businesses that are best suited to the proprietorship and partnership forms of organization.
- Indicate some of the legal points to be considered when selecting a name for a business.

An important characteristic of business in the United States is that nearly all businesses are owned by individuals. One person, or a group of persons, invests savings in a business with the hope of obtaining profits from its activities. Profit, however, is not guaranteed just because one enters business. Whether a new business makes a profit or suffers a loss depends in part on an owner's understanding and acceptance of the responsibilities of ownership.

The responsibilities of business ownership must be weighed before one decides to go into business. Then, the legal form of ownership must be selected. The most common forms are the proprietorship, the partnership, and the corporation. The form of ownership selected depends on several factors, such as the nature and size of the business, the capital needed, the type of managerial services desired, the tax laws, and the financial liability the owners are willing to assume. Two legal forms of business ownership—the proprietorship and the partnership—are discussed in this chapter. Also discussed is the selection of a legally acceptable name for a business.

RESPONSIBILITIES OF BUSINESS OWNERSHIP

The decision to enter business is not an easy one to make. In addition to meeting financial, legal, and other general requirements, a great many other responsibilities must be assumed. A single owner has many more responsibilities than an ordinary employee. Assume, for example, that you are employed as a truck driver. Your duties include making pickups and deliveries. After obtaining several years of valuable work experience, you decide to start your own trucking firm.

As the owner your duties not only include those of a driver, but you must also perform many other duties. Even if you run the business from your home, you will have added expenses for an office, a garage, and perhaps a telephone answering service. You must find customers, persuade those customers to pay a fair price for your services, and collect from those customers. Furthermore, you must assume responsibility for damage that may occur to the merchandise hauled. Fees for various licenses, taxes, insurance premiums, gasoline, truck repairs, and other operating expenses must be paid. Additionally, it may be necessary to hire, train, and supervise employees.

These many responsibilities of ownership cannot be overlooked when one considers opening a business. These responsibilities may be seen as a disadvantage by some people, but as an advantage by others. Persons who enjoy being leaders and making decisions find great satisfaction in running a business. Opportunities to make decisions and to experience other rewards are found in business ownership. Some of these rewards will be identified in the section that follows.

PROPRIETORSHIP

The most common form of business organization is the proprietorship, of which there are over 11 million in this country. A business that is owned and managed by one person is known as a **sole proprietorship,** or a **proprietorship,** and the owner-manager is the **proprietor.** In addition to owning and managing the business, the proprietor often performs those day-to-day tasks that make a business successful. Under the proprietorship form of organization, the owner furnishes money, management, and perhaps part of the labor. For assuming these responsibilities, the owner is entitled to all profits earned by the business.

Provided that no debts are owed, a proprietor has full claim to the **assets** (property) of the business. If the proprietor has business debts, however, **creditors** (those to whom money is owed) have first claim against the assets. Illus. 5–1 is a simple financial statement of Jane York, who is the proprietor of a small retail grocery store and fruit market.

ILLUS. 5–1
Balance sheet (Jane York).

Assets		**Claims Against Assets**	
Cash	$ 7,400	Accounts Payable (Debts)	$ 6,000
Merchandise	13,200	J. York, Capital	85,000
Equipment	10,400		
Land and Building	60,000		
	$91,000		$91,000

This simple financial statement, known as a **statement of financial position**, or **balance sheet**, shows that the assets of the business are valued at $91,000. Since York has debts of $6,000, her capital is $85,000 ($91,000 – $6,000). In accounting, **capital**, **net worth**, and **equity** all mean assets less claims against assets. If there are any earnings, she gets the total amount. She must also absorb any losses. Since she owns the land and the building, she does not have to pay any rent, although she must pay the cost of maintenance and taxes for the property.

ILLUS. 5–2
A proprietor is the sole owner of a business.

Advantages of Proprietorship

The fact that almost three out of four businesses today are proprietorships indicates that this form of organization has definite advantages. Can you list any of the advantages before reading further?

Owner Is Boss. When one is the sole owner of a business there usually is a certain satisfaction in being one's own boss and of being responsible only to oneself. The proprietor feels there is a better chance to be inventive and creative in working out ideas. This feeling stimulates the owner to work hard to make the business a success.

Owner Receives All Profits. Very closely related to this first advantage is the fact that all the profits belong to the sole proprietor. As the sole gainer, the owner is more likely to work overtime and to think continually of how the business can be operated more efficiently.

Owner Personally Knows Employees and Customers. Because most proprietorships are small, the proprietor and the employees know each other personally. This relationship can lead to mutual understanding and interest between employer and employees. These same benefits should also result from the close ties that the proprietor has with customers.

ILLUS. 5–3
A proprietor is entitled to all of the profits of the business.

Owner Can Act Quickly in Decision Making. The sole proprietor is not blocked in making decisions. As there is no need to consult others, the owner can act promptly in emergencies. If an unusual opportunity to buy merchandise or equipment arises, or if the owner wishes to change the location of the business or to sell on credit terms rather than on a cash basis, there are no dissenting partners to stop such action. Thus, the management of a proprietorship is flexible and can adjust itself easily to changing conditions.

Owner is Free from Red Tape. One can usually begin or end business activities as a sole proprietor without legal formality. One does not need to consult a lawyer and go through a large amount of red tape in order to organize a proprietorship. In some types of businesses, however, such as a restaurant, it is necessary to obtain a license before operations can begin.

Owner Usually Pays Less Income Tax than a Corporation. In most sole proprietorships the income tax is usually less than in the corporation type of business. This is explained in the next chapter.

Disadvantages of Proprietorship

There are many advantages to owning your own business. However, there are also some disadvantages facing the sole proprietor.

Owner May Lack Special Skills and Abilities. Each person usually has a special aptitude or ability. One person may be able to sell merchandise. Another person may be more talented at purchasing goods or keeping records. Still a third person may have the ability to supervise employees. All of these activities are important to the success of a business, but the proprietor is likely to be weak in one or more of them. It is, therefore, easy to understand why many proprietorships end in failure within a short time.

Owner May Lack Funds. Often there is need of additional funds (capital) for emergencies. Financial assistance on a large scale may be difficult to obtain when so much depends upon one person. The expansion of the business may be slowed because of the owner's lack of capital.

Owner Bears All Losses. A proprietor assumes a great deal of risk. It is true that a sole owner receives all the profits of the business; but, too, a sole owner bears all the losses if the business fails. Should this happen and the owner is unable to pay the debts of the business, the creditors have a claim against any assets of the proprietor. The owner may therefore lose not only the money invested in the enterprise, but also personal possessions such as a car or home.

Illness or Death May Close the Business. It is possible that the owner of a business could become ill. If the illness lasts for a long time or results in death, the business would have to close.

Kinds of Businesses Suited to the Proprietorship Form of Organization

The kind of business that is primarily concerned with rendering personal service is well suited to the proprietorship form of organization. Dentists, accountants, auctioneers, landscape gardeners, carpenters, painters, tourist camps, barber shops, beauty shops, shoe repair shops, and radio and television service stores are examples of businesses frequently organized as proprietorships.

Another type of business that seems to be well adapted to the proprietorship form of business is the one that sells merchandise or service on a small scale. Newspaper and magazine stands, roadside markets, restaurants, flower shops, gasoline stations, small grocery stores, meat markets, clothing stores, parking lots, and dry cleaners are examples of this type. In general, the type of business that can be operated suitably as a proprietorship is one that (a) can be managed by the proprietor or by persons hired by the proprietor, and (b) does not require a great amount of capital.

PARTNERSHIP

Jane York, who operates the proprietorship mentioned earlier, is faced with the problem of expanding her business. She is now 55 years old and has operated the business successfully for many years. She sees new opportunities in the community for increasing her business, but she does not wish to assume full responsibility for the undertaking. She realizes that the expansion of the business will place on her considerable financial and managerial responsibilities. She also realizes that in order to expand the business she needs additional capital, but she does not wish to borrow the money. Because of these reasons she has decided that it will be wise to change her business from a proprietorship to a **partnership**, a business owned by two or more persons.

Robert Burton operates an adjoining meat market. He is younger than Jane York and has proved to be honest and to have considerable business ability. Combining the two businesses could result in more customers for both groceries and meats. Customers who have been coming to the meat market will possibly become grocery customers also. And those who have been buying at the grocery and fruit market may become meat market customers. A discussion between Jane and Robert leads to a tentative agreement to form a partnership if a third person can be found who will invest enough cash to remodel the present two stores to form one large store and to purchase additional equipment. The financial statement of Burton's business is shown in Illus. 5–4.

The net worth of Burton's business is $64,000. In other words, after deducting the amount of his debts ($3,000) from the total value of his assets ($67,000), he has a net ownership of $64,000. According to the balance

ILLUS. 5–4
Balance sheet (Robert Burton).

Assets		Claims Against Assets	
Cash	$ 4,400	Accounts Payable	
Merchandise	3,000	(Debts)	$ 3,000
Equipment	9,600	R. Burton, Capital	64,000
Land and Building	50,000		
	$67,000		$67,000

sheet on page 89, York's business is worth $85,000. In order to have an equal investment in the partnership, Burton must invest an additional $21,000 in cash.

They find Carl King, a person with accounting experience, who has $60,000 and is able to borrow the remaining amount of $25,000 to be an equal partner. The partnership agreement, shown in Illus. 5–7 on page 95, is then written and signed by the three people.

Once the partnership is formed, a statement of financial position (balance sheet) must be filled out. This statement shows the total assets, liabilities, and capital of the owners at the start of the business. The partnership's balance sheet is shown in Illus. 5–5.

ILLUS. 5–5
Balance sheet (partnership of York, Burton and King).

Assets		Claims Against Assets	
Cash	$117,800	Accounts Payable	
Merchandise	16,200	(Debts)	$ 9,000
Equipment	20,000	J. York, Capital	85,000
Land and Building	110,000	R. Burton, Capital	85,000
		C. King, Capital	85,000
	$264,000		$264,000

In operating the partnership, York, Burton and King divide the responsibilities. York supervises the grocery department, Burton supervises the meat department, and King has charge of finances and records.

During the year the three partners combine the stores and remodel them. They also buy some new equipment. At the end of the year the financial statement, shown in Illus. 5–6 on page 94, is prepared to show the status of the partnership.

Has the partnership had a successful year? Each partner has received a salary of $2,000 a month (according to the terms of the partnership agreement); in addition, the capital or net worth of each partner has increased from $85,000 to $94,000 as a result of profits made during the year. This increase of the total capital from $255,000 to $282,000 amounts to

ILLUS. 5–6
Balance sheet (partnership of York, Burton and King), end of first year.

Assets		Claims Against Assets	
Cash	$ 24,000	Accounts Payable	
Merchandise	48,000	(Debts)	$ 8,000
Equipment	45,000	J. York, Capital	94,000
Land and Building	173,000	R. Burton, Capital	94,000
		C. King, Capital	94,000
	$290,000		$290,000

$27,000 and is an increase of over 10 percent. King, who had to borrow some of the money used for his investment, had to pay 8 percent interest. His investment in the partnership has brought him a return that is considerably more than the interest on his loan.

Advantages of the Partnership

Many business firms are organized as partnerships at the very beginning. There are over one million businesses operating as partnerships in the United States. While most partnerships have only two or three partners, there is no limit set on the number of partners. In some businesses, there are as many as ten or more. Some of the advantages of the partnership form of business organization are discussed below.

Skills and Abilities Pooled. A partnership is likely to be operated more efficiently than a proprietorship because two or more persons share in the management. One partner may have special sales ability; another may have an aptitude for buying the right kind, quality, and quantity of merchandise. One partner may propose a change in the business, and another partner may be able to point out disadvantages in the plan and suggest modifications that were not apparent to the one who made the original proposal. The combined abilities of the partners should result in a more efficient operation than would be the case if each were conducting a business as sole proprietor.

Sources of Capital Increased. When a business is started, more capital can be supplied through the investments of two or more people than can ordinarily be obtained by one person. Some business firms require a greater amount of capital for equipment and merchandise than one person may be able to supply; but enough beginning capital can be obtained if several persons enter into a partnership. Generally the additional capital needed for expansion is obtained more easily if there are several partners.

Credit Position Improved. The partnership usually has a better credit reputation than the sole proprietorship. This is because there are several owners responsible for the ownership and management of the business.

PARTNERSHIP AGREEMENT

This Contract, made and entered into on the first day of June, 19--, by and between Jane L. York, of Olean, New York, party of the first part, Robert R. Burton, of Olean, New York, party of the second part, Carl O. King, of Ceres, New York, party of the third part:

WITNESSETH: That the said parties have this day formed a partnership for the purpose of engaging in and conducting a retail grocery-fruit market and meat store under the following stipulations, which are made a part of the contract:

FIRST: The said partnership is to continue for a term of ten years from date hereof.

SECOND: The business shall be conducted under the firm name of Y B & K Fine Foods, at 4467 Goodson Street, Olean, New York.

THIRD: The investments are as follows: Jane L. York: Cash, $7,400; Merchandise, $13,200; Equipment, $10,400; Land and Building, $60,000; Total Assets, $91,000, less Accounts Payable, $6,000, equals Net Investment, $85,000. Robert R. Burton: Cash, $25,400; Merchandise, $3,000; Equipment, $9,600; Land and Building, $50,000; Total Assets, $88,000, less Accounts Payable, $3,000, equals Net Investment, $85,000. Carl O. King: Cash, $85,000.

FOURTH: All profits or losses arising from said business are to be shared equally.

FIFTH: Each partner is to devote his or her entire time and attention to the business and to engage in no other business enterprise without the written consent of the others.

SIXTH: Each partner is to have a salary of $2,000 a month, the same to be withdrawn at such time as he or she may elect. No partner is to withdraw from the business an amount in excess of his or her salary without the written consent of the others.

SEVENTH: The duties of each partner are defined as follows: Jane L. York is to supervise the grocery-fruit department. Robert R. Burton is to supervise the meat department. Carl O. King is to have charge of finances and records.

EIGHTH: No partner is to become surety for anyone without the written consent of the others.

NINTH: In case of the death, incapacity, or withdrawal of one partner, the business is to be conducted for the remainder of the fiscal year by the surviving partners, the profits for the year allocated to the withdrawing partner to be determined by the ratio of the time he or she was a partner during the year to the whole year.

TENTH: In case of dissolution the assets are to be divided in the ratio of the capital invested at the time of dissolution.

IN WITNESS WHEREOF, The parties aforesaid have hereunto set their hands and affixed their seals on the day and year above written.

In the presence of:	Jane L. York (Seal)
Barbara Hemmelgarn	Robert R. Burton (Seal)
Christopher Barks	Carl O. King (Seal)

ILLUS. 5–7

A clearly written and understood partnership agreement can prevent problems later.

Contribution of Goodwill. Each partner is likely to have a large personal following. Some people will be more likely to do business with the newly formed partnership because they know one of the owners. This is known as goodwill.

Increased Concern in Business Management. Each owner of the business will have a greater interest in the firm as partners than as employees. Much of this is due to the greater financial responsibility each person has as a partner.

Less Tax Burden Than Corporations. Partnerships usually have a tax advantage over corporations. You will learn more about this in Chapter 6. Partnerships prepare a federal income tax report but do not pay a tax on their profits as do corporations. However, partners must pay a personal income tax on their individual share of the profits.

Elimination of Competition. Two or more proprietors in the same line of business may combine by organizing a partnership. This move may substantially decrease, or even eliminate, competition.

Retirement from Management. A sole proprietor may wish to retire. However, the proprietor may not want to close the business. In such a case, the owner may form a partnership and allow the new manager to manage the business.

Operating Economies. It is often possible to operate more efficiently by combining two or more business firms. Combining firms reduces certain operating expenses, such as advertising, supplies, equipment, fuel, and rent.

Disadvantages of Partnership

While there are many advantages of partnerships, there are also many disadvantages. The following discussion points out some of the disadvantages of the partnership form of business organization.

Unlimited Financial Liability. According to law each member of the partnership has an **unlimited financial liability** for all the debts of the business. Partners are responsible for their share of the business debts; but, if some of the partners are unable to pay their share, one partner may have to pay all the debts. Suppose that the partnership of York, Burton and King should fail and that, after all the business assets have been changed into cash, the amount due the creditors of the partnership is $9,000 more than the amount of cash. Each partner should contribute $3,000 to the partnership so that there will be enough money to pay the remaining business debts. The creditors, however, may choose to enforce their claims only against York because she may own more property outside the partnership than the other two partners. If York pays the entire $9,000, she then has a claim against each of the other two partners for $3,000.

Disagreement Among Partners. There is always danger of disagreement among partners. The majority of the partners may want to change the nature of the business but are unable to do so because of the refusal of one partner. For example, a partnership may have been formed for the purpose of conducting a retail stereo business. After a while the majority of the partners may think it wise to stop selling stereos and handle home computers instead. As long as one partner disagrees, however, the partnership cannot make the change, although the change may seem very desirable. Furthermore partners sometimes feel that they are not properly sharing in the management. This situation may cause disagreements which could hurt the business. Such a condition may be partly prevented if the partnership agreement states the duties of each partner.

Each Partner Bound By Contracts of Others. Each partner is bound by the partnership contracts made by any partner if such contracts apply to the ordinary operations of the business. There is always the possibility of friction and ill will between partners if one partner makes a contract that turns out to be unprofitable to the partnership.

Uncertain Life. The life of a partnership is uncertain. Sometimes when the contract for a partnership is drawn up, a definite length of time, such as ten years, is fixed for the existence of the business. If one partner dies, however, the partnership ends. The deceased partner may have been the principal manager, and, as a result of his or her death, the business may suffer. The heirs of the dead partner may demand from the surviving partners an unfair price for the share of the deceased partner; or they may insist upon the complete end of the partnership so that they can obtain the share belonging to the dead partner. In the latter case, the assets that are sold usually do not bring a fair price, and, as a result, all the partners suffer a loss. (Insurance on the life of a partner can be carried to provide money to purchase the interest of a partner who dies.) Under the laws of most states, the bankruptcy of any partner or the entrance of a new partner are other causes that may bring a sudden end to the partnership just at a time when the business is beginning to do well.

Limited Sources of Capital. The amount of funds that a partnership may obtain is limited by the contributions of the partners, the earnings of the business, and the amount that can be borrowed. It is difficult for a partnership to obtain enough capital to carry on a large business unless each member of the partnership is wealthy or unless there are many partners. Too many partners, however, may be the cause of inefficiency in operation.

Unsatisfactory Division of Profits. Sometimes there is not a satisfactory distribution of the partnership profits according to the ability and efforts of the individual partners. The profits are shared on the basis of the partnership agreement, such as 60 percent to one partner and 40 percent to the other. If no provision is made in the agreement, the law requires an equal division of the profits.

Difficulty in Withdrawing from Partnership. If a partner wishes to sell his or her interest in a business, it may be difficult to do so. Even if a buyer is found, the person may not be acceptable to the other partners.

Limited Partnership

In an ordinary (general) partnership each partner is personally liable for all the debts contracted by the partnership. The laws of some states, however, permit the formation of a type of partnership in which not all the partners have unlimited financial liability for the partnership debts. This type of partnership is known as a **limited partnership.** However, at least one partner must be a general partner who has unlimited liability. In many states the name of a limited partner may not be included in the firm name.

Usually the law requires that a certificate of limited partnership be filed in a public office of record and that proper notice be given to each creditor with whom the limited partnership does business. If these requirements are not fulfilled, the limited partners have unlimited liability in the same manner as a general partner.

The limited partnership is a useful form of business organization in situations where one person wishes to invest in a business but does not have the time or interest to participate actively in its management. The owner of a sole proprietorship may find a limited partnership useful when more capital is needed to expand the business but the owner does not wish to share the management of the business. Any business that is formed as a proprietorship can usually be formed as a limited partnership.

Kinds of Businesses Suited to the Partnership Form of Organization

The partnership form of organization is found in many businesses that furnish more than one kind of product or service. Each partner usually looks after a specialized phase of the business. For example, car dealers often have sales and service departments. One partner may handle the sale of new cars, and another partner may be in charge of servicing and repairing cars. Still another partner could be in charge of used car sales or the accounting and financial part of the business. Similarly, if a business operates in more than one location, there can be a partner in charge of each location. Businesses that operate longer than the usual eight hours a day, such as restaurants and gasoline stations, find the partnership organization desirable. Each partner can be in charge for part of the day.

Partnerships are often found in the same types of businesses that are formed as proprietorships, particularly in selling goods and services to consumers.

ILLUS. 5–8
Sign used to indicate YB and K partnership.

BUSINESS NAME

A proprietorship or a partnership may be conducted under the name or names of the owner or owners. In many states the law prohibits the use of *and Company* or *& Co.* unless such identification indicates additional partners. For example, if there are only two partners, it is not permissible to use a firm name such as Jones, Smith & Co., for that name indicates at least three partners. The name or names comprised in the term *company* must be identified by registration at a public recording office, usually the county clerk's office. Usually one can do business under a trade, or artificial, name such as The Superior Shoe Store or W–W Manufacturing Company. Likewise, proper registration is usually required in order that creditors may know the person or persons responsible for the business. Operating under a trade name, therefore, does not reduce the owner's liability to creditors.

In forming an enterprise, then, one must be concerned not only with what to call the business but with the responsibilities involved and with the advantages and disadvantages of various forms of legal ownership. In addition to the sole proprietorship and partnership forms, one must examine the corporate form, which is discussed in the next chapter.

NEW TERMS AND CONCEPTS

Define the following terms, which may be found in boldface type on the page shown in parentheses.

sole proprietorship, or proprietorship (88)
proprietor (88)
assets (88)
creditors (88)
statement of financial position, or balance sheet (89)
capital, or net worth, or equity (89)
partnership (92)
unlimited financial liability (96)
limited partnership (98)

CHAPTER REVIEW

1. What are the three most common legal forms of business ownership?
2. What types of persons enjoy the responsibilities of business ownership?
3. List the major advantages of proprietorships.
4. List the major disadvantages of proprietorships.
5. Which kind of business is most suited to a proprietorship?
6. List the major advantages of partnerships.
7. List the major disadvantages of partnerships.
8. Under what types of situations is a limited partnership found to be useful?
9. In which types of businesses is the partnership form of organization found?
10. Why is it usually necessary for proprietorships and partnerships to register their company names with local authorities?

QUESTIONS FOR CLASS DISCUSSION

1. You have been working part-time and summers at a local gas station during your school years. You have performed just about every major task from pumping gas to making car repairs and even handling some of the book work. Discuss how your responsibilities as an employee will change if you become the owner of the station.
2. The proprietor is not hindered by associates in making decisions. What disadvantages could result from not having partners to help in making decisions?
3. If a proprietorship needs additional capital but the owner cannot furnish it from personal funds, from what sources might it be secured?
4. Why is it a good plan to include in a partnership agreement a clause such as the seventh clause shown in Illus. 5–7?
5. Why is it a good plan to include in a partnership agreement a clause such as the fifth clause shown in Illus. 5–7?
6. Why is it desirable that the partnership agreement be in writing?
7. A partner signed a partnership contract for television advertising while the other two partners were on vacation. Upon returning, the two claimed that the partnership was not bound to the contract because both of them disapproved of television advertising. Was the partnership legally bound?
8. What effect is there on the life of a partnership when (a) a partner dies, (b) a partner quits, or (c) a new partner is added?
9. Why are proprietorships so much more popular than partnerships?

PROBLEMS AND PROJECTS

1. Prepare a list of the advantages of the sole proprietorship on a sheet of paper and a list of the disadvantages on a second sheet of paper. Show the lists to the sole proprietor of a small business in your community. After asking the proprietor the following questions, summarize the answers and make a report to the class:
   a. Are there any advantages you would want to add to the existing list of advantages?
   b. Are there any advantages with which you disagree?
   c. Which one advantage is the most important in your business?
   d. Are there any disadvantages you would want to add to the list of disadvantages?
   e. Are there any disadvantages with which you disagree?
   f. Which one disadvantage is the most important in your business?
2. Form a committee of three to five students in order to (a) discuss the situation below, and then (b) prepare a summary of your committee's recommendations to the two people involved. Here is the situation:

   Bob Kickish plans to go into business for himself operating a men's clothing store. He believes that he has adequate experience in this area, having managed a clothing department in a large local department store for several years. Bob thinks that he has sufficient capital, but it may be a little tight financially getting through the first year of operation.

   Phyllis Banda, a long-time friend of Bob's, is also planning to open a business. Her women's clothing store will be located next to Bob's, in the same busy shopping area. Although Phyllis has almost no experience in the clothing business, she did work part time one summer in a fashion shop. And now she has a degree in finance from the local university. Her uncle is willing to lend her all the money needed to start the business.

   Both Phyllis and Bob have learned of each other's plans. The idea of forming a partnership has been mentioned, but they are not quite sure what to do.
3. Adams invested $40,000 and Cook invested $30,000 in their partnership business. They share profits and losses in proportion to their investments. What amount should each receive of the $16,800 profit earned during a certain year?
4. Carlton and Baker had invested equal amounts in a partnership business. Later the business failed with $40,000 in liabilities (debts) and only $15,000 in assets (property). In addition to a share of the assets of the business, Baker had $35,000 of other personal property at the time of the failure; but Carlton had only $5,000 of additional personal property. What amount of property other than the partnership property will be required of each partner to pay the debts of the partnership?

5. Assume that the balance sheet of the partnership of Davis and Miller at the time they closed the business appeared as follows:

Assets		Claims Against Assets	
Cash	$ 9,000	Accounts Payable	
Merchandise	20,000	(Debts)	$ 5,000
Fixtures and Equipment . . .	12,000	B.S. Davis, Capital . . .	45,000
Land and Building.	54,000	T.C. Miller, Capital . . .	45,000
	$95,000		$95,000

In selling the assets the merchandise was sold for $16,000, the fixtures for $9,000, and the land and building for $55,000. After paying their debts, what amount of the remaining cash should each partner receive?

CASE 5–1

Jesse Rosenblum, who is 27 and single, had just completed his fifth year of employment as a carpenter for a very small home builder. His boss, the sole owner of the company, is Fred Helms. A few days ago Fred asked Jesse if he would like to become a partner, which he could do by contributing $35,000 for which he would receive 40 percent of all profits earned by the business. Jesse had saved $15,000 and could borrow the balance needed from his grandmother at a low interest rate, but he would have to pay her back within 15 years.

Jesse was undecided about becoming a partner. He liked the idea but he also knew there were risks and concerns. To help him make up his mind, he decided to talk to Fred at lunch. Here is how the conversation went:

Jesse: I have been giving your offer a lot of thought, Fred. It is a tough decision, and I do not want to make the wrong one. So I would like to chat with you about some of the problems involved in running a business.

Fred: Sure. I struggled with the same problem about 25 years ago. When you own your own business, you are the boss. No one can tell you what to do or push you around. You can set up your own hours and make all the decisions. I enjoy the feeling of ownership.

Jesse: I do not know if I am ready to become part-owner of a business. I am still young and single, and I like working for you. I am not sure I want all those responsibilities—getting customers, paying bills, buying tools and lumber. You say you set your own hours, but I know you are already working when I arrive each morning, and you are still here when I leave in the evening. I know you spend some nights in the office, because I see the lights on when I drive by.

Fred: Well, I do put in many hours. That goes with the territory. But I don't mind all those hours because I like making the decisions. And, when you join me as a partner, we will share the work.

Jesse: Then, I will be working longer hours. Both of us could go to work for that big new contracting firm on the other side of town. They could struggle with all the problems and decisions. Then, we could work shorter hours and have more time to relax.

Required:

1. Do you think Jesse is seriously ready to become a partner? Explain your answer.
2. If you were in Jesse's position, how would you decide? Explain.
3. If Jesse decides to accept Fred's offer, what action should be taken?

CASE 5–2

Janell Bragg is the owner and operator of Bragg's Boats, a small business at a large lake resort area. She rents and sells sailboats and canoes. Because it has just become permissible to operate small motor boats on the lake, she would also like to rent row boats and motors that can be attached. However, she lacks the $10,000 additional capital needed to expand unless she borrows against her home.

She has limited knowledge of boat motors and the repair of them. Bragg operates the business with two full-time employees during the peak season, mid-June through August. She closes down completely from November through April. For the rest of the year, she runs the rental business by herself.

Required:

1. What choices are available to Janell Bragg if she wishes to expand? Discuss them.
2. If she decides to form a partnership with one other person, what characteristics should influence the selection of a partner?

CASE 5–3

The York, Burton, and King partnership, described in this chapter, has been operating six months. This combination grocery-fruit market and meat market has been doing much better than expected. Jane York and Bob Burton, however, have become somewhat unhappy with Carl King.

York, Burton, and King are supposed to work Monday through Friday and alternate working on Saturdays. York and Burton claim that King, who is in charge of finances and records, has only been working Monday through noon Friday. He has, however, always taken his turn managing the store on Saturdays. When King was approached about the unfairness of his taking Friday afternoons off, he had a quick response.

"By noon Friday I have all the book work done. Therefore, I meet the terms of our partnership agreement, Item 7 (See Illus. 5–7). Rather than make it look as though I'm working Friday afternoons, I arrange to play golf or to fish with some business people. For example, last week I went fishing with the sales representative of our biggest supplier of canned goods. From that trip I learned a great deal about how we can better display our products and how to have better control over our inventory. Friday afternoon is as much work for me as being at the store."

Required:

1. How can the business benefit from Carl King's Friday activities?
2. Is King living up to Items 5 and 7 of the partnership agreement?
3. York and Burton also play golf, but not on business time. Therefore, personal relationships are becoming strained. What can be done to improve this situation?

Have You Thought About Becoming . . .

. . . A PART-TIME ENTREPRENEUR?

Can you wear two hats? Some people who have good jobs, which they do not care to lose, also have an interest in owning their own business. How can you do both? Perhaps you could become a limited partner. Or, you could operate a part-time business, perhaps on weekends or during special times of the year. For example, you may be an accountant for a corporation and run a concession stand at a seasonal resort area. Or you could work on an assembly line days and run a tennis shop evenings and weekends. Occasionally, the part-time business becomes so successful and preferred that you may wish to give up working full-time for someone else to work full-time for yourself.

Being an employer and an employee has some real advantages. You find out if you are the type of person who enjoys running a business. You also discover whether your part-time business has possibilities of becoming profitable on a full-time basis. Further, you gather a great deal of valuable experience about running a business. Finally, in most new enterprises, profits are very small or nonexistent for a few years. By remaining an employee while also being an employer, you can have a basic income while your new business venture becomes better known to your customers. Yes, you can wear two hats. Many people do.

6

CORPORATE FORMS OF BUSINESS OWNERSHIP

After studying this chapter you will be able to:

- Identify the basic rights of stockholders.
- Describe how a corporation is formed.
- Point out how a close corporation and an open corporation differ.
- List some of the major advantages and disadvantages of the corporate form of business.
- Describe the cooperative form of business organization.

In Chapter 5 you learned about proprietorships and partnerships as legal forms of organizing a business. This chapter will consider two other organizational forms—corporations and cooperatives. You will soon learn that both corporations and cooperatives serve vital roles in business in the United States.

CORPORATIONS

Corporations are towers on the business landscape. While proprietorships are many in number, they are generally small in size. In comparison, corporations are few in number, but generally large in size. Because corporations tend to be large, they play a powerful role in the economy of our country. For example, corporations employ millions of people and provide consumers with many of the goods and services they need and want. In a recent year, corporate sales of goods and services were over ten

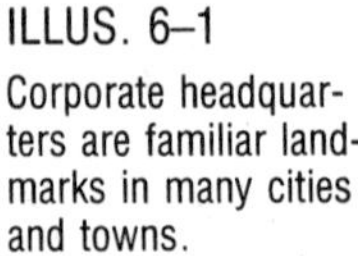

ILLUS. 6–1
Corporate headquarters are familiar landmarks in many cities and towns.

times more than sales from proprietorships, and over twenty times more than sales from partnerships.

Because the corporation plays so important a role in business, it is necessary to understand its basic features as well as its advantages and disadvantages. To gain an understanding of the basic features of the corporation, we can follow York, Burton and King as they consider incorporating their fast-growing food store business.

Basic Features

Karen Ritter, a lawyer, helped York, Burton and King prepare the partnership agreement under which they now operate. As their attorney, she has been asked by the partners to describe a corporation. She stated that a **corporation** is a business owned by a group of people and authorized by the state in which it is located to act as though it were a single person. To get permission to form a corporation, a charter is needed. A **charter** (often called a **certificate of incorporation**) is the official document granted by a state giving power to run a corporation.

A corporation is, in a sense, an artificial person created by the laws of the state. A corporation can make contracts, borrow money, own property, and sue or be sued in its own name. Any act performed for the corporation by an authorized person, such as an employee, is done in the name of the business. For example, the treasurer of a corporation has the power to borrow money for the business. An unauthorized employee, such as a clerk who was hired to file papers and type letters, could not borrow money for the corporation.

Ritter further explained the important parts played by three key types of people in corporations: stockholders, directors, and officers.

Stockholders. **Stockholders** (often called **shareholders**) are the owners of a corporation. Ownership is divided into equal parts called **shares.** One need only buy a share in order to become a stockholder. Therefore, thousands of people can own a corporation. Each stockholder receives a certificate from the corporation which shows the number of shares owned. Stockholders have a number of basic rights, including the following:

- To transfer ownership to others.
- To vote for members of the ruling body of the corporation and other special matters that may be brought before the stockholders.
- To receive dividends. **Dividends** are profits that are distributed to stockholders. The decision to distribute profits is made by the ruling body of the corporation.
- To buy new shares of stock in proportion to one's present investment should the corporation issue more shares.
- To share in the net proceeds (cash received from the sale of all assets less the payment of all debts) should the corporation go out of business.

ILLUS. 6–2
Each stockholder receives a certificate showing the number of shares of stock owned.

A stockholder does not have the same financial responsibility as a partner; that is, there is no liability beyond the extent of the stockholder's ownership. If the corporation fails, a stockholder may lose only the money that is invested. Creditors cannot collect anything further from the stockholder.

Directors. The **board of directors** (often shortened to **directors** or the **board**) is the ruling body of the corporation. Board members are elected by the stockholders. Directors develop plans and policies to guide the corporation and then appoint officers to carry out the plans. Often directors are stockholders who hold many shares. But directors need not be stockholders. People who hold few or no shares are sometimes elected to the board because they have valuable knowledge that is needed by the board of directors in making sound decisions.

Officers. The **officers** of a corporation are the top executives who are hired to manage the business. They are appointed by the board of directors. The officers of a small corporation often consist of a president, a secretary, and a treasurer. In addition, large corporations may have vice-presidents in charge of major areas, such as marketing, finance, and manufacturing.

Formation of Corporations

Over several months the partners asked their attorney, Karen Ritter, many questions. Only after careful thought did York, Burton and King then decide to form a corporation. Ritter was again consulted. She told them that there were basically three steps involved. First, a series of decisions had to be made about how the corporation would be organized. Second, the proper legal forms had to be prepared and sent to the state office that handles such matters. And, third, the state would review the incorporation papers and issue a charter if it approved. The formation of a new corporation for York, Burton and King is now presented in detail.

Preparing the Certificate of Incorporation. Each state has its own laws for forming corporations. No federal law exists. To incorporate a business, it is necessary in most states to file a certificate of incorporation with the appropriate state office. The certificate of incorporation prepared by Ritter for York, Burton and King (the organizers) is shown in Illus. 6–3.

Notice the general type of information called for in the certificate of incorporation. In addition to the firm name, purpose, and capital stock, information about the organizers is requested.

Naming the Business. When naming the business, it is usually required by law to clearly indicate that a corporation has been formed. Words or abbreviations such as *Corporation, Corp., Incorporated,* or *Inc.* are used. Taylor Co., Incorporated, and Bell Company, Inc., are examples. The organizers have decided to name their corporation York, Burton and King, Inc.

Certificate of Incorporation

OF

York, Burton and King, Inc.

Pursuant to Article Two of the Stock Corporation Law.

State of New York }
County of Cattaraugus } ss.

We, the undersigned, for the purpose of forming a Corporation pursuant to Article Two of the Stock Corporation Law of the State of New York, do hereby make, subscribe, acknowledge and file this certificate for that purpose as follows:

We, the undersigned, do hereby Certify

First.—That all the undersigned are of full age, and all are citizens of the United States, and all residents of the State of New York.

Second.—That the name of said corporation is York, Burton and King, Inc.

Third.—That the purpose for which said corporation is formed is to operate a retail food business.

Fourth.—That the amount of the Capital Stock of the said corporation is Four Hundred Thousand Dollars ($400,000) to consist of Four Thousand (4,000) shares of the par value of One Hundred dollars ($100) each.

Fifth.—That the office of said corporation is to be located in the City of Olean, County of Cattaraugus and State of New York.

Sixth.—That the duration of said corporation is to be perpetual.

Seventh.—That the number of Directors of said corporation is three.

Eighth.—That the names and post office addresses of the Directors until the first annual meeting are as follows:

Jane L. York 1868 Buffalo Street, Olean, NY 14760-1436
Robert R. Burton 1309 Main Street, Olean, NY 14760-1436
Carl O. King 4565 Erie Avenue, Ceres, NY 14721-2348

Ninth.—That the names and post office addresses of the subscribers and the number of shares of stock which each agrees to take in said corporation are as follows:

NAMES	POST OFFICE ADDRESSES	NO. OF SHARES
Jane L. York	1868 Buffalo Street	
	Olean, NY 14760-1436	940
Robert R. Burton	1309 Main Street	
	Olean, NY 14760-1436	940
Carl O. King	4565 Erie Avenue	
	Ceres, NY 14721-2348	940

Tenth.—That the meetings of the Board of Directors shall be held only within the State of New York at Olean

In Witness Whereof, we have made, subscribed and executed this certificate in duplicate the tenth day of September in the year One thousand nine hundred and --

Jane L. York
Robert R. Burton
Carl O. King

ILLUS. 6–3

A certificate of incorporation includes information about the organizers of a corporation.

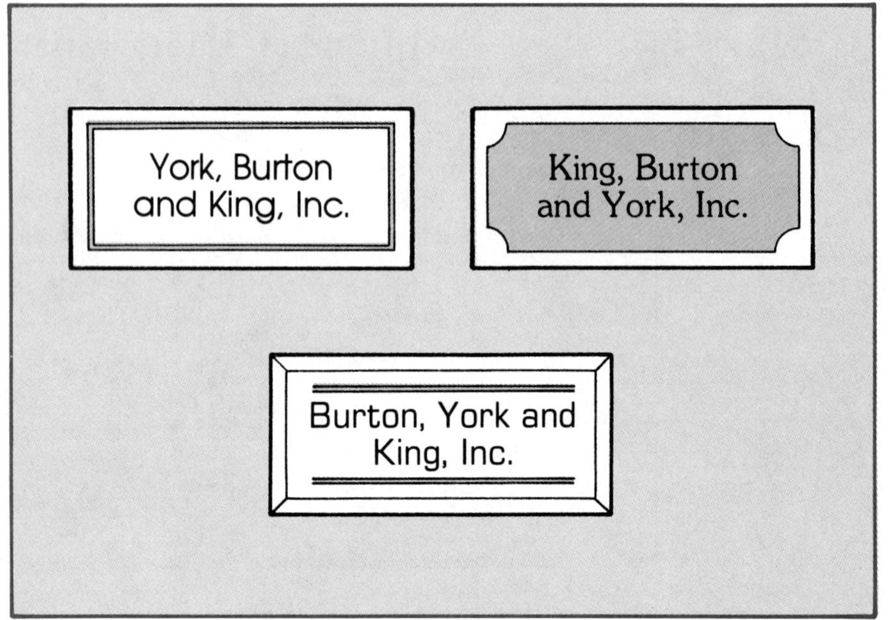

ILLUS. 6–4
Organizers must select a name for the business to be recorded on the certificate of incorporation.

Stating the Purpose of the Business. The state requires that the corporation's purpose be clearly expressed. The purpose, "to operate a retail food business", by our organizers is precise. It allows the corporation to expand into new food lines, but it does not allow it to start nonfood type operations. For major changes in purpose, a new request must be submitted and approved by the state.

Investing in the Business. The certificate of incorporation could not be completed until York, Burton and King decided how to invest their partnership holdings in the corporation. They agreed that the assets and debts of the partnership should be taken over by the corporation. They further agreed that their capital (net worth or equity) of $94,000 each should be invested in the corporation. **Capital stock** is the general term applied to the shares of ownership of a corporation.

Here is how the details were worked out. The organizers requested authorization from the state to issue $400,000 in capital stock, as can be seen in Illus. 6–3. Shares were valued at $100 each at the time of incorporation; there were 4,000 shares in all ($400,000 ÷ $100 = 4,000). York, Burton and King agreed to purchase 940 shares each as shown in Illus. 6–5.

The 1,180 unissued shares, the difference between the 4,000 authorized shares and the 2,820 shares bought by the organizers, can be sold at a later date and can be used to expand the business.

Paying Incorporation Costs. Usually a new business must pay an organization tax—based on the amount of its capital stock—and a filing fee before the state will issue a charter entitling the business to operate as a

ILLUS. 6–5
Division of stock shares of York, Burton and King, Inc.

York	940 shares × $100 per share = $ 94,000
Burton	940 shares × $100 per share = $ 94,000
King	940 shares × $100 per share = $ 94,000
TOTAL	$282,000

corporation. In some states, the existence of the corporation begins when the application or certificate of incorporation has been filed in the Department of State.

Operating the New Corporation. York, Burton and King, Inc., received approval to operate as a corporation. Their attention was next turned to getting the business started.

Getting Organized. York, Burton and King had a statement of financial position prepared. This was the first step in getting the new corporation underway. An example of the new corporation's balance sheet is shown in Illus. 6–6.

ILLUS. 6–6
Balance sheet of York, Burton and King, Inc.

Assets		**Claim Against Assets**	
Cash	$ 24,000	Accounts Payable (Debts)	$ 8,000
Merchandise	48,000	Capital Stock	282,000
Equipment	45,000		
Land and Building	173,000		
	$290,000		$290,000

The ownership of the corporation is in the same hands as was the ownership of the partnership. The ownership of the corporation, however, is evidenced by the issued capital stock. The former partners have received a stock certificate indicating that each owns 940 shares of stock with a value of $100 a share.

The three stockholders own the business and elect themselves directors. The new directors select officers. York is appointed president; Burton, vice-president; and King, secretary and treasurer. A simple organization chart of the new corporation is shown in Illus. 6–7.

Handling Voting Rights. It was agreed that each stockholder will have 940 votes on matters arising in the meetings of the stockholders. Voting stockholders usually have one vote for each share owned. Should King sell 472 of his shares to Burton, Burton would own 1,412 shares, or more than

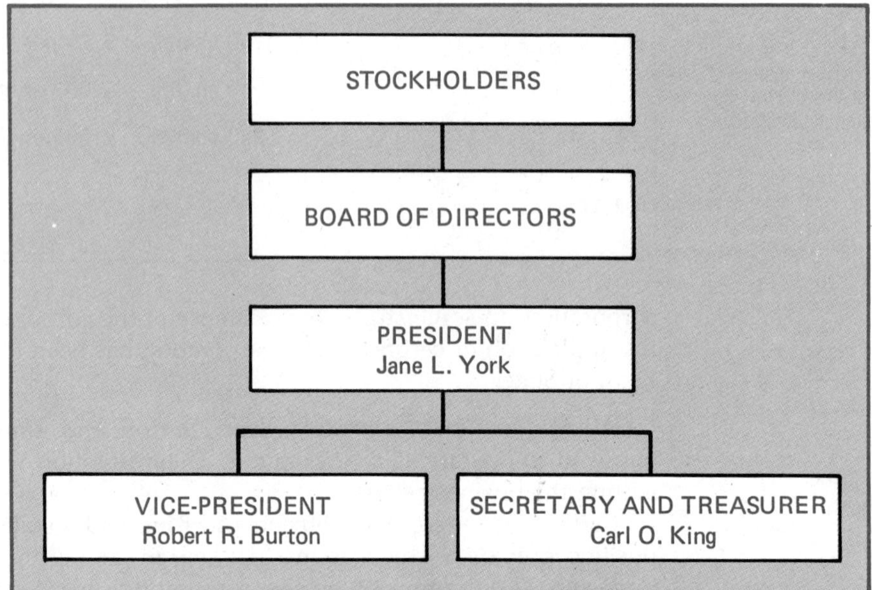

ILLUS. 6–7
An organization chart of a corporation.

50 percent of the total 2,820 shares of stock that have been issued. Then Burton could control the corporation.

The officers of the corporation were told by their lawyer that they must send each stockholder notices of all stockholders' meetings to be held. Even stockholders with just one share must receive notices of meetings. If stockholders cannot attend the meetings personally, they may be represented by a proxy. A **proxy** is a written authorization for someone to vote in behalf of the person signing the proxy. It is common practice for a proxy form to be included in the letter announcing a stockholders' meeting. One example of a proxy which a corporation might use is shown in Illus. 6–8.

BRUMWAY EASTMONT POWER CORPORATION – PROXY – Annual Meeting, Nov. 7, 19- -

The undersigned hereby appoints Henry T. Brumleve III, Dean G. Rehme, D. A. Dromboski, and Donald F. Stark, and any of them, proxies of the undersigned, with power of substitution, to vote at the Annual Meeting of Stockholders of Brumway Eastmont Power Corporation, at Kenwood, Ohio, on November 7, 19--, at 11:00 a.m., and at any adjournments thereof,

This Proxy is Solicited by Management

(1) FOR [X] or NOT FOR [ ] the election of a Board of Directors;

(2) FOR [X] or AGAINST [ ] the proposal to increase the number of authorized shares of Common Stock; and

(3) for the transaction of any other business properly brought before the meeting.

Dated October 25, 19--

RAYMOND L COOKE
349 MIDPINES DRIVE
BUFFALO NY 14202-4449

Raymond L. Cooke

Signature of Stockholder

(PLEASE GIVE YOUR FULL TITLE WHEN SIGNING AS ATTORNEY, TRUSTEE, EXECUTOR, ADMINISTRATOR, OR GUARDIAN, ETC.)

If no preference is indicated, this proxy will be voted FOR items (1) & (2).

ILLUS. 6–8
A proxy signed by a stockholder.

Close and Open Corporations

A **close corporation** (also called a **closely held corporation**) is one that does not offer its shares of stock for public sale. It is owned by just a few stockholders, some of whom may help run the business in the same manner as partners operate a business. York, Burton and King, Inc., is an example of a close corporation. The three former partners own all the stock and operate the business.

In most states a close corporation does not need to make its financial activities known to the public. Its stock is not offered for general sale. It must, however, prepare reports for the state from which it obtained its charter. And it must, for tax purposes, prepare reports for all states in which it operates.

An **open corporation** (also called a **public corporation**) is one that offers its shares of stock for public sale. For the benefit of prospective investors, an open corporation must furnish to the public information regarding its earnings, assets, and debts. These reports must be provided in keeping with federal and state laws.

Open corporations often have a very large number of stockholders, some having a million or more. Many of the stockholders in these large corporations own only a few shares. But because of the great number of stockholders, such a corporation has a very large amount of capital. Naturally these large corporations are not as simple in organization as York, Burton and King, Inc. The form of organization becomes more complicated as the business grows.

ILLUS. 6–9
An open corporation must offer its shares for sale to the public.

Advantages of the Corporation

The corporation has a number of advantages as compared with the proprietorship and partnership. Some of these are given next.

Available Sources of Capital. The corporation can obtain money from several sources. One of those sources is the sale of shares to stockholders. This special privilege helps to raise enough capital for running large-scale businesses. Because corporations are regulated closely, people usually invest more willingly than in proprietorships and partnerships. Also, corporations usually find borrowing large sums of money less of a problem than do proprietorships or partnerships.

Limited Liability of Stockholders. Except in a few situations, the owners (stockholders) are not legally liable for the debts of the corporation beyond their investments in the stock. Thus, people—whether they have only a few dollars to invest or whether they have thousands of dollars—may invest in a corporation without the possibility of incurring a liability beyond their original investment.

Permanency of Existence. The corporation is a more permanent type of organization than the proprietorship or the partnership. It may continue to operate indefinitely, or only as long as the term stated in the charter. The death or withdrawal of an owner does not affect the life of a corporation.

Ease in Transferring Ownership. It is easy to transfer ownership in a corporation. A stockholder may sell stock to another person and transfer the stock certificate, which represents the ownership, to the new owner. When shares are transferred, the transfer of ownership is indicated in the records of the corporation. A new certificate is issued in the name of the new stockholder. Millions of shares are bought and sold every day.

Disadvantages of the Corporation

Although we have seen that there are several distinct advantages to the corporation, there are also several disadvantages. A discussion of some of the major disadvantages follows.

Taxation. The corporation is usually subject to more taxes than are imposed on the proprietorship and the partnership. Some taxes that are special to the corporation are a filing fee, which is payable on application for a charter; an organization tax, which is based on the amount of authorized capital stock; an annual state tax based on the profits; and a federal income tax.

The federal income tax rate for corporations is based on the taxable earnings (total yearly receipts less allowable deductions). A corporation, for example, with taxable earnings of $105,000 will pay $28,550 in federal income taxes as shown in the following calculations, which are based on tax rates in a recent year:

Taxable Earnings	Tax Rate	Tax
from $ 0 to $ 25,000	16%	$ 4,000
$ 25,001 – 50,000	19%	4,750
50,001 – 75,000	30%	7,500
75,001 – 100,000	40%	10,000
$100,001 or more ($5,000 × 46%)	46%	2,300
		$28,550

Another tax disadvantage for corporations is that profits distributed to stockholders as dividends are taxed twice. This double taxation occurs in two steps. The corporation first pays taxes on its profits as just described. Then it distributes some of these profits to shareholders as dividends, and the shareholders pay taxes on the dividends they receive.

Government Regulations and Reports. The regulation of corporations by states and by the federal government is extensive.

A corporation cannot do business wherever it pleases. York, Burton and King, Inc., has permission to conduct business only in the state of New York. Should it wish to do business in nearby states, it will probably be required to obtain in each state a license as a **foreign corporation** and to pay a fee to do business in that state.

A corporation must file special reports to the state from which it received its charter, as well as to other states in which it may be doing business. As a result, there is an increased need for detailed financial records and reports.

Stockholders' Records. Corporations that have many stockholders have an added problem—and expense—in communicating with and keeping the records of stockholders. Stockholders are guaranteed by law to be kept informed of corporate matters, to be notified of meetings, and to be given the right to vote on important matters. Letters and reports must be sent to them on a regular basis. In addition, each time a share of stock is bought or sold and whenever a dividend is paid, detailed records must be made. The keeping of records of the millions of stockholders of the American Telephone & Telegraph Company, for example, is a time-consuming and costly task.

Charter Restrictions. A corporation is allowed to engage only in those activities that are stated in its charter. Should York, Burton and King, Inc., wish to add to the business a department selling hardware, they would have to go to the state to obtain a new charter or change the old one. As a partnership they could have added the other department without governmental approval.

Types of Businesses Organized as Corporations

Even though the corporation has major disadvantages, a survey of business firms shows that almost every kind of business exists as a corporation. The corporate form of ownership is especially suited to certain types of business firms. The following types of business firms most frequently organize as corporations:

1. Those that require large amounts of capital, such as airlines, construction firms, automobile manufacturers, and iron and steel firms. To start a 500-room hotel, for example, requires millions of dollars for buying land and for constructing and furnishing the building.
2. Those that may have uncertain futures, such as mining companies, amusement parks, publishers of new magazines, and makers of novelty goods. The publisher of a new magazine, for example, takes a great risk in assuming that the magazine will be popular enough to make a profit. Organizers of business firms with uncertain futures do not wish to assume the added financial risks that fall upon a proprietor or a partner in case the business fails.

Each form of business organization has special advantages to owners of different types of businesses. While the corporate form of organization is suited to those firms that have uncertain futures or that require large amounts of capital, the partnership is especially suited to small, growing business firms. The proprietorship, in comparison, has great appeal to the person who wants to run a small business. The cooperative, about which you will learn next, is yet another form of organization designed to meet the special needs of still another kind of business owner.

COOPERATIVES

Proprietorships, partnerships, and corporations are by far the most popular forms of business organization. There is yet another form of organization that is small in number but which serves a very useful purpose. This particular type of business is called a cooperative, and it is somewhat like a corporation.

Nature of Cooperatives

A **cooperative** is a business owned and operated by its user-members for the purpose of supplying themselves with goods and services. The members, who are much like stockholders in a corporation, usually join a cooperative by buying shares of stock. The members elect a board of directors, which appoints officers to run the business. Much like a corporation, a cooperative must also obtain a charter from the state in which it is organized in order to operate. Some types of cooperatives need authorization from the federal government.

The purpose of cooperatives is to provide its members with cost and profit advantages that they do not otherwise have. For example, a group of people believe that individually they can save money by forming a food-store cooperative. Once the business is organized and operating, the members (owners) become the customers of the store and buy food at prices that are slightly less than at other food stores. In addition, as owners they share in any profits of the business. Thus, the members of the cooperative save by buying food at lower prices and by receiving dividends declared by the board of directors.

The amount of dividend earned by each member is based on how much the member buys from the cooperative. For example, assume that you spent $2,000 at the cooperative during the year and that the cooperative earned a profit and paid a dividend. Your dividend would be twice as large as that of another member who spent only $1,000 at the cooperative.

Types of Businesses Organized as Cooperatives

Of the 14 million businesses in the United States, only a small portion are cooperatives. This small number, however, does not reduce their importance. Cooperatives generally serve two large groups—consumers and business firms.

Many consumers use the services of the most common type of cooperative: the credit union. **Credit unions,** which permit members to borrow at low interest rates, have become popular. These cooperatives are often formed by labor unions or associations of employees for the benefit of employee members. Many people buy insurance from mutual insurance companies. A **mutual insurance company** is a form of business organization that is much like a cooperative. Many health insurance plans are formed as cooperatives. A number of U.S. citizens live in apartment buildings which are organized as cooperatives, and buy their food from food-store cooperatives of which they are members.

There are thousands of cooperatives that have been formed to serve individual companies as well as consumers. Small retail store owners often form cooperatives to buy goods at a savings for resale to customers. Cooperatives that buy such supplies as seed and fertilizer and store, ship, and sell harvests for farmer members are rather common in agricultural areas. Small fruit farmers, for example, find it profitable to join a cooperative to market their crops. Cooperatives can be found in almost every type of business venture.

NEW TERMS AND CONCEPTS

Define the following terms and concepts, which can be found in boldface type on the page shown in parentheses.

- corporation (106)
- charter, or certificate of incorporation (106)
- stockholders, or shareholders (107)
- shares (107)
- dividends (107)
- board of directors, or directors, or board (108)
- officers (108)
- capital stock (110)
- proxy (112)
- close corporation, or closely held corporation (113)
- open corporation, or public corporation (113)
- foreign corporation (115)
- cooperative (116)
- credit unions (117)
- mutual insurance company (117)

CHAPTER REVIEW

1. Which form of business is smallest in total number but biggest in terms of total sales of goods and services?
2. What are the five basic rights of stockholders?
3. How does one become a stockholder in a corporation? a director? an officer?
4. What three steps must be taken to form a corporation?
5. By what means can stockholders vote on matters affecting the corporation even when they cannot be present at meetings?
6. How is a close corporation different from an open corporation?
7. Give the major advantages of corporations.
8. Give the major disadvantages of corporations.
9. What is the purpose of cooperatives?
10. List five kinds of goods or services that are handled through the cooperative form of business ownership.

QUESTIONS FOR CLASS DISCUSSION

1. Why can a corporation be described as an artifical person?
2. Illus. 6–8, page 112, shows a proxy. If the person receiving the proxy only signed the card but did not vote for or against the numbered items, would the proxy be valid?
3. Compare the financial responsibility of owners of a corporation with that of owners of a partnership.
4. Why would a corporation request in its certificate of incorporation more shares of capital stock than are needed to get started?

5. The following people own all the shares of stock in the same corporation: Brower, 100; Garroway, 70: Forcina, 30; and Hall, 10. If all have an interest in running for the board of directors, how could it be possible for the largest stockholder not to be elected?
6. Under what conditions would you be able to buy stock in York, Burton and King, Inc.?
7. Why are cooperatives popular in agricultural regions?
8. Provide two major differences between cooperatives and corporations.

PROBLEMS AND PROJECTS

1. A corporation's taxable earnings for federal income tax purposes amounted to $300,000 for a recent year. Using the tax rates given in this chapter, answer the following questions.
   a. What was the total federal income tax for the year?
   b. What was the profit after taxes that could be available for distribution as dividends to stockholders?
   c. What percentage was the total federal income tax of the total earnings?
2. The board of directors of Melby Company, Inc., decided to distribute $40,950 as dividends to its shareholders. There are 27,300 shares of stock held by stockholders.
   a. What is the amount of the dividend to be distributed on each share?
   b. John Taylor owns 240 shares. What amount of dividends should he receive?
3. On the statement of financial position of the Fenwick Company, the assets have a value of $117,000; the debts are listed as $37,000; the capital stock, $80,000. The company has decided to go out of business. The assets are converted into $97,000 cash. What amount of cash will the stockholders receive?
4. The net profit of a retail cooperative is $4,000, and the purchases made by members amount to $100,000. If the profit is divided in proportion to the purchases, how much should be given to a member who made purchases of $1,000?
5. George Thompson purchased stock in the Erie Manufacturing Co., Incorporated, for $76 a share. During a year he received quarterly dividends of $1, $1, $1, and $.80 on each share. His total dividends for the year amounted to what percentage of the price he paid for each share?

CASE 6–1

Kim Chan owns 15 shares of stock in the Shale Oil Company, a very large corporation that deals with oil and gas products. Tom Breslin, a friend of Kim's, owns 20 shares. Today they both received an invitation to attend the annual stockholders' meeting in Chicago, which neither can attend. This conversation occurred during the evening when they were having dinner at a local restaurant:

Kim: Since I cannot attend the meeting, I am going to sign the proxy card and answer "for" regarding the two proposals that are to be voted upon. Of course, I do not know any of the board members who are up for election, but they must be good.

Tom: You should not just give your vote away to management, Kim. You not only do not know the board members, but you probably do not know anything about the second item asking for approval to increase the number of shares of stock that can be sold.

Kim: I do not have time to do homework on the company. They make a profit; therefore, they deserve my vote.

Tom: None of the stockholders do their homework on the company, and not many go to the meetings. So, management always has its own way. Why bother sending a proxy statement at all? I am not going to waste my time sending the proxy back.

Kim: I am still going to vote, Tom. Besides the company pays the postage.

Tom: You are doing what everyone else does. Management always wins. But since you are going to vote, I will too. The difference is that I am going to vote against the two items . . . No, on second thought, I will just sign the proxy. That will really confuse them.

Required:

1. How many votes may Kim and Tom cast whether they vote "for" or "against" the proposals listed on the proxy statement?
2. If the proxy statement is like the one shown in Illus. 6–8 and Tom signs it but does not mark "for" or "against" the two proposals, how will management use the proxy?
3. If Tom or Kim wanted an important proposal to be made known to the stockholders and voted upon, how could they achieve their goal?
4. Should Kim and Tom have received information about each of the proposals from management that would enable them to vote with adequate information?

CASE 6–2

The Snorkel Company was operated as a partnership for years by Ann Bird, Pat Rossi, and Ron Shaffer. Primarily to gain added capital, they converted their partnership to a corporation. It then became known as Snorkel Company, Inc. Five friends invested large sums of money by buying shares of stock in the new corporation. The company remained a close corporation.

All eight shareholders have been extremely satisfied with the profits over the last five years. But, as the firm has continued to improve its profit picture, the owners have become more and more upset. Ron Shaffer summed up the feelings of everyone when he said, "That double taxation is killing me." The stockholders have become so upset that they are seriously thinking about reorganizing again into a partnership.

Required:

1. Why was the *Inc.*, added to the title of the company?
2. What did Shaffer mean by double taxation?
3. If they do form a partnership, what corporate advantages will they surrender?

CASE 6–3

Mark Friedman, Eleanor Meade, Charles Nemeth, and Joanne Walls are the only stockholders in Accounting Company, Inc. The firm keeps the financial records of many small business firms in Trenton, New Jersey. Each stockholder, except Meade, is an accountant who works full time for the company. Friedman, Nemeth, and Walls are also officers and members of the board of directors. Meade is a friend of Walls who invested in the company to help it get started. She is a board member but not an officer.

Because the business has expanded rapidly in the last two years, Friedman and Walls believe the company should find a better location and perhaps construct a new office building. Meade and Nemeth strongly disagree, believing the firm should wait a few more years. The funds available are not sufficient unless some of the remaining unissued capital stock is sold. But none of the owners think they can afford to buy more shares. Thus, new investors will have to be found if the owners decide to expand now. Each stockholder holds the following number of shares:

Friedman	50	Nemeth	40
Meade	60	Walls	30

A meeting of the board of directors will be held in one month to make decisions regarding this company expansion.

Required:

1. Is this a close or an open corporation in its present form?
2. Which people will decide whether the unissued stock should be sold? Why?
3. Which people will decide whether the proposed office building will be constructed? Why?

4. Is it possible that official approval could be obtained for the office building, but not for the sale of unissued stock? Explain.

Have You Thought About Becoming . . .

. . . AN EXECUTIVE?

Every corporation has several top-level managers called executives. Their titles may be chief executive officer, president, or vice-president. A superintendent of schools, a mayor of a city, and a chief hospital administrator are also examples of executives. While titles may differ among organizations, top executives all have something in common—they make major decisions affecting an entire organization.

One gets to be an executive by possessing certain characteristics and skills. Generally, executives are excellent thinkers who are especially good at setting objectives, planning, making decisions, and solving problems. Most successful executives have college degrees and a great deal of management experience. Their experiences are usually quite varied, though most have specialized backgrounds in such areas as marketing, engineering, law, and finance. Because they are outstanding in their specialized areas and can work well with people, they are usually promoted faster than others.

No single career path exists for becoming an executive, because executives must excel at nearly everything. They are usually good students, good at making friends, and good at leading others. The high school honor student who is voted class officer for several years may one day become an executive. The college student who graduates with honors while having served as president of a student organization is also likely to become an executive. Upon graduation, such individuals often start careers in organizations as management trainees and rise steadily to the top of the corporate ladder.

Executives often earn high salaries. In fact, executives are usually the highest paid individuals in an organization. While the number of executive positions is limited, there are always job openings for those who possess the right combination of skills and abilities.

UNIT 3

Production and Marketing

Imagine yourself living on an island—a modern day Robinson Crusoe, for example—without all the products and services you now use and enjoy. That is what life would be like today without the efforts of business. Production and marketing are the primary activities of our economy. Those activities are directly responsible for what we buy, where we buy, from whom we buy, and how much we pay. The standard of living we enjoy is a result of production and marketing activities.

The important roles played by producers, marketing businesses, and consumers are examined in this unit. You will also learn about the importance of marketing activities and the many marketing techniques used by businesses.

Barbara Proctor, whose biographical profile appears on the next page, has devoted her efforts to one particular field in marketing—the field of advertising. The contributions to marketing made by her advertising company are typical of contributions made by other advertising agencies.

BARBARA GARDNER PROCTOR

A leading business magazine selected Barbara Gardner Proctor one of the country's one hundred top corporate women. The first woman in the country to open a full service advertising agency that specializes in marketing to black communities on a local, regional, and national basis, she is the founder, chairperson, president, and creative director of Proctor & Gardner Advertising, Inc., which she started in Chicago in 1970. She is a prominent executive, civic leader and human rights advocate.

Born into poverty in a North Carolina shack, Barbara Proctor struggled to become a success and to earn numerous business and community service awards. She completed her college studies in psychology, sociology, English literature, and education, and came into the advertising business in 1964 after working for a real estate office and a recording company. For the next seven years, she held various positions in several advertising agencies. With this valuable experience and a great deal of courage, she formed her own company with the help of loans from a local bank and a government agency.

It took seven months to land her first customer, but within a few years total sales for the business were more than $1 million. Her business continues to grow as she handles the advertising for some of the country's largest companies who sell brand name products.

Ms. Proctor still finds time to talk to others, especially about responsible advertising. She enjoys talking to students, urging them to develop self-initiative in preparing for the future and to get a good education. She once challenged students in an audience to reach their potential by pointing out the "importance of strong and healthy bodies and minds, the quest for knowledge, economic gain, strong family ties, a sense of decency, and a quest for freedom." Ms. Proctor is a living example of her philosophy.

7

PRODUCT PLANNING AND PRODUCTION

After studying this chapter you will be able to:

- Describe how research is used to develop new products.
- Identify the steps in planning a new product.
- Explain the four types of manufacturing processes.
- Discuss factors to be considered in locating a manufacturing business.
- Discuss the importance of production scheduling.
- Describe differences between manufacturing and service businesses.

As consumers, we are offered a number of choices of products and services to satisfy our wants and needs. Businesses also have a choice of what products or services to sell. Businesses are most successful when they (1) are able to offer products or services that consumers want to purchase, and (2) can produce them at prices that consumers are willing to pay.

The development and manufacture of new products is a very difficult and expensive task. For example, it took one manufacturer about ten years and many millions of dollars to develop a new type of potato chip. Typically, one out of every three new products introduced will fail within five years. A producer or manufacturer risks a large amount of money in buildings, equipment, materials, and personnel in order to provide the products that we consume.

NEW PRODUCT DEVELOPMENT

Production is the process of developing or improving a product or service. As a result of many factors, products are continuously changing—old products go out of use or are improved, and new products are developed. It is estimated that most of the products you will be using within ten years are not even available today. For a company to survive, it must continually search for ways to improve even its most successful products and regularly consider the development of new products.

Ideas for new products can come from many sources. People inside and outside the company may suggest new product ideas. A company may get ideas from sales and production personnel, from other business people, and from research projects. Many companies employ people whose primary responsibility is to create and test new products.

One of the best sources of new product information is a company's customers. They have used the company's products and know what they like and do not like. Customers can give useful information on how to improve products and on the types of new products they would like to see. There are many ways companies can get this information from customers. Some companies send questionnaires to people who recently bought a product asking for their opinions. Other companies have telephone numbers that customers can call when they have questions or problems.

If a company wants to get a great deal of information from consumers about possible new products, it might form a **consumer panel**—a group of people who offer opinions about a product or service. The panel is made

ILLUS. 7–1
A taste test is an effective way for a company to get product information directly from its customers.

up of several people who have bought or are likely to buy the company's products. The panel members meet regularly with the company representatives to discuss their feelings about new products and tell the representatives what they think the company can do to improve its current products.

Salespeople can also be used to gather information from customers. Since salespeople regularly talk to customers, they collect valuable information that can help the company improve its products. Salespeople should be encouraged to learn as much as they can about customer likes and dislikes.

PRODUCT DEVELOPMENT RESEARCH

No matter what the source of new product ideas, it is very risky for a company to go ahead with the development of a new product without completing some research. **Research** is the systematic search for and interpretation of facts in an effort to solve problems. A company must invest a great deal of money, time, and other resources in a new product. Most companies are not willing to invest that much without being sure that they can produce the product successfully, and that there are customers who will buy the product. Business now spends billions of dollars a year on research. In addition, universities and the federal government are continually conducting research that results in new products. On the average, about 2 percent of a firm's annual sales is spent on new product research. Some firms spend as much as 10 percent of their sales dollars each year to discover new products.

Several types of research can be done to help firms decide whether to produce and sell new products. Two broad categories are product research and marketing research.

Product Research

Product research is research done to develop new products or to discover improvements for existing products. Researchers need to create products which customers will prefer over the products of other companies. Therefore, companies will try to use information about the needs and wants of potential customers while new product research is being conducted.

There are two types of product research—pure research and applied research. These will be discussed in the next two sections.

Pure Research. One type of product research is called **pure research**—research done without a specific product in mind. Scientists and researchers in many companies are continually searching for new processes, materials, or ideas. They are experts in specific areas such as chemistry,

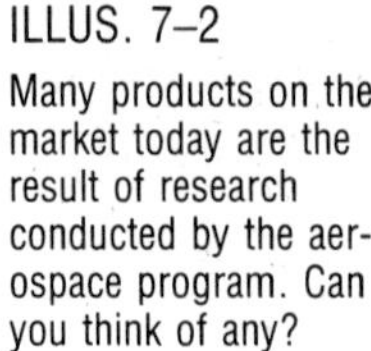
ILLUS. 7–2
Many products on the market today are the result of research conducted by the aerospace program. Can you think of any?

mechanical engineering, electronics, or energy sources. They conduct experiments and tests in order to make discoveries that might lead to new products.

Many products that we use today have been developed as a result of such research. Microcomputers, digital clocks, and electronic games are the results of several pure research projects. Much of the material used in the clothing we wear today has been developed through chemical research. Some examples include dacron, rayon, and nylon. Insulation used in refrigerators and beverage coolers is a result of research conducted by scientists involved in the space program.

Scientists are conducting pure research in many areas today. Products will likely be developed in the near future that effectively use solar energy, find new uses for laser technology, or result in the improved treatment of diseases.

Applied Research. **Applied research** studies existing product problems or design improvements for current products. For example, automobiles are more fuel-efficient today than just a few years ago. Telephone calls are now often completed using satellite communications. Self-correcting features on typewriters allow typists to correct errors neatly and quickly. Soft contact lenses are designed to be more comfortable than hard lenses. All of these improvements are the result of on-going applied research.

Changes and improvements in products are necessary if the products are going to be successful for a long time. Many types of improvements result from product research. Changes can be made in the physical product, or new features can be added to existing products. Sometimes changes in the package can improve a product. Such improvements include aluminum and plastic soft drink containers, safety caps on medicine containers, and packaging materials that use air to prevent product damage during shipping.

Marketing Research

Marketing research is the study of all activities involved in the exchange of goods and services between businesses and consumers. Many companies have developed products that were well designed and manufactured and were needed by consumers, but they were not successful.

Many factors contribute to the success or failure of a product. Those factors include the many marketing decisions that determine the best ways to sell the product to consumers. Effective marketing decisions are as important to a product's success as are product decisions. Marketing research is conducted to assist business managers in making those decisions.

Think of all the decisions that have to be made when marketing a product: Who will buy the product? What are the buyers' needs? What companies offer competing products? What brand name should be used? How should the product be packaged? Where will it be sold? What price should be charged for the product? What type of advertising will be most effective? The list is almost endless, but each of these questions must be answered. Marketing research can provide information to help answer such marketing questions. Some common types of marketing research are shown in Illus. 7–3.

ILLUS. 7–3
Common types of marketing research.

Market Research	The study of the people or businesses who buy a company's products or who may buy a new product. Market research is used to locate and describe potential customers.
Motivation Research	The study of consumer buying behavior. Motivation research helps businesses determine why people buy and what influences their decisions.
Advertising Research	Research done to test advertisements and the media that carry advertisements. It is used to determine if the company's advertising is effective in informing the public of available products and services.

PLANNING A NEW PRODUCT

Planning, producing, and marketing a new product must be approached carefully by a business. All of the major units in the business including production, finance, accounting, and marketing should be involved.

The product should be designed to meet the needs of the customers. Customers should be able to identify features of the product that are different from and better than those of competing products. Also, products need to be safe and easy to use.

If marketing research shows that a company has a new product idea needed by enough customers to make it successful, the company can begin to design the product. In this step, engineers and researchers build models of the product and test them to be sure that a quality product can be produced. Once a model has been built, it can be used for additional market research, as well as for determining what resources the company will need to produce larger quantities of the product. At this time, the firm may decide not to produce the product at all; especially if consumer reaction has not been favorable or if the product cannot be produced and sold profitably.

If the new product has survived the research and testing process, the company can begin producing and marketing it. This will usually be an expensive step. Manufacturing facilities may need to be built or remodeled; raw materials will need to be purchased; enough people must be available to produce the product; and the product must be promoted, distributed, and sold. However, if the product has been carefully planned and produced, it has a better chance of being successful, and the company will be able to make a profit when the products are purchased by consumers.

MANUFACTURING AND PRODUCTION PROCESSES

Product manufacturing is a complex process even if only one product is being produced. Look carefully at any product you have purchased recently. Very likely, it is made of several smaller parts or pieces. Those parts either have to be manufactured by the company or purchased from other companies. The manufacturer needs to store the parts until they are needed. Then the parts need to be assembled by machinery or people. Once assembled, the product will usually be packaged. Many products will be packed together for shipping and then stored in a warehouse for delivery to the places where the product will be sold.

In addition to the activities just discussed, many other things must happen during the manufacturing process. Equipment must be maintained and repaired, supplies must be available, and people must be trained to operate the equipment.

As you can see, manufacturing just one product is a complicated process. Often, manufacturers produce many products at the same time. So you can easily understand how complicated it can be to operate a manufacturing business.

When you think of a manufacturing business, you may have an image of a large factory with a long assembly line. Workers perform specific activities on the assembly line as the product moves past. Many products, all looking exactly alike, are produced on the assembly line each day. While assembly lines are one way to manufacture products, there are many other methods.

Projcct Manufacturing

Often there is a need to build only one or a very small number of units of a product. The product may be very large or complex, and take a long time to build. This type of product is often designed and built to meet the specific needs of the purchaser. Houses, buildings, bridges, and highways are all examples of manufacturing projects. If a company needs a special piece of equipment built, a project manufacturer must be used.

A project manufacturer must be able to work with a customer to develop a unique product. The company must be flexible enough to build a different product each time, and it may need to build part or all of that product at a new location each time.

Repetitive Activities

Some companies manufacture a product using a repetitive activity. They do the same thing over and over to produce a product. The activity is usually rather simple and can be completed in a short time. The product developed may be slightly different for each customer. Examples of companies that use a repetitive activity are printers and photographers.

Continuous Processing

Raw materials and natural resources usually need to be processed before they can be consumed. Companies that work with raw materials to make them more useable are involved in continuous processing. Steel mills, for example, convert iron ore into steel to be used by other manufacturers. Oil refineries change crude oil into a variety of petroleum products including gasoline and oil. Cereal manufacturers process many different kinds of grain into the cereals you eat for breakfast.

Mass Production

Earlier you read about companies that use assembly lines to produce products. **Mass production** is an assembly process in which a large number

of products is produced, each of which is identical to the next. Many products you use are assembled through mass production procedures. Automobiles, cameras, calculators, appliances, and wristwatches are examples of mass-produced items.

Mass production has allowed companies to manufacture products at a low cost and in large quantities. Many changes have occurred in mass production since it was first used in the early 1900s. Long conveyor belts and moving chains now move the product through the factory. New tools and equipment make assembly easier. Many businesses are using robots on the assembly line to complete such tasks as painting, welding, and product testing.

ORGANIZING A MANUFACTURING BUSINESS

When a new manufacturing business is organized, a number of important decisions must be made. The company must be able to get the materials needed to build products. Buildings, machinery, and equipment must be purchased and arranged so that quality products can be produced rapidly and at a low cost.

People must be hired with the skills to operate the business. If people with the proper skills cannot be found, others must be trained. Finally, after the products are completed they must be distributed and sold.

Locating the Business

One of the first decisions of the manufacturing company is where to locate the business. While it might seem that a business could locate anywhere it wants to, it is a very complicated procedure to find the best location. A discussion of several factors that influence the decision follows.

Availability of Raw Materials. If a company uses a large quantity of raw materials, it must make sure they are available at a low cost. The owners, therefore, may choose to locate close to the source of the raw materials to make them easier to obtain and to keep the cost of transporting the raw materials as low as possible. Furniture and textile manufacturers, steel mills, and food processing companies are examples of industries that are located close to the source of needed raw materials.

Transportation Methods. A company must decide how to obtain needed materials and how products will be shipped to customers. The choice of transportation method can determine whether raw materials are received and products are delivered on time. The major transportation methods include air, railroad, truck, water, and pipeline. Each has specific advantages based on time, cost, and convenience.

Supply and Cost of Energy and Water. The costs of energy used by manufacturers have increased by over 100 percent during the past several years. Natural gas, oil, and gasoline have all been in short supply at certain times. In many parts of the country, water supplies are limited as well. A company must be sure to locate where it will have enough energy and water to be able to operate for many years in the future.

Land and Building Costs. While some companies can operate in small buildings, others may need several hundred acres of land. Land and buildings can be purchased or leased. As a business grows, it must plan for possible future expansion. Many companies have had to expand several times since they started business. Expansion is easier if enough land is available close to the existing buildings.

Labor Supply. Well trained employees are an important part of most manufacturing companies. In selecting a location, a company should look at the supply of workers, the training that might be necessary, and the cost of labor. It will make a big difference whether the company needs highly skilled employees, or if it can use unskilled labor.

Location of Customers. Just as some companies need to locate near the source of raw materials, others may consider the location of their customers. Manufacturers that supply parts for the auto industry usually locate near Detroit. Some companies locate near seaports if they have important markets in other countries. Soft drink bottlers have plants in most cities to reduce transportation costs. The location of a firm's customers is an important factor when most of them can be found in one part of the country or when transportation costs will be very high.

Economic and Legal Factors. A company should consider the type and amount of taxes that must be paid in a given location. Some cities offer reduced tax rates or may even remove some taxes for several years to encourage new businesses to locate there. Most towns and cities today also restrict the location and operation of businesses. Zoning laws identify where specific types of businesses can operate. Environmental regulations control the use of water and other resources.

Factory Layout

Facilities, equipment, and materials all must be organized so products can be produced efficiently. Products must move through the building, parts must be added, and employees must be able to work on the product easily and safely. Raw materials, parts, and supplies must be received and stored. Once products are finished, they need to be stored or loaded for shipment.

The type of layout used by a manufacturer will depend on the product and the assembly process. One company that builds tractors has a continuous assembly line that is nearly a mile long. Many of the parts have to be stored long distances from the place they are needed. The parts are delivered to the assembly line with overhead conveyor belts and chains.

Another small company that builds electric motors has all of the needed parts brought to each assembler's work area. The assembler puts all of the parts together to finish the motor. The motor is then moved to the shipping area to be packaged and stored for delivery.

In addition to the type of product and the assembly process used, other factors influence the layout of the business. Products and people must be able to move around the building. Product testing may be needed. The layout should be designed to make product assembly easy and safe.

Companies should be able to build products rapidly and keep costs down. For most companies the layout should be flexible so new machinery and equipment can be added. Also the layout may need to be expanded if the company grows.

ILLUS. 7–4
Future expansion opportunities should also be considered in plant location and layout decisions.

Production Scheduling

There are three steps in efficiently scheduling production. First, it is necessary to list the various steps in the production process to determine the jobs that must be performed. The second step is to arrange the plant and equipment so production can be carried out smoothly. It is important that production moves from one process to another without interruption or delay, and with a minimum of labor and machinery to do each job. Third, a production schedule must be developed to make sure all activities occur at the proper time. A **production schedule** lists the resources and materials needed in production, and the dates they will be ordered, delivered, and used. One example of a production schedule is shown in Illus. 7–5.

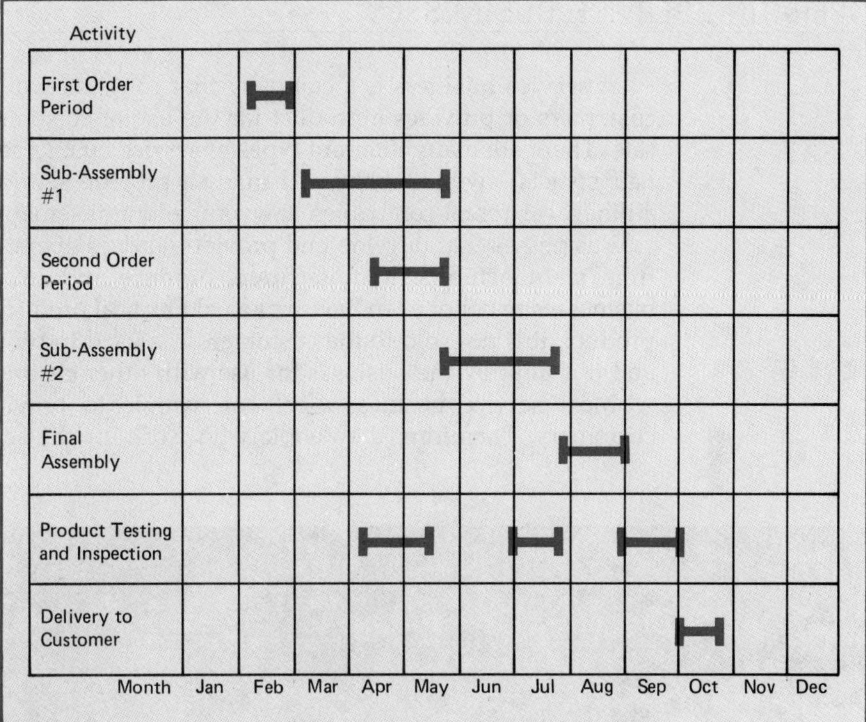

ILLUS. 7–7
A production schedule helps a business operate efficiently.

Developing a production schedule could be compared to planning a meal. All ingredients must be available in the right quantities and at the right time. Cooking utensils need to be assembled. Since some foods require longer cooking times than others, preparation of each item must begin at the correct time. If scheduled and completed correctly, all foods can be served at the same time.

When developing a production schedule, a company estimates the need for labor, materials, and equipment. If calculations have been made correctly, all resources needed for the first assembly will be available at the same time. Those needed for the second assembly can be available later. In most cases, some spare time will be allowed in the schedule so there will be no costly delay in production if one part is not delivered on time.

Sophisticated planning systems are used by managers to help them develop production schedules. Computers are very useful in scheduling production and insuring that production schedules are being followed.

The manufacturing of products is an important part of our economy. However, nearly half the money spent by consumers today is used to pay for services. Just as manufacturers must carefully plan the production of products, service businesses need to develop effective procedures. In the next section we examine the operation of service businesses.

OPERATING SERVICE BUSINESSES

A **service business** is a company that completes an activity to benefit customers or provides a product for the use of customers rather than for sale. There are many different types of service businesses. Movie theaters, hair stylists, swim clubs, and banks all provide services. So do motels, airlines, car rental companies, lawyers, and amusement parks.

Businesses that develop and provide services operate much differently from manufacturers. Manufacturers produce and sell products. Service businesses may not even have an actual physical product. If they do have a product, it is not sold to the customer. It is used in providing the service, and it is kept by the business for use with other customers.

Most service businesses rely on people to provide the service to customers. Therefore, the people who work for the service business are

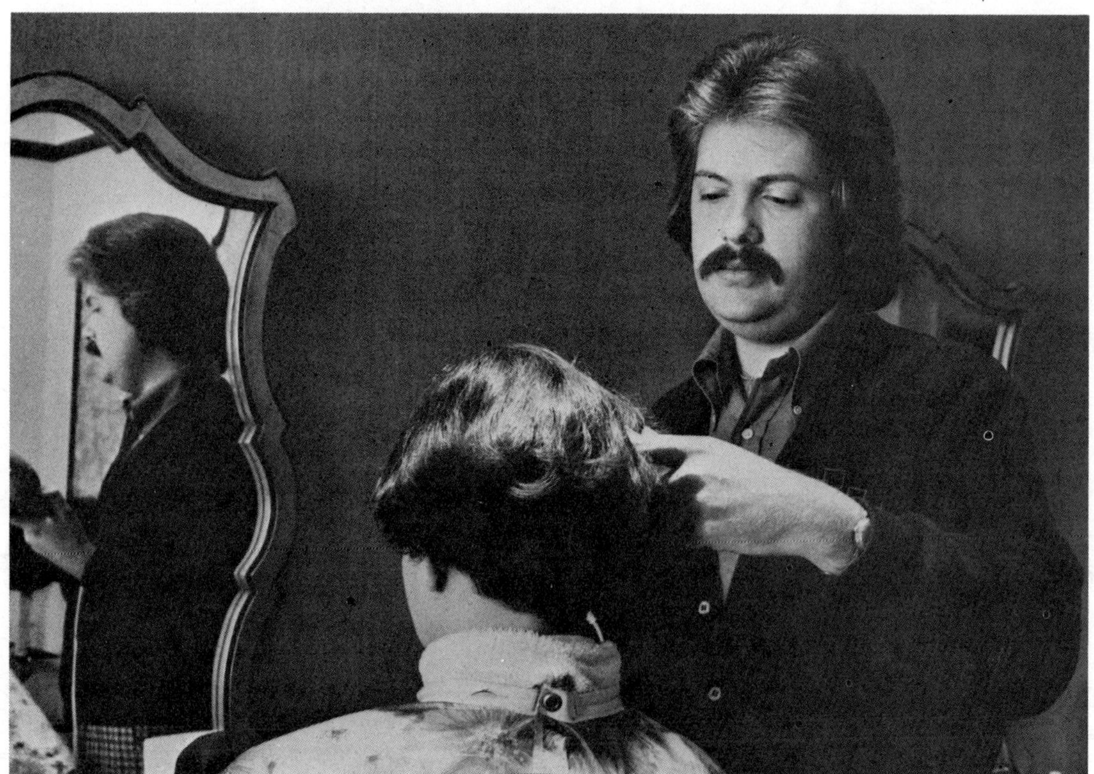

ILLUS. 7–6

Meeting the needs and expectations of customers is especially important in service businesses.

very important. If they do not do a good job of providing the service, customers will not be satisfied. It is difficult to get the customers to return to the business if they are not happy with the service provided. Employee selection and training are an important part of the operation of a service business.

The owner of a service business must study the needs and wants of customers. Services should be designed to meet customer needs and they must be available when and where customers want them. Companies need to look continually for ways to improve the services they offer.

Over $600 billion is spent on services in the United States each year. Many service businesses have total sales of hundreds of millions of dollars each year. While from a production standpoint it may be easier to provide services than to manufacture a complex piece of equipment, service businesses are not easy to operate. To be successful, service businesses need to develop effective procedures just as manufacturers need to carefully plan the production of their products.

NEW TERMS AND CONCEPTS

Define the following terms and concepts, which may be found in boldface type on the page shown in parentheses.

production (126)
consumer panel (126)
research (127)
product research (127)
pure research (127)
applied research (128)
marketing research (129)
market research (129)
motivation research (129)
advertising research (129)
mass production (131)
production schedule (134)
service business (136)

CHAPTER REVIEW

1. Why is new product development important to a successful company?
2. Identify four sources of new product ideas for a business.
3. How is pure research different from applied research?
4. Give three examples of marketing research.
5. Why should a company produce a model of a new product before it begins to produce large quantities of the product?
6. What is the difference between continuous processing and mass production?
7. Why is it desirable for some businesses to locate close to the source of raw materials?

8. When would a company want to locate a business near its customers?
9. Explain the importance of a well organized factory layout for a manufacturer.
10. List the three steps necessary to efficiently schedule production.
11. Give four examples of service businesses.
12. How can a business provide products to customers and still be a service business?
13. Why is employee selection and training so important to a service business?

QUESTIONS FOR CLASS DISCUSSION

1. Why should companies study customers' needs, likes, and dislikes before they begin to develop a new product?
2. Some estimates suggest that at least six of every ten new products introduced will never be successful. In your opinion what are several reasons for this high rate of failure?
3. Why would a company invest money in pure research rather than applied research?
4. Under what circumstances might a company decide to go ahead with the production of a new product rather than spend time developing and testing a model?
5. List several examples of businesses that use each of the major types of manufacturing: project, repetitive activity, continuous processing, mass production.
6. In addition to the factors listed in the chapter, what should an owner look for when selecting a specific location for a new business?
7. Identify several ways that computers can be used to improve the process of manufacturing products.
8. Why are the number and size of service businesses increasing in the U.S. economy?
9. How does the concept of production scheduling apply to a service business?

PROBLEMS AND PROJECTS

1. The Hi-Tech Corporation spent $337,250 on research last year. Of the total, 10 percent was spent on pure research, 25 percent on marketing research, and the remainder on applied research. The annual sales of the company for the last year were $9,500,000.
   a. What percentage of sales was spent on research?
   b. How much was spent on each of the three types of research by Hi-Tech?

2. The Autostart Company manufactures automobile batteries. During one year it produced 46,000 batteries and had the following expenses:

materials	$320,000
labor for production	$112,000
equipment	$ 51,000
depreciation	$170,000
utilities	$175,000
insurance	$ 69,000
marketing costs	$483,000

   a. What was the total cost of producing and marketing the batteries?
   b. What was the cost per unit?
   c. What percentage of total costs was spent on marketing?
3. A business is considering making changes in one of its products—a microwave oven. It wants the product to be more efficient and durable and have features that make it very easy for people to operate.
   a. Identify several ways that the business could study its old product to find improvements.
   b. If the company cannot make the product more efficient and durable, should it continue to sell its old product?
4. Develop a chart that lists the four types of manufacturing (project, repetitive activity, continuous processing, and mass production). Under each of the headings, list as many products as you can identify that are manufactured in that way. After you have completed the chart, identify the differences among the products that indicate the type of manufacturing that was used.
5. Interview the owner or manager of a service business. Find out what the manager does in order to develop the service for the customers. Then write a short report comparing those activities to the activities that would be completed in producing a product.

CASE 7–1

Gene and Levi were discussing their company's efforts to test new products before the products were introduced into the market. Their conversation went like this:

Levi: I cannot believe we have already spent almost $500,000 on research for the new computer.

Gene: It does seem like a lot of money for a product we believe is needed.

Levi: Much of the consumer research seems to be wasted. Most of the people told us they did not know enough about computers to tell us what they did or did not like.

Gene: The research by our engineers shows that our computer is faster than most others and that it is easier to service and repair. That should be enough to convince people to buy our brand.

Levi: Now they say we have to put the computer into three test markets before it can be sold nationwide. That will take another four months.

Gene: The last time we used a test market for a product, one of our competitors got their brand into the national market before we did. Does the company want that to happen again?

Required:

1. Is $500,000 too much to spend on research for a new computer? How could a company determine the amount to spend?
2. What could be done with the information the company learned from the consumer research?
3. Is the information gathered from the engineers' research more useful than the consumer research?
4. What is meant by the term test market? What are some of the advantages and disadvantages of using a test market?

CASE 7–2

Jackie Duea owns a small business that designs and manufactures decorative stained glass windows. When building a product for a customer, Jackie uses a project manufacturing process. She and the customer plan the colors, shapes, and sizes of the windows needed. Then one of four employees is given the plans and individually creates the windows as they have been designed.

Jackie has been in business for five years and the company is very successful. In fact, she has to turn away about half of all customers because she does not have the time or space to build all of the windows they request.

Recently Jackie has been thinking about changing to a mass-production process. She believes that if she uses one basic design and size she can produce twice as many windows as she does now. Customers still could have their choice of the colors used in the stained glass windows.

Required:

1. What changes would Jackie have to make in her business if she went from project manufacturing to mass production?
2. List the advantages and disadvantages of the change for (a) Jackie, (b) her employees, and (c) her customers.

Have You Thought About Becoming . . .

. . . A NEW PRODUCT MANAGER?

Companies that introduce many new products often have a position for a product manager. That person is responsible for supervising many of the activities needed to create and market a new product.

When a new product idea arises, a product manager is given the responsibility to develop and test it. The product manager must work closely with engineers and production, finance, and marketing managers as the new product takes form.

The product manager must be able to interpret research results, prepare cost estimates and budgets, and decide if the product needs to be test marketed. Sales forecasts must be made, and production facilities must be developed. The product manager needs to coordinate all of those activities and keep top management informed of the progress being made. The product manager will then make a recommendation as to whether or not the product should be produced.

You can see that the product manager's job is very complicated, but also very interesting. If you would like to be a product manager you will need a strong background in mathematics, statistics, and accounting. You will also need to understand all parts of business operations, and be able to manage people and coordinate their activities. If you think the development of new products would be challenging, think about a career in product management.

8

NATURE AND SCOPE OF MARKETING

After studying this chapter you will be able to:

- Discuss the importance of marketing and its role in the economy.
- List the activities that are a part of marketing.
- Describe the four elements of marketing.
- Explain the four stages of the product life cycle.
- Identify the consumer goods classifications.

After a product is manufactured, many things must happen before it can be consumed. As you learned in Chapter 1, **marketing** involves getting the goods or services from the producer to consumers. The definition may make you think that marketing is simply the transportation of products. However, it is much more than that. Products must be packaged, brand names must be developed, and prices must be determined. Often products must be stored until customers are ready for them. Someone must finance the product until it is sold. Most products require some type of promotion. Marketing is involved in all of these activities and many more. Much time and effort must be spent by firms in marketing their goods and services.

IMPORTANCE OF MARKETING

Every consumer comes into contact daily with marketing in one form or another. Whenever you see a commercial on television, read an advertisement in the newspaper, notice a truck being unloaded at a store, or view an

ILLUS. 8–1
Store displays may not only be attractive, but may also encourage buying.

attractive store display, you are exposed to the marketing efforts of business. Each retail establishment, each form of advertising, each salesperson, and even each package in which a product is sold is a part of marketing. A great deal of business activity centers around marketing.

Almost four million business establishments are directly involved in marketing activities. These establishments include retailers—businesses that sell directly to consumers, and wholesalers—businesses that buy from manufacturers and sell to retail stores or other businesses. Many businesses that sell services, rather than products, are also included. In addition, companies such as advertising agencies, finance companies, and transportation firms that support the marketing efforts of other businesses are involved in marketing. Many manufacturing firms have marketing departments with employees involved in marketing jobs. For example, employees are hired to work on market research, to help in the design of products, and to sell the products. There are many other types of marketing jobs, such as advertising and sales promotion, customer service, credit, and insurance. The many jobs range from clerk to vice-president in charge of all marketing activities. Well over one third of all workers in the United States are employed in a marketing job or a marketing business.

NATURE OF MARKETING

When many people think of marketing, they think only of advertising and selling. Many marketing activities must occur before a product can be advertised and sold. To better understand marketing, we will examine the major marketing activities, the cost of marketing activities, and the role of marketing in business.

Marketing Activities

The most common marketing activities are shown in Illus. 8–2. They include the following:

- **Buying**—obtaining goods to be sold. This activity involves finding suppliers who can provide the right goods in the right quality and quantity at a fair price.
- **Selling**—providing information to customers and helping them buy the goods they need.
- **Transporting**—moving goods from where they were made to where consumers can buy them.
- **Storing**—holding goods until needed by consumers, such as on shelves, in storage rooms, or in warehouses.
- **Financing**—providing money that is needed to perform various marketing activities, such as obtaining credit when buying and extending credit when selling.
- **Researching and information gathering**—studying buyer interests and needs, testing products, and gathering facts needed to make good marketing decisions.
- **Risk-taking**—assuming the risk of losses that may occur from fire, theft, damage, or other types of loss.
- **Grading and valuing**—grouping goods according to size, quality, and color, and determining an appropriate price for products.

Cost of Marketing

Whether the product is paper clips for offices or huge generators for power companies, all eight marketing activities just described must be performed as the product moves from producer to customer. Because performing these activities requires many workers and special equipment, the cost of marketing a product is sometimes higher than the cost of making that product. According to one study, all marketing activities cost the customer between 42 and 59 cents for each dollar spent. There does not appear to be any major difference in marketing costs whether producers sell directly to consumers or whether they sell through retail stores. No matter how the goods get to the consumer, on the average, marketing represents about 50 percent of the total cost, and production represents the other 50 percent. Although this amount may appear to be high, the

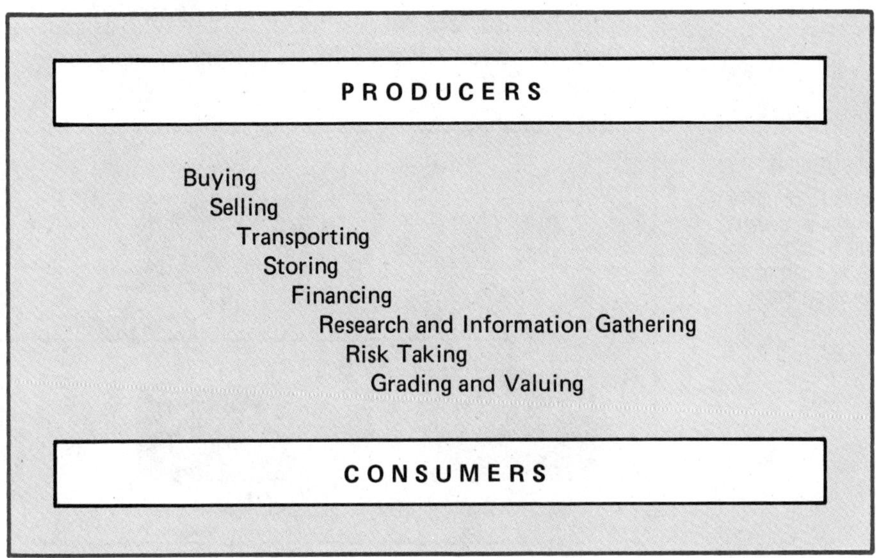

ILLUS. 8–2
Marketing activities are necessary to get goods and services from producers to consumers.

marketing dollar that is well spent contributes much to the success of products and businesses, as well as to the satisfaction of customers.

ROLE OF MARKETING

Marketing has not always been an important part of business. In the early 1900s, business conditions were much different than they are now. Customers had only a few products to choose from and a limited amount of money to spend. Usually only a few producers manufactured a product, and the manufacturing process was not very efficient. Demand for most products was greater than supply. As a result, most producers concentrated on making more kinds of products in greater quantities. Firms were production oriented. Production decisions received the most attention. Firms did not have to worry a great deal about marketing.

However, in time, the standard of living increased, and consumers had more choices of products to purchase. Many businesses were competing with each other to sell the same product. Companies began to realize it was not enough just to produce a variety of products. They had to produce the *right* products. Those companies that produced what customers wanted and made it easier for customers to buy were more successful than those that did not.

Since about 1950, more and more businesses have become customer oriented. A customer-oriented company tries to satisfy the customers with its products or services. Keeping the needs of the consumer upper-most in mind during the design, production, and distribution of a product is called the **marketing concept.** A company that has adopted the marketing concept will have a marketing manager who is part of top management and who is involved in all major decisions, as shown in Illus. 8–3.

ILLUS. 8–3
When a company is customer oriented, the marketing manager is a part of top management.

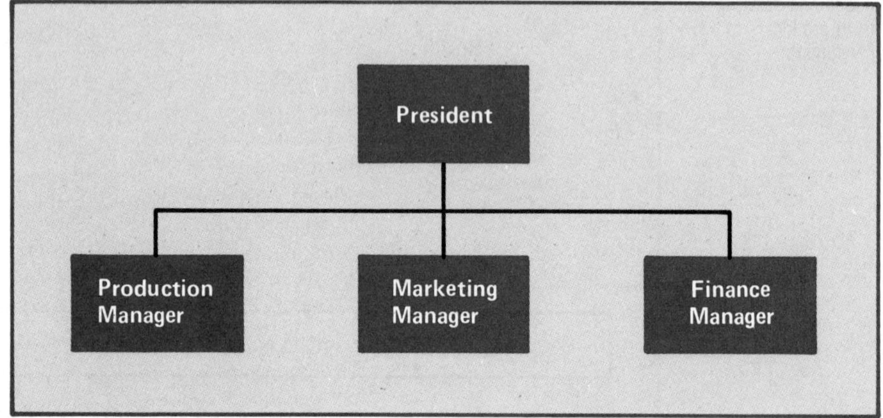

Market Determination

Before a producer decides to make and distribute a product to consumers, it is necessary to determine the market to be served. Here, **market** refers to the types of buyers a business wishes to attract and where such buyers are located. All companies need to clearly identify their markets.

Whom to Serve. A manufacturer has many potential customers for every product. Some people may be searching for the product, while others will have to be convinced to buy it. Some people will be very easy to reach, while others will be located long distances from the company. For cost reasons it is usually not wise to attempt to reach all potential customers. Therefore, a business tries to identify groups of potential customers and then decide which group or groups will be the best markets for a product.

Population characteristics, such as age, sex, family status, education, income, and occupation, are often used to group consumers. A clothing manufacturer, for example, could handle women's clothing or men's clothing, clothing for children or adults, casual clothing or formal clothing, and so on. The producer of a small pocket calculator may want to attract students, engineers, or accountants. Producers can decide to serve one or more markets. The market chosen is based on the opportunities available, including the competition that exists, the number of customers and their needs, the amount of money they spend, and other factors.

Where to Serve. Producers often limit the scope of their business operations to certain areas. Marketing managers study the geographic sections of a region or country to determine whether a product might sell successfully. Climate, for example, may cause a small producer of air conditioners to concentrate its marketing efforts on southern markets; whereas the maker of skis may concentrate on northern markets. Some products may sell better on the East Coast than on the West Coast. Finding the best marketing locations enables a business to operate more efficiently.

Characteristics of Good Markets

Companies find it easier to produce goods and services that meet the needs of consumers if they know who their customers are and what their customer's wants and needs are. Many companies spend a great deal of money on market research before they begin to develop products. As you remember from Chapter 7, market research is the study of the people who buy a company's products or who may buy a new product. Market research is used to identify target markets. **Target markets** are groups of customers with very similar needs to whom the company can sell its product.

If a company can find a group of people with very similar needs, it will be much easier to produce a product that will satisfy them. On the other hand, if a group of people have needs that are quite different, it will be almost impossible to develop a product that will satisfy each of them.

Imagine developing a product like a bicycle. It can be made in a variety of sizes and shapes with a number of special features. There is not one bicycle that will satisfy every consumer's needs. However, if you could find a group of people with very similar needs, you could successfully design a bicycle for them. If several groups are identified, each with unique needs for a product, the company can design a different product for each group it decides to serve.

A company that has adopted the marketing concept will use research to identify markets before products are developed. The research can help the company determine who the best possible customers are, what their needs are, and where they are located. That information should allow companies to make better production and marketing decisions.

ELEMENTS OF MARKETING

Marketing managers have many decisions to make. These decisions usually center around four elements of marketing; namely, product, price, place, and promotion. Each element involves a series of important questions that need answers. For example, assume that you want to market a new product. You will need to answer the following questions related to the four elements of marketing: (a) Will the product be made in one size and color, or in several? (b) Will the product be high priced, medium priced, or low priced? (c) Will the product be sold door-to-door or through retail stores? (d) Will newspaper, radio, or television advertising be used?

The blending of all decisions that are related to the four elements of marketing is called the **marketing mix.** The marketing mix for a new product may be to design an item for young adults which will be low priced, sell the item through retail stores, and advertise it on radio. Or it could be to produce a medium priced item to be advertised on television and sold door-to-door to senior citizens. The marketing mix for any one product can be quite different because many different decisions are possible. Furthermore, these decisions need to be reviewed frequently because conditions are constantly changing. Changes in general economic conditions, changes in consumer needs, and the appearance of new or improved products by competitors are factors that may demand a change in the marketing mix. Because the four elements of marketing and the decisions related to them are so important, each needs to be discussed individually.

Product

The first marketing element is the product. **Product** can be defined as everything offered by a business to satisfy its customers. It includes services as well as physical products. A principal question relating to the product is: What do customers want? Product planning and development activities deal with finding answers to that question. Marketers examine consumer behavior and use special marketing research techniques as discussed in Chapter 7.

ILLUS. 8–4
Consumers can express their opinions about a company's offering through market surveys.

By knowing the market or markets for a product and knowing what customers want, the production department can manufacture a better item. The marketing department can help the production department make such product decisions as:

- The number of items to produce.
- The physical features the product should possess, such as the size, shape, color, and weight.
- The quality preferred by the target market.
- The number of different models needed to serve the different markets the company is trying to attract.
- The packaging features of the item, such as the color and the shape of the package, as well as the information printed on the package, in order to attract customers to the displayed item.
- The brand name to be used.
- Product guarantees and services the customers would like.

Price

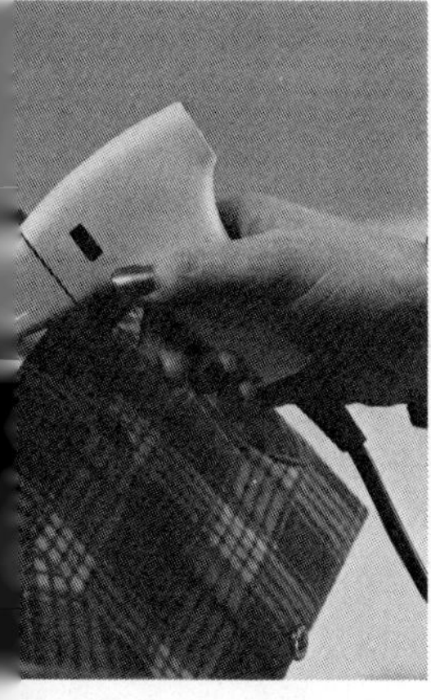

The second element around which marketing decisions are made is price. Price is influenced by the many decisions that are arrived at during the development of the product. First, the costs of producing and marketing the product must be determined. If a decision is made to manufacture a high-quality product, the price is likely to be higher than that for a low-quality product. The prices and number of competing products, the demand for the product, and the credit terms to be offered are some of the many factors that influence price decisions.

When making price decisions, a company must do more than just set a price that customers will pay for the products. Decisions must be made about prices to charge to retailers and wholesalers who buy and resell the product. Will the company extend credit to customers? Will customers be allowed to bargain for a lower price or trade in a used product for a new one? As you can see, pricing is not an easy marketing decision.

Promotion

The third marketing mix element for which decisions must be made is promotion. **Promotion** is providing information to consumers that will assist them in making a decision to purchase a product or service. The major methods of promotion are advertising, personal selling, and product displays (showing or exhibiting goods). Promotional decisions for a camera might involve selecting the kind of advertisements to use and deciding whether to advertise on television, radio, or in magazines. Then it must be decided whether to use sales demonstrations in stores, displays of the cameras, or both. Promotional decisions, of course, are influenced by the type of product and its price. The strategy for promoting an expensive piece of jewelry is likely to be much different from that of promoting tennis shoes.

While the product and its price provide general guides for promotion, many other factors must be considered before developing the actual promotions to be used. For example, a certain amount of money will be available to use for promotion. A business must decide when to spend the money, and how much to spend for advertising, displays, and other types of promotion. The company must consider what promotions competitors are using, and what information consumers need in order to decide to buy.

Place

The fourth and final element around which marketing decisions are made is place. This marketing decision refers to place utility as discussed in Chapter 3, which means the product must be in a place where it is needed or wanted by customers. **Place** (or distribution), therefore, deals with the methods of transporting and storing goods, and making them available to customers.

Decisions must be made regarding the types of businesses that will handle goods as they move from the producer to the consumer. Relatively few consumers buy directly from manufacturers. The various paths or routes that goods follow and the places where they are sold are important marketing decisions.

The Marketing Plan

It is difficult for a business to keep track of all the marketing decisions that must be made. To help deal with the problem, most businesses develop a marketing plan. The **marketing plan** is a detailed description of all marketing activities that a business must accomplish in order to sell a product. It describes the goals a firm wants to accomplish, the target markets it wants to serve, and the marketing mix it will use. The marketing plan is written for a specific time period (often one year).

The marketing plan is developed by the top marketing executive, who needs to get assistance and information from many other people. Market research will be very important in developing a marketing plan. Once a written plan is completed, it can be used by all of the people involved in marketing activities as they make decisions about each of the marketing mix elements.

MAKING MARKETING DECISIONS

A company wants to put together a successful mix for every product. Executives must carefully examine two types of information when they decide on the best marketing mix for a product: the product's life cycle and the type of good being sold.

The Product Life Cycle

The type of competition that a new product will face influences the marketing mix to be used. The amount of competition can be estimated by looking at the product life cycle. The **product life cycle** predicts the sales and profit performance of a given product. There are four stages in the life cycle of a product: introduction, growth, maturity, and decline. A typical life cycle is shown in Illus. 8–5.

ILLUS. 8–5
Sales and profits change during each of the stages of the product life cycle.

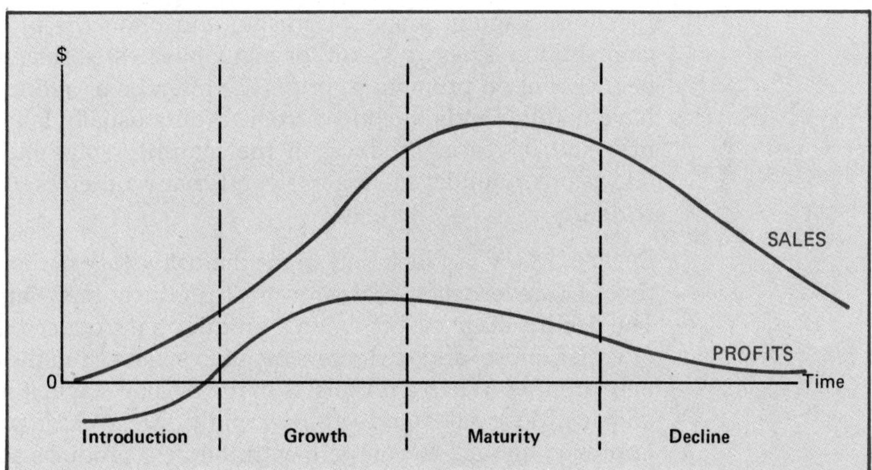

Introduction. In the **introduction stage** a brand new product enters the market. At this time there is only one brand of the product available for consumers to purchase. The new product is quite different from, and hopefully, better than products customers are currently using. While every product has gone through the introduction stage at some time, examples of products that were recently in that stage include microwave ovens and computer games.

When a product is being introduced, the company is concerned about getting it distributed and informing customers about the product and its uses. There is no competition from the same type of product, but customers will probably be using other older products. The customers must be shown how the new product is better than the products they are currently using. The costs of doing so are high, very likely resulting in a loss or very low profits for the firm.

Growth. When several brands of the new product are available, the market is in the **growth stage** of the life cycle. If customers like the new product, they will begin buying it regularly. When competitors see the success of the new product, they also will want to get into that market.

In the growth stage, each of the brands is trying to attract customers. Companies try to improve their brands by adding features that they hope will satisfy customers. Profits should begin to appear and increase in this stage. Examples of products that have been in the growth stage recently are automatic drip coffee makers, radial tires, and mopeds.

Maturity. A product in the maturity stage has been purchased by large numbers of customers and has become quite profitable. The **maturity stage** has many competing brands with very similar features. Customers have a hard time finding important differences among the brands.

In this stage companies emphasize promotion including their brand name, packaging, a specific image, and often the price of the product. Competition is very difficult for many businesses since so much money is being spent on promotion, prices are often being reduced, and customers have many brands to choose from. Profits usually fall even though sales may still increase. Products in the maturity stage include automobiles, televisions, laundry detergents, and many other products that you use regularly.

Decline. Many products stay in the maturity stage of the life cycle for a long time. However, sooner or later most products move into a decline stage. The **decline stage** occurs when a product is introduced that is much better or easier to use, and customers begin to switch from the old product to the new product. When a product is in the decline stage, it has to be improved or it will lose sales and profits rapidly. Most older products cannot be improved enough to compete with the new products so usually they will drop from the market after a short time.

Some companies have been able to move old products out of the decline stage by finding new uses for them. For example, baby oil is now being used as a suntan product, and baking soda is used to remove odors from refrigerators.

If a product cannot be saved from the decline stage, the company should continue to sell remaining products to customers who still prefer them. Companies should spend as little money as possible while marketing the remaining products and certainly should not produce any more.

Types of Goods

When making marketing decisions, executives need to understand how customers shop for and use products. Products can be classified as either industrial goods or consumer goods. **Industrial goods** are products that are to be used by another business. Frequently industrial goods are purchased in large quantities, are made to special order, or are sold to a selected group of buyers located within a limited geographic area. Examples of industrial goods include bricks purchased by a building contractor, steel purchased by a machine manufacturer, and cash registers purchased by retailers. Many, but not all, industrial goods are used to make consumer goods.

Consumer goods are produced for sale to individuals and families for personal use. Toothbrushes, chairs, fruit, aspirin, and combs are some of the many products used by consumers. Consumer goods require much marketing attention because there are so many products and brands and so many possible customers located throughout the country.

Depending on who buys the goods, however, certain merchandise may be both a consumer good and an industrial good. Gasoline and typewriting paper, for instance, may be purchased by consumers in small quantities or by business firms in large quantities.

Consumer goods can be categorized to help make marketing decisions easier. There are four categories of consumer goods: convenience goods, shopping goods, specialty goods, and unsought goods. The categories are based on (1) how important the product is to the customer, and (2) whether the customer is willing to shop to compare products and brands.

Convenience Goods. **Convenience goods** are inexpensive items that consumers purchase regularly without a great deal of thought. Consumers are not willing to shop around for these products because they are purchased often and customers have many choices. Therefore, convenience goods need to be sold through many retail outlets conveniently located to where people work and live. Products that are usually treated as convenience goods are candy, milk, soft drinks, pencils, soap, and many other inexpensive household items.

Shopping Goods. Goods that are bought less frequently than convenience goods, that usually have a higher price, and that require some buying thought are called **shopping goods.** Customers see important differences between brands of these products in terms of price and features. Therefore, they are willing to shop at several stores and compare products and brands before they make a purchase. Shopping goods do not have to be sold in as many stores as convenience goods. They need effective promotion so customers can make informed decisions. Cars, furniture, large appliances, and houses are all examples of shopping goods for most people.

Specialty Goods. **Specialty goods** are products that customers insist upon having, and are willing to shop for until they find them. The customer has decided that only one product or brand is satisfying, so he or she will shop until that brand can be found and purchased. Specialty goods are found in fewer retail outlets, can be priced higher than competing brands, and may need very little promotion. Examples of specialty goods for many consumers are designer clothing, expensive jewelry, and certain brands of stereo equipment or automobiles.

Unsought Goods. There are certain products that many customers will not shop for because they do not have a strong need for the product. Such products are known as **unsought goods,** and they present a difficult marketing problem. Life insurance, encyclopedias, and funeral services are unsought by most consumers. A company marketing unsought goods will usually have to go to the customer and use personal selling to discuss the need for the product. Unless the customer recognizes a need that can be satisfied with the product, it will remain unsold.

Improving Marketing

Many of the complaints consumers have about business today involve marketing activities. Misleading advertisements, poor customer service, high prices, and poor delivery are all marketing problems. Businesses must be as careful in making marketing decisions as they need to be in producing a quality product.

In the next three chapters, we will examine the marketing mix in more detail. You will learn how businesses use marketing activities to satisfy customers and attract them from competing businesses.

NEW TERMS AND CONCEPTS

Define the following terms and concepts, which may be found in boldface type on the page shown in parentheses.

marketing (142)
marketing concept (145)
market (146)
target markets (147)
marketing mix (147)
product (148)
promotion (149)
place (150)
marketing plan (150)
product life cycle (151)
introduction stage (151)
growth stage (151)
maturity stage (152)
decline stage (152)
industrial goods (152)
consumer goods (153)
convenience goods (153)
shopping goods (153)
specialty goods (153)
unsought goods (153)

CHAPTER REVIEW

1. What are the two major categories of businesses that are directly involved in marketing?
2. List five types of companies that provide special marketing services to support other companies.
3. What are the eight common marketing activities?
4. On the average, what percent of the consumer's cost of a product applies to marketing costs?
5. Why have businesses had to change from a production orientation to the marketing concept?

6. What two questions must a firm answer about its customers when identifying a market to serve?
7. How can marketing research improve production decisions for a business?
8. Identify the four elements of marketing.
9. How can marketing decisions about a product and its price influence decisions about how the product will be promoted?
10. What should be included in a marketing plan?
11. How does the amount of competition change during the stages of the product life cycle?
12. List several products that are both industrial goods and consumer goods.
13. What are the two factors that determine the categories of consumer goods?
14. Why do companies have problems marketing unsought goods?

QUESTIONS FOR CLASS DISCUSSION

1. How can transportation firms, finance companies, and insurance businesses be considered marketing establishments?
2. Before a producer decides to make and distribute a product, how is the market to be served determined?
3. Explain how valuing and grading are used in the marketing of food products.
4. For what types of products would you expect the cost of marketing to be well over 50 percent of the total cost of the product?
5. Do you believe the number of firms directly involved in marketing will increase or decrease during the next five years? Why?
6. Identify several products that would sell well only in specific geographic locations.
7. Why should companies that have adopted the marketing concept be more successful than those that have not adopted it?
8. How can a product's package be used to satisfy customers?
9. Discuss a number of the products used in your own home that could be classified as industrial goods as well as consumer goods.
10. How do convenience goods differ from shopping goods?

PROBLEMS AND PROJECTS

1. Select any product that you use regularly. Using the eight marketing activities listed in the chapter, give an example showing how each of the activities was completed between the time the product was produced and the time it was purchased.

2. Use the same product that you selected to answer question 1. Describe how each of the four elements of the marketing mix (product, price, place, promotion) has been developed for the product.
3. Jan Shepard produced 100 bushels of potatoes for sale. She could have sold them in their ungraded condition to a city wholesale produce business at $4.00 a bushel. That would have required one trip to the city and four hours of her time. Instead she decided to sell them door-to-door in the city. It took Jan 12 hours to sort, grade, and put the potatoes into bushel baskets. She had to make one trip to the city (2 hours) to purchase the baskets, which cost $1.00 each. Jan spent 15 hours more traveling to the city and selling the potatoes. She sold 80 bushels of large size potatoes for $6.00 per bushel, and the remainder for $5.00 per bushel. Assume that the cost of driving a truck to the city was $20.00 for each trip, and Jan's time is worth $3.50 an hour. Did she receive more or less by marketing the potatoes directly than she would by selling them to the wholesaler? How much?
4. Go to a department store or discount store. Identify two products that you believe fit into each stage of the product life cycle. What evidence can you see in the store that supports your decision for each product?
5. Interview ten people to determine how they purchase jeans. Ask each of them the following questions:
   a. Where do you usually buy your jeans?
   b. What product features are important to you when you are deciding to buy?
   c. Is there one brand that you usually buy?
   d. Do you usually look in several stores before you buy a pair of jeans?

   Based on each person's answers, determine whether he or she is treating jeans as a convenience, shopping, specialty, or unsought good.

CASE 8–1

Pamela Minton is the new marketing manager for the McCullough Manufacturing Company, a firm that makes stereo sets. These high-quality sets are now sold to wholesalers and retail outlets that buy in large quantities. She thinks the company could do much more business if she could identify the different markets for stereo sets. Then the production department could make different models for the different markets. Perhaps the channels of distribution might even be changed.

In a chat with Tim McCullough, the production manager, she learned that even if the target audience for the product is identified, a problem still exists. Tim expressed his point of view by saying, "Our profits are not that good right now, Pam, but our customers—whoever they are—want quality and they know us for quality. Our production department will not sacrifice quality for anything. If we concentrate on making and selling one excellent model, customers will buy it and they will be satisfied."

In response to his comment, Pam replied, "We can still have quality, Tim, but we have to meet the competition by providing what the customer wants. Our competitors are drawing away our customers. There is no question that there are customers who want different model designs, colors, and other special features. We should be able to offer different models and still give the public top quality."

Required:

1. Compare the views of Tim McCullough and Pamela Minton as they apply to the marketing concept.
2. Do you agree with Pam Minton that you can sell quality products and still provide customers with what they want? Explain?
3. How would you approach the problem of determining the market for the stereo sets?

CASE 8–2

Sandy and Beth wanted to buy a video recorder to attach to their television set. They had seen advertisements for the recorders but knew very little about them. Sandy suggested that they go to several stores and look at all of the brands available before making a decision. Beth felt that the machines had so many differences that it would be hard for them to determine which brand to buy. She suggested that they buy the same brand as their television. The television had performed well for them for five years, and Beth thought they could trust that brand better than others they had not used before.

Required:

1. Which goods classification best describes Sandy's method of buying the video recorder?
2. Which classification best fits Beth's buying method?
3. Describe how customers would shop for a video recorder for each of the remaining goods classification not described in questions 1 and 2.
4. Do you believe Sandy and Beth should be included in the same target market?

Have You Thought About Becoming . . .

. . . A MARKETING MANAGER?

One of the fastest growing career areas in business today is marketing management. However, the requirements for a job in marketing management are increasing as well.

Many large companies now have an executive in a top level of management known as the marketing manager. That person is responsible for all marketing decisions and activities in the firm. The marketing manager helps other top executives make generalized plans for the entire business. Then specific plans must be made for the promotion, pricing, and distribution of every product. To accomplish this, the marketing manager will often have a budget of millions of dollars and hundreds of people to control.

Being a marketing manager today usually requires a college degree. Many marketing managers have a master's degree in business. You will need skills in mathematics, communications, and financial analysis and decision making, as well as in marketing. Marketing managers must understand all parts of the business, and they usually have many years of experience in other marketing jobs such as selling. With the appropriate education and experience, you can find many exciting and challenging jobs in marketing management.

DISTRIBUTION FUNCTIONS AND INSTITUTIONS

After studying this chapter you will be able to:

- Explain the various channels for distributing products from the producer to consumers.
- Identify factors to be considered in selecting channels of distribution.
- Describe some of the transportation problems businesses face when distributing products.
- Discuss the advantages of the major methods of shipping goods.
- Show how product storage is an important part of distribution.

Do any of these situations sound familiar? They are all the result of failures in the distribution system.

Customer A: This is my third store. I hope you carry Marvelous Muffins!
Clerk: Sorry, we do not carry that brand.

Customer B: May I have a package of Marvelous Muffins? They were advertised in Thursday's newspaper.
Clerk: No. We sold out and will not have more until next week.

Customer C: Please give me my money back for these Marvelous Muffins. The package is torn and they are stale.
Clerk: I can see that the package is torn.

Distribution systems are designed to get products to customers where they want them, when they want them, and in the form they want them. In this chapter, we examine the businesses that are involved in the distribution of products from the producer to the product user, and the activities involved in distribution.

CHANNELS OF DISTRIBUTION

The various avenues taken by goods in getting from the producer to the consumer are called **channels of distribution,** or **trade channels**. Businesses that aid in transferring goods from the producer to the user are called **channel members**. The most common types of channel members are retailers and wholesalers. A **retailer** sells directly to the consumer. A **wholesaler**, on the other hand, supplies goods to retailers, industrial users, schools, hospitals, and government agencies. Wholesalers, retailers, and other channel members serve important roles in distributing goods.

Customers also influence the number of businesses in a trade channel. When developing a channel of distribution, businesses must consider the location of customers, the number of customers wanting the product, and the ways in which customers purchase the products.

Types of Trade Channels

The trade channels used by producers of both consumer and industrial goods may result in a short or long path for merchandise to follow. The shortest path is for the producer to sell directly to consumers; the longest path can include a retailer, a wholesaler, and even other businesses, as shown in Illus. 9–1. The most common types of trade channels are described next.

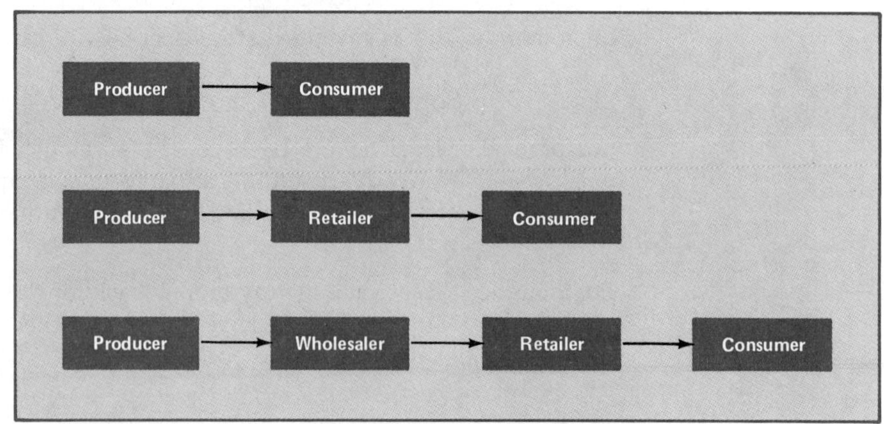

ILLUS. 9–1
Common types of trade channels for consumer goods.

Producer Directly to Consumer. Certain producers prefer to sell directly to consumers rather than through other businesses. A farmer can sell vegetables at a roadside stand, an airplane manufacturer can sell planes directly at airlines, and a publisher can sell books through the mail to consumers. When producers sell directly to the ultimate customer, it is called **direct marketing**; distribution through channel members is called **indirect marketing**.

ILLUS. 9–2
Door-to-door selling can be very challenging and rewarding.

Direct marketing is accomplished in a number of ways. One way is for sales representatives to call on users in person. Door-to-door selling, for instance, has been used successfully by cosmetic, insurance, and encyclopedia companies. Another form of direct marketing is by mail. Letters and advertising brochures or catalogs are sent to prospective customers through the mail. Customers can use a mail-order form or telephone to buy a single product or a series of products. Mail-order companies have operated for many years selling a variety of merchandise and are a very popular form of marketing today.

Generally the majority of producers of industrial goods sell directly to users, whereas fewer producers of consumer goods sell directly to consumers. Consumer goods are usually sold to large numbers of customers in many locations. Most customers will buy only one or a very few products at one time, which makes marketing very difficult. Most manufacturers avoid the expanded operations necessary for the direct marketing of consumer goods. In fact, one estimate is that only about 4 percent of all consumer goods go directly from producer to consumers. Indirect trade channels are needed for most consumer goods.

Producer to Consumer Through Retailers. When a producer does not wish to maintain a large sales force to sell to consumers, the need for an indirect channel arises. Producers can maintain a small sales force and simplify some of their marketing operations by selling to retailers. A small sales force is satisfactory because there are fewer retailers than consumers, and retailers buy in large quantities. The retailer specializes in marketing activities, which allows the producer to specialize in manufacturing activities. As you learned in Chapter 1, specialization leads to improved efficiency, which benefits consumers through lower prices and added or improved services.

Retailers benefit consumers in several ways. Unlike producers, retailers can be conveniently located near consumers and can provide the products of many manufacturers in one place, thereby permitting consumers to make comparisons. Furthermore, a retailer can offer several kinds of products that consumers may need, convenient shopping hours, credit terms, merchandise exchanges, and other special services that producers may not be able to provide. Some of the types of retail stores that serve consumers are shown in Illus. 9–3.

Producers prefer to sell products to those retailers who buy in large quantities, such as department and discount stores. Retailers who deal in small quantities usually buy from other channel members rather than from producers.

ILLUS. 9–3
Types of retail stores.

convenience stores	Primarily neighborhood stores that handle convenience goods, such as basic foods, drugs, stationery, and housewares.
department stores	Generally large stores that carry many types of goods, such as furniture, appliances, clothing and household items.
discount stores	Usually handle a variety of items that sell for less than the price at which they may be sold in other types of stores because fewer services are provided.
specialty stores	Generally handle one type of good, such as shoes, jewelry, hardware, clothing, or furniture, but offer a wider choice of colors, sizes, and brands.
supermarkets	Generally large food stores that are well stocked with a variety of food and related items.

Producer to Consumer Through Wholesalers and Retailers. The most commonly used trade channel for consumer goods involves the use of wholesalers and retailers. Many producers distribute goods to a wholesaler who then distributes them to retailers. Some common types of wholesalers are shown in Illus. 9–4.

ILLUS. 9–4
Common types of wholesalers.

merchant wholesaler	A wholesaler who takes legal title to goods, offers credit to retailers, and provides other services, such as help with advertising and displaying merchandise.
cash-and-carry wholesaler	A wholesaler who operates much like a merchant wholesaler, except that the buyer must pay cash and transport the product from the wholesaler's business. This type of wholesaler is often used by retailers who buy in small quantities.
rack jobber	A wholesaler who takes legal title to goods and who usually works through large retail stores, especially food stores that carry nonfood items. These wholesalers furnish racks or displays, stock shelves, price-stamp goods, fix displays, and keep inventory records. The retailer only provides space for the product.
specialty wholesaler	A wholesaler that specializes in one or only a very few types of merchandise—grocery items, automotive products, apparel, and the like.
manufacturer's agent	An independent salesperson who is given the sole privilege of selling a business's product in a given geographic area. An agent usually has the authority to set the price or the terms of sale for the product, but does not take title to or possession of the goods.

In certain cases, a product may even go through two wholesalers. For example, a small leather belt producer may distribute belts first through a leather goods wholesaler who then distributes them to a larger wholesaler. The larger wholesaler then distributes the belts to retailers.

Wholesalers provide valuable services that producers may not provide. They sell to retailers in small quantities and can usually deliver goods quickly. In addition, many wholesalers offer credit terms to retailers and provide help in promoting the sale of goods. These special services make wholesalers a popular part of a trade channel.

The importance of wholesalers is indicated by the fact that in a recent year there were nearly 400,000 wholesaling establishments employing over four million people in the United States. These businesses handle thousands of different products ranging from convenience goods, such as food and drug items, to other types of consumer and industrial goods. While consumers generally do not come into contact with wholesalers, their importance to the consumer rivals that of retailers.

Factors Involved in Choosing A Trade Channel

From the available trade channels shown in Illus. 9–1, producers must decide which channel or channels will best fit their needs. Producers generally prefer to use as few trade channels as possible. Sometimes it is necessary, however, to use more than one channel if the product is to get the widest distribution. Goods such as razor blades, ballpoint pens, and soap are stocked by so many different kinds of retail stores that the producers of such items must use several trade channels to reach most consumers. Some manufacturers may also find it profitable to use more than one trade channel for the same product so they can reach different types of customers. For example, a magazine publisher may sell magazines through news agencies, newsstands, and magazine subscription agencies, as well as directly through the mail to subscribers as shown in Illus. 9–5.

Many factors must be considered by a producer in deciding which channel or channels to select for distributing the company's products. Some of the main factors are discussed here.

- Perishability of the product. Highly perishable articles, such as baked goods and ice cream, are usually marketed directly to the consumer or through few channel members.
- Geographic distance between the producer and the consumer. There will often be more businesses involved in handling a product as the distance increases from producer to consumer.
- Need for the special handling of the product. If the product requires costly procedures or equipment for handling, it is likely to pass through as few channel members as possible. Gasoline, which requires special tanks and tank trucks for handling, is moved from the refiner to the retailer as directly as possible. Often the retail outlet is owned by the refiner.

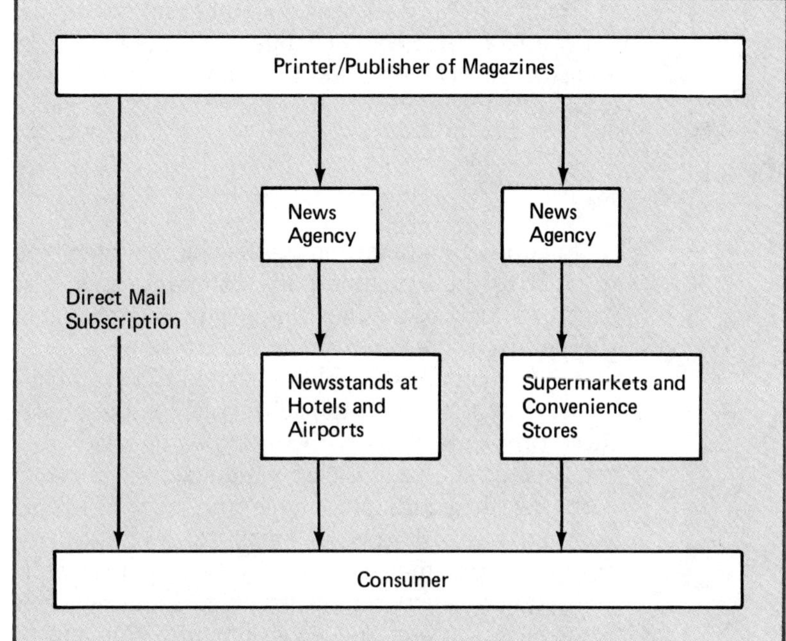

ILLUS. 9–5
Three possible trade channels for the sale of magazines to consumers.

Products that are highly complex in nature and which need experts to install and repair also require short channels. Manufacturers of large computers, for example, sell directly to users.

- Number of users. The greater the number of users of a product, the more channel members there probably will be. For instance, the manufacturer of steel is likely to sell directly to a few large users, whereas a shoe manufacturer may sell to wholesalers.
- Number of types of products manufactured. A producer who has only one product, such as pottery, will probably sell to a wholesaler. It is too expensive to maintain a sales force large enough to contact all retailers in the country. But if a producer has a large number of electrical products, such as irons, clocks, heaters, and toasters, it might sell directly to large retailers who will handle all products. The marketing costs can be distributed over many products.
- Financial strength and interests of the producer. Large companies that are strong financially are better able to perform the marketing activities required to move goods from producer to consumer through the least number of channel members. Some financially strong companies, however, are not interested in performing many of the marketing activities. For these companies other channel members are used.

Trade channel decisions, like other marketing decisions, require careful study and are subject to change. Changes in technology, in transportation and storage facilities, and in retail methods are reasons why producers are constantly looking for more efficient ways to market their goods.

PRODUCT DISTRIBUTION

In addition to determining the channel members who will help sell the product to the consumer, the company must also make other channel decisions. One of the most important decisions is how the product will be shipped from the producer to the consumer.

Several common problems related to the transportation of goods must be faced by the buyer, the seller, or both the buyer and the seller. One of these problems deals with the types of goods to be shipped. Factors to consider in shipping include the size, shape, and weight of the goods. Also, certain goods are fragile and may need special care in handling. Transporting 100 tons of steel, for example, requires much different treatment from that required for moving a carton of glassware.

Another transportation problem is the time needed to deliver goods. Some buyers expect or need shipment within a matter of hours, and others may not need or expect delivery for several weeks. Still another shipping problem is that of cost. In addition to the basic transportation charges, there are the costs of packaging the goods, insuring the goods, and occasionally storing the goods at a warehouse before final delivery can be made to the buyer.

Those companies which do not perform their own shipping activities must first decide on a method of shipment. Then, they must select a firm to transport the goods.

TRANSPORTATION PROCEDURES

To deal effectively with transportation problems, it is necessary to be familiar with transportation procedures. We next examine the procedures related to methods of shipping, the contracts for shipping, and the shipment of small packages.

Methods of Shipping

The most commonly used methods of transporting goods are by railroad, truck, and airplane. A business may find that it is feasible to use more than one type of transportation, depending on the type of shipment involved.

Railway Freight Shipments. Railway transportation is one of the most common forms of shipping in the United States. It includes carload freight

(CL) and less-than-carload freight (LCL). The principal advantage of rail transportation is low cost for moving heavy and bulky goods long distances. Often there are delays along the route when it is necessary to drop off cars that have arrived at their destination or to add cars to the train. There are many communities that are not served directly by railroads. For an extra charge, railroads in many cities will pick up goods at the shipper's place of business, load the goods in railroad cars, ship them to the destination city, unload them, and deliver them to the business which ordered them.

Railroad shipment rates are generally expressed in rates per hundred pounds or per ton. Rates for less-than-carload freight shipments are much higher than those for carload shipments. The rates are not the same for all products that weigh the same and are shipped the same distance. For instance, products of a high unit value and subject to damage, such as television sets, have a higher rate than those of a low unit value that cannot be easily damaged, such as coal.

Truck Shipments. Trucks are often used for short-distance shipping. Trucks are of great importance for communities with infrequent or no railroad service. Shipments made by truck generally are picked up at the shipper's place of business and delivered directly to the receiver's place of business. Some trucking companies load their own trucks or trailers and place them on railroad cars to be shipped close to the final destination. This service is called **piggyback service**. Some railroads own trucking lines to provide this service.

Truck shipment rates are usually based on the weight of the shipment and the distance to be transported. In most cases, the rates are higher than those charged by railroads.

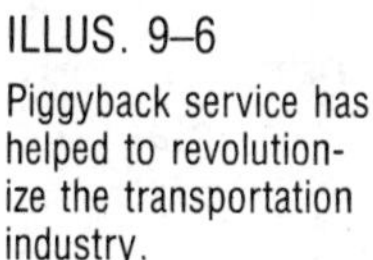

ILLUS. 9–6

Piggyback service has helped to revolutionize the transportation industry.

Air Shipments. The shipment of products by air has grown rapidly. Hundreds of different products are shipped by air every day. Because airplanes provide the most rapid form of transportation and because their rates are extremely high, they are used principally for long-distance shipments and for the shipment of items of relatively small bulk, high value, or quick perishability. Airlines are used for shipping cut flowers, high-fashion clothing, seafood, film, and jewelry. Air shipments are also used for items needed in emergencies, such as medicines and parts for machines needing quick repairs. The airlines have special cargo planes to handle large shipments.

Other Transportation Methods. Water transportation (ocean, lake, and river) is the slowest method of transporting goods. However, it is also the cheapest for bulky goods such as coal, iron ore, oil, lumber, grain, and cotton, which are the principal items transported by water.

In the United States, there is a network of approximately 250,000 miles of pipelines. The principal items transported are petroleum and natural gas. Pipelines are being considered in some parts of the country for the movement of coal slurry (coal chips mixed with water) from coal mines.

Contracts For Shipments

Three parties are involved in the process of shipping: the business or person that is shipping the goods (the **consignor**), the transportation company (the **carrier**), and the business or person to which the goods are being shipped (the **consignee**). The formal contract between the shipper and the transportation company is the **bill of lading**. Illus. 9–7 shows the front side of the bill of lading used by a trucking company. The terms of the contract are stated on the reverse side and include statements about losses for which the transportation company will not be liable. Three copies are made. The original copy goes to the consignee, one copy is kept by the carrier, and one copy is kept by the consignor. Upon presenting the copy of the bill of lading and signing for the goods, the consignee can obtain the shipment from the carrier.

Small Shipments

When an order for goods involves only a small quantity of a product or when the product itself is very small, businesses must use a different type of shipment. The shipment of such small packages is usually called a **parcel shipment**. Various delivery services are available for sending these small packages by air, rail, bus, or truck. The speed of delivery ranges from one to a few days. The cost can vary a great deal depending on the carrier selected. In most cases there is a limit to the size or weight of a parcel. Some airlines for example, limit parcel size to 50 pounds while bus companies limit parcel size to 100 pounds. The United States Postal

ILLUS. 9–7

Can you identify the consignor, the carrier, and the consignee?

STRAIGHT BILL OF LADING—SHORT FORM—ORIGINAL—NOT NEGOTIABLE

RECEIVED, subject to the classifications and tariffs in effect on the date of the issue of this Bill of Lading,

AGENT'S NO. ____

FROM FRANK'S ELECTRIC COMPANY AT CINCINNATI, OHIO, February 6 19--

CONSIGNED TO AND DESTINATION
John Kelley & Son
604 Regent Blvd.
Detroit, Michigan 48205-1923

CUST. ORDER NO. L409-3

DELIVERING CARRIER ASSOCIATED TRUCK

CAR INITIAL AND NO.

the property described below, in apparent good order, except as noted (contents and condition of contents of packages unknown), marked, consigned, and destined as indicated below, which said carrier (the word carrier being understood throughout this contract as meaning any person or corporation in possession of the property under the contract) agrees to carry to its usual place of delivery at said destination, if on its route, otherwise to deliver to another carrier on the route to said destination. It is mutually agreed, as to each carrier of all or any of said property over all or any portion of said route to destination, and as to each party at any time interested in all or any of said property, that every service to be performed hereunder shall be subject to all the terms and conditions of the Uniform Domestic Straight Bill of Lading set forth (1) in Official, Southern, Western and Illinois Freight Classifications in effect on the date hereof, if this is a rail or a rail-water shipment, or (2) in the applicable motor carrier classification or tariff if this is a motor carrier shipment.

Shipper hereby certifies that he is familiar with all the terms and conditions of the said bill of lading, including those on the back thereof, set forth in the classification or tariff which governs the transportation of this shipment, and the said terms and conditions are hereby agreed to by the shipper and accepted for himself and his assigns.

NO. PACKAGES	DESCRIPTION OF ARTICLES	WEIGHT	RATE	CHK.
3	cartons electrical appliances	350 lbs.		

*If the shipment moves between two ports by a carrier by water, the law requires that the bill of lading shall state whether it is "carrier's or shipper's weight." Note—Where the rate is dependent on value, shippers are required to state specifically in writing the agreed or declared value of the property. **The agreed or declared value of the property is hereby specifically stated by the shipper to be not exceeding** ____ per ____

FRANK'S ELECTRIC COMPANY

Per B. L. K. ____ Agent, Per ____

PERMANENT POST-OFFICE ADDRESS OF SHIPPER: 10 Mesa Street, CINCINNATI, OHIO 45227-1492

YOUR INVOICE MUST SHOW OUR BILL OF LADING NUMBER

Subject to Section 7 of conditions of applicable bill of lading, if this shipment is to be delivered to the consignee without recourse on the consignor, the consignor shall sign the following statement:
The carrier shall not make delivery of this shipment without payment of freight and all other lawful charges.

FRANK'S ELECTRIC COMPANY
(Signature of Consignor)

If charges are to be prepaid, write or stamp here, "To be Prepaid."

TO BE PREPAID

Received $ ____
to apply in prepayment of the charges on the property described hereon.

Agent or Cashier

Per ____
(The signature here acknowledges only the amount prepaid.)

Charges Advanced: $ ____

†Shipper's imprint in lieu of stamp; not a part of bill of lading approved by the Interstate Commerce Commission.

† The fibre boxes used for this shipment conform to the specifications set forth in the box maker's certificate thereon, and all other requirements of Uniform Freight Classification.

SHIPPER'S NO.

1 36644

Service, which operates a parcel post service, limits the weight of a package to 40 pounds and the length and girth to 84 inches. Shippers must contact individual carriers to obtain their shipping rates and requirements.

Some parcel services require that packages be delivered to their business. Also, the person or business ordering the merchandise may need to pick up the package upon arrival. Door-to-door service, if available, will usually cost more than the normal service.

Product Storage

Storage is an important part of the marketing process. Usually consumers do not buy products as soon as they are produced. Producers and channel members may want to accumulate a large quantity of products to make shipping more efficient. Some products are purchased more during one time of the year than another. Lawnmowers, air conditioners, snowmobiles, and skis are examples of such products. Most companies will produce those products throughout the year and store them until they are to be sold.

Buildings used to store large quantities of products until they can be sold are known as **warehouses**. Warehouses are usually large buildings with racks, shelves, or bins for storing products. They may be controlled

ILLUS. 9–8

Adequate inventory storage allows channel members to meet the demand for products quickly.

for temperature or humidity if products need special protection. Products must be carefully handled and stored to prevent damage. Accurate records must be kept so that products being stored can be located. Many companies are using computers to keep those records. When an order is received, the computer is used to determine the quantity of a product available, and the location of that product in the warehouse.

Many changes have occurred in the way warehouses are operated. It is expensive to handle products several times and store them for a long time. There are many opportunities for products to be damaged while they are being stored. Some companies use mechanical equipment and robots to handle the products in their warehouses. Computers control both the equipment and the robots as products are moved into storage and subsequently removed for shipment. The use of equipment in the warehouse has reduced the cost of storage as well as the amount of product damage.

Wholesalers and retailers that handle a variety of products and sell them through a number of outlets may use distribution centers. A **distribution center** is a warehouse used to accumulate and redistribute products. A wholesaler or retailer may buy products from a number of manufacturers. Each of these products is shipped to a distribution center in large quantities. They are then repackaged into smaller quantities, combined with products from other manufacturers, and shipped to a store where they can be sold to consumers. Distribution centers can save a great deal of money for a business. Individual stores can order larger quantities than if they had to order merchandise from each manufacturer.

NEW TERMS AND CONCEPTS 

Define the following terms and concepts, which may be found in boldface type on the page shown in parentheses.

channels of distribution, or trade channels (160)
channel members (160)
retailer (160)
wholesaler (160)
direct marketing (161)
indirect marketing (161)
convenience stores (162)
department stores (162)
discount stores (162)
specialty stores (162)
supermarkets (162)
merchant wholesaler (163)
cash-and-carry wholesaler (163)
rack jobber (163)
specialty wholesaler (163)
manufacturer's agent (163)
piggyback service (167)
consignor (168)
carrier (168)
consignee (168)
bill of lading (168)
parcel shipment (168)
warehouses (170)
distribution centers (171)

CHAPTER REVIEW

1. Name three ways in which distribution can help satisfy customers' needs for a product.
2. Identify the two most common types of channel members between the producer and the consumer.
3. What is the difference between a direct and an indirect channel of distribution?
4. Why do producers of industrial goods generally use direct channels more than producers of consumer goods?
5. What advantages does a producer gain by selling products through a retailer?
6. What is the most typical channel for consumer goods?
7. Give an example of a possible trade channel where two wholesalers and a retailer could be used by a producer.
8. Why might a producer choose to use more than one trade channel?
9. List several characteristics of a product that would indicate the need for a direct or a very short channel of distribution.
10. Explain how railroads and trucks combine their services in providing freight transportation.
11. What types of items are typically shipped by air?
12. How does a company shipping goods insure that the correct company receives the goods from the carrier?
13. What are the usual methods of shipping small parcels?
14. In what ways can a computer be a useful tool in a warehouse?
15. In what ways is the operation of a warehouse changing?

QUESTIONS FOR CLASS DISCUSSION

1. Three producers make the same type and quality of cosmetics for sale. Producer A sells through wholesalers to retailers; Producer B sells to retailers; Producer C sells through door-to-door sales representatives. Why will the selling price be about the same even though the channels of distribution are different?
2. How can methods of distribution affect the form in which a consumer receives a product?
3. Provide examples showing that the ways in which consumers purchase a product influence the type of trade channel used.
4. Could catalog sales be a part of an indirect trade channel?
5. Why might a manufacturer choose to sell products through a department store rather than a discount store?
6. What are some reasons that businesses are more concerned about transportation today than they were in the past?
7. Why would a company choose to use a

truck to haul products from the East Coast to the West Coast when railroad shipping is available and is cheaper?

8. Make a list of products you purchase that were probably stored for a length of time before they were purchased. Then make a similar list of products that were not stored or were stored only a short time before they were purchased. Discuss the differences among the products.

9. In what ways could the procedures used in a warehouse help to reduce the prices of products to consumers?

PROBLEMS AND PROJECTS

1. The Better Bakers Business manufactures a line of cookies, cakes, and pies that it distributes directly to retail grocers within a 60–mile area with its own trucks. The company is considering doubling its baking facilities and marketing its products over a 200–mile area.

a. If the distribution area is going to be much wider, will the Better Bakers have to use an indirect channel of distribution? What would be the advantages and disadvantages of an indirect system?

b. Are there other possible outlets, other than retail grocers, for the company's products? Does the number of outlets help determine whether a direct or indirect channel is better?

2. The common types of trade channels used to distribute consumer goods are: (1) producer directly to the consumer, (2) producer to the consumer through retailers, and (3) producer to the consumer through wholesalers and retailers.

a. For each of the three types of trade channels listed, identify two products sold in your community that are distributed through that type of trade channel. You may need to interview business people or complete some research in the library to identify the products.

b. Study the products you have identified for each of the trade channels. Discuss the advantages of each of the trade channels for distributing the products identified.

3. An appliance store can purchase a certain brand of electric heater for $35.00 from a firm in City A or for $35.50 from another firm in City B. The transportation cost from City A for the appliance store is $3.88 per heater. From City B, the transportation cost is $2.77 per heater. How much money will be saved if 50 heaters are purchased from the firm in City B?

4. In each of the following situations, identify the consignor, the carrier, and the consignee.

a. Great West Manufacturing Co. uses its own trucks to move products to a railroad loading area six blocks from its warehouse. The North Track Railroad delivers the shipment 1,500 miles where it is picked up by Homeowned Wholesaling Co.

b. The McDonald Store, a retail firm, is returning a parcel of merchandise to A.B. Manufacturing. The Allstates Parcel Service provides door-to-door service.
c. Carlos Perez owns an independent trucking firm. He has been contacted by Shelly Dawes, a manufacturer's agent, to deliver merchandise from the Landes Company to Discount Wholesaling, Inc.

5. A product weighs 30 pounds and needs to be delivered to a place 500 miles from your community. Identify three ways the product could be shipped. Then, determine the cost and time it would take for delivery using each delivery method.

CASE 9–1

John Allen is an artist who specializes in sketches of flowers, fruit, and small plants. People hang the sketches in their homes or apartments. By limiting his work to a dozen of the most popular sketches, he is able to produce about two original sketchings each day, or about ten sketchings a week.

Up to now, he has sold the sketches to his sister, Carla Allen, who sells them in her women's clothing shop. Because he now has a fairly large inventory of sketchings on hand, John feels that selling to his sister is not the best way to distribute the sketches. He has been thinking about (a) opening his own small shop where he could continue to sketch and also wait on customers, or (b) selling the sketches in quantity to a friend who owns a retail art shop.

Required:

1. Describe the current channel of distribution.
2. Select the type of store shown in Illus. 9–3 that John's friend operates.
3. Are sales of sketches likely to increase over current sales if John distributes through his friend's shop? Explain.
4. If John opens his own shop and sells directly to customers, will he be performing more or fewer marketing activities than he does by selling to Carla Allen or his friend? Explain.
5. Would you recommend that John Allen sell his sketches to his friend or open his own shop? Explain your answer.

CASE 9–2

The Erickson Machine Company, based in Cincinnati, makes large machinery for other manufacturers. The company built a machine for the

Corrado & Sons Company of Detroit. An important part of that machine has broken. The cost of replacement is $200. The part weighs 75 pounds. Production on the machine has stopped and 20 people are out of work. It is important to get the machine back into production. A new part has been ordered from the Erickson Machine Company. Corrado & Sons Company needs to have the part as soon as possible.

Required:

1. What transportation choices does the Erickson Machine Company have in sending this part from Cincinnati to Detroit, a distance of approximately 300 miles?
2. How should Erickson Machine Company ship the new part? Why?
3. If Erickson Machine Company had to ship the part to Los Angeles rather than to Detroit, would your answer change? Why?
4. Suppose the replacement part weighed 1,800 pounds and cost $2,500. What do you think the shipping decision should be?

Have You Thought About Becoming . . .

. . . A TRAFFIC MANAGER?

It is very important for a manufacturer to have all of the raw materials and equipment available when they are needed to produce specific products. If they are not received on time, the company may have to stop production. If they arrive too early, the company may not have enough storage space.

Because so many decisions have to be made about the transportation and delivery of products, large companies have a traffic manager to make those decisions. The traffic manager must be very familiar with all of the transportation methods. The traffic manager must select the best method to get products delivered undamaged, at the right time, and at the lowest possible cost.

If products are lost or damaged, the traffic manager will need to make adjustments with customers, the transportation company, or an insurance company. Deliveries will often need to be made to other states and even to other countries, so the job can become very complicated.

While a college degree is not always needed for this career, some colleges are now offering degrees in transportation management. Traffic managers need to understand all parts of a business since they will be working with production, sales, shipping and receiving, accounting, and even the legal department of a company.

10

PURCHASING AND PRICING

After studying this chapter you will be able to:

- List common purchasing decisions a business must make.
- Identify the steps involved in ordering and receiving goods.
- Explain the major terms and discounts related to the purchase of goods.
- Identify factors that affect the price of goods and services.
- Discuss differences among various pricing policies firms might choose.

All firms are involved in purchasing and pricing decisions. Whether a firm is buying goods for resale, raw materials for use in manufacturing, equipment to operate the business, or supplies to be used in its operation, that firm must make careful purchasing decisions. When goods are sold, a price must be agreed upon by both the buyer and the seller. The procedures and problems of purchasing and pricing are discussed in this chapter.

PURCHASING

Employees charged with the responsibility for buying must make several decisions. They must decide what to purchase, when to purchase, how much to purchase, and from whom to purchase.

What to Purchase

To be successful, a business must keep the right kind of goods in stock. Manufacturers buy products to be used in the production of goods. Retail businesses purchase products that will satisfy their customers. Several factors that must be considered in making decisions about the types of goods to be purchased are discussed here.

Quality. Many buyers harm their businesses by thinking more about quantity than about quality. They are so eager to sell more products than their competitors, that they do not consider the quality of their products. In other words, the price factor is most important in their minds. Winning and keeping the confidence of customers are the principal factors in the success of any business. Customers may be fooled for a short time, but when they find that products are not as good as expected, they look for other places to buy.

Brand Names. The person who is just beginning a business is confronted with the problem of deciding what brand or brands of goods to handle. Well-known **national brands** (brand names established by the manufacturer) are probably the best for a new business. Customers are more aware of the national brands and are willing to buy those brands from a new business. After the business is well established and has earned a good reputation, customers might be willing to try **private brands** (brand names

ILLUS. 10–1
Retailers must decide how many brands of a product to stock.

established by the retailer), which usually yield a larger profit per item for the business.

A business must also decide how many different brands of similar products to carry in stock. For instance, a grocer must decide on the number of brands of canned corn to carry. A study of the customers and the competition could help the grocer make this decision. If the grocer decides to carry three or four brands instead of two, a larger amount of capital must be tied up. For some products only one brand will need to be carried. For other products, customers will expect a choice of two or three brands.

Product Variety. A business must determine the variety of products to be handled. The number will vary with each type of business. Should a new men's clothing store handle suits only, or should shoes, shirts, underwear, socks, neckties, and hats also be stocked? There are two factors that should be considered in reaching a decision. The type of competition is one factor. If a number of nearby stores carry the same type of merchandise, the owner of the men's clothing store will want to determine what items to handle in order to be competitive. If a survey determines that none of the nearby men's stores sell leisure clothes, it is probably wise to consider carrying those lines in addition to suits.

The second factor to consider in reaching a product variety decision is the financial ability of the business to handle many items. It costs a great deal to keep a wide selection of products available. Keeping in mind these two factors, the business should handle those items that will meet customers' needs and can be sold profitably.

Size and Quantity. Because many items come in different sizes, the business person has to decide which sizes of various items should be stocked. For example, should a supermarket carry sugar in two-pound, five-pound, or ten-pound packages? Similarly, the manager of a shoe store must determine the sizes and quantities of each shoe style and color that should be purchased.

Guides in Determining What to Purchase

There are several guides that a business can use in determining what to purchase. Catalogs and salespeople are valuable tools. Trade associations and their publications can also help. Two information sources readily available to every business are company records of past purchases and sales, and comparison surveys.

Company Records. An important guide to buying is found in the records of past purchases and sales. These records show factors that affected sales in past seasons. They must be interpreted in connection with new circumstances that may affect future sales.

Comparison Surveys. Studies of what competitors are doing also help a business make purchasing decisions. A study of the advertising and merchandising of competing businesses can be helpful. Many large retailers send someone to competitors' stores to find out what merchandise, prices, and services are offered by those stores. This person is usually known as a **comparison shopper**. Such a person may actually buy goods in a competitor's store to compare price and quality.

When to Purchase

The determination of when to purchase is influenced by the type of merchandise, the type and location of the supplier, and style and price trends. Orders often have to be placed well in advance so that products will be available when they are needed. For example, orders for summer shoes are usually placed in January or earlier. A manufacturer must schedule purchases to be sure raw materials are available when they are needed to meet production schedules. Should buyers believe that prices for certain goods are likely to be much higher in the near future, they may wish to place the order for the goods before the price rises.

How to Purchase

Through trade associations and magazines, a buyer should be able to obtain information about important sources of supply. The commonly used methods of buying are (1) ordering from sales representatives, (2) making personal trips to the market, (3) ordering through buying offices, and (4) ordering by catalog.

Traveling Sales Representatives. Many manufacturers and wholesalers use sales representatives to contact prospective customers. The representatives can provide product information, demonstrate how products are used, and help the customer select appropriate merchandise.

Trips to the Market. The buyers for large retail stores usually go to the cities where a number of suppliers are located. In this way the buyers have a chance to visit several suppliers at one time and to compare their merchandise before ordering. Usually the buyers order the merchandise needed for an entire season during one buying trip.

Buying Offices. For some products, buyers can visit a buying office. A **buying office** represents the products of many manufacturers and assists buyers in making purchases. A buying office is useful for small manufacturers or for manufacturers located in a different geographic area.

Ordering by Catalog. Repeat orders of regularly purchased goods are most often made through catalogs. Catalogs are best for supplies or products that are low priced, and are purchased by a large number of companies on a regular basis.

Choice of Suppliers

Most business firms have several different suppliers from whom they can purchase merchandise. Therefore, the decision as to which supplier or suppliers to choose can pose a problem.

One of the most important considerations is the reputation of the supplier in such areas as dealing with customers, filling orders exactly as requested, and providing necessary services. Other considerations are the price and credit terms that a supplier will provide.

A business must decide whether to buy most of the goods from a few suppliers or to spread the orders among many suppliers. Most business firms find it practical to concentrate their buying among a few suppliers. This plan usually develops better relationships between the suppliers and the purchaser. Better prices and better credit terms, as well as better service, are also likely to result.

Sources of supply do not remain the same. Some firms go out of business. New businesses start up. Some businesses develop new products or improve old ones. The successful business will be constantly looking for better sources from which to buy. A business that relies on only one supplier may run into problems if the supplier changes products, increases prices, or goes out of business.

How Much to Purchase

After deciding what to buy, when to buy, how to buy, and from whom to buy, someone in the business must determine how much to buy. A business should have sufficient goods available to meet demand. If customers cannot be supplied with the goods they want when they want them, sales will be lost. If the business is engaged in manufacturing and the necessary raw materials and parts are not available when needed, the manufacturing process is delayed.

If a business has a much larger inventory of goods than is usually needed, large amounts of money will be tied up in inventory. The large inventory also requires extra storage space. If only small quantities of goods are kept in stock, the danger of loss from spoilage, changes in design, or changes in demand will be small. When it comes to buying small quantities, however, the transportation costs should be considered. Transportation costs for a small amount of a product may be as much as or, in some cases, even more than the cost of shipping a larger quantity. Shipping companies may give discounts for full trucks or railroad cars and charge higher prices when smaller quantities are shipped.

The length of time required to replenish the stock is another important consideration. If the suppliers are located nearby, there is less need for the business to purchase large quantities.

Demand can affect the quantity purchased. If the demand is seasonal—garden tools, antifreeze, fur coats, or summer clothes—the merchandise should be purchased in quantities that will assure their complete sale by the end of the season.

The amount and kind of storage space that is available limit the quantity that should be purchased. Stoves require more storage space than do kitchen clocks. Special storage equipment is needed for frozen foods, dairy products, eggs, fresh meats, and similar products.

A study of the records of previous purchases and sales of an item can help determine the correct quantity to reorder. The economic outlook also affects the quantity of merchandise that should be ordered—a favorable economic outlook encourages more purchases, while a poor outlook discourages customers from purchasing.

If a business owner decides to purchase a new product, it may be wise to buy only a small quantity on the first purchase. If the product proves to be a good seller, larger quantities can be purchased later.

PURCHASING PROCEDURES

In a small business the purchasing is usually done by the owner. In a partnership the purchasing is often done by one of the partners, usually in consultation with the other partner. Usually in very large business firms, a purchasing department is used with many people participating in the purchasing function. It is necessary, therefore, that the procedures involved in purchasing be organized carefully.

A business that has a well-organized purchasing procedure obtains and keeps detailed information on supplies, consumption, quality, and prices. For each product that is purchased, there should be information on sources, product descriptions, quantities purchased in the past, time required for delivery, prices, price trends, and so forth.

The Purchasing Department

Many business firms have a department that handles all purchases. Each person in the department has specialized duties to perform. The person in charge of the purchasing department is known as the **purchasing agent.** The procedures involved in the purchasing and receiving of goods also involve departments other than the purchasing department. The departmental interrelationships which result from the purchase and receipt of goods in one large company are shown in Illus. 10–2 on page 182. Illus. 10–3 describes each of the steps in the purchasing process.

Ordering and Receiving Goods

Two important parts of the purchasing process are ordering goods and receiving goods. The following discussion explains how these operations are handled in large and small business firms.

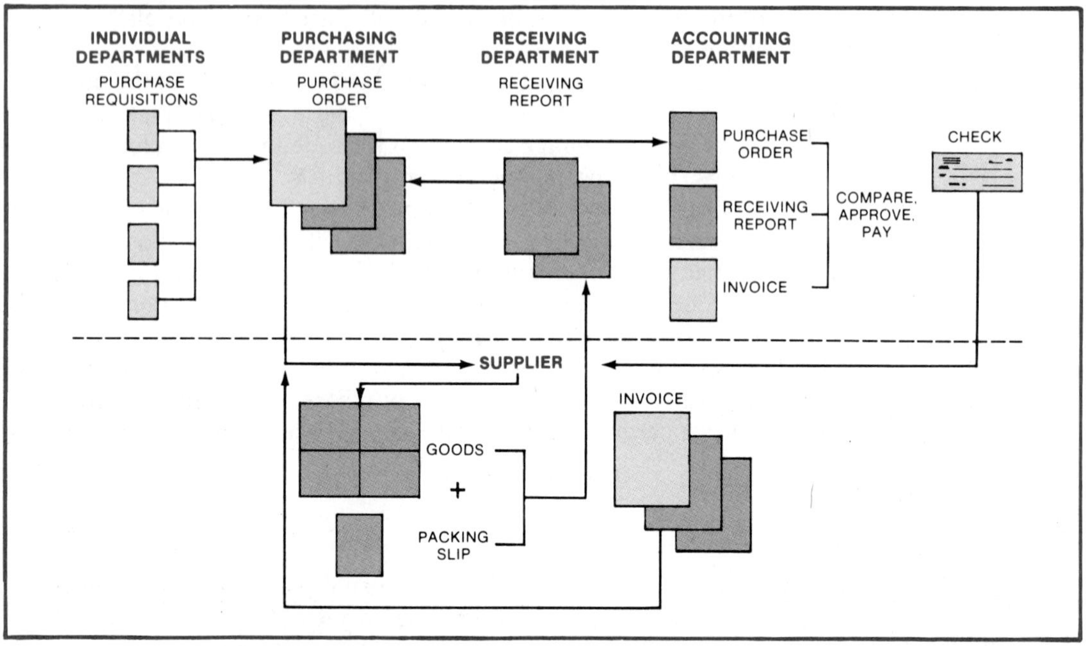

ILLUS. 10–2
Several departments within a firm may be involved in the purchasing process.

Placing the Order. The manager of a small business must watch the stock to determine when additional orders should be placed. As an aid, the manager should keep a list of products to be purchased. When the order is placed, the items ordered should be recorded.

It is impossible for the owner or even the purchasing department of a large business to know when all goods should be ordered. For that reason purchase requisitions are needed. **Purchase requisitions** are forms requesting the purchasing agent to buy the items listed. A department head, or stockkeeper, usually fills out and signs the requisition. Illus. 10–4 on page 184 shows a purchase requisition. The original is sent to the purchasing agent, and one copy is kept by the department requesting the purchase. The purchasing agent uses the information from the purchase requisition to complete a purchase order. A **purchase order** is a form that lists the merchandise being ordered from a supplier. Such a form is shown in Illus. 10–5 on page 184. Several copies of a purchase order are made by the purchasing department.

The original is sent to the **vendor,** the company from which goods are being ordered. One copy is kept in the purchasing department files, and another is sent to the department that prepared the purchase requisition to indicate that the goods have been ordered. A copy may be sent to the receiving department, and another is sent to the accounting department.

Handling Incoming Goods. After products are sent from the vendor to the purchaser, several operations must be carried out in preparation for the

Who Performs the Task	Steps Taken to Accomplish Task
individual departments	1. Prepare purchase requisition. 2. Send purchase requisition to purchasing department.
purchasing department	3. Collect purchase requisition and prepare purchase order. 4. Send copies of the purchase order to the following: (a) supplier (b) requisitioning department (c) accounting department
supplier	5. Upon receipt of purchase order, supplier will do the following: (a) prepare invoice and send to accounting department. (b) send goods with list of goods sent to receiving department.
receiving department	6. Receive goods—count items and check quality. 7. Prepare receiving report and send to purchasing department.
purchasing department	8. Compare receiving report with purchase order as to quantities and prices. 9. Send completed purchase order and receiving report to accounting department with approval for payment of invoice.
accounting department	10. Receive approval for payment together with purchase order and receiving report from purchasing department. 11. Compare purchase order with the supplier's invoice. 12. Send payment to supplier.

ILLUS. 10–3
Purchasing procedures for a business firm.

resale or use of the goods. All incoming shipments should be received at a specific place in the business and a complete receiving record should be made there. Before signing the receipt of the transportation company, the receiving clerk should examine each shipment to see if the goods are damaged and if they match the description on the bill of lading. If the shipment appears to be damaged or incomplete, a statement of the condition in which it is received should be written on the receipt. This will aid in establishing a claim for damaged or lost merchandise.

The next step in the receiving process is unpacking and checking the merchandise. The goods should be counted and checked against a copy of the purchase order. In some firms the checker does not receive a copy of

ILLUS. 10–4
A purchase requisition.

The George D. Barbey Co., Inc. PURCHASE REQUISITION
Charlotte Avenue and Third Street Fort Dodge, IA 50501-4379

Requisition No.: 27994
Date Issued: August 22, 19--
Date Required: September 24, 19--

Deliver to: Assembly Dept.
Location: Basement
Job No.: 584-31
Approved by: A.M.G.

Quantity	Description	Unit Price	Total
2 boxes	3½" Loose leaf fasteners	4.75	9.50
50	Pressboard folders, half cut tab	.58	29.00
5	8½ x 11 Ring binder	3.10	15.50
20	8½ x 11 Analysis pads	.70	14.00
5	8½ x 14 Analysis pads	.75	3.75
			71.75

M. S. McGraw
Department Supervisor

the purchase order for comparison with the contents of the shipment. Instead the checker lists the contents on a form. One copy of the form goes to the purchasing department and one to the department that placed the order. This list is then checked against the **invoice,** which is a form prepared by the vendor listing the goods shipped, the price, and the terms of sale. An invoice is shown in Illus. 10–6 on page 185.

ILLUS. 10–5
A purchase order.

The George D. Barbey Co., Inc. PURCHASE ORDER
Charlotte Avenue and Third Street Fort Dodge, IA 50501-4379

To: Fordson Office Supplies Co.
212 East Main Street
Webster City, IA 50595-3118

Date: August 23, 19--
Order No.: 14518
Ship by: Truck
Terms: net 30 days

Quantity	Cat. No.	Description	Unit Price	Total
2 boxes	485-X	3½" Loose leaf fasteners	4.75	9.50
50	280-Z	Pressboard folders, half cut tab	.58	29.00
5	141-A	8½ x 11 Ring binder	3.10	15.50
20	926-J	8½ x 11 Analysis pads	.70	14.00
5	929-J	8½ x 14 Analysis pads	.75	3.75
				71.75

By Doris Hayes

ILLUS. 10–6
An invoice.

Fordson Office Supplies Co. INVOICE
212 East Main Street
Webster City, IA 50595-3118

Sold to: The George D. Barbey Co., Inc.
Charlotte Avenue and Third Street
Fort Dodge, IA 50501-4379

Date: August 29, 19--
Our Invoice No.: 102658
Your Order No.: 14518
Shipped By: Truck
Terms: net 30 days

Quantity	Description	Unit Price	Total
2 boxes	3½" Loose leaf fasteners	4.75	9.50
50	Pressboard folders, half cut tab	.58	29.00
5	8½ x 11 Ring binder	3.10	15.50
20	8½ x 11 Analysis pads	.70	14.00
5	8½ x 14 Analysis pads	.75	3.75
			71.75

Checked by *Ray Evans* Salesperson *Abrams*

Dating and Terms

Since the dating and terms of a purchase offered by sellers vary a great deal, a business should be familiar with those most commonly used. Choosing the best terms can have an important effect in reducing the cost of products.

FOB. When purchases are made, a free delivery point is indicated by the seller. Ordinarily merchandise is bought **FOB (free on board) shipping point**. This means that the seller pays only the expense of delivering the goods to the carrier, such as a railroad, in the city in which the seller is located. **FOB destination** means that the seller will pay the transportation charges to the destination. These transportation charges do not include the charges for trucking the goods from the railroad to the purchaser's business. Most trucking lines do, however, provide door-to-door delivery.

As an example of shipping practices, consider the following case: Zimmerman, who operates a store in Buffalo, orders a machine from a Chicago business. The price is $300, FOB Chicago (the shipping point). The transportation charges from Chicago to Buffalo are $25. Zimmerman, therefore, pays the transportation company $25 and the seller in Chicago $300. If Zimmerman purchased the machine for $300 FOB Buffalo, Zimmerman would not have to pay the transportation cost.

There is a legal point in connection with these two situations that the buyer should keep in mind. In the first situation, when goods are purchased FOB shipping point, the title to the goods passes to the buyer as soon as the seller delivers the goods to the carrier. Thus, if the goods sold to Zimmerman should be damaged enroute to Buffalo, the loss would fall upon Zimmerman, the buyer. Only in some cases might Zimmerman be able to collect damages from the transportation company. In the second situation, however, when goods are sold FOB destination, the title to the goods and the risk of damage remain with the seller until the time the goods reach their destination.

Net 30 Days. Companies that extend credit to customers can list their credit terms on the invoice. A common way for the credit terms to be stated is **net 30 days**, which means that payment is to be made within 30 days from the date on the invoice. The date on the invoice is usually the date of shipment of the goods. Some businesses offer longer terms, such as net 60 days. The longer the terms, the better for the buyer, who will then have a chance to sell some or all of the goods by the time payment is due.

EOM. Another form of credit dating is EOM (end of month). **EOM** means that the time of payment is computed from the end of the month in which the merchandise is shipped. If goods are shipped on May 14 with terms of EOM 30 days, payment need not be made until June 30.

Discounts

Business firms may be offered discounts on goods that they purchase. **Discounts** are reductions from the price of the product to encourage customers to buy. Common types of discounts are trade discount, quantity discount, seasonal discount, and cash discount.

Trade Discount. A **trade discount** (or **functional discount**) is a special deduction from the **list price** (price quoted in price lists and catalogs) that is given to certain types of buyers, such as wholesalers or retailers. The discounts are given because the buyers perform certain functions for the seller. For example, a manufacturer may give retailers a 30–percent discount but may give wholesalers a 45–percent discount. Sometimes a series of trade discounts may be offered. For instance, in a manufacturer's catalog, a particular article may be quoted as $40, less 25 percent, less 10 percent. The net cost would be figured as follows: $40 less $10 (25 percent of $40), or $30; less $3 (10 percent of $30), or $27.

The use of a trade discount serves as a simple method of adjusting prices. For example, when prices are rising, the manufacturer can drop one or more discounts from a series, or replace a larger discount with a smaller one, without publishing an entirely new price schedule or catalog. Likewise, when prices are falling, manufacturers can adjust prices by increasing the rate of discount.

Quantity Discount. A **quantity discount** is used by sellers to encourage customers to buy in large quantities. One kind of quantity discount applies to individual shipments. For example, a retail paint store which orders 200 gallons of paint from a wholesaler is charged a certain price per gallon. However, if the store orders 1,000 gallons at one time, the price per gallon is lower. The manufacturer can afford to sell the larger quantity for a lower price because such a sale reduces the amount of money invested in inventory, the amount of storage space needed, the insurance costs, and the clerical records needed. Another kind of quantity discount applies to the total purchases by a business over a period of time. Quantity discounts may be based on the number of units purchased or on the value of the order.

Seasonal Discount. A **seasonal discount** is given to the buyer for ordering or taking delivery of goods in advance of the normal buying period. It encourages the buyer to purchase earlier than is really necessary. An example is a discount offered on snowmobiles if they are purchased in the summer.

ILLUS. 10–7
Buying in the off-season can save consumers money.

Cash Discount. To encourage early payments, most manufacturers and wholesalers offer a discount known as a cash discount or time discount. A **cash discount** (or **time discount**) is given if payment is received by a certain date. It may be offered with various datings and credit terms. For example, the terms of a purchase may be net 30 days with a 1–percent discount for payment within 10 days. If the invoice is dated May 1, the buyer will be permitted to deduct 1 percent off the total price of the purchase provided that payment for the merchandise is made on or before May 11; otherwise, the full amount must be paid by May 31. It is customary in business to express such terms as 1/10, n/30. Most businesses try to take advantage of cash discounts because they produce important cost savings.

PRICING TERMS AND PROCEDURES

Knowing the general factors that affect prices is helpful, but this knowledge alone is not enough to enable a business person to set fair and profitable prices. The person must also be familiar with many specific pricing terms and procedures.

Terms Used in Pricing

There are many terms and concepts used in pricing that are not commonly used in other areas of business. The following sections discuss some of these terms, and Illus. 10–8 explains the makeup of the selling price of an item.

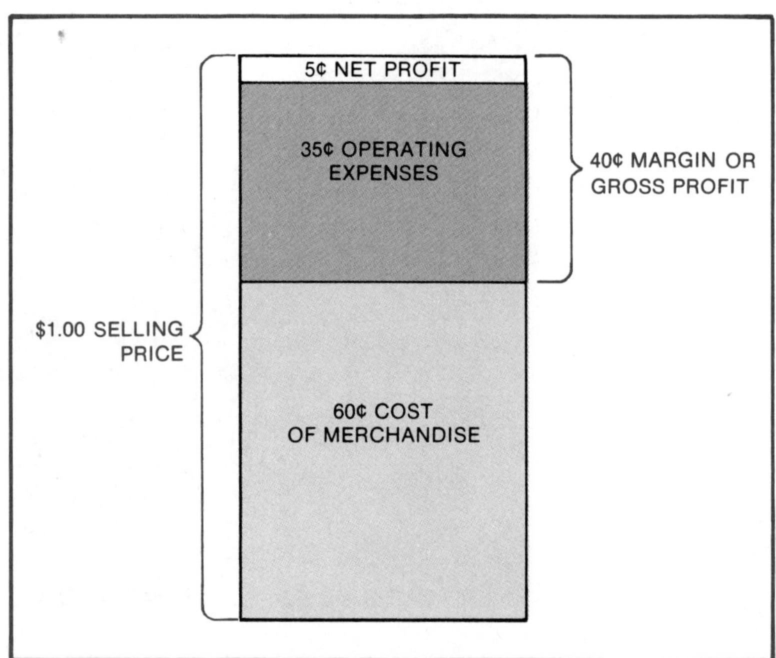

ILLUS. 10–8
Component parts of the selling price of the customer's sales dollar.

Cost of Goods Sold. The basic factor in determining the selling price of a product is the **cost of goods sold** (the price of the product when delivered from the vendor). To determine the total cost of a product, it is customary to add the transportation charges to the price of the product as shown on the invoice. For example, if the invoice price of an article is 55 cents and the transportation charge is 5 cents, the total cost of that article is 60 cents.

Operating Expenses. **Operating expenses** are the costs of operating a business. Many expenses fall into this category. Some of the more common operating expenses are listed in Illus. 10–9.

ILLUS. 10–9
Some common operating expenses.

Rent	Depreciation of furniture, fixtures, and delivery equipment
Taxes	Uncollected accounts and collection expense
Interest paid on borrowed money	Delivery costs
Repairs and maintenance	Advertising
Salaries	Utilities
Supplies	Donations
Telephone service	Insurance
Allowance of inventory losses due to theft, spoilage, or breakage	

Net profit. **Net profit** is the difference between the selling price and all costs and expenses of the business. Net profit can be expressed in the following formula:

Net Profit = selling price − cost of merchandise sold − operating expenses

Margin. **Margin** is the term used to indicate the difference between the selling price and the cost of the goods. Sometimes it is called the gross profit. In Illus. 10–8, the margin is 40 cents. Margin is the term usually used when referring to the operating level of a store. For example, a store may operate on a 20– to 25–percent margin.

Markup. **Markup** is the amount added to the cost of a product to determine its selling price. It is similar to margin. When both are spoken of in dollars and cents, they are identical. For example, in Illus. 10–8, the markup is also 40 cents. The markup may be expressed as a percentage of the cost or as a percentage of the selling price. Thus, the markup in Illus. 10–8 is 66 2/3 percent (40 cents ÷ 60 cents) if expressed as a percentage of the cost. If the markup is expressed as a percentage of the selling price, it is 40 percent (40 cents ÷ 100 cents). It is, therefore, very important that business people are certain of the exact meaning intended when these terms are used. Markup is the term usually used when referring to a given product rather than to the whole store. While the store may operate on a 25–percent margin, the markup on the store's products may range from 5 percent to 50 percent.

Markdown. **Markdown** is any amount by which the original selling price is reduced before an item is sold. Markdowns are used to clear out unwanted inventory.

Evaluating Prices

In order for a business to compare figures that are related to sales, it is necessary to have a common base for computations. If salaries are figured as a percentage of cost of goods sold and the net profit is figured as a percentage of sales, an accurate comparison cannot be made. Since selling price includes everything (cost of goods, operating expenses, and net profit), it is generally used as the base, or 100 percent. Then the cost of the goods, the various operating expenses, the net profit, the margin, and practically all financial items can be stated as percentages of the sales of the business.

The cost of selling different kinds of merchandise varies. Competition and other factors, which are discussed later in this chapter, affect the prices of many kinds of merchandise. These factors make it difficult to have the same margin on all items. It is necessary, therefore, that the business keep records of sales and operating expenses by departments or by kinds of merchandise. Only when such information is available is it possible to price each kind of product so that it will be sold profitably.

PRICING DECISIONS

Products purchased by wholesalers and retailers must be priced for resale to the business' customers. Since a business is operated for profit, the owner will want to set prices very carefully. In this section we will discuss pricing methods and policies that businesses use to determine the prices of products.

A company may establish high prices and sell very few articles. As a result of that decision, the firm may make very little profit or may actually lose money. On the other hand, some businesses establish very low prices in the hope of selling merchandise in quantities large enough to result in a desirable profit, even though the percentage of profit for each item is lower. Consider the following two examples:

Example A: An article that costs a business $50 is offered for sale at $100. The company sells four of these in a month making a **gross profit** (revenue minus cost of goods sold) of $200.

Example B: Another business, selling the same item, attempts to sell a greater quantity at a lower price. This company offers the item for $80. During a month, six of these are sold at a gross profit of $180.

If we assume that all other factors are equal, the company in Example A makes a greater gross profit than the one in Example B, although each may fail to make a net profit (revenue minus cost of goods sold and operating expenses). In many cases more expense will be involved in selling six items than in selling four items. The cost of doing business, therefore, will be greater when the larger volume of business is handled.

Businesses must be careful about setting extremely high or extremely low prices. At one extreme, prices are set so high that a sufficient quantity will not be sold to yield a fair net profit; at the other extreme, prices are set so low that a sufficient gross profit will not be made. Between these two extremes there is a reasonable price. But there are many factors influencing the choice of that price. Businesses can make better pricing decisions if they understand their customers, competitors, and the costs of operating the business.

Pricing To Meet Competition

The amount of competition among companies handling similar goods or services is an important factor in establishing prices. If one company has much higher prices than competitors, some of the company's customers are likely to buy from the competitors. Even business firms in separate locations may be influenced by competition. If prices are too high in one area, many people will travel to nearby communities to purchase goods or services. For example, if a service station in one neighborhood is selling a certain brand of gasoline for $1.40 a gallon and a station two miles away is selling the same brand for $1.30, a customer may travel to buy where the price is lower.

A business may need to offer some of its merchandise at a price below that which will yield a fair profit because a competitor has established a lower price. However, it is not always necessary to have a lower selling price than competitors. If a product has some distinct advantages or if the company provides services that customers want, such as charge accounts and delivery, the company may be able to charge a higher retail price without losing customers.

When competition is strong, a company will usually set prices at a level to cover only the actual costs of doing business. Net profits are made, therefore, only by the most efficient business firms. Even if there is little or no competition, a company that sets its prices too high finds that people will try to do without its products or services or find substitutes, rather than pay prices that seem to give that company an unduly large profit. For example, a car wash that asks too high a price for its services will find that many of its customers will wash their cars less often or will wash their cars at home.

When introducing a new product, the manufacturer should become acquainted with competitive products on the market and check the prices at which they sell. Gaps in the prices of competing products may be discovered that can be filled by pricing the new product accordingly. For example, if a competing manufacturer is selling shoes in the $50 to $60 range, the new product may be designed to sell in the $30 to $45 price range and thus hit a price bracket that is not being filled.

Pricing To Earn A Specific Profit

When they introduce a new product, many businesses base their selling price on a specific profit they want to make. The costs of producing and marketing the product are determined. The price is then set by adding an amount necessary to make a profit. This policy can help a company determine prices, but the actual profit earned will be influenced by how well customers like the product and by the prices of competing products.

Pricing Based On Consumer Demand

The owner of a business that carries fashion merchandise knows that at certain times the goods will be in great demand, and at other times the demand will be very low. A retailer will find that swimsuits sell readily early in the season, but that late in the season it is almost impossible to sell them unless the prices are greatly reduced. Since the exact number of suits that a business will sell cannot be estimated accurately, the retailer will, at the beginning of the season, set a selling price that should ensure a net profit on the entire lot of swimsuits, even though prices may have to be reduced drastically late in the season so that no suits are carried over to the next year.

Sometimes a business may buy a group of similar items at the same price but, because of variations in designs, colors, and styles, charge different prices for the various items. Since certain colors or designs are more attractive than others, customers are willing to pay higher prices for them.

A manufacturer of a new article that suddenly becomes popular may want to sell at a high price while the demand is great. When new competitors come into the field and the demand begins to subside, the original manufacturer will need to sell the product at a much lower price.

The introduction of new products on the market presents an interesting study in price decisions. When digital wrist watches were first introduced, they sold for several hundred dollars. Within a few years, competitors entered the market and prices rapidly dropped to as low as $30. Digital wrist watches now can be purchased for $10 or less. During the process of introducing a product of this type, a business needs to use large amounts of money for advertising and promotion. In the early stages of a product's life cycle, there are few, if any, competitors. The price that is established at this time may, therefore, be the highest price at which the manufacturer can sell a reasonable quantity.

As the manufacturer increases production facilities and develops more economical methods of producing the item, the price can be reduced and, in many cases, gross profit can be increased. As new competitors come into the field, there is usually a tendency to lower prices. The additional sales promotion of several competitors helps create a greater total demand. With this greater demand, a larger volume of sales often results. But, in spite of the greater volume, a large reduction in price may decrease profits for many businesses.

Pricing To Sell More Merchandise

Articles that are marked at higher prices usually sell more slowly than articles that cost the same but are marked at lower prices. For example, an article that cost $4 may be sold at a price of $6, but remains in stock for nearly six months. Another article that also cost $4 may be marked at $5.50, but remains in stock for only two months. Because more of the second product can be sold, it may yield a larger net profit to the business at the end of the year. The number of times during a year that a business is able to sell its average inventory is known as its **merchandise turnover rate.** Some businesses (such as discount stores) attempt to increase their rate of merchandise turnover by setting lower prices.

The following methods are used in computing the rate of merchandise turnover:

1. Divide the cost of goods sold by the average inventory valued at the cost price.
2. Divide the net sales by the average inventory valued at its retail price.
3. Divide the total number of units sold by the average number of units in stock.

If a business has a low rate of merchandise turnover, higher prices will need to be charged. The higher prices are needed to cover the cost of the inventory and the operating expenses of the business. For instance, the merchandise in a jewelry store is usually sold and replenished at the rate of once a year or less. The jeweler, therefore, finds it necessary to mark the retail price of merchandise very high in relation to its cost.

Pricing To Provide Customer Services

A business that has a policy of extending credit to its customers and of delivering goods may have higher operating expenses than one that sells on a cash-and-carry basis. Higher operating expenses require a higher selling price to yield the same net profit as that earned by a store with lower expenses. Other services, such as free parking and gift wrapping, also have an effect on prices. Retail stores established as self-service stores are able to reduce the number of employees and many operating expenses and, therefore, reduce prices.

CONTROLLING PRICES AND PROFITS

Businesses are not always able to increase prices if they are not making a profit. Costs of merchandise and operating expenses for the business often increase, while prices charged to customers cannot be increased due to competition. Businesses have to make careful purchasing and operating decisions to avoid unnecessary expenses. Three important areas that can affect costs are markdowns, damaged or stolen merchandise, and merchandise returns.

Markdowns

In many cases businesses are forced to sell part of their products at lower prices then they had planned. This can happen because companies purchase products that customers do not want, that go out of style, or that are damaged or soiled. Businesses also have to sell products at lower prices when too much of the product has been purchased.

Markdowns cannot be avoided totally, but they should be controlled. Careful purchasing can eliminate many markdowns. Proper product handling and marketing practices can also reduce the number of markdowns.

Damaged or Stolen Merchandise

Some products may be damaged so much that they cannot be sold. Other products may be stolen through shoplifting or employee theft. These situations have a serious effect on profits.

Assume that a product with a selling price of $5.00 is damaged or stolen from a business. The product cost the business $4.00, and operating expenses amounted to $.75 for each product. Expected net profit was $.25.

In order to recover the cost of the damaged or stolen product, the business will have to sell 16 more products than first planned. Another 3 products will have to be sold to cover operating expenses. The business will not earn a profit on the sale of the 19 products if just one product out of 20 is damaged or stolen.

Returned Merchandise

If customers are not satisfied with their purchases, they may return the products to the business. This adds to expenses in two ways. If the merchandise can be resold, it will have to be sold at a reduced price. Also, many expenses are involved in again handling and reselling the returned merchandise.

If businesses fail to consider the expense of returned merchandise, they may well find themselves operating at a loss. A business should consider its record of returned merchandise when buying and pricing merchandise. The study of merchandise returns is another important type of marketing research.

When business managers give close attention to the three problem areas of markdowns, damaged or stolen merchandise, and returns, it is possible to keep operating expenses at a minimum. As a result, profits can be maintained and the percentage of markup may be lowered.

NEW TERMS AND CONCEPTS

Define the following terms and concepts, which may be found in boldface type on the page shown in parentheses.

national brands (177)
private brands (177)
comparison shopper (179)
buying office (179)
purchasing agent (181)
purchase requisitions (182)
purchase order (182)
vendor (182)
invoice (184)
FOB shipping point (185)
FOB destination (185)
net 30 days (186)
EOM (186)
discounts (186)
trade (functional) discount (186)
list price (186)
quantity discount (186)
seasonal discount (187)
cash (time) discount (187)
cost of goods sold (188)
operating expenses (188)
net profit (189)
margin (189)
markup (189)
markdown (189)
gross profit (190)
merchandise turnover rate (193)

CHAPTER REVIEW

1. How can a person be hurt by thinking more about quantity than about quality when making purchasing decisions?
2. When is a store likely to be successful using private brands?
3. What information is available to a business in determining what to purchase?
4. What types of products do businesses usually purchase by use of a catalog?
5. Why should businesses usually concentrate their buying among a few suppliers?
6. What are the disadvantages of buying products in very large quantities?
7. What is the value of a purchasing department to a large business?
8. How can a purchase order be used when goods are received by a business?
9. How does the use of FOB affect the point at which the title to the goods is passed from seller to buyer?
10. Why is selling price typically used as the base when comparing pricing figures?
11. What must happen in order for a business to reduce the selling price of a product and still increase its gross profit?

12. In what situation can a business have a higher selling price for its products than for the products of its competitors?
13. Why does the price for a new product often decrease very rapidly in the first few years it is on the market?
14. What effect does self-service usually have on prices charged by businesses?
15. Why are the amounts of markdowns, stolen merchandise, and returned merchandise important to a business manager?

QUESTIONS FOR CLASS DISCUSSION

1. What types of businesses usually carry both national and private brands?
2. Why would a business want to use a buying office to sell its products?
3. Are there situations where a business should purchase a large quantity of a new product?
4. Why should a small business use a purchase order?
5. What should a firm do if the quantity of merchandise listed on the invoice is not the same as listed on the purchase order?
6. Should a business ever borrow money to take advantage of a cash discount?
7. How could a small grocery store successfully compete with a supermarket whose prices are lower?
8. A business has no competition in the same town. It, therefore, sets its prices quite high and makes a large profit. What will probably be the effect of this policy?
9. Why does the rate of merchandise turnover affect profits?
10. Why might customers return merchandise to stores?

PROBLEMS AND PROJECTS

1. The bookkeeper for the Downtown Store has the following invoices to pay today, November 30. For each invoice, determine (a) how much discount may be taken, if any, and (b) the amount the check should be made out for in payment of the invoice.

Invoice No.	Amount	Invoice Date	Terms
A-4371	$100	Nov. 17	2/10, n/30
A-8235	$450	Nov. 19	1/15, n/60
D-0071	$135	Nov. 21	2/10, n/45

2. A dress shop purchased 200 dresses at $50 each. The dresses were priced to sell at $75 each, and 100 dresses were sold at that price. For those dresses that had not been sold, the price was reduced to $56; 60 dresses were sold at that price. The remaining dresses were then sold for $35. What was the total gross profit (ignoring operating expenses) on the dresses?
3. Suppose a merchant estimates that sales in a year will be $1,000,000 and that operating expenses will be $200,000.
   (a) What will be the amount of the margin if a net profit of 5 percent of sales is expected?
   (b) What is the percentage of margin?
   (c) What percentage of the total sales is the cost of merchandise?
   (d) If an article costs $15, what should its selling price be?
   (e) What is the rate of markup on the cost?
4. During a year a merchant sold 180 kerosene heaters. The number of heaters on hand during the year was as follows: January 1, 22; February 1, 28; March 1, 36; April 1, 30; May 1, 42; June 1, 55; July 1, 50; August 1, 50; September 1, 48; October 1, 43; November 1, 66; December 1, 70. What was the rate of turnover?
5. A hobby shop has been selling each month an average of 10 model airplane motors that cost $20 each. The regular selling price has been $28. By reducing the selling price to $24, the number of sales was increased to 15 each month. If the average monthly operating expenses were increased $10 by the change, how much was the monthly net profit increased or decreased by the change in price?

CASE 10–1

The Touring Bicycle Shop is currently selling a racing bicycle that costs $160 for $305. On the average, 5 of the bicycles are sold each month. The owner thinks that if the selling price were reduced $25, more sales and more profit could be made. The owner believes that operating expenses would not increase even if more bicycles were sold.

Required:

1. How many additional bicycles will have to be sold during the year at the lower price in order to keep the same amount of gross profit?
2. Does it seem reasonable that the owner could expect to sell the additional bicycles if the price was reduced by $25?
3. Comment on the owner's belief that operating expenses would not increase.

CASE 10–2

Kuen Young is planning to open a small convenience grocery store in a town of 50,000 people. The town also is served by two well-known supermarket chains. One chain is a cash-and-carry supermarket where customers must sack their own merchandise. The store offers no special services and stocks private brands.

The second supermarket offers a selection of three or four national brands for most products. Its prices are much higher than the prices of the first chain, but it offers many customer services including check cashing, a place to pay utility bills, and a small package wrapping and mailing service.

Kuen's store will be located in a new housing development on the opposite end of town from the two supermarkets.

Required:

1. What type of grocery products and services should Kuen offer to compete with the two supermarkets?
2. Are there other products that Kuen might carry in addition to grocery items to attract customers from the supermarkets?
3. How should Kuen decide on the prices to charge for the products carried in the new business?

Have You Thought About Becoming . . .
. . . A PURCHASING AGENT?

In this chapter you learned about the procedures businesses must complete to purchase products and materials. Most businesses, large or small, have a person, the purchasing agent, who is responsible for buying the supplies and materials needed by the business. Larger businesses have purchasing departments where many people work to complete the purchasing activities.

A purchasing agent can work for a manufacturer, wholesaler, or retailer. The purchasing agent is responsible for identifying available suppliers, working with departments to determine what needs to be purchased, negotiating price and delivery, and processing the paperwork associated with the purchasing process.

Information from potential suppliers must be collected and updated. The information (catalogs, price lists, delivery schedules, etc.) must be organized and indexed so it can be easily used. Computers are frequently used to store and retrieve this information.

The purchasing agent must determine exactly what needs to be ordered and be sure that funds are available to pay for the purchase. Negotiation skills are needed to insure that the best terms of sale are received from the supplier. Purchase orders and invoices must be checked to be sure that products are delivered as ordered.

If you are interested in a career in purchasing, you will probably start work as a clerk in the purchasing department. If successful, you might one day manage a large purchasing department.

11

PROMOTION

After studying this chapter you will be able to:

- Identify the major methods of promotion.
- List the sources of advertising.
- Identify information sources for planning an advertising program.
- Discuss factors involved in managing promotion including cost, timeliness, and legality.
- Explain how understanding customers can improve personal selling.
- Show how a salesperson can use product knowledge.
- Describe four methods of suggestion selling.

Before a business can be successful, it must interest people in buying its goods or services. Even though a company has a good product, the product will not automatically sell itself. Consumers may not know that the product is available or where it can be purchased. They will not usually know what the product does or how it is better than other products they are currently using.

Promotion is used to communicate the features and benefits of a product or service to consumers. There are many types of promotion used by businesses. The two primary methods are advertising and personal selling. Other methods include sales promotion, displays, and publicity. In this chapter we examine the major types of promotion and determine how each can be used to sell products and satisfy customers.

ADVERTISING

Advertising includes all forms of paid promotion that deliver a message to many people at the same time. Because the message is prepared for many people it will be rather impersonal. However, since the message will be seen by thousands of people, the cost of communicating with each person is very low.

More money is spent each year in the United States on advertising than on any other type of promotion. The average business spends 5 percent of total sales annually on advertising. While not every business uses advertising, there are many ways that advertising can help a business communicate with its customers. The major purposes of advertising are shown in Illus. 11–1.

ILLUS. 11-1
Advertising can be used to accomplish many tasks for a business.

1. To inform and educate consumers.
2. To introduce a new product or business.
3. To announce an improvement or product change.
4. To reinforce important product features and benefits.
5. To increase the frequency of use of a product.
6. To increase the variety of uses of a product.
7. To convince people to enter a store.
8. To get a list of prospects.
9. To make a brand, trademark, or slogan familiar.
10. To improve the image of a company or product.
11. To gain support for ideas or causes.

Kinds of Advertising Media

Most businesses use some form of advertising and sales promotion to attract prospective customers. **Advertising media,** the methods of delivering the promotional message to consumers, are quite varied. A few of the most widely used media, grouped by categories, are as follows:

- Publication advertising: newspapers, general magazines, business magazines, trade journals, directories, and various kinds of programs.
- Mass advertising: billboards, signs, posters, electrical displays, radio, and television.
- Direct advertising: sales letters, catalogs, booklets, folders, and inserts.
- In-store advertising: window displays, counter displays, and self-service merchandising.

Some large companies use practically all of these forms of advertising, but many small business firms must be content to use only a few. For instance, a business in a small town may use only the local newspaper or radio station.

Billboards and local radio and television programs are good methods of advertising for many local companies. Such advertising is effective in attracting the general public within a particular area. It is doubtful, however, that a neighborhood grocer in a large city will find television advertising profitable. The cost is so great that the results will not justify the expense. Television advertising in this case is not effective because such a small percentage of the listeners or viewers are potential customers of the business. However, a supermarket chain in a metropolitan area might find it profitable.

Almost any business, particularly the small retailer, can use most forms of direct advertising. The cost and number of people reached with direct mail advertising can easily be controlled by adding to or eliminating people from mailing lists. A comparison of advertising expenditures for the major media are shown in Illus. 11–2.

Radio Advertising. There are approximately 7,000 radio stations in the United States. Most of these broadcast advertising commercials. Rates for advertising on radio are much lower than those for advertising on television. An advertiser can get a message broadcast on the same day that it is prepared. For instance, a retailer can advertise snow blowers on the day of the first snow when consumers might have a strong need for the product.

Most radio stations offer businesses a choice of 60-, 30-, or 10-second commercials. The most expensive commercial time on many radio stations is known as **drive time.** That is the time during the early morning and late afternoon when many people are in their cars and are likely to be listening to the radio.

Television Advertising. During the last 40 years, the number of households having one or more television sets has increased from approximately 10

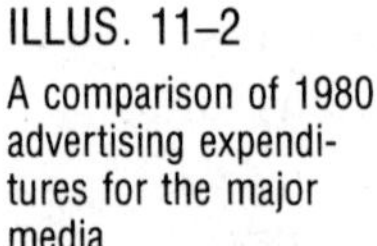

ILLUS. 11–2

A comparison of 1980 advertising expenditures for the major media.

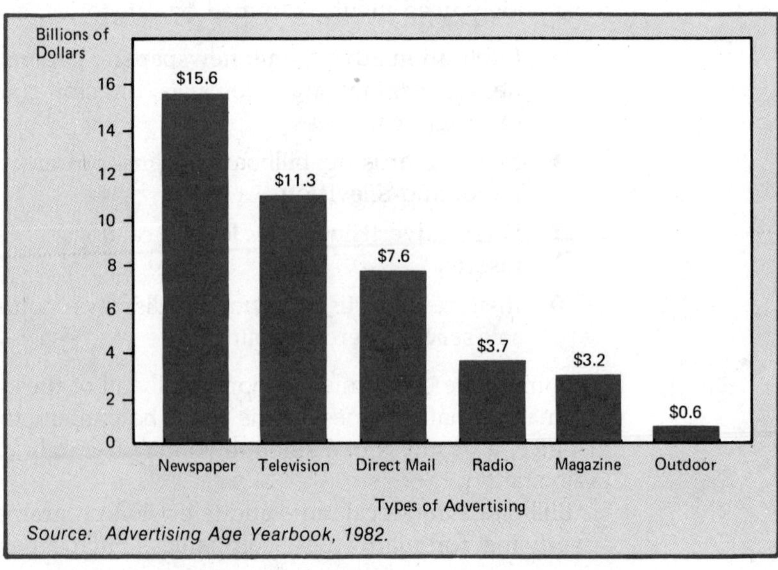

Source: *Advertising Age Yearbook, 1982.*

percent to over 98 percent. Nearly half of all homes have two or more television sets. Because of this increase, many large business firms find television a profitable medium for advertising. A principal advantage of television advertising is that it communicates both sound and sight simultaneously. Most television stations are affiliated with one of three networks—ABC, CBS, or NBC. However, cable television is a rapidly growing part of the television medium.

The cost of television advertising varies depending on the time of the telecast, the number of stations carrying the telecast, and the nature of the program during which the advertising appears. The most expensive time is between 6 p.m. and 11 p.m., which is usually referred to as **prime time.** Commercials prepared by and used only on local stations are much less expensive than network advertisements because they reach fewer people. The time needed and the cost of preparing television advertising is a major limitation in its use.

Newspaper Advertising. Newspapers are read by over 75 percent of all people over the age of 18. Since people use newspapers to get a variety of information, they are a good place for advertising.

Most large newspapers are daily papers so advertising reaches consumers frequently. It also can be changed rapidly if needed. Smaller newspapers are published once or twice a week.

Newspaper advertising is quite inexpensive when compared to other media and, therefore, is used by many businesses. More advertising dollars are spent for newspaper advertising than for any other type of advertising.

Magazine Advertising. The first type of national advertising was magazine advertising. It was first used in the late 1800s when magazines were distributed on trains. Today, magazines are very specialized and often relate directly to their readers' occupations, hobbies, or interests.

The major advantage of magazines is the high quality of the advertisements. They are usually printed on heavy, glossy paper using several colors. Also, magazines are often read by more than one reader and each reader may see the ad several times. However, advertising in national magazines can be very expensive. A two-page, full-color advertisement in one national magazine costs over $70,000.

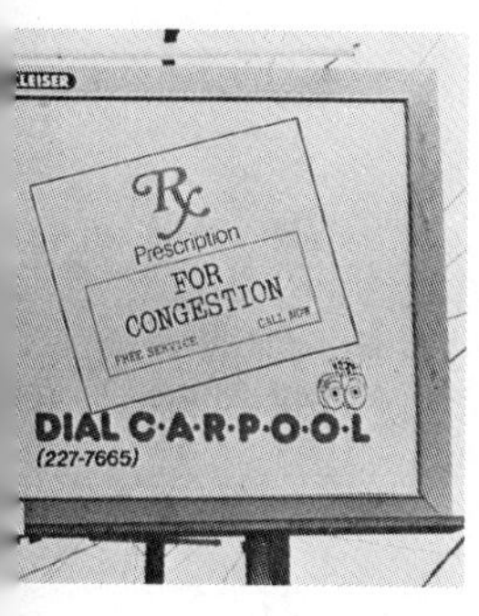

Outdoor Advertising. Outdoor advertising is the oldest form of advertising. Billboards allow simple, brief messages to be presented to everyone who passes by. If the right location is chosen for an outdoor advertisement, thousands of people can see a business' message every day as they pass the billboard.

Direct Mail Advertising. Promotions sent directly to a consumer's home through the mail are known as **direct mail advertising.** This type of advertising allows a company to direct its message to specific people through the use of specially selected mailing lists.

Direct mail advertising can be used to provide detailed information to consumers about products or services. Because the consumer receives the advertisement through the mail, the message may get more attention than if it were placed in a magazine or newspaper.

There are many forms of direct mail advertising ranging from quite inexpensive to very expensive. A business can send a one-page flyer to all residents of a small town at a very low cost. A national retailer that sends a mail-order catalog to thousands of customers will spend a great deal of money on that form of advertising.

One-page advertising pieces can be placed in customers' packages or enclosed in the envelope containing the monthly statements mailed to charge account customers. In these instances, however, the promotion will only reach current customers.

Planning and Managing the Advertising Program

The preceding discussion points out the various types of advertising and evaluates their usefulness. Every business, however, has an individual problem in determining what kind of advertising program to follow. In many cases the business will imitate its competitors or at least follow a similar plan, but the marketing department should always be looking for a new and more effective means of advertising.

Small businesses often have little help in making their advertising plans and in writing their advertisements. The printer may help in writing the copy and designing the advertisement for direct mail. Newspaper publishers may offer suggestions in preparing newspaper advertisements. Radio and television station marketing people might also help plan advertising.

Other sources of help in planning and carrying out an advertising program are as follows:

- Salespeople
- Manufacturers
- Advertisements of competitors
- Trade associations
- Exchange of ideas with other business friends
- Free-lance artists and writers
- Advertising agencies
- Marketing instructors at schools and universities

As the business grows, the owner has the option of hiring someone to handle the advertising or of placing all of the company's advertising planning in the hands of an advertising agency. For their services, advertising agencies usually charge a percentage of the total amount spent for the advertising.

ILLUS. 11–3
Advertising can be developed in-house or by an agency.

Cost of Advertising. The amount that a business can spend for advertising should be determined when the company's budget is developed. Most businesses plan the advertising program for one year. Of course, emergencies may arise that require a quick decision; but, unless some planning has taken place, the budget may be misused.

A person engaged in business should know what constitutes a reasonable expenditure for advertising. Most trade associations provide information on average advertising expenditures for their types of business. Advertising expenses range from 1 to 2 percent of sales in some businesses to 10 percent or more in others.

Firms that advertise nationally or in large areas have a wide variation in the amount that they spend for advertising. Manufacturers of drugs, soaps, and toiletries often spend 10 to 15 percent of the sales dollar for advertising purposes. This large amount of advertising helps increase demand for the company's brands, which permits the company to sell low-cost products at a profit.

Timeliness of Advertising. In almost every type of business there are certain times when advertising can be more effective than at other times. A company should determine the times when potential customers are most willing and able to buy the goods or services advertised.

A single advertisement may produce only temporary results, but advertising is important in building a steady stream of customers. If advertising does not appear often enough, customers tend to forget about a business. It is practical for most business firms to spread their advertising over the entire year as shown in the advertising budget in Illus. 11–4. A company can use smaller and less expensive advertisements more frequently, rather than spend all advertising funds on a few expensive advertisements.

ILLUS. 11–4
Most businesses spend some money on advertising throughout the year.

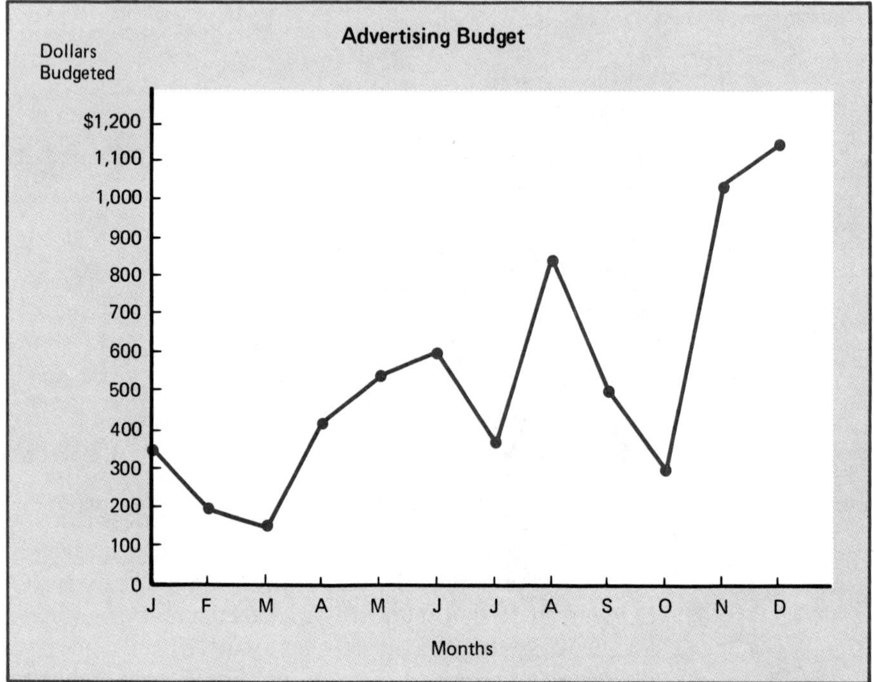

PERSONAL SELLING

Personal selling is promotion through direct, personal contact with a customer. The salesperson makes direct contact with the customer by a letter, a telephone call, or a face-to-face meeting. Most personal selling is through face-to-face contact, which better enables the salesperson to answer the customer's questions and to explain how goods or services can benefit the customer. In personal selling there are four elements: the customer, the business, the merchandise or service, and the salesperson. The salesperson bridges the gap between the customer and the business. The success of the business depends, to a great extent, on the quality and price of the goods or services, but its success is also very dependent on the selling skills of the sales force.

What do customers like about a business? A customer survey identified seven factors customers believe to be important. Those factors are shown in Illus. 11–5. Since Items 3 and 5 in Illus. 11–5 are related to the actions of salespeople, it is evident that personal selling plays a very important part in the success of a business.

ILLUS. 11-5
Characteristics customers look for in a business.

- A sufficient variety of products from which to choose.
- Prices comparable to the quality of the merchandise.
- Pleasant and helpful employees.
- Willingness to make adjustments in case of errors and returns.
- Truthful statements about the goods and services.
- Attractive premises (including lighting, ventilation, equipment, and arrangement).
- Service features, such as delivery, charge accounts, and free parking.

Understanding The Customer

There are many types of customers, and a salesperson must be able to adjust to each. Some customers know exactly what they want. They do not want to listen to a long explanation about the product. Some customers constantly change their minds when being shown merchandise. Some people who come into retail stores are not interested in any particular article but are just looking around. Some customers are talkative, some are quiet, some are irritable, some are suspicious of salespeople, and some always want a lower price. The successful salesperson must be able to recognize and successfully serve all types.

Studying the Wants of Customers

The salesperson who attempts to sell candy to a child by emphasizing the quality probably will not succeed. On the other hand, the salesperson who emphasizes the quantity of candy that can be purchased for a quarter probably will make a sale simply because that salesperson understands the important reason that usually causes a child to prefer one kind of candy to another. An individual who wishes to be successful in satisfying customers must study and understand human nature. Why do people buy? What wants do they have? How can those wants be satisfied?

Buying motives are the reasons people buy. Many motives cause people to buy. Some of the most important buying motives are listed in Illus. 11–6.

To be successful the salesperson must know what is likely to be the buying motive of a particular customer and then make the sales talk and demonstration appeal to that motive. In many cases the salesperson can make appeals to more than one buying motive. For instance a laundry company representative, in attempting to sell laundry services to a couple with three children and an income that is a little above average, may talk about the comfort and convenience of having the laundry done outside the

ILLUS. 11-6
Salespeople must be able to identify buying motives.

Imitation	Amusement
Desire for ease and comfort	Desire for bargains (thrift)
Affection	Desire for good health
Appetite	Pride of possession
Love of beauty	Desire for recognition
Desire for money	Envy
	Fear

home rather than doing it themselves. The salesperson may also explain that it is less expensive to send the laundry to a professional laundry because of all the expenses that are involved in doing it at home.

Suppose that this same laundry representative calls on the owner of a barber shop or beauty salon. Here the salesperson can place emphasis on the special sterilizing treatment given to linens and the high degree of whiteness in the laundered linens.

If a customer has several buying motives, the salesperson can often make brief appeals to different motives and carefully observe the reaction of the customer. As soon as the most important motive is discovered, the salesperson can emphasize it.

In other words, it is a sound policy in selling to determine a customer's wants and buying motives and then satisfy those motives with the product. Providing customer satisfaction through a sale is the ultimate goal of a salesperson. This method of selling does not require high-pressure selling; it requires intelligent selling.

Giving Information about the Product

Effective personal selling requires that the salesperson understand the wants or needs of the customer. In addition, it is necessary that the salesperson have a thorough knowledge of the company's goods or services to suggest those which best fit the customer's needs.

Customers are interested in what the products or services will do for them and how they can be used. It is important that salespeople have a thorough knowledge of the various uses of products, as well as their limitations.

The primary uses of products are usually known to the customer, but the salesperson should be able to convince the customer that a particular brand is best suited for the customer's particular purpose. The salesperson should also point out the versatility of the product by explaining its secondary uses. For example, the primary use of a vacuum cleaner is to clean rugs and carpets; but a particular cleaner may also be used to clean curtains or upholstery and even to remove lint from clothing.

A thorough knowledge of the merchandise is necessary so that the salesperson may answer questions that are asked about the product. The following questions are examples of those that customers might ask: "How much paint will I need for a bathroom six feet by eight feet?" "Which paint is best for a concrete basement floor?" "Can these slacks be laundered?" "Why is this pair of shoes $48 and that pair $45?"

One of the best ways for a salesperson to provide service to the customer is to obtain information concerning the kind, quality, cost, and source of materials used in making the product. These factors affect the price, quality, durability, appearance, uses, and the care of an article. For example, the fact that a certain piece of clothing is made of cotton, wool, rayon, nylon, orlon, dacron, silk, or a combination of two or more of these fabrics determines the care that should be given the article in cleaning. It also has a definite influence on the quality, appearance, and price. A salesperson should be aware of important information, such as knowing that certain products are handmade and that others are not touched by human hands.

Different items of information about the same product may appeal to different people. For instance, a safety shut-off switch on a washing machine will appeal to some people, while the simplicity of operation or the availability of a certain color may be more important to others. Salespeople should study the products they sell as well as competing products, and they should always be prepared to explain why their products are worth the price that is being asked for them. Some useful sources of product information are shown in Illus. 11–7.

ILLUS. 11-7
Salespeople can obtain merchandise information from many sources.

- Examination and use of the merchandise.
- Booklets, circulars, and training provided by the manufacturer or company training programs.
- Magazine and newspaper advertisements.
- Representatives of the manufacturer or distributor.
- Technical books and magazines.
- Customers that have already had experience with the product.
- Other salespeople who are acquainted with the merchandise.
- Selling points that competitors make for their products.

In addition to giving customers information about the merchandise, salespeople should effectively demonstrate the merchandise so customers can determine whether or not the product will fit their needs. It is usually a good idea for salespeople to demonstrate the article as they provide information about it. The customer's attention is then focused on the product as its features and advantages are being explained.

A product should be shown to its best advantage. By handling it carefully and showing respect for it, the salesperson enhances the value of the product in the customer's mind. For example, the value of a piece of sterling silver is enhanced when the salesperson handles it very carefully and admiringly places it on a piece of velvet.

An effective way of convincing the customer to buy an object is to show it in use as it would be used by the customer. A sewing machine may be demonstrated by sewing some samples for the customer; a furniture polish, by actually polishing a piece of furniture.

Whenever possible, the customer should be encouraged to participate in the demonstration—to operate the vacuum cleaner, to type on the typewriter, to try on a coat, or to drive the automobile. Such activity often changes the customer's interest to a desire to own the product.

In certain selling situations, such as selling very large or bulky products or selling services, sales representatives demonstrate without having the actual product. They use such items as photographs, charts, drawings, catalogs, projectors, and films.

Suggestion Selling

Have you ever had the experience of buying a ball-point pen and having the salesperson suggest that you buy a mechanical pencil to match the pen? Or have you ever observed a man purchasing a shirt and the salesperson suggesting a necktie to match? Such activity on the part of salespeople is known as suggestion selling. **Suggestion selling** occurs when the salesperson calls the customer's attention to goods that were not requested. Four common types of suggestion selling are:

- Suggesting an item related to the one the customer has just purchased.
- Recommending that a larger quantity be purchased.
- Suggesting a substitute item or brand.
- Calling attention to a featured item or a special purchase.

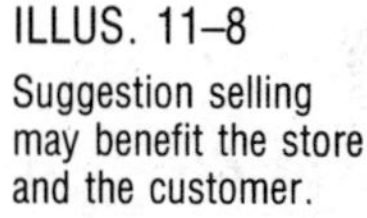

ILLUS. 11–8
Suggestion selling may benefit the store and the customer.

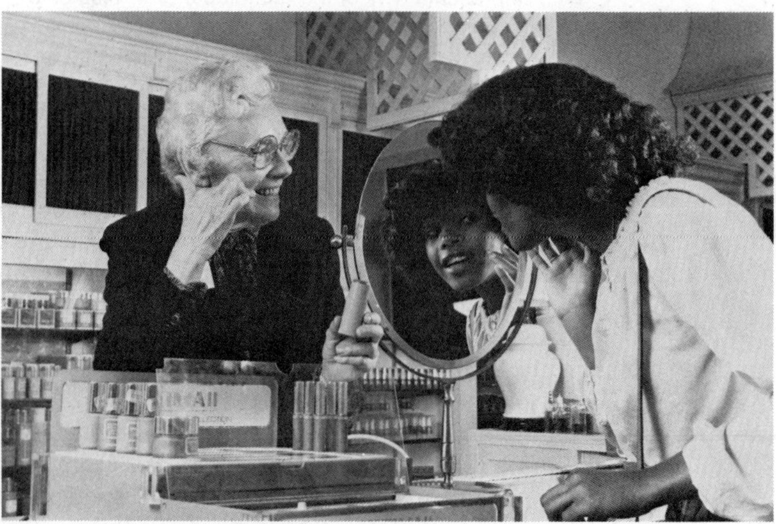

If the salesperson really uses suggestion selling to benefit the customer and does not attempt to force unwanted goods on the customer, then suggestion selling is desirable. Calling attention to related goods may save the customer from making an extra trip to the store later to buy the related article. It may also provide goods that more closely complement the original purchase than goods that are purchased elsewhere. Likewise, suggesting the purchase of a large quantity in order to get a low price, suggesting high-priced merchandise when it means better quality, and suggesting a substitute brand may be of value to the customer and should be considered part of the service a salesperson gives.

To a business, suggestion selling has great possibilities for increasing sales by getting customers to purchase related items now instead of buying them later from competitors. The increased sales should result not only in larger net profits, but also in a greater percentage of net profit because the additional sales cause only a little increase in overhead expenses.

Selling by Telephone

There is a growing use of the telephone to sell goods and services. The telephone provides a quicker and less expensive method of calling on customers than making face-to-face calls. The telephone is also a convenient method for the customer to use in placing an order. Many businesses now have people who devote all of their time to telephone selling. These people must have a thorough knowledge of the products or services of the business and possess an excellent telephone voice and manner.

The telephone can be used by a business as a follow-up to its advertising, as a method of reviving inactive accounts, and as a way of calling attention to special items that may be of interest to customers. It is frequently used in industrial selling and in selling magazine and newspaper subscriptions.

OTHER PROMOTIONAL METHODS

Businesses have other ways to promote their products in addition to advertising and personal selling. Several of these methods are discussed next.

Coupons

Coupons are used extensively to promote the sale of goods. Coupons are an effective method of increasing sales of a product for a short time. They are used principally to introduce a new product or to maintain and increase a company's share of the market for established product brands. Coupons usually appear in newspaper and magazine advertisements, but they are also distributed by direct mail.

ILLUS. 11–9
Manufacturers use coupons to promote both old and new products.

Manufacturer and Dealer Aids

Manufacturers often cooperate with retailers by providing certain materials to be used in promoting products. Some of these promotional materials, commonly furnished without cost or at a low price, include window displays, layouts and illustrations for newspaper advertisements, mail enclosures, counter displays, and demonstration aids.

It is advisable for manufacturers and wholesalers to aid retailers with their promotional campaigns. Local retailers can tie their advertising and promotion to a national campaign by keeping themselves informed on advertising and advertising programs, and by obtaining all the free materials and suggestions that are available. For example, when a dealer who distributes phonograph records or cassettes learns that a particular artist is appearing on a national television program or is performing locally, it is advisable to feature the records and tapes of this artist and obtain all the displays that are available.

When producers are introducing a new product, they may distribute samples through the mail. The purpose of this is to familiarize people with the products so that there will be a demand for them in local stores.

Producers and distributors also cooperate with retailers by arranging special displays and demonstrations within stores. Samples are given to customers as they enter the store. This practice usually helps the retailers sell the new product. The retailer, of course, gives this merchandise a preference over other competing products. Sometimes distributors pay

ILLUS. 11–10
Displays should encourage customer buying.

merchants for the privilege of giving demonstrations or offer special inducements for such a privilege.

Store Displays

Many prospective customers get the first impression of a retail store chiefly by its windows; such windows are a very valuable part of a retail store. Windows are considered so valuable by large department stores that the various departments are charged for the window display space they use. Using windows to display merchandise alerts passersby that the store handles these items, and should result in increased sales of the items. Stores have estimated increases of 30 to 50 percent in the sale of items that are effectively displayed in windows. To the small store located in a large city, the window display may be the chief means of advertising.

The interior of a business can be used for promotion as well. In planning an **interior display,** a display within the store, it is necessary to take into consideration a whole interior and not just an individual area. In order to obtain a harmonizing effect from displays, the interior planning should include the decoration of the store, layout, and merchandise.

Self-Service Merchandising

Modern store fixtures and packaging methods have resulted in such effective displays of merchandise that the use of self-service merchandise has increased greatly. In **self-service merchandising,** customers select the

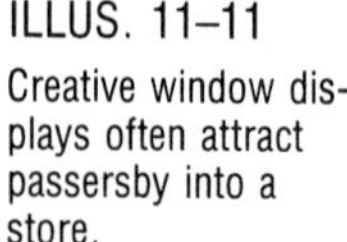

ILLUS. 11–11
Creative window displays often attract passersby into a store.

goods they wish, take them to a cashier or checkout counter, and pay for them. Self-service stores have only a few clerks to aid customers in making selections. Most employees are used to receive and stock merchandise in the store.

Marketing specialists generally agree that successful self-service merchandising requires products which do not need to be demonstrated or explained, which have well-known brand names, and which are packaged so that they can be easily handled.

The display of merchandise in self-service stores should attract attention and make it convenient for the shopper to examine the merchandise. The labels on the merchandise should provide adequate information about the merchandise for the shopper.

TRUTH IN ADVERTISING AND SELLING

False advertising in interstate business is prohibited by federal law. False advertising, as defined by federal law, is "misleading in a material respect," or in any way that could influence the customer's purchase or use of the product. The Federal Trade Commission is responsible for enforcing laws that regulate advertising.

Long-term business success must be built on honesty and fair practices. A business person may be tempted occasionally to exaggerate or to imitate a competitor who seems to be stretching the truth. In the long run it does not pay, however, to destroy the confidence of customers.

The Council of Better Business Bureaus has established standards to be followed in selling and advertising. Particular attention is given to misleading statements. Illus. 11–12 summarizes the Fair Trade Code for Advertising and Selling adopted by the Council of Better Business Bureaus.

ILLUS. 11-12
Fair Trade Code for Advertising and Selling.

1. Serve the public with honest values.
2. Tell the truth about what is offered.
3. Tell the truth in a forthright manner so that its significance may be understood by the trusting as well as the analytical.
4. Tell customers what they want to know—what they have a right to know about what is offered—so that they may buy wisely with maximum satisfaction from their purchases.
5. Be prepared and willing to make good as promised and without quibble on any guarantee offered.
6. Be sure that normal use of merchandise or services will not be hazardous to public health or life.
7. Reveal material facts, the deceptive concealment of which might cause consumers to be misled.
8. Advertise and sell merchandise or service on its merits and refrain from attacking your competitors or reflecting unfairly upon their product, services, or methods of doing business.
9. If testimonials are used, use only those of competent witnesses who are sincere and honest in what they say about what you sell.
10. Avoid all tricky devices and schemes such as deceitful trade-in allowances, fictitious list prices, false and exaggerated comparative prices, bait advertising, misleading free offers, fake sales, and similar practices that prey upon human ignorance and gullibility.

NEW TERMS AND CONCEPTS

Define the following terms and concepts, which may be found in boldface type on the page shown in parentheses.

advertising (200)
drive time (202)
advertising media (201)
prime time (203)
direct mail advertising (203)
personal selling (206)
buying motives (207)
suggestion selling (210)
interior display (213)
self-service merchandising (213)

CHAPTER REVIEW

1. Name four categories of advertising media and give three examples for each category.
2. About how much was spent for magazine advertising in 1980?
3. Compare the advantages and disadvantages of newspaper advertising with direct mail advertising.

4. Explain the importance of frequency of advertising.
5. State six characteristics consumers look for in a business.
6. What are some of the most common buying motives?
7. Where can a salesperson obtain information about the products he or she sells?
8. Name four kinds of suggestion selling.
9. State two ways in which a business can use suggestion selling.
10. List five promotional aids that manufacturers often provide for retailers.
11. Explain the main purpose of window displays.
12. How are most employees used in self-service merchandising?

QUESTIONS FOR CLASS DISCUSSION

1. Why is the cost for television advertising between 6 p.m. and 11 p.m. the most expensive?
2. Name some types of business firms that could benefit from advertising in a school newspaper.
3. Announcements in newspapers of engagements and approaching weddings could be a mailing list source for what kinds of businesses?
4. Discuss several characteristics that you believe would be desirable in a salesperson and give a specific example of the importance of each.
5. Explain how a salesperson's lack of knowledge about products can cause problems for a company.
6. What should the training of salespeople include?
7. Why are some stores using less self-service merchandising and more personal selling today?
8. Why are coupons an effective booster of sales?
9. Why should manufacturers and wholesalers help retailers with promotions?
10. Mention some types of promotional practices you think are unfair.

PROBLEMS AND PROJECTS

1. A book and gift store that has average annual sales of $700,000 spends 3 percent of its sales for advertising. The store's advertising budget is divided as follows: catalogs, 30 percent; calendars and other sales promotions, 7 percent; window displays, 15 percent; newspaper advertising, 15 percent; direct mail, 20 percent; and miscellaneous, 13 percent.
   a. How much is the average annual advertising budget?
   b. What is the amount spent on each type of advertising?
2. Obtain a sample of direct mail advertising. Evaluate it concerning its effectiveness in the following areas: (a) attractiveness, (b) ability to

attract attention, (c) specific information, and (d) effectiveness of promotion.

3. From a local newspaper office find out (a) what types of help they will provide for a business in preparing advertising, and (b) the costs of advertising in the newspaper.
4. Assume that you are a salesperson in a furniture store. Explain how you can make appeals to several buying motives when selling a sofa sleeper to a homeowner.
5. You are opening an auto repair business that specializes in speedy oil changes and engine tune-ups.
   a. From what sources could you obtain names and addresses of potential customers?
   b. Write a one-page letter you could send to prospective customers inviting them to try your new business.

CASE 11–1

Jared and Chris were discussing how companies use advertising. Their conversation follows:

Jared: Companies spend too much money on advertising. If they would spend less, the prices of products would be a great deal lower.

Chris: Advertising is used to get people to buy products they do not want. Companies should not have to advertise good products.

Jared: The worst thing about advertising is that businesses can say anything they want to about products, even if the statements are wrong. You will not know what is wrong with the product until you have bought it, and then it is too late.

Required:

1. Do you believe product prices would decrease if companies did not advertise? Explain.
2. Do good products need to be advertised?
3. What types of controls are there on what a business can say in its advertising? Can customers do anything if they have been misled by advertising?

CASE 11–2

Peter Ponticello is manager of the Denim Duds Shop, a retail store in a shopping center that specializes in selling jeans and related clothing to young people. The town is served by a daily newspaper, three radio stations, and one television station. Mr. Ponticello has budgeted $8,000 to be spent on advertising for the year.

Required:

1. Identify the method or methods of advertising Mr. Ponticello should use and give reasons for your choice.
2. If Mr. Ponticello is going to use radio advertising, how should he select the radio station to use?
3. Suggest one idea for a window display that would encourage young people to come into the store.
4. List the types of training Mr. Ponticello should provide for his salespeople.

Have You Thought About Becoming . . .
. . . AN ADVERTISING AGENCY WORKER?

Most of the advertisements you see or hear each day are created by advertising agencies. Advertising agencies are hired by companies to develop advertising ideas, prepare the actual advertisements, and place the advertisement in the medium that best reaches the right consumers.

There are many types of jobs in an advertising agency. Probably, most people would first think of the creative specialists. They are responsible for creating ideas for advertisements, writing ads, and planning illustrations. To be a creative specialist, you need a good background in English, speech, or art.

Once the advertisements are completed, they must be placed in the media. Media-buying specialists get the ads placed in the best media at the right time to reach consumers. It is a difficult job to be aware of all of the media requirements and their costs, and to get the best price for a series of advertisements. Media specialists need to be skilled in planning, budgeting, and communications.

A third major job area in an advertising agency is marketing. The marketing division is responsible for working with the businesses that need the services of the agency. Marketing specialists make presentations to potential clients, help clients determine their advertising needs, and then work with other agency departments to make sure the advertising is completed correctly. Marketing specialists must be effective salespeople and managers.

Other jobs found in most advertising agencies are accounting, research, and administration. As you can see, there are many different kinds of job opportunities available if you decide to work for an advertising agency.

UNIT 4

Finance

Other than the weather, perhaps nothing is more frequently discussed than financial matters. As individuals, we need money to buy things, to pay loans, and to provide savings for later use. Business firms need money to purchase materials, to pay banks for money they have borrowed, and to distribute earnings to owners. These and other types of financial requirements are treated in Unit 4.

Early in this unit you are presented with a foundation for understanding financial terms commonly used by managers, accountants, and others. Borrowing money, extending credit, budgeting income and expenses, and keeping financial records are also examined. Finally, the topic of insurance is treated because it provides protection against the risk of financial loss caused by such things as fire and theft.

Competition among firms offering financial services has been undergoing much change in recent years. James D. Robinson III, whose biographical profile appears on the next page, works for a business that has led the way in offering financial services to meet nearly everyone's needs.

12. Financial Records in Business
13. Financial Analysis of a Business
14. Financing a Business
15. Financial Services
16. Credit and Collections
17. Business Risks and Insurance

JAMES D. ROBINSON III

What company first comes to mind when you hear "travelers cheques"? Most people would likely answer "American Express." Travelers cheques, however, represent only a small part of the total services offered by the American Express Company. Major subsidiaries of this large company include travel-related services, investment services, insurance services, and international banking services.

This dynamic company, over 130 years old, is headed by James D. Robinson III. Mr. Robinson was born into the world of finance. Both his father and his grandfather were bankers in his hometown of Atlanta, Georgia. He attended Georgia Institute of Technology before earning a master's degree in business at Harvard University. Mr. Robinson joined American Express in 1970 after having gained much managerial experience by working for investment banks. Within five years he was elected president of American Express Company.

Under James Robinson's leadership, American Express has strengthened its position as a leading financial services institution. In August of 1982, it became the first financial services company to be added to the Dow Jones Industrial Index, a leading stock market indicator. Mr. Robinson presided over the acquisition of a successful Wall Street brokerage firm—Shearson Loeb Rhoades—now known as Shearson/American Express, Inc. His goal is to make American Express a leading provider of payment systems, stocks and investment service products, insurance, travel services, and international banking services.

Although Mr. Robinson is a busy corporate leader, he shares his expertise in other ways. For example, he assists many distinguished nonprofit business groups. He is national chairman of the U.S. Savings Bonds Volunteer Committee. He is also chairman of the U.S. Services Advisory Committee for the Office of the U.S. Trade Representative. Equally important, he serves as a member of the board of directors for the United Way of America.

12

FINANCIAL RECORDS IN BUSINESS

After studying this chapter you will be able to:

- Discuss why business firms need good record systems.
- Identify some of the types of records business firms need.
- Distinguish between depreciation and obsolescence.
- Provide reasons why business records should be protected.
- Describe how budgets are used to run business firms efficiently.

Clearly the most tangible reward that business owners get is a financial reward, namely profits. Without profits, it would be impossible for companies to remain in business. Some method, therefore, is needed to determine how a business is doing financially. **Accounting records** are financial records of the transactions of the business. Because accounting information is used to make numerous important decisions, these records must be carefully kept. Some valuable information obtained from accounting records includes:

- Kinds and values of assets.
- Amounts of various debts owed by the business.
- Amounts owed to the business.
- Cash balance in the bank and cash on hand.
- Amount of cash sales and credit sales.
- Kinds and amounts of expenses.

- Amount of merchandise bought.
- Profit or loss.
- Trends in sales, expenses, profits, and net worth.
- Comparisons with other similar businesses.

Financial records are handled in various ways. The business owner can keep the records personally, employ a full-time or part-time accounting clerk, use an accounting service organization, or establish an accounting department. The way records are handled is determined, in part, by the record system adopted.

ILLUS. 12–1
Many businesses hire part-time accounting clerks to handle financial records.

RECORD SYSTEMS

Systems for keeping accounting records may be simple or complex, and may require no equipment or be highly automated. In addition to providing reliable and accurate information, the system must be easy to use and designed to provide timely information. The type of record system used is based on the nature of the business. Therefore, we will look at manual and computer systems and at systems for small and large businesses.

Manual System

Accounting records are not difficult to keep. Standardized forms can be purchased at office supply stores. Trade associations, such as those of oil dealers and hardware stores, supply their business members with standard forms. Model sets of records are available from some cash register manufacturers. In most of these systems, no special equipment is needed; the records are kept by hand. When a business has only a small number of records, manual systems can be practical and rather inexpensive to maintain.

Computer System

In many offices computer-type equipment is used to perform tasks that were formerly done manually or by simple machines. Whenever it is necessary to perform repetitive clerical operations and to store large amounts of information, computers are useful because the time, and possibly the cost, of handling these operations is reduced. Depending on the volume of information to be processed, a business must decide whether to process the information manually, purchase computer equipment, or hire the services of a data processing service center.

A **data processing service center** is a special type of business that processes data for other businesses for a fee. A business delivers data to the service center on a daily, weekly, or monthly basis. In return, the service center processes the data and prepares reports that the business needs. Many business firms use a data processing service center to perform such tasks as preparing bills for customers, keeping track of inventory bought and sold, and preparing payroll records and checks. A business can have many routine operations processed efficiently by a service center.

Various types of computers and computer-like equipment are available. A discussion of data processing and computers is found in Chapter 19.

Systems in Small Businesses

Small business firms, especially retail stores, do not need elaborate records. Many such businesses use a cash register as a basis for obtaining most of the information for their financial records. An example of a financial record which might be kept by a small retail business is shown in Illus. 12–2. If a cash register that shows detailed kinds of transactions is used in the business, this information can be taken from the cash register tape (or audit strip) and copied in the daily balance form.

A special form listing the daily cash payments should be kept. Many cash registers provide for these amounts to be shown on the daily audit slip. In the absence of an adequate cash register, a written record should be made throughout the day of all types of sales, other receipts, and payments, and these should be formally recorded at the end of the day.

ILLUS. 12–2
The cash register slip often provides the information shown on this daily balance form.

DAILY BALANCE FORM

Store Name 04 Prepared By Hal Vogel Date Mar. 8, 19--

	RESET TOTALS OF REG. (SALES)	RESET TOTALS OF REG. (RETURNS AND VOIDS)	NET REGISTER TOTALS
DEPT. 1 Meat	5,200.00	80	5,120 00
DEPT. 2 Produce	1,560.00	40	1,520 00
DEPT. 3 Deli	1,040.00	-0-	1,040 00
DEPT. 4 Grocery	15,600.00	60	15,540 00
DEPT. 5 Frozen Food	2,080.00	20	2,060 00
DEPT. 6 Household	520.00	10	510 00
DEPT. 7			
TAX			
TOTAL			
CASH	26,000.00	210.00	25,790 00
CHARGE	500.00	-0-	500 00
TOTAL	26,500.00	210.00	26,290 00
ACCT. NO.	CH0079		
REC'D ON ACCT.			-0-
CASH			-0-
TOTAL			
CASH RETURNS	(X Read Cash Total) →	210.00	OTHER INCOME
ACCT. NO.			TOTAL
LAYAWAY PAYMENTS REFUND	(X Read R. A/C) →		
TOTAL			
PAID OUTS		RETURNS AND VOIDS / MDSE. AND EXP.	( )
CASH TO BE ACCOUNTED FOR			26,290 00
ACTUAL CASH			26,290 00
CASH OVER OR SHORT			-0-

PAID OUTS TO DR. & CR.	$ KEPT ON RET.	P. O. AMOUNT	DR. CODE
#1			
#2			
#3			
#4			
#5			
#6			
#7			
#8			
#9			
CREDIT CODE	CR. MISC. INC.		
AUDITOR'S CREDIT *			
MARK DOWNS OR UNITS			
PURCHASES AT RETAIL OR SALES AT COST			
Register Totals			

ACCOUNTS RECEIVABLE CONTROL	
BEGINNING ACCTS. RECEIVABLE	-0-
NET CHARGES TODAY	500 00
TOTAL	500 00
LESS: NET REC'D ON ACCT. TODAY	-0-
ENDING ACCTS. RECEIVABLE	500 00
* DATA PROCESSING NO.	
* TODAY'S DATE	—
* CASH SHORT DR.___CR.___	-0-
* CASH OVER DR.___CR.___	-0-
*	

Systems in Large Businesses

Complicated systems for keeping records are generally required in large firms. Many people, usually organized into an accounting department, maintain these records. An accounting department is commonly divided into several sections. Each section is usually responsible for handling one or more phases of accounting, such as cash records, receipt and payment records, depreciation records, and tax and payroll records.

Many large firms, and some small ones, use cash registers that are connected to computers. Such a register is called a **point-of-sale terminal.** When cashiers ring up sales transactions, for example, each item sold is subtracted from the inventory recorded in the computer. The computer calculates when merchandise reordering is necessary (based on predetermined inventory needs) and provides other valuable information for management. Some point-of-sale terminals have scanners that electronically read product codes stamped on the merchandise, thereby speeding the checkout service provided customers. You have probably seen these in the grocery store.

TYPES OF RECORDS

Accounting records in all types of businesses have many points of similarity, but they differ in some respects because of the nature of each business. The kinds of records that a business uses also depend on the size of the business. Some of the more common records a business uses include those for accounting for cash, receipt and payment records, depreciation records, special asset records, tax records, and payroll records.

Accounting for Cash

A cash register is used in most retail businesses for handling cash transactions. Regardless of whether a business employs a bookkeeper or whether the records are kept by the owner of the business, similar procedures must be followed in accounting for cash. Several suggestions for the safe handling of cash are listed in Illus. 12–4 on page 226.

In accounting for cash a special problem arises when a business wants to make payments of small amounts of money. There are two ways in which small payments are usually made by business firms. When a cash register is used and there is no special petty cash fund, the usual practice is to pay the amount and put a petty cash voucher, such as the one shown in Illus. 12–3, in the cash register drawer. When money is put aside (often in a

ILLUS. 12–3
A petty cash voucher.

PETTY CASH VOUCHER

NO. 6 DATE February 9, 19--

PAID TO Sims Typewriter Service AMOUNT

FOR Repairing typewriter 28 | 50

CHARGE TO Miscellaneous Expense

PAYMENT RECEIVED: REED AND MALLOCH

Helen Jones APPROVED BY George Ajax

ILLUS. 12-4
Suggestions for the safe handling of cash.

1. A petty cash fund, adequate for small emergency payments, should be kept in a safe place with someone responsible for it. A written record of all money put into the fund and all money paid out must be kept. Receipts for payments should be obtained where possible, and the fund should be replenished by check to provide a further record.
2. If a cash register is used, small emergency payments can be made out of cash register funds instead of through a petty cash fund; but adequate records of payments must be made and receipts obtained.
3. If a cash register is used, there should be a daily change fund of a fixed amount, which is never deposited in the bank but is kept available to start each day's operations. This fund should be counted and verified daily.
4. All receipts should be deposited in a bank account.
5. Make payments by check for all items except small emergency payments.
6. Verify by a double check any cash overages or cash shortages in the daily transactions.
7. Do not keep any more cash in the office than is necessary and, if convenient, make more than one deposit in the bank daily.
8. Pay salaries by check instead of by cash.
9. Audit regularly the amounts received on account.
10. Audit regularly the receipts by comparing them with the bank deposits you have made.
11. Audit regularly the actual cash paid out by comparing the check stubs with bills paid.
12. Endorse all checks for deposit with a company rubber stamp or, when signing checks for endorsement, write "For deposit only."
13. Reconcile the monthly bank statement promptly and regularly as explained in Chapter 15.

special box or drawer) for a petty cash fund, a petty cash record is kept which shows why the cash was paid and to whom it was given.

It is very important to keep a careful watch on one's bank account in accounting for cash. A bank always provides a monthly statement that should be compared with the checkbook. If the checkbook balance does not agree with the bank's monthly statement balance, the reasons for the difference must be determined. The process of bringing the checkbook balance and bank statement balance into agreement is discussed in Chapter 15.

Receipt and Payment Records

All business firms must deal with money that is received as a result of the sale of goods or services to customers. Because many businesses sell on credit, careful records must be kept showing what each customer owes and pays. This record is called an **accounts receivable record.** When a sale is made, the salesperson completes an appropriate form, such as the one shown in Illus. 12–5. The information on this form is transferred to the accounts receivable record. Money owed to the business and money received from customers are recorded daily on these records.

ILLUS. 12–5
The information found in the accounts receivable record is obtained from sales slips like this one.

NO. 24108 DEPT. Furniture DATE Feb. 12 19 --

NAME Dr. Anthony W. Hantjis

ADDRESS Continental Lane

CITY Princeton, NJ 08540-1245

SOLD BY	CASH	C.O.D.	CHARGE	ON ACCT.	MDSE. RETD.	PAID OUT
Kingston				✓		

		DESCRIPTION	PRICE	AMOUNT	
4	1	Chairs, No. 75-A	50.00	200	00
1	2	Table, No. 120-B	300.00	300	00
	3				
	4				
	5				
	6				
	7				
	8				
	9			500.	00
	10	Tax		25	00
	11				
	12			525	00
	13				

CUSTOMER'S ORDER NO. REC'D BY

REDIFORM 5S 34 **KEEP THIS SLIP FOR REFERENCE**

A record must also be kept to show money owed and payments made by a business. When a business buys such items as supplies and merchandise, it often does so on account. As a result, an **accounts payable record** must be kept showing money owed to other businesses and payments made by the business. A file, such as the one shown in Illus. 12–6, can be used for this purpose. The unpaid invoices are placed behind tabs indicating the date on which payment is due in order to take advantage of cash discounts or to avoid additional fees if payments are not made within the time allowed. When invoices are paid, the payment is recorded in the accounts payable file under the creditor's name (those to whom money is owed).

Depreciation Records

Every business person should recognize the problems that result from a decrease in the value of property through use. For example, a service station owner buys a piece of equipment that costs $600. The owner knows

ILLUS. 12–6
Many firms file unpaid invoices according to the date payment is due.

from experience that at the end of five years the equipment will not be worth any more than its value as junk, about $50. It is estimated, therefore, that the equipment will wear out at the average rate of $110 a year. ($600 − $50 = $550; $550 ÷ 5 years = $110.) When this asset loses its usefulness, it must be replaced.

Fixed assets, or **plant assets,** are material assets that will last a long time—land, equipment, and buildings, for example. Except for land, fixed assets tend to lose their value over time. Fixed assets are recorded on the books of a business when they are purchased. They become part of the property owned by the business. As they wear out or become less valuable, the business is allowed by law to charge the loss in value each year as an operating expense.

The general term that is applied to such a decrease in the value of an asset is **depreciation.** Property may also decrease in value because of **obsolescence;** that is, the asset may become out of date, or it may become inadequate for a particular purpose. For all practical purposes, however, any decrease in the value of an asset can be considered depreciation. A cash register, for instance, may wear out gradually, or it may become obsolete.

The loss due to depreciation is very real, although it usually cannot be computed definitely. Any business that fails to recognize depreciation is failing to observe good business principles. The depreciation of assets is part of the cost of doing business. When equipment is worn out, it must be replaced. If money is not available to replace the equipment, the business may be seriously handicapped.

Special Asset Records

Financial statements provide information on such items as insurance, fixed assets, and real property, but they do not provide detailed information about these assets. As a result, a business must keep special records. For example, a business should maintain a precise record of insurance policies showing such details as the purchase and expiration dates of the policies and the amount to be charged each month as insurance expense. A detailed special record should also be maintained for all fixed assets, such as filing cabinets and fork lifts, providing such information as asset description, cost, monthly depreciation expense, and **book value**—original cost less accumulated depreciation. Special records provide additional information that is helpful to management.

Tax Records

The federal income tax law requires every business to keep satisfactory records so that its income and expenses can be reported. Preparation of an income tax return for a small business is relatively simple; however, both small and large firms use the services of tax accountants. The information needed for the income tax return of a business can be obtained from any good set of business records.

Employers are required to withhold a certain percentage of the wages of each employee for federal income tax purposes. Each employee is required to fill out a card regarding family status. From a table furnished by the Internal Revenue Service, the employer can determine the amount to withhold from each paycheck. Periodically these withholdings must be paid by the employer to the Internal Revenue Service.

Most employers have to pay social security taxes for old-age benefits and unemployment compensation payments. The employer is also required to withhold taxes from each employee's wages for social security purposes. The business is required to pay to the federal government its own taxes and those withheld from employees. Further discussion concerning federal payroll taxes is found in Chapter 22.

Payroll Records

In order to keep satisfactory payroll records to provide the information needed by the business owner and to satisfy federal and state authorities, businesses must keep complete records for all employees, and show the hours worked, regular wages paid, overtime wages, and all types of deductions from wages for each employee. It is from these records that an employer makes regular reports. A simple set of payroll records is shown in Illus. 12–7.

USING AND KEEPING RECORDS

Business records should be accurately maintained and always up to date. A convenient filing system that permits quick and accurate storage and retrieval of financial records is essential. Common filing systems are arranged in one or more of the following ways: alphabetically, numerically, geographically, and by subject. Office supply firms and filing equipment companies usually recommend appropriate filing systems for various kinds of businesses.

The financial records, including the accounts of customers and all other vital information, should be protected from such hazards as fire and theft. Many records, such as the accounts of customers, might not be stolen but could easily be destroyed by fire. Every office, therefore, should have a fireproof safe or vault for such records. Fireproof filing cabinets are also available. Valuable documents, such as deeds, leases, and contracts should be placed in safety deposit boxes if there is no adequate protection in the office.

Information stored in computers and in computer files should also be protected from damage or loss caused by weather conditions. For example, computers must usually be placed in climate-controlled settings, such as

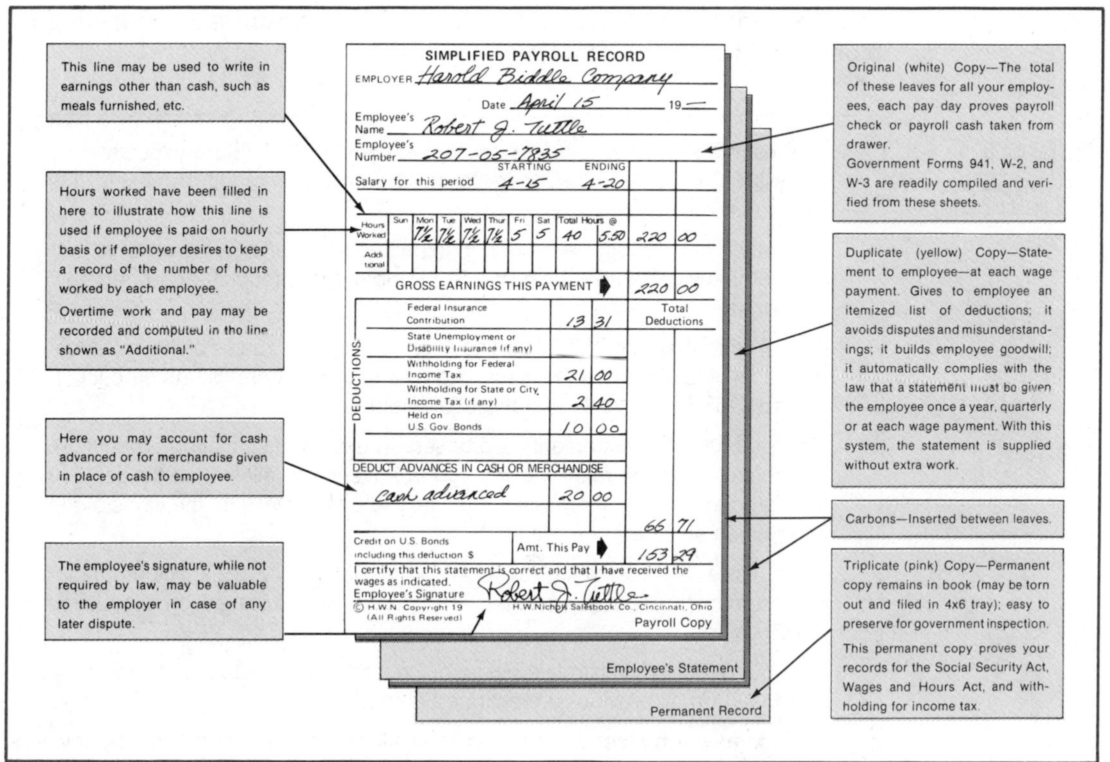

ILLUS. 12–7
A simplified payroll record.

air-conditioned offices. Damage to computer information may also be caused by people. For this reason, business firms usually restrict entrance to computer centers to authorized workers only.

BUDGET SYSTEMS

Budgeting has become very important. A study conducted by the United States Department of Commerce reveals that stores that budget their financial operations are more successful than stores that do not budget. The stores that are most successful are those that (a) keep recommended accounting records, (b) have their accounts audited or checked by an experienced accountant, (c) take an inventory of merchandise more than once a year, and (d) operate under a financial budget.

In its simplest form, a **budget** is an estimated plan for the future that helps keep expenses in line with income. Use of a budget should prevent overbuying and help to anticipate when borrowing is necessary.

The actual procedures used in budgeting will depend on the type of business. For a small business, the process is mostly one of budgeting sales, expenses, purchases, and cash. For large businesses, budgeting is more complicated, as is indicated in Illus. 12–8.

ILLUS. 12-8
Budgeting procedure for a manufacturing business.

1. The estimate of sales is based on past experience and future expectations. As will be explained later, there is more than one method of making this estimate.
2. The advertising budget is based on expected sales and on the amount that the company can afford to spend to promote new products and open new territories.
3. The production plans should be based on the expected sales of the individual products. It is, therefore, necessary to take into consideration the production capacity of the business and the equipment needed.
4. The purchasing requirements are based on expected sales and production. Purchases must be made far enough in advance to allow time for delivery and production. It is, therefore, necessary to be familiar with the times of the year when sales are the greatest.
5. In a large manufacturing business it is necessary to anticipate labor requirements. The labor budget must, therefore, be based on production requirements.
6. The budget of administrative costs, office costs, and costs of supplies must be based on all previously mentioned factors.
7. The complete budget is made up after all of the preceding budgets have been made.
8. The cash budget, which is explained later in this chapter, is a budget that shows the manager of the business or the treasurer the cash balance that can be expected at any particular time. Such a budget is necessary for a company to anticipate borrowing.

TYPES OF BUDGETS

The final overall budget for a business is made up of several other budgets, such as the sales budget, the merchandising budget, the advertising budget, the cash budget, the capital budget, and the budgeted income statement. Most individual budgets are based on sales projections. At times, however, in some types of businesses, either the production capacity or the financial capacity must be determined first. Sales and all other estimates are then based on the ability to produce.

The traffic manager, the office manager, the employment manager, and the engineer in a large production plant must know about all of the individual budgets because their departments are affected by the budget requirements. The small business obviously will not have such a detailed budget as that described previously. It will, in all cases, however, be concerned with budgeting sales, purchases, expenses, and cash.

Sales Budget

The **sales budget** is strictly a forecast of the sales for a month, a few months, or a year. Estimated sales may be figured on the basis of sales territories, sales representatives, branch offices, departments, or particular products or services. Sometimes independent estimates are made on all of these bases and, after some discussion, a final sales budget is prepared. Sometimes sales estimates are prepared with the idea of developing sales quotas or goals for sales representatives and territories. These estimates provide a goal for the sales department, as well as a basis for preparing the merchandising, purchasing, and other operating budgets.

Illus. 12–9 shows sales estimates determined in two different ways for the same company. Since the two sets of estimated figures are not the same, someone must be responsible for combining them into one satisfactory estimate that can be followed.

ILLUS. 12-9

Two ways of budgeting sales.

Budget Based on Analysis of Sales Representatives

Sales Representative	Year 1 Sales (actual)	Year 2 Sales (estimate)
T. A. Nader	$ 71,344	$ 76,000
H. E. Loch	69,676	72,000
C.D. Heidel	94,248	88,000
J. H. Sharmon	88,588	88,000
C. F. Powell	85,396	88,000
J. G. Dunbar	81,672	80,000
Total	$490,924	$492,000

Budget Based on Analysis of Products

Product	Year 1 Sales (actual)	Year 2 Sales (estimate)
Washers	$128,568	$136,000
Dryers	40,464	40,000
Ranges	37,852	36,000
Lamps	41,872	40,000
Refrigerators	242,168	260,000
Total	$490,924	$512,000

Numerous factors influence sales estimates. General business conditions have an important bearing. Although one company may enjoy brisk sales, another, at the same time and under the same conditions, may suffer a decline in sales. If a good harvest and favorable prices for crops are anticipated in a certain section, there should be good prospects for selling farm machinery in that section. A retail store located in such an area should expect increased sales. A flood or drought may affect certain businesses unfavorably but others favorably. These are examples of some of the influences that should guide a manager in making a sales estimate.

The following is suggested as a checklist of factors to be used as a guide in preparing a sales budget:

- Previous sales
- Economic trends
- Factors such as weather conditions
- Population shifts
- Sales force
- Availability of merchandise
- Buying habits
- Season of the year

When a person is starting a new business, it is advisable to investigate the experiences of other people in the same line of business and secure whatever information can be obtained from wholesalers, manufacturers, trade associations, and government agencies.

Merchandising Budget

The **merchandising budget** is a means to plan and control the supply of merchandise to be sold to customers. If a business has too little merchandise, sales might be lost. On the other hand, if a business has too much merchandise, valuable cash may be tied up that could be better used elsewhere. Furthermore, excess merchandise has to be stored, protected, and insured. These expenses add to the cost of doing business. It is important, therefore, to properly manage the purchase of merchandise in relation to sales.

The business must determine the kinds of stock to have on hand at all times. Maximum and minimum levels of supplies are set. Purchases are planned and information is given to the financial department so that cash needs can be estimated. Sources of supply are checked, and delivery dates are scheduled. The receiving department is notified of the delivery dates. Careful procedures must be set so that all departments and personnel are fully aware of the merchandise needed, on hand, and ordered.

Advertising Budget

The **advertising budget** is a plan of the amount of money a firm should spend for advertising based on estimated sales. Advertising should be kept within reasonable bounds, for it is not true that sales will always be in direct proportion to advertising. In other words, if estimated sales are pretty well known, it is unwise to spend a large amount of money for advertising. Such a plan may result in a loss. On the other hand, a special advertising campaign, properly planned, may increase the sales of a certain product, if only temporarily; and the advertising budget will, as a result, have an influence on the sales budget. These two budgets should, therefore, be planned together. Likewise, the finance department should be aware of the advertising budget in order to control those expenses and to have the necessary cash at the proper time.

Cash Budget

The **cash budget** is an estimate of cash income from all sources and of cash payments. Budgeting cash is a matter of making certain there is enough cash available to meet payments as they come due. Cash comes from either or both of two sources: (1) from the income of the business, or (2) from borrowing. When money is borrowed, it must eventually be paid back. In the cash budget, therefore, borrowed money should be included as a special item under receipts. When it is to be repaid, it should be included in the cash budget under payments.

The form in Illus. 12–10 on page 236 may be used for the cash budget of a small business. A cash budget, however, should be prepared by every business, regardless of size. It should show the anticipated necessity of borrowing and the possibilities of repaying borrowed money. For instance, it is possible for a business to make a sizable profit; but at some particular time during the year it may not have enough cash for its operations and may, therefore, have to borrow.

Capital Budget

Every business that plans to continue in operation must give thought to replacing worn-out or obsolete fixed assets. For instance, a van used by a firm will have to be replaced at some future date. Also, if the business is highly successful, it is possible that the firm may wish to buy a second van. A plan must exist for replacing the old van, or buying a new one.

A **capital budget** is a financial plan for replacing fixed assets or acquiring new ones. Capital budgeting is important because large sums of money are tied up for long periods of time. A wrong decision can be costly. For example, a decision to buy a new van that will last five years involves a large expenditure of money. The manager must plan well in advance if the money is to be available when the van is needed. Assume that the van is purchased based on a forecast that future sales will justify the need for the van. However, if sales do not increase as expected, profits will be lowered as a result of added costs related to the van.

ILLUS. 12-10
A cash budget.

Cash Budget
For Three Months Ending March 31, 19--

	January	February	March
Net Sales	$40,000	$40,000	$40,000
Beginning cash balance	16,750	2,000	3,500
Collections from customers	35,000	35,000	40,000
Total cash available	51,750	37,000	43,500
Payments			
Accounts to be paid	22,500	22,500	30,000
Labor	4,750	6,000	8,000
Salaries and administrative expense	3,500	3,500	3,500
Sales expense	7,500	7,500	7,500
Other operating expense	6,500	9,000	12,000
Purchase of fixed assets		5,000	5,000
Repayment of bank loan	5,000		
Total cash payments	49,750	53,500	66,000
Expected cash shortage		16,500	22,500
Bank loans needed		20,000	25,000
Ending cash balance	2,000	3,500	2,500
End-of-month situation:			
Materials purchased	22,500	30,000	40,000
Accounts receivable	75,000	80,000	85,000
Accounts payable	22,500	30,000	40,000
Bank loans		20,000	45,000

Income Statement Budget

An **income statement budget** is a plan showing projected sales, costs, and individual expense figures for a future period, such as for one month, three months, or a year. The projected total sales, less total projected costs and expenses, permit a business to estimate its net profit. Like other budgets, the income statement budget is based on past experience and many other considerations.

ADMINISTERING THE BUDGET

No budget can be followed exactly in a business. Remember that a budget is an estimate, and that it, therefore, cannot be exact.

A budget is merely a guess of what may happen. If sales increase more than was expected, all elements of the budget can be adjusted, particularly

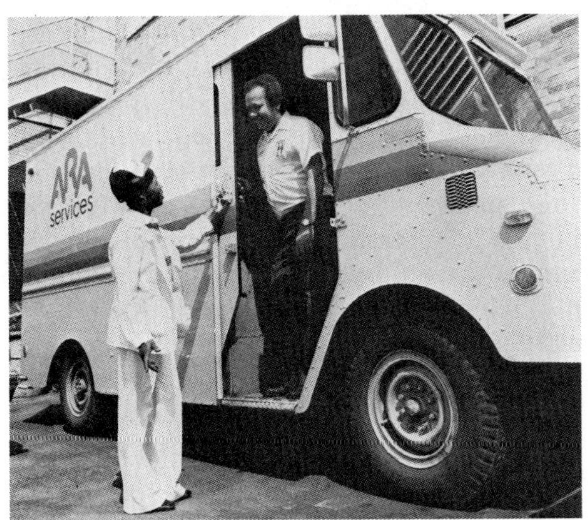

ILLUS. 12–11
Budgets must anticipate new equipment purchases.

purchasing. If sales decrease more than was anticipated, the amounts set for the merchandising and purchasing budgets can be reduced accordingly.

The operations of the business should be checked periodically, preferably monthly but in some cases weekly, to determine whether the business is making a profit and whether the budget is being followed. If the budget is not being followed closely enough to insure a profit, it may be necessary to reduce some items of expense or to find new ways of promoting business.

The budget must be checked periodically to see how the actual operating performance compares with the budgeted estimates. Illus. 12–12

ILLUS. 12-12
A comparison of estimated figures with actual figures.

Items	Estimated Sales First Quarter	Actual Sales First Quarter	Estimated Advertising First Quarter	Actual Advertising First Quarter
Radios	$ 4,000	$ 3,750	$ 75	$ 71
Televisions	15,000	14,250	325	349
Ranges	7,000	7,500	120	115
Refrigerators	8,250	8,430	120	115
Lamps	6,900	7,100	100	98
Furniture	20,000	19,670	475	425
Home furnishings	9,100	9,400	260	292
Household equipment	6,000	5,200	90	80
Total	$76,250	$75,300	$1,565	$1,545

shows a comparison of actual sales and advertising expenditures for the first quarter of a year with estimated sales and advertising for the same quarter. If a comparison of actual operating performance with the budget estimates reveals that the business will not make the expected profit or will have a loss, the manager must review the expenses to determine what can be done to reduce them. Savings can result when businesses budget the inventories carefully to avoid buying unnecessary new merchandise and to reduce the quantity of old items in inventory. If sales are considerably below the anticipated level, it may be necessary to make drastic adjustments, such as reducing delivery service, discharging a few workers, or canceling certain purchases.

The use of budgets and a budgeting system cannot guarantee the success of a business, but these management devices may help reduce losses or increase profits. The entire budgeting process is valuable in planning and controlling operations. But whether a business is a success or not can only be determined after the budget time periods have passed. A business measures past success by preparing and analyzing financial statements. A few of the most commonly used financial statements are discussed in the next chapter.

NEW TERMS & CONCEPTS

Define the following terms and concepts, which may be found in boldface type on the page shown in parentheses.

accounting records (221)
data processing service center (223)
point-of-sale terminal (225)
accounts receivable record (226)
accounts payable record (228)
fixed assets, or plant assets (229)
depreciation (229)
obsolescence (229)
book value (229)
budget (231)
sales budget (233)
merchandising budget (234)
advertising budget (234)
cash budget (235)
capital budget (235)
income statement budget (236)

CHAPTER REVIEW

1. Name at least five kinds of information that a manager or owner of a business should expect to obtain from the accounting records.
2. How can a business use a data processing service center?
3. What do many small business firms use as a basis for obtaining most of the information for their financial records?
4. From the daily balance form of a small retail business shown on page 224:
   a. What is the amount of cash sales?

b. What is the amount of charge sales?
c. What is the cash register total?
d. What are the total cash returns?

5. Give at least three suggestions for the safe handling of cash.
6. Why is it desirable for a business to file its unpaid bills by date, as shown in Illus. 12–6?
7. Why is depreciation a part of the cost of doing business?
8. What kind of information is shown in an insurance record? in a fixed assets record?
9. Is an employer required by law to make income tax deductions from the wages of employees?
10. Name the types of information that must be recorded for social security and payroll tax purposes for each employee and for all employees as a group.
11. Name two ways in which information stored in computers could be damaged.
12. What should the use of a budget achieve?
13. List six types of budgets that are a part of the final overall budget for a business.
14. Name some classifications or bases on which it is possible to estimate the sales of a business.
15. Is a budget ever changed after it has been prepared?

QUESTIONS FOR CLASS DISCUSSION

1. Regardless of the type of record system a company selects to use, what features should the system have?
2. Discuss why the safe handling of cash is so important to a business.
3. How could a truck be a fixed asset? Under what circumstances would land not be a fixed asset?
4. Could a piece of equipment, such as a computer, both depreciate and become obsolete? Explain.
5. What are some of the advantages of keeping an insurance policy record?
6. What problems would be created if a business had a fire and all the records of customers were destroyed?
7. Why must the production manager know the estimated sales budget?
8. Explain why the advertising budget should be prepared at the same time that the sales budget is prepared.
9. Why is the cash budget so important from the viewpoint of the owner of a small business or the director of a large business?
10. Of what value is it for a business to compare budgeted amounts with actual amounts?

PROBLEMS AND PROJECTS

1. L. A. Hendricks has assets as follows: (a) a store building that was bought two years ago at a cost of $40,000, not including the value of the land; (b) store equipment that cost $6,000 and was installed when the building was bought; and (c) a used delivery truck that was bought two years ago for $4,000. Assume the following with regard to depreciation: (a) the building decreases in value at the estimated rate of 5 percent a year; (b) the store equipment decreases at the estimated rate of 10 percent a year; and (c) the truck will last one year and can be traded in then for $600. What is the depreciated value of the assets now?

2. A list of certain items kept by the Fine Fabrics Shop, a small retail store, follows. Decide where each item should be kept for safekeeping. Make three columns across a sheet of paper and place these headings at the top: Office Safe, Fireproof Filing Cabinet, Bank Safe Deposit Box. Write the items below in the column where they best belong.
   a. Office lease
   b. Petty cash
   c. Customers' accounts
   d. Contracts
   e. Bills owed suppliers
   f. Checks received from customers and not yet deposited
   g. Insurance policies

3. The sales budget by product for the Gonzalez Supply Company for this year was estimated to be as follows:

Product A	$25,000
Product B	10,000
Product C	30,000
Product D	35,000

   a. What are the estimated total sales?
   b. If total sales the prior year were $80,000, what percentage of increase does the company expect this year over last year?
   c. What percentage of this year's total sales will Product A provide?
   d. The actual sales for this year for Products A, B, and D were as shown, but the sales for Product C were only 50 percent of the budgeted amount. What are the actual total sales for the year?

4. Visit a gasoline service station or other familiar business and obtain copies of three forms the business uses; for example, for credit sales, for daily cash sales, and for inventory. Ask the manager how the forms are used in the business. Then give a report to your class showing the forms and explaining how they help in running the business effectively.

5. Interview the manager of your local school store or other business and determine which of the suggestions listed in Illus. 12–4 are used for handling cash. Also, find out if there are other steps the manager takes

to protect the cash that the store handles each day. Make a report of your findings to the class.

CASE 12–1

George Gorski operates his own restaurant, which is called George's Place. His accountant, Rosalind Quinn, is quite concerned about the way George handles cash.

Each morning before opening the business, George counts all the money in the cash drawer that was taken in the day before. He then leaves all the coins in the cash drawer so that there will be enough on most days for making change. On days when the change runs low, he sends a worker to the nearby bank to get some. All the paper money in the cash drawer is put in a file cabinet that can be locked. When restaurant supplies are bought, George uses the money in the file cabinet to pay cash for them. On Friday of each week, the money in the file drawer is deposited in the bank.

George cannot understand why Rosalind Quinn is upset with his cash practices. "It has been working fine for years," he says.

Required:

1. Which of George's procedures are improper business practices? Why?

2. What methods should George follow to correct the improper business practices?

CASE 12–2

Karen Kline and Joe Kim are both accounting clerks in a medium-sized manufacturing firm called Electrical Home Products, Inc. The head accountant, Brooke Shenker, has just asked Karen to provide the sales budget for next month's annual budget meeting. Joe was asked to construct the cash budget. Neither was happy about the request, though neither complained directly to the head accountant. Karen did, however, let her feelings be known to Joe.

Karen: We spend weeks developing these budgets and all the budget committee does is argue for two days and change our estimates. You just wonder why they ask for our figures in the first place.

Joe: I agree. What is worse is that we never come in on target. Those credit sales projections are never right, and it makes me look bad because my cash budget is off.

Karen: Why don't they just agree to try to improve sales? The company should put a little more money in advertising expenses to help boost sales, and then hope for the best. I am sure that would be just as good a way to plan and everyone would be happier. I hate all that arguing that goes on.

Joe: Last year they argued for three days and look what happened. They were so far off budget that I heard Brooke say a child could have done a better job forecasting. Budgeting is a waste of time.

Karen: I will start on the sales budget tomorrow, but if I were smart my vacation would begin then too!

Required:

1. If budget figures are prepared by Karen and Joe, why is it necessary for management to discuss them?
2. Do you agree with Joe that when budgeted amounts and actual figures do not agree, the budgeting process is not worthwhile? Explain your answer.
3. Do you agree with Karen that by increasing the advertising budget, sales will increase?

CASE 12–3

The Jetworth Manufacturing Company had the following income statement for the past year:

Sales (10,000 units)		$400,000
Cost of Merchandise Sold		240,000
Gross Profit		$160,000
Selling Expense	$80,000	
General Expense	72,000	
Total Expense		152,000
Net Income		$ 8,000

Management was not happy with this low profit and asked the sales manager to make a study. The manager's recommendation was to reduce costs through a 50 percent increase in production with a promise to sell the increased number of units if the price was reduced 10 percent.

Estimates were then made, and it was determined that the cost of each unit would decrease 15 percent, the total selling expense would increase 20 percent, and general expenses would increase 5 percent.

Required:

Prepare a budget for the next year based on these estimates.

Have You Thought About Becoming . . .
. . . AN ACCOUNTING CLERK?

Do these tasks sound exciting to you? Verify the calculations on a purchase order. Record a payment in a customer's account. Prepare a bank deposit. Reconcile the bank statement. Pay bills. Calculate the payroll for the week. Mail bills to customers. Post to a ledger. Draw up a financial statement.

Accounting clerks perform these and many other tasks that are similar in nature. Accounting clerks are office employees who, while often found working in accounting departments in large firms, are found in all types of businesses, large and small. They work with financial records related to business transactions.

If you want to be an accounting clerk, you should take courses in accounting, computers, and business arithmetic while still in high school. Some course work at a college or postsecondary school would help boost your career. Above all, accounting clerks should enjoy working with numbers. Accuracy and attention to details are important. Interest and ability to work with computers and other electronic equipment is becoming an important aspect of an accounting clerk's job. Successful accounting clerks who continue with their education are building a good foundation for becoming accountants and managers of accounting departments.

13

FINANCIAL ANALYSIS OF A BUSINESS

After studying this chapter you will be able to:

- Describe a balance sheet and explain how it can be useful to a business.
- Point out the usefulness of the income statement in making business decisions.
- Describe the importance of working capital and cash flow.
- Explain several useful financial ratios.
- Describe how various financial experts can assist business managers.

Business activity is in large part measured in terms of money, and the amount of money a business earns is one way to judge its success. Because success is judged in dollars-and-cents terms, every business must (a) keep thorough and accurate records, (b) prepare important financial reports on a regular basis, (c) interpret the financial information in the reports, and (d) make decisions that will affect future financial results.

While the importance of keeping good financial records was presented in Chapter 12, this chapter deals with financial reports and how information from financial reports is used. Though there are many types of financial reports, the two most used by business will be examined: the balance sheet and the income statement. These reports must be carefully understood if the best financial decisions are to be made.

Financial reports have many uses in the business world. Executives use financial reports on a regular basis as a means to run an efficient, profitable business. Suppliers, lenders, unions, governments, and owners also use financial reports when making various types of decisions about a business. The purposes for which financial information is needed by various users are shown in Illus. 13–1.

ILLUS. 13-1
The financial records of a business serve a variety of purposes.

User	Needs financial data to . . .
Managers	make day-to-day decisions. review past results. plan for the future.
Owners	decide whether to increase or decrease ownership investment. decide whether to continue business operations.
Suppliers	decide whether to extend credit. decide how much credit to extend.
Lenders	decide whether to lend a business money. decide on the terms of a loan to a business (amount, time period, and interest rate).
Unions	determine fair increases in wages, salaries, and fringe benefits.
Government	arrive at fair tax rates. detect fraudulent practices.

While a general understanding of financial matters is necessary for all users of financial information, there are times when it is necessary to hire experts who have special skills in handling financial matters. Some of these experts, such as accountants, are identified and discussed in this chapter.

FINANCIAL STATEMENTS

Financial statements are comprehensive summaries of a firm's financial data over a period of time, such as a month, three months, a year, or even the life of the business. We now turn attention to two types of financial statements—the balance sheet and the income statement.

Balance Sheet

The balance sheet is also known as a statement of financial position. You will recall that a balance sheet lists the assets, liabilities, and capital of a business. **Assets** are those things owned, such as cash and buildings. **Liabilities,** on the other hand, are claims against assets or things owed—the debts of a business. And capital (also called owner's equity or net worth) is what a business is worth after subtracting the liabilities from the assets. The total of the assets equals the combined total of the liabilities plus capital. In fact, the **basic accounting formula** is represented in the balance sheet as Assets = Liabilities + Capital.

Each balance sheet has a heading that includes the name of the person or business, the title "Balance Sheet," and the date. The information in the balance sheet presents a picture of the financial position of a business on the date shown in the heading. Balance sheets are prepared at least once a year. Some business firms, however, prepare balance sheets more often.

Because a balance sheet reveals the basic financial position on a given date, it has value to anyone who needs such information. Therefore, a balance sheet can be as useful to individuals as it is to businesses.

Personal Balance Sheet. Illus. 13–2 is an example of a personal balance sheet for Bob Santry. The balance sheet is followed by a discussion of the data found in it.

ILLUS. 13-2
A balance sheet is a useful financial statement for individuals.

Bob Santry
BALANCE SHEET
December 31, 19—

ASSETS		LIABILITIES AND CAPITAL		
Cash	$ 250	Liabilities:		
Motorcycle	2,400	Owed a Friend	$ 100	
Stereo Set	550	Owed on Motorcycle	1,800	
Clothing	400	Total Liabilities		$1,900
Other Assets	100	Capital		
		Bob Santry, Net Worth		1,800
Total Assets	$3,700	Total Liabilities and Capital		$3,700

Kinds of Data. On December 31, Bob Santry listed everything he owned and the amount he paid for each item. These items were placed under "Assets." As can be seen in Illus. 13–2, the total assets are $3,700. Then he listed his debts—the $100 that he borrowed from a friend and the unpaid $1,800 for the motorcycle. These two items were placed under "Liabilities," which totaled $1,900. When he subtracted the total liabilities from the total assets, he learned that his capital (net worth) amounted to $1,800.

Value of Data. From the balance sheet, Bob Santry learned that he owns assets of $3,700, owes $1,900, and is worth $1,800 on December 31. Each major asset and each liability is identified. While this summary information is valuable, he can learn even more by comparing some of the individual assets and liabilities. For example, he can see that if his friend were to demand the $100 owed, he could pay it. But he does not have enough cash to pay for the motorcycle. He still owes $1,800 on the motorcycle which he bought for $2,400.

His motorcycle is his biggest asset and his biggest debt. Because the motorcycle is so important to his financial picture, he knows that he should protect it. Insurance, which is discussed in Chapter 17, is one means of protection. If his motorcycle were destroyed or stolen, Bob Santry would be in financial difficulty without insurance.

Business Balance Sheet. A balance sheet for a business and a personal balance sheet are alike in many ways. An example of a business balance sheet for a jewelry store, the Crown Corporation, is shown in Illus. 13–3.

Crown Corporation
BALANCE SHEET
December 31, 19—

ASSETS		LIABILITIES AND CAPITAL		
Cash	$ 12,000	Liabilities:		
Accounts Receivable	4,000	Accounts Payable	$16,000	
Merchandise Inventory	32,000	Owed on Land and		
Equipment	40,000	Building	52,000	
Land and Building	180,000	Total Liabilities		$ 68,000
		Capital:		
		Stockholders' Net Worth		200,000
Total Assets	$268,000	Total Liabilities and Capital		$268,000

ILLUS. 13-3
The balance sheet shows the financial position of a company on a given date.

Kinds of Data. On December 31 the accountants for the Crown Corporation prepared a balance sheet. From the records, all the assets and all the liabilities were listed. The total liabilities ($68,000) when subtracted from the total assets ($268,000) equaled the total capital ($200,000).

Bob Santry's balance sheet is much like that of the Crown Corporation. Both balance sheets show assets, liabilities, and capital. Only the amounts and types of items listed in each category differ.

There are two items listed for the Crown Corporation that are not listed on Bob Santry's balance sheet. The items are accounts receivable and merchandise inventory. The Crown Corporation purchases jewelry from a manufacturer, displays it in the store, and then sells it to customers. Until the jewelry is sold, it is listed as an asset called merchandise inventory. **Merchandise inventory** refers to goods that are purchased for the purpose of selling to customers at a profit. Merchandise is sold on a cash or credit basis. For credit sales, the Crown Corporation allows customers 30, 60, or 90 days to pay for purchases. The amount owed by customers is an asset called **accounts receivable.** It is an asset because the business has a legal right to obtain cash for the goods sold and can sue customers who do not pay. The store will eventually collect cash from the customers.

In the same sense, the accounts payable item that is found under liabilities on the balance sheet means the Crown Corporation owes money for purchases made on credit. Money owed for credit purchases is a liability called **accounts payable**. In this example, the store bought jewelry on credit from a manufacturer and may take up to a month to pay for it.

Value of Data. The balance sheet for the Crown Corporation provides a great deal of useful data. Specific types and amounts of assets and liabilities are listed. The balance sheet also shows that the business owns assets of $268,000, owes $68,000, and is worth $200,000 on December 31. The total figures on the balance sheet agree with the basic accounting formula as follows:

Assets	=	Liabilities	+	Capital
$268,000	=	$68,000	+	$200,000

A careful look at the specific items reveals other valuable information. For example, the Crown Corporation cannot now pay the $16,000 that is owed under accounts payable because only $12,000 in cash is available. Hopefully adequate cash sales will be made, and certainly some of those customers listed under accounts receivable will soon pay. Even though the money owed under accounts payable is not likely to become due all at once, the company could possibly have trouble meeting other day-to-day expenses. The company would be in trouble if a sudden emergency arose that called for much cash.

The Crown Corporation may use its balance sheet to compare financial results with prior time periods or with other companies. Because a yearly balance sheet is prepared, the business can review its financial progress by comparing this year's results with last year's results. It may find, for example, that the amount of capital increased over last year without an increase in liabilities. If the Crown Corporation wished to do so, it could also compare some information on its balance sheet with that of other business firms of similar size and kind. Published information is available from several sources, such as trade associations. With comparative figures, the business can make judgments about its success and perhaps even find ways to improve its financial picture in the future.

Income Statement

The **income statement**, also known as a **profit and loss statement**, is a financial document that reports total revenue and expenses for a specific period, such as a month or a year. Income statements have three major parts:

1. **Revenue**—income earned for the period, such as from the sale of goods and services.
2. **Expenses**—all costs incurred that helped to earn the revenue.
3. **Profit or Loss**—the difference between total revenue and total expenses.

When the revenue is greater than expenses, a profit results. When the expenses are greater than revenue, a loss occurs. The income statement shows a picture of success or failure (profit or loss) for a specific period of a year or less. The balance sheet, on the other hand, shows the financial condition of a business at a particular point in time. Both types of financial statements serve useful but different purposes.

Personal Income Statement. An example of an income statement for an individual—Bob Santry—is shown in Illus. 13-4. The date in the heading indicates that the period covered is for the month of October only. Separate statements could be prepared each month, or one statement could be prepared covering the entire year.

ILLUS. 13-4
The income statement provides helpful information to individuals.

Bob Santry
INCOME STATEMENT
For the Month of October, 19—

Revenue (Income):		
Full-Time Job	$ 1,500	
Part-Time Job	300	
Total Revenue		$ 1,800
Expenses:		
Rent	$ 450	
Food	360	
Motorcycle (gas and repairs)	234	
Recreation	216	
Clothing	180	
Insurance	144	
Other	54	
Total Expenses		1,638
Net Profit		$ 162

Kinds of Data. On the October income statement, Bob Santry recorded how much he earned from his full-time and part-time jobs. These were listed under "Revenue," and his total revenue or income was $1,800.

Bob Santry next made a list of all expenses for the month. These expenses totaled $1,638. He then subtracted the expenses $1,638, from the revenue, $1,800, and got $162. Because revenue exceeded expenses, the

$162 is profit. The net result of the business activity reported in the form of revenue, expenses, and profit on the income statement will appear in one form or another on the balance sheet. For Bob Santry, the asset cash and his net worth will be increased by $162. The basic accounting formula will still show that assets equal liabilities plus capital.

Value of Data. As with the balance sheet, the income statement presents useful data. Revenue ($1,800), expenses ($1,638), and profit ($162) for the period are shown. Comparisons can also be made each month or year to see whether revenue, expenses, and profit are increasing or decreasing. The actual amount of each item can also be compared with the budgeted amount.

A detailed analysis of the income statement is especially helpful in controlling individual expenses from month to month and in budgeting future expenditures. A fair way to analyze individual items on the income statement is to use percentages. For example, the percentage of revenue spent on rent, food, and other items can be found easily. Let total revenue equal 100 percent. Then, by dividing total revenue into each deduction from revenue, percentages can be computed for making comparisons.

For instance, to find the percentage of income spent on rent, divide $450 (rental payment) by $1,800 (total revenue). This equals .25, a decimal, which is changed to a percentage by multiplying by 100. The result shows that October's rent was 25 percent of revenue.

The same type of calculation and comparison can be made for each expense. In addition, profit percentage can be determined. This is done by dividing revenue, $1,800, into net profit, $162, and multiplying by 100, which equals 9 percent. The 9 percent profit can be compared with last month's or last year's percent of profit. For example, a 7 percent profit last year and a 9 percent profit this year indicate an improvement in one's financial condition.

From such calculations, Bob Santry can better manage his personal finances. He may want to save more than 9 percent of his revenue. If he wishes to save 10 percent, for example, he has clues as to how to reach the new goal. He can try to increase revenue, or he can plan to reduce one or more of the expenses by a certain amount. Business firms, too, look at the income statement as a way to judge success and to meet new goals.

Business Income Statement. The income statements for a business and for an individual provide the same general types of information. An example of a business income statement is shown in Illus. 13–5. The period covered for the Crown Corporation is one year, as shown in the heading.

Kinds of Data. The revenue for the Crown Corporation comes from one source—the sale of jewelry. Total revenue for the year was $400,000. If the company earned other income, such as from the repair of jewelry, it would be listed separately under revenue.

In order to earn revenue in a retail goods business, goods are purchased from suppliers and sold to customers at a profit. As you learned in Chapter

ILLUS. 13–5
The income statement shows profit or loss for a specified period of time.

Crown Corporation
INCOME STATEMENT
For the Year Ending December 31, 19—

Revenue from Sales	$ 400,000	
Cost of Goods Sold	220,000	
Gross Profit		$ 180,000
Operating Expenses:		
Salaries and Wages	$ 80,000	
Advertising and Promotion	24,000	
Depreciation	16,000	
Utilities	10,000	
Supplies Used	6,000	
Other	4,000	
Total Operating Expenses		140,000
Net Profit (before taxes)		$ 40,000

10, the net price paid for merchandise bought and sold is called cost of goods sold. Generally the cost of goods sold is a rather large deduction from revenue. To highlight the cost of goods sold, it is kept separate from other deductions and is used to arrive at gross profit. Gross profit should not be confused with net profit. Gross profit for the Crown Corporation is $180,000, which is found by subtracting the cost of goods sold ($220,000) from sales ($400,000).

Expenses needed to operate the business during the year are listed next on the income statement. When the total of these operating expenses, $140,000, is subtracted from the gross profit, $180,000, the net profit, $40,000, is obtained. It is the net profit that is used as a basis for determining income taxes for a firm. Such taxes are often shown right after net profit to arrive at net profit after taxes.

Value of Data. The manager of Crown Corporation can learn a great deal about the business from the income statement. Specifically, the total deductions from the $400,000 in revenue are $360,000, which consists of cost of goods sold, $220,000, and operating expenses, $140,000. It can also be observed that the net profit before taxes—$40,000—is a rather small part of the total revenue.

The Crown Corporation can improve its financial controlling and budget planning by doing an item-by-item analysis of the income statement, such as that shown in the first two columns of figures in Illus. 13–6. Each expenditure can be compared with the total sales to get percentage calculations, as was illustrated earlier with the personal income statement of Bob Santry. Once the percentages are obtained, they can be compared with similar figures from prior months and years.

Crown Corporation BUDGETED INCOME STATEMENT For Twelve Months Ending December 31, 19—				
Income, Expense, and Profit	**Amounts for Past 12 Months**	**Percentage of Sales**	**Amounts Budgeted for Next 12 Months**	**Estimated Percentage of Sales**
Sales	$400,000	100.00%	$480,000	100.00%
Cost of Goods Sold	220,000	55.00	264,000	55.00
Gross Profit	180,000	45.00	216,000	45.00
Operating Expenses				
Salaries and Wages	80,000	20.00	91,200	19.00
Advertising/Promotion	24,000	6.00	29,280	6.10
Depreciation	16,000	4.00	16,000	3.33
Utilities	10,000	2.50	14,400	3.00
Supplies Used	6,000	1.50	7,200	1.50
Other Expenses	4,000	1.00	4,800	1.00
Total Operating Expenses	140,000	35.00	162,880	33.93
Net Profit	40,000	10.00	53,120	11.07

ILLUS. 13-6
Income statement budgets can be prepared from income statements.

For instance, the first and largest operating expense is $80,000 for salaries and wages. When $80,000 is divided by total sales, $400,000, and the answer is changed to a percentage, the result is 20 percent. If last year the total wages and salaries expense amounted to only 18 percent of sales, the business would know that this expense had increased in relation to total sales. If possible, the company can try to correct this 2 percent increase for the next year by trying to increase sales or reduce expenses in some way. The same type of calculation and analysis can be made for each of the remaining expenses on the income statement. In addition, it is possible to determine the percentages of gross profit and net profit in relation to sales.

ANALYSIS OF FINANCIAL DATA

The financial statements that have just been presented are not always sufficient to enable the manager to interpret the condition of the business. Other information that can be used to assist in interpreting financial data follows.

Cash Flow

Regardless of the size of a business, cash is both a short-term and a long-term concern. Businesses must have cash on hand to pay bills when they are due and to plan ahead for large cash payments, such as the purchase of equipment or the launching of a promotion campaign.

Cash flow refers to the movement of cash into and out of a business. Money comes in immediately as a result of the sale of goods and services for cash and later from customers who buy on credit. Money goes out to pay for various costs and operating expenses. Because money does not always flow in at the same rate it flows out, cash needs must be budgeted as described in Chapter 12.

The planning of cash flow needs is shown in Illus. 13–7 by an example for a retail piano store. While some pianos are sold for cash, most are sold on credit. The bulk of piano sales occurs during the December holiday season. The need for cash is greatest during September, October, and November when pianos are purchased. Large sums of cash are needed to pay for the pianos, for sales promotions such as advertising, and for regular operating expenses. The cash flowing out of the company from October through December is greater than the cash flowing in. Large amounts of cash start to flow in during December from customers who pay cash for their purchases. Credit customers who purchased in December, however, will make cash payments in January, February, and March. During these three months, the flow of cash coming into the business will

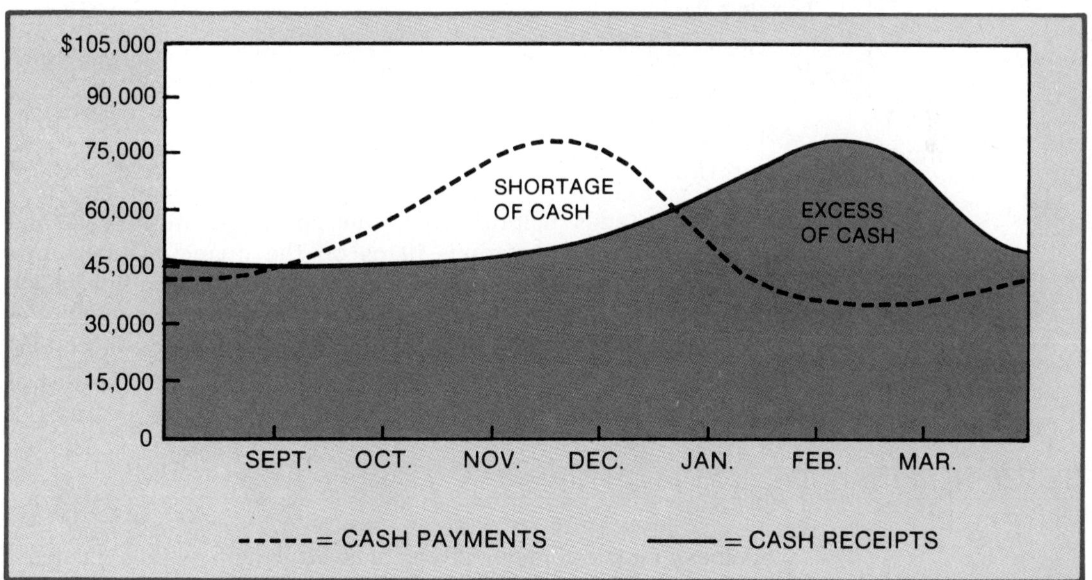

ILLUS. 13–7

Cash flow needs change each month. Businesses must plan their spending around their cash shortages and cash excesses.

be greater than the cash going out. Knowing the cash needs of the business enables the manager to plan accordingly.

Working Capital

Closely related to cash flow is the concept of working capital. **Working capital** is the difference between current assets and current liabilities. The word *current* refers to those assets and liabilities which have a life of one year or less. When current assets are much larger than current liabilities, business firms are more readily able to pay current liabilities. The amount of working capital is one possible indicator that a business can pay its short-term debts. Businesses with large amounts of working capital usually find it easier to borrow money than those with little working capital. The working capital for the Crown Corporation is shown in Illus. 13–8.

ILLUS. 13-8
Working capital can be obtained from the balance sheet by subtracting current liabilities from current assets.

Crown Corporation
WORKING CAPITAL
DECEMBER 31, 19—

Current Assets:		
Cash	$ 12,000	
Accounts Receivable	4,000	
Merchandise Inventory	32,000	$ 48,000
Current Liabilities		
Accounts Payable		16,000
Total Working Capital		$ 32,000

Financial Ratios

Managers find ratios helpful when interpreting financial data and especially when comparing various items on the financial statements. Some of the more important ratios and their uses are found in Illus. 13–9. Once a ratio is calculated for a business it can be compared with prior period ratios, with ratios from other firms, and with other types of ratios. Organizations such as Dun & Bradstreet, Inc., publish a standard list of average ratios for various types of businesses.

SECURING FINANCIAL INFORMATION

If a business needs general advice or special help with a financial problem, experts are available. Types of experts who are called upon to help solve financial problems are accountants, bankers, consultants, and the federal government.

Frequently Used Financial Ratios

Ratio	Calculation	Crown Corporation*	Purpose
Return on Sales	Net Profit / Sales	$ 40,000 / 400,000 = 10.0%	Shows how profitable a firm was for a specified period of time.
Inventory Turnover	Sales / Mdse. Inventory	400,000 / 32,000 = 12.5	Shows whether the average monthly inventory might be too large or small.
Current Ratio	Current Assets / Current Liabilities	48,000 / 16,000 = 3.0	Shows whether a firm can meet its current debts comfortably.
Return on Owners' Equity	Net Profit / Owners' Equity	40,000 / 200,000 = 20.0%	Shows whether the owners are making a fair return on their investment.
Return on Investment	Net Profit / Total Assets	40,000 / 268,000 = 14.9%	Shows rate of return on the total money invested by owners and others in a firm.

*See Illus. 13-3, 13-5, and 13-8 for sources of figures for calculations.

ILLUS. 13-9

Ratios that can be easily calculated help judge the financial condition of a business.

Accountants

Accountants establish systems for collecting, sorting, and summarizing all types of financial data. They prepare and explain in detail the many figures found on financial statements. Accountants also help managers interpret financial data and make suggestions for handling various financial aspects of a business. Large firms have full-time accountants, while small firms usually hire part-time accountants.

Bankers

Bankers also assist business organizations with financial decisions. Bankers are not only well informed about the financial condition of businesses, but they provide advice on how and where to get loans. Since bankers frequently work with business firms, they are aware of businesses' problems and needs.

Consultants

Consultants also assist businesses. A **consultant** is an expert who is called upon to study a special problem and to offer solutions. Consultants usually are not employees. They are outside experts with specialized knowledge.

A financial consultant is valuable to persons thinking about starting a business. For example, consultants provide advice on the amount of money needed to get started and advice on handling finances during the early years of operation. Professors of accounting, finance, and management at local colleges or universities often serve as consultants. There are even business firms that sell consulting services. Large as well as small firms use the many services offered by consultants.

Small Business Administration

Still another source of financial information and advice is the federal government. Of particular value is the Small Business Administration (SBA). The SBA is a branch of the federal government that provides helpful literature on money matters and on other aspects of running a business. The SBA can assist small firms in getting loans under special conditions. And the SBA can also recommend consultants to businesses.

NEW TERMS AND CONCEPTS

Define the following terms, which may be found in boldface type on the page shown in parentheses.

financial statements (245)
assets (245)
liabilities (245)
basic accounting formula (246)
merchandise inventory (247)
accounts receivable (248)
accounts payable (248)
income statement, or profit and loss statement (248)
cash flow (253)
working capital (254)
consultant (255)

CHAPTER REVIEW

1. For each of the following, state two purposes for which financial information is needed: (a) managers, (b) owners, and (c) suppliers.
2. What are the two most used financial statements?
3. Name the three parts to a balance sheet.
4. How is it possible that accounts receivable is listed on the balance sheet as an asset when the customers have not yet paid?
5. Give an example of what a business can learn by comparing one year's balance sheet figures with another's.
6. Name the three major parts to an income statement.

7. Does the income statement show results for the same period of time as the balance sheet?
8. How can a percentage for an income statement expense be calculated?
9. Is net profit likely to be larger than gross profit?
10. Why is cash flow a concern for most businesses?
11. If current liabilities are larger than current assets, is this an indication that a business might have trouble paying some of its debts in the short run?
12. How are ratios helpful to business firms?
13. What do accountants do?
14. Why would a business want to use a consultant?
15. What is the SBA and what does it do?

QUESTIONS FOR CLASS DISCUSSION

1. If, in Illus. 13–2, Bob Santry had forgotten to include a guitar that was recently purchased for $250 cash, how would this affect his total assets, total liabilities, and net worth?
2. If, in Illus. 13–3, all the customers paid their bills, which are shown in accounts receivable, what effect would it have on the total assets, total liabilities, and the stockholders' net worth?
3. Discuss the accuracy of this statement: The balance sheet tells you whether you made a profit or a loss for the year.
4. If, in Illus. 13–4, Bob Santry suffered a net loss of $80, what would happen to his net worth on the balance sheet?
5. Why is gross profit likely to be so much larger than net profit?
6. From Illus. 13–6, which two operating expenses helped make it possible for the estimated total operating expenses to decrease from 35 percent to 33.93 percent?
7. If a business that previously sold on a cash basis now permits customers to buy on 30-day credit terms, how will the cash flow be affected during the first month of credit sales?
8. Discuss whether it would be possible for working capital to ever go below zero.
9. If the average return on sales for all jewelry stores reported by the trade association is 7 percent, how would you judge the success of the Crown Corporation? See Illus. 13–9.
10. What experts would you contact for help if you were planning to open a gift shop, but you were having trouble deciding where to get financial help and how much to borrow?

PROBLEMS AND PROJECTS

1. Use the following items to prepare a balance sheet dated today for the Acorn Corporation. Use Illus. 13–3 as a model.

Cash, $5,000
Accounts Receivable, $8,000
Merchandise Inventory, $15,000
Land and Buildings, $120,000
Accounts Payable, $12,000
Owed on Land and Buildings, $90,000
Stockholders' Net Worth, $46,000

2. Use the following items to prepare an annual income statement dated today for the Home-Rite Corporation. Use Illus. 13–5 as a model.
   Revenue from Sales, $250,000
   Cost of Goods Sold, $80,000
   Operating Expenses:
     Wages, $40,000
     Advertising, $13,000
     Depreciation, $10,000
     Insurance, $6,000
     Supplies Used, $3,000
     Other, $2,500

3. Prepare a balance sheet for yourself or your family making certain to list all your assets and liabilities before finding your net worth. You may find it more convenient to use the price you paid for the assets. If you cannot remember the prices paid, guess as closely as possible or find out from a store or catalog what the item would cost. Group similar items under one name and amount, such as providing only the total value for all your clothing.

4. The following is a portion of an income statement for a local retail store. Calculate the percentage that each item represents of the total sales so that the manager can use the information to help prepare next year's budget.

Revenue from Sales		$500,000
Cost of Goods Sold		300,000
Gross Profit		$200,000
Operating Expenses:		
Wages and Salaries	$90,000	
Advertising	15,000	
Supplies Used	30,000	
Other	20,000	
Total Operating Expenses		155,000
Net Profit (before taxes)		$ 45,000

5. Use the following information that was obtained from the balance sheet and income statement of the Waxwing Company to calculate the following financial ratios: (a) inventory turnover, (b) current ratio, (c) return on owners' equity, and (d) return on investment. See Illus. 13–9.

Revenue from Sales, $320,000
Net Profit, $25,000
Current Assets, $36,000
Total Assets, $200,000
Current Liabilities, $15,000
Owners' Equity, $150,000
Merchandise Inventory, $20,000

CASE 13–1

Carla and Juan Sanchez have been making leather-type items, such as belts, purses, and wallets, for several years in their home as a hobby. They have sold many items to friends and neighbors. Because Juan has just lost his regular job, he and Carla have decided to go into business full time making leathercraft items. The items will be sold to retailers and, perhaps later, to wholesalers. A great deal of money will be needed, some of which they have saved. Both agree that they know a great deal about how to make leather items, but very little about financial matters.

Carla believes they should hire a consultant before they do anything else to start the business. Juan, on the other hand, believes they should go to a bank to borrow as much as they can and then start business. Juan believes that they can hire an accountant after they have gotten the business started. Juan does not believe the consultant will know enough about the leather business to give advice. "Besides," he adds, "consultants are too expensive."

Required:

1. Do you agree with Carla or Juan about whether a consultant is needed? Explain.

2. How could a consultant help them?

3. Could the Small Business Administration be of help? How?

CASE 13–2

Katie Jackson finished the first year of operating her new dry cleaning business. Her accountant gave her an income statement and a balance sheet. The income statement showed that the total revenue from sales was $72,000 and the net profit was $2,880. The balance sheet follows and shows total assets, total liabilities, and capital.

While her profits were not that large, she was certain that she would do much better next year. "After all," she said, "there were extra expenses in getting started the first year; and now that people know me, I will be getting more and more business." Even so, she is concerned about her financial status. Because you are a friend and you have had some business training, she calls you as a consultant to answer a few questions.

Katie's Cleaners
BALANCE SHEET
December 31, 19—

ASSETS		LIABILITIES AND CAPITAL		
Current Assets:		Current Liabilities:		
Cash	$ 12,000	Accounts Payable		$ 28,000
Accounts Receivable	8,000	Other Liabilites:		
Supplies	4,000	Owed on Equipment	$ 4,000	
Other Assets:		Owed on Land and Building	60,000	64,000
Equipment	20,000			
Land and Building	160,000	Capital:		
Total Assets	$204,000	Katie Jackson, Net Worth		112,000
		Total Liabilities and Capital		$204,000

Required:

1. What was the return on sales for the first year?
2. How much is Katie's working capital?
3. If she were to go to a bank to borrow $20,000 to expand the business, would the bank give her the loan? Explain.

CASE 13–3

Philip Crone started a lumber and building materials business. He invested $40,000 of his own money and borrowed $10,000 from a bank. He bought $2,000 of equipment and purchased $45,000 of merchandise. His sales for each of the first two years amounted to about $90,000, but he was always short of cash and had difficulty paying his bills.

Required:

1. If the average inventory turnover ratio for the lumber and building materials industry is 5, do you think merchandise turnover is a cause of difficulty for the business? Explain.
2. What can Philip do to improve his financial situation?

Have You Thought About Becoming . . .
. . . AN ACCOUNTANT?

If you enjoy working with financial statements of the type you studied in this chapter, you should consider becoming an accountant. Organizations need people who can design accounting systems and carefully analyze detailed financial information upon which important decisions are based.

Many types of accountants are needed. Generally the field of accounting is divided into private, public, and government accounting. Those in private accounting handle the financial records of a single business and work for a salary. Public accountants, on the other hand, offer their services to the general public for a fee, much like lawyers. Many small businesses often have a full-time bookkeeper and obtain the occasional services of a public accountant. Government accountants work for local, state, and federal offices and provide financial data for administrators. Still other accountants serve as consultants, researchers, and professors.

All accountants must possess certain skills. In addition to good mathematical skills, accountants must be able to analyze and interpret financial data and communicate the data to employers or clients in a meaningful way. Because accountants work with numbers for long periods of time, accuracy and patience are also extremely important traits.

To become an accountant, you need at least several years of college training. Most accountants who fill responsible positions have graduated from a four-year college with a major in accounting. Some even have master's degrees with a specialization in such fields as tax or cost accounting. Public accountants, moreover, must usually obtain several years of work experience with a public accounting firm and pass a difficult examination in order to obtain a license to become a Certified Public Accountant (CPA). The CPA license is of special importance because it is a mark of distinction that few accountants achieve. While some accountants obtain jobs in government, most are private accountants working in business firms.

The demand for accountants is high and is expected to remain high for many years. Most accounting graduates find jobs; however, outstanding graduates are usually offered jobs at above-average salaries and are usually promoted to top-level positions.

14

FINANCING A BUSINESS

After studying this chapter you will be able to:

- Distinguish between owned capital, retained earnings, and borrowed capital.
- Explain how common stock is different from preferred stock.
- List various sources of short-term borrowed capital.
- Describe the differences between bonds and common stock.
- Provide reasons why a business might need long-term capital.
- Discuss three factors that a business should consider before deciding which source of capital to use.

When an existing business wishes to grow or when a new business wants to get started, capital is needed. In financing a business, the term **capital** refers to the money and credit required to run a business. Capital comes from many sources. It may be provided by the owners, by those who lend money to the business, by credit extended to the business, and by earnings left in the business.

In this chapter, you will learn about the various sources of capital and about factors to consider when deciding upon sources of capital. In addition, you will learn how stocks and bonds, which are often called **securities**, are marketed to the public.

SOURCES OF CAPITAL

It is necessary to determine where capital will come from to start and to operate a business. First, money invested in the business by its owner or owners is called **owned**, or **proprietary capital**. This capital may be from personal funds, such as from accumulated savings, or from money obtained by borrowing on a home or on personal property. As shown in Illus. 14–1, small businesses rely heavily on owned capital.

ILLUS. 14-1
Sources of initial capital investment.

Sources	Percentage of Total
Cash and Savings of Operator	52.5
Loans from Banks and Other Institutions	15.7
Previous Investment in the Business	8.1
Loans from Family	6.9
Credit from Suppliers	6.0
Loans from Friends	4.7
Loans from Previous Owners	2.7
Loans from Surrendered Insurance	0.1
Other Unspecified Sources	3.3

Source: Small Business Administration.

A second source of capital is from retained earnings. **Retained earnings** are the profits that are put aside to run a business. A successful business generally uses retained earnings as a source of capital.

A third source of capital is **borrowed capital**, which is capital loaned to a business by others. Banks and other types of lending institutions usually will not loan money to a business unless the owned capital exceeds the borrowed capital. As a result, businesses in financial difficulty often have trouble getting borrowed capital. Illus. 14–2 shows the relationship between owned and borrowed capital.

ILLUS. 14-2
Relationship between borrowed and proprietary capital.

McGraw's Pet Shop
BALANCE SHEET
July 31, 19—

Assets	$20,000	Liabilities:	
		Borrowed Capital Obtained from Bank	$ 8,000
		Capital:	
		Proprietary Capital Invested by Owner	12,000
	$20,000		$20,000

Owned Capital

To finance a business by acquiring owned capital, the individual proprietor has several alternatives. The owner can sell personal assets, borrow from an individual, mortgage the business property, or mortgage personal property.

The sole owner of a business may also obtain additional money by (a) forming a partnership and requiring the new partner to invest money in the business, or (b) forming a corporation and bringing in owners by selling stock. A business that expands in one of these ways may increase its sales and profits, but the percentage of profits based on the invested money may decrease. The owner of the business must, therefore, estimate whether it will be more profitable to remain a sole owner or to get additional money by forming a partnership or a corporation and bringing more owners into the business.

Let us say that the proprietor decides to secure additional proprietary capital by incorporating and selling shares of stock. A copy of a stock certificate is shown in Illus. 14–3. The two kinds of stock most frequently issued by a corporation are common stock and preferred stock.

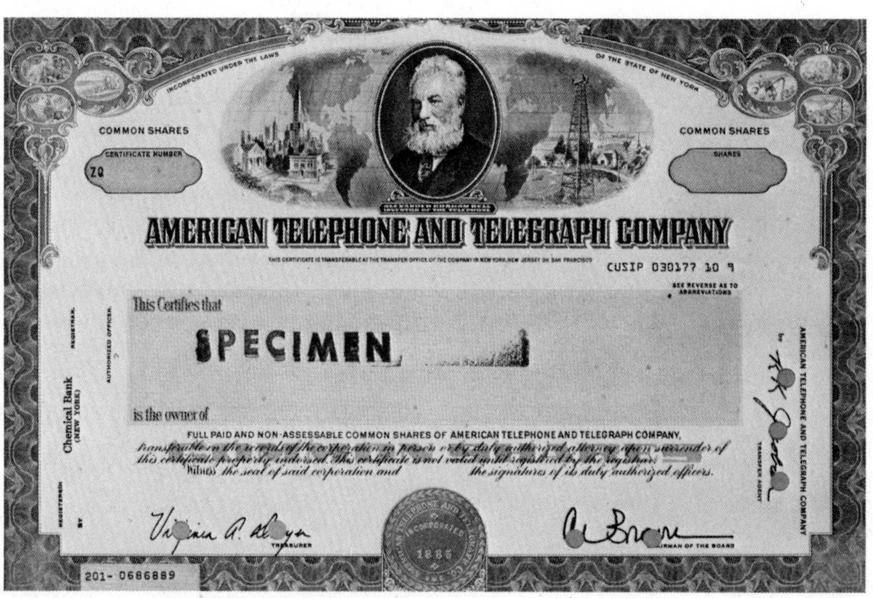
INCORPORATED UNDER THE LAWS OF THE STATE OF NEW YORK

COMMON SHARES | COMMON SHARES

CERTIFICATE NUMBER | SHARES

ZQ

AMERICAN TELEPHONE AND TELEGRAPH COMPANY

CUSIP 030177 10 9

This Certifies that

SPECIMEN

is the owner of

FULL PAID AND NON-ASSESSABLE COMMON SHARES OF AMERICAN TELEPHONE AND TELEGRAPH COMPANY,

Chemical Bank (NEW YORK)

201- 0686889

ILLUS. 14–3
A corporation obtains capital by selling stock.

Common Stock. **Common stock** represents a type of ownership that gives holders the right to participate in managing the business by having voting privileges and to share in the profits (called dividends) if there are any. Holders of common stock, however, do not receive dividends until all other investors have been paid. Furthermore, the dividend rate on common stock can vary over time.

Preferred Stock. **Preferred stock** represents a type of ownership that gives holders preference over the common stockholders of a corporation in payment of dividends and in claims against assets. Common stockholders receive dividends, if any remain, after the preferred stockholders are paid. A corporation must, of course, pay its regular debts and interest on borrowed money before paying any dividends. Holders of preferred stock usually receive a fixed dividend based on a stated percentage of the face value of the stock.

Let us see just how this plan works. Suppose that a corporation has issued $100,000 of 14 percent preferred stock and $100,000 of common stock, and that the profits for the year are $16,000. The preferred stockholders will receive 14 percent of $100,000, or $14,000. There is only $2,000 remaining for the holders of the common stock.

But suppose that the same corporation earns $31,000 in profits during the following year. In this case, the preferred stockholders will be paid their fixed rate of dividends (14 percent of $100,000), or $14,000; and there will be $17,000 left for distribution to the holders of the common stock. If this entire amount is distributed, subject to approval of the board of directors, the holders of the common stock will receive a dividend of 17 percent ($17,000 ÷ $100,000).

It is usually not a good policy to distribute all of the profits. It is better to keep some of the profits as a reserve or surplus (retained earnings). If all of the profits are paid out in the form of cash, a company may later need to borrow money in order to carry on its operations. As shown in Illus. 14–4, some corporations prefer to leave retained earnings in the business so that, if no profit is earned during a particular period, dividends can be paid out of retained earnings (the reserve or surplus that was previously earned). If a corporation pays out all of its earnings and profits, it may have serious difficulty if a loss is suffered in a later year.

Ordinarily the preferred stockholders do not have any voting privileges in managing the business. However, the ownership of certain types of preferred stock does permit the stockholders voting privileges when

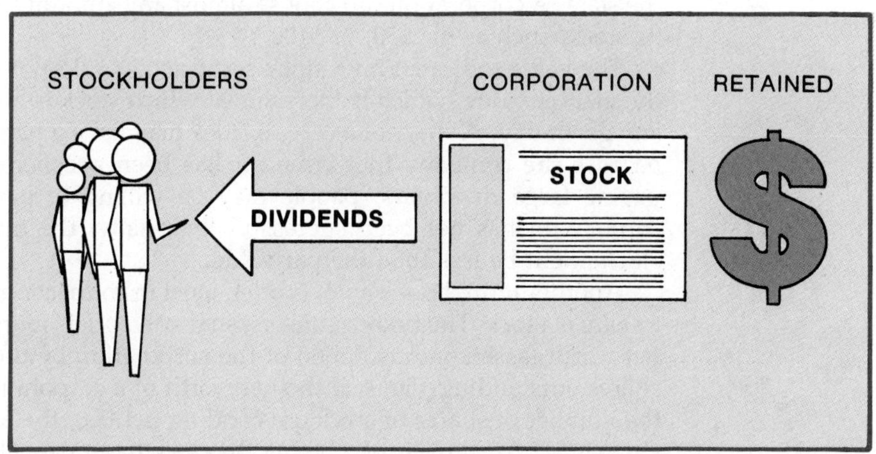

ILLUS. 14–4
A corporation distributes some profits to stockholders and retains the rest.

dividends are not declared and paid regularly. Most kinds of preferred stock carry a special privilege with regard to claims against the assets. For instance, if the corporation ceases operations, the preferred stockholders must be paid before the common stockholders are paid. Suppose that a corporation has outstanding $50,000 of common stock and $50,000 of preferred stock. The preferred stock carries a claim against the assets when the corporation goes out of business. After all of the assets are sold for cash and after all of the creditors of the corporation are paid, assume that $80,000 in cash still remains. The sum of $50,000 (the face value of the preferred stock) must be paid to the preferred stockholders because their stock is preferred as to assets. As a result, the holders of common stock receive only $30,000, which is 60 percent of the full face value of their stock ($30,000 ÷ $50,000). Had there been no preference as to assets, both common and preferred stockholders would have shared equally, with each group receiving $40,000.

When a corporation goes out of business, however, preferred and common stockholders seldom get much from the assets. The assets often do not sell for enough to pay the creditors who must be paid before stockholders receive any money.

Par Value and No-Par Value Stock. In many states, corporations have the privilege of issuing par value stock or no-par value stock. These two types of stock are explained in the following sections.

Par Value Stock. Each stock certificate must show the number of shares it represents. In addition, it may show a par value or stated value. The **par value** of a stock is simply an amount used for bookkeeping purposes on the balance sheet of the issuing company. A par value or stated value shown on the certificate does not indicate the current worth of the stock. For example, a stock with a par value of $10 may be worth $50, or it may be worth nothing.

A par value on shares of stock may be required by the corporate laws of the state. A corporation can choose almost any amount for the par value of its stock, such as $1, $50, or $100.

The value indicated on a stock certificate should not be confused with the **market value**, which is the value at which stock is bought and sold on any given day. A share of a certain stock may have a par value of $50; but, because the company that issued it has been prosperous and has been paying large dividends, people may be willing to pay $60 for it. If a corporation has not been successful financially, the market value of its stock might be less than the par value.

Another term, book value, is often used in connection with the value of a share of stock. The **book value** of a share of stock is found by dividing the net worth (assets minus debts) of the corporation by the total number of shares outstanding. Thus, if the net worth of a corporation is $75,000 and the number of shares of stock outstanding is 1,000, the book value of each share is $75, regardless of whether the stock has a par value of $50 or $100, or whether it has no par value. Book value is used in special situations, such as to help determine the price of an entire business that is about to be sold. It may also be used, in part, to determine the amount of money to give to shareholders when a business is dissolved.

No-Par Value Stock. **No-par value stock** is essentially the same as par value stock except that it has no value stated on it. This is done to avoid assuming that the stock is worth a certain amount. Dividends on no-par value stock are always stated as a certain amount per share, such as $6 per share.

Which Kind of Stock to Issue. Corporations must determine the kind of capital stock to issue. The certificate of incorporation states whether all the stock is to be common or whether part is to be common and part preferred. Corporations can issue no other stock unless authorization is received from the government.

It is usually a good plan to issue only common stock when starting a business. Even though profits may be made from the very beginning, it is often wise to use those profits to expand the business, rather than to distribute the profits as dividends. Although a corporation often pays dividends to holders of common stock, it is not required to do so. When preferred stock is issued, however, the corporation is under an obligation to pay the specified dividend from its profits. If only common stock is initially issued and the corporation later wants to expand, it may then issue preferred stock in order to encourage others to invest in the business.

Retained Earnings

Rather than distribute all profits earned as dividends, a business should reserve some of its earnings to reinvest in the business. This is called "plowing back" earnings. A business plows back earnings for some or all of the following reasons:

- Replacement of buildings and equipment as the result of depreciation (wearing out).
- Replacement of equipment as a result of obsolescence (becoming out of date).
- Addition of new facilities for expanding the business.
- Financial protection during periods of low sales and profits.

Even when the business is not making a profit, it should plan to replace the assets that decrease in value because of depreciation or obsolescence. For instance, a car rental company may start operations with new cars. The company may not make a profit, but there may be considerable cash available each month. If the owners of the business take out all of the available cash, there will be no funds with which to buy new cars when the present ones are worn out.

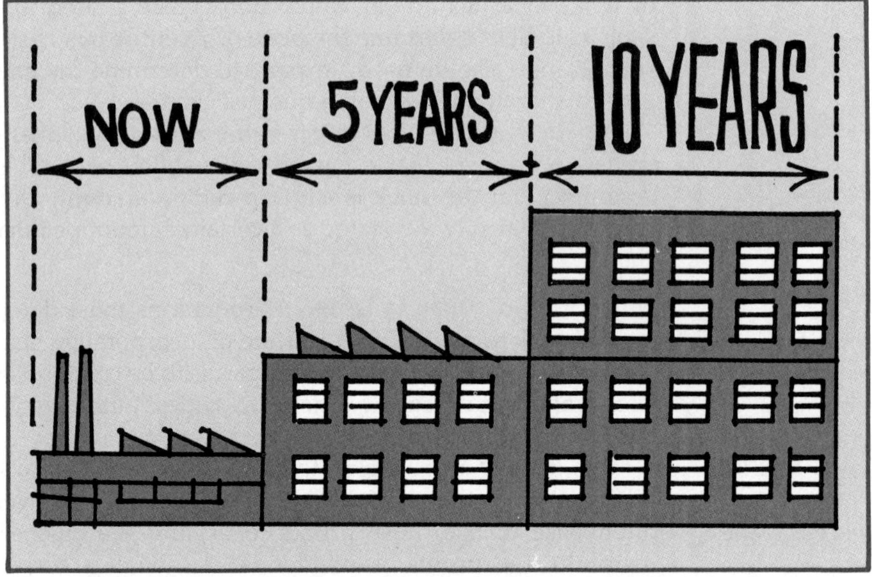

ILLUS. 14–5
Some of a business' earnings should be retained for future expansion.

Retained earnings are not kept in the form of cash only. Cash may be tied up in such current assets as inventories and accounts receivable, which are later converted to cash. Since retained earnings are a part of owned capital, the earnings can be used for investment purposes and for future expansion.

Borrowed Capital

Regardless of size, businesses often borrow capital to pay expenses, buy materials, or purchase equipment. Much of this capital is made available from the savings of individuals. Millions of people deposit their savings in banks and in other financial institutions that then loan these funds to businesses.

Since a business can borrow for as few as 30 days or for several years or longer, borrowed capital is of two types: short term and long term. Sources for these two kinds of capital are listed in Illus. 14–6.

Short-Term Capital. **Short-term capital** is borrowed capital that must be repaid within a year, and often in 30, 60, or 90 days. Short-term capital may be obtained from a bank or other lending agency.

Obtaining Funds From Banks. Banks want to be certain that a loan will be repaid. Some of the questions that may be asked about the borrower are listed in Illus. 14–7. If satisfactory answers are given to these questions, the bank may grant a loan or it may also grant an **open line of credit**, which will permit borrowing up to a specified amount for a specified period of time. For example, a business may be allowed a line of credit up to $50,000

ILLUS. 14-6

Borrowers can get capital from many sources.

Sources of Borrowed Capital

1. Banks
2. Small loan companies
3. Factoring companies (which will purchase the accounts receivable and notes receivable of a business at less than face value)
4. Commercial credit companies (that will lend money on securities, such as accounts receivable and notes receivable or warehouse receipts)
5. Sales finance companies (which are used primarily when installment sales are involved and will purchase the installment sales contracts)
6. Insurance companies
7. Individual investors
8. Corporations that are seeking branches or outlets (and will, therefore, lend to a small business to set it up or help finance it in order to serve as a branch or outlet)
9. Investment bankers
10. Community industry-development groups (which are formed in some communities to encourage new business and which will lend to a new business getting started or help an old one expand)
11. Equipment manufacturers (which will not actually lend money, but will sell needed equipment on an extended-time payment plan)
12. Loans from the federal government

ILLUS. 14-7

There are many things people need to know before lending money.

Questions That May be Asked About a Borrower

1. Is the borrower of good character?
2. Is the borrower putting up enough cash?
3. What experience has the borrower had in this business?
4. Will the loan be secured properly? Will payments on debt be made from profits only?
5. Will financing be sound? (Lender will want to see the net worth to debt and the cash-to-cash needs ratios; also the debt payments to income ratio.)
6. Is enough cash being raised to supply needs—
   - for repairs on buildings and equipment?
   - for modernization, new equipment?
   - to build up accounts receivable?
   - for build-up of inventory expansion?
7. How good is the estimate of salaries, wages, utilities, advertising, supplies, taxes, insurance, and other expenses?
8. What are the terms of the lease? What amount must be paid in taxes?
9. Does the borrower have good accounting knowledge?
10. Does the borrower keep proper accounting records?

for a year. Whenever it needs to borrow, it may do so up to the $50,000 limit. If the business borrowed $10,000, it could still borrow up to $40,000 more during the year.

When a business wants to borrow money from a lending institution, whether the business has a line of credit or not, a promissory note must be signed. A **promissory note** (see Illus. 14–8) is an unconditional written promise to pay a certain sum of money, at a particular time or on demand, to the order of the one who has obtained the note. The business or person who promises to pay the amount of the note is the **maker**. The one to whom the note is payable is the **payee**.

If there is some doubt about the ability of the business to repay a loan, the bank may require the business to pledge its accounts receivable or merchandise inventory as security for the loan. If the loan is not repaid, the bank can then claim the money collected from the accounts of customers or can claim the merchandise and sell it.

Warehouse receipts are also used as security on bank loans. A business stores goods in a public warehouse and receives a receipt for the goods. If funds are needed, the business gives the warehouse receipt to the lending bank as security for the loan. When a warehouse receipt is used to secure a loan, the goods used as security cannot be used or sold until the loan is repaid.

Obtaining Funds From Other Sources. Depending upon the type of business, there may be other sources of short-term capital. Owners with life insurance policies can borrow from funds paid to the insurance company. Small businesses may be able to borrow through the federal government (Small Business Administration). Funds are available at favorable rates from some states, cities, counties, and towns in order to

DUE August 10, 19–– NO. 528

$ 500.00 MUNCIE, IND., May 10 19––

Three months –––––––––––––––––– AFTER DATE, WE, OR EITHER OF US, PROMISE TO PAY

TO THE ORDER OF J. J. McKissick ––––––––––––––––––––––––––––––

Five hundred and 00/100 –––––––––––––––––––––––––––––––––– DOLLARS

WITH ATTORNEY'S FEES. NEGOTIABLE AND PAYABLE AT **INDUSTRIAL TRUST & SAVINGS BANK OF MUNCIE, IND.,** FOR VALUE RECEIVED, WITHOUT RELIEF FROM VALUATION OR APPRAISMENT LAWS. THE DRAWERS AND ENDORSERS SEVERALLY WAIVE PRESENTMENT FOR PAYMENT, PROTEST, NOTICE OF PROTEST AND NOTICE OF NON PAYMENT OF THIS NOTE, WITH 9 PER CENT INTEREST AFTER DATE, AND TEN PERCENT INTEREST AFTER MATURITY UNTIL PAID.

T Oliver Reese

1145 South High J. B. Burton

ILLUS. 14–8

A promissory note.

encourage businesses to locate in a particular area or to encourage businesses not to leave.

In addition, **factoring companies**, or **factors**, specialize in loaning money to businesses based on their accounts receivable. The usual practice, however, is that the factor will purchase the accounts receivable at a discount and then collect the full amounts when due.

A **sales finance company** engages in purchasing installment sales contracts from businesses. The contracts are purchased at a discount, thereby giving the business cash immediately, and the finance company makes the collections. For example, a customer buys a refrigerator on the installment plan and signs a contract. This contract may then be sold to a finance company for less than the amount that is owed on the contract when it becomes due. The finance company collects the full amount of the contract, which enables it to make a profit for handling the transaction. However, in some cases, finance companies lend the money to the business with the installment contracts as security, and the business—rather than the finance company—continues to collect the installments.

Long-Term Capital. **Long-term capital** is capital that is borrowed for longer than a year. A business usually obtains such capital by issuing long-term notes, bonds, or mortgages.

Notes. Notes are a significant source of capital in modern business. Written for periods of 1 to 15 years, they are often **long-term notes** or **term loans**. Because the term loans extend for such a long period, lending institutions require the principal and interest to be repaid on a regular basis over the life of the note.

Long-term notes are often used to purchase equipment. Rather than borrow large sums of money to buy a piece of equipment, however, a company may prefer to lease it. A **lease** is a contract that allows the use of an asset for a fee. Leasing is a practical substitute for long-term financing, especially if capital is difficult to obtain. For example, large computers are often leased because they are costly, are constantly changing, and are soon out of date. Even though a business does not legally own the leased asset, it has full use of it for the life of the lease. Furthermore, the maintenance of the asset is often included in the leasing agreement.

Bonds. The **corporation bond** is a long-term written promise to pay a definite sum of money at a specified time. It contains an agreement to pay interest at a specified rate at certain intervals. Bonds do not represent a share in the ownership of the corporation; they are evidence of debt owed by the corporation. Bondholders are creditors, and have a preferred claim against the earnings of the corporation. Bondholders must be paid by the company before stockholders share in the earnings.

There are two general types of bonds: (a) mortgage bonds, and (b) debenture bonds. The issuer of **mortgage bonds** pledges specific assets as a guarantee that the principal and the interest will be paid according to the terms specified in the bonds. Land, buildings, and machinery are commonly used as security for such bonds.

Debenture bonds have no specific assets pledged as security. They are secured by the faith and credit of the corporation that issues them. Public corporations, such as city, state, and federal governments, usually issue debenture bonds when they need to borrow money. Private corporations usually find it difficult to sell debenture bonds, although they probably prefer to issue debenture bonds instead of mortgage bonds. If a mortgage bond is issued and the corporation is unable to meet some of the interest payments as they fall due, the bondholders may start foreclosure proceedings against the corporation.

Bonds may be further classified as (a) coupon bonds, (b) registered bonds, (c) convertible bonds, and (d) warrants. They are discussed in more detail in the following sections.

Coupon bonds are generally payable to the bearers (holders) who cash in coupons to collect interest. Thus, the corporation that issues coupon bonds has no way of identifying the owners of the bonds at the time interest payments are due. Coupons are attached to such a bond for each date that interest is due (see Illus. 14–9). The owner of the bond may collect the interest by clipping a coupon and presenting it to the designated office on or after the date shown on the coupon.

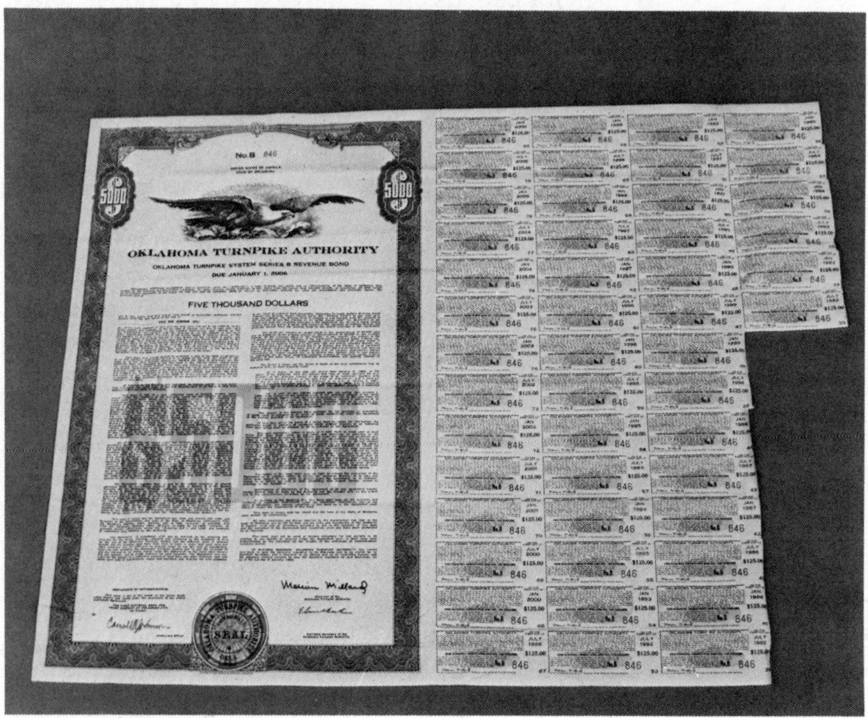

ILLUS. 14–9
The owner of this bond has collected interest by clipping coupons.

If **registered bonds** are issued, the corporation keeps a record of each owner and pays the principal and the interest by check to the registered owner. This type of bond creates more clerical work for the corporation, but it is preferred by many people who buy bonds. These bondholders do not have to clip and mail coupons to receive their interest payments.

Sometimes **convertible bonds** are issued. The holders of such bonds carry the privilege of exchanging them for a definite number of shares of stock. This feature is attractive to holders. They receive a fixed rate of interest as long as they hold the bonds. Later, if the corporation begins to earn large profits and to pay large dividends, holders may exchange the bonds for stock and begin receiving dividends instead of interest.

Another way to encourage investors to purchase bonds is to offer warrants. A **warrant** gives the bond investor the right to buy a specified number of shares of common stock at a set price. Thus, a bond might be sold with the right to buy 300 shares of common stock at $40 a share. If the price of the stock goes to $45, the bond buyer (investor) may still buy 300 shares of stock at $40 each. Rather than buy the stock, the bond buyer may also sell the warrant. Warrants are also offered with other securities.

Mortgages. Mortgage loans are given to firms that have some type of property to use as security for the loan. Property often used as security includes real estate, equipment, stock and bond certificates, and life insurance policies. Lending agencies which make many of the mortgage loans are insurance companies and commercial banks.

If the loan and interest are not paid when due, the lender may take legal action against the firm to collect the value of the debt. Sometimes the lender may cause the property to be sold in order to recover the amount of the loan. Often, however, property cannot be sold for the amount of the loan. The lender may choose to attach (or claim) other assets of the firm instead of the property originally used as security.

DETERMINING WHICH SOURCE OF CAPITAL TO USE

Three important factors should be considered in deciding the source from which capital should be obtained: (a) the original cost of obtaining the capital, (b) the interest rate, and (c) the authority exercised by the various contributors of capital.

Original Cost of Obtaining Capital

It can be costly for a business to obtain capital by selling bonds, long-term notes, and new stock issues. A new bond issue, for example, is expensive to launch. Forms must be filed, approvals obtained from government authorities, agreements made, bonds printed, buyers found, and careful records kept. These costs are usually so high that only large or highly successful firms even consider obtaining capital by issuing new stocks or bonds. It is far less costly to obtain capital from a mortgage or a note.

Interest Rates

As suggested in Illus. 14–10, interest rates can vary from day to day and from week to week. Borrowing when rates are low will cost less than borrowing when rates are high. If a business needs money when interest rates are high, it will usually borrow for a short time with the hope that rates will drop. If the rates drop, long-term obligations may then be issued and a portion of the capital obtained may be used to pay the short-term obligations. In this way, the company has to pay the high interest rate for only a short time. In following this plan, however, a business exposes itself to possible difficulty in obtaining funds when the short-term obligations fall due, and to the possibility that interest rates may rise even higher.

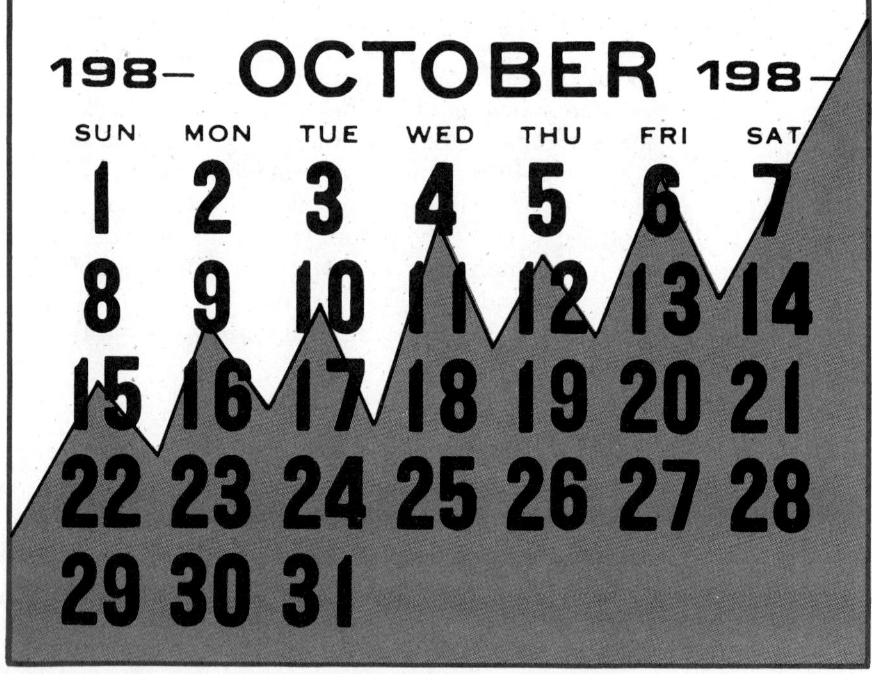

ILLUS. 14–10
Because interest rates change somewhat from day to day, the cost of borrowing also changes.

Authority Exercised by Contributors of Capital

If short-term creditors contribute capital, they usually have no control over the affairs of the business. If the obligations are not paid, the creditors may then bring a legal action to recover the amount due. Otherwise, the owners of the business are in no way restricted by short-term creditors in their conduct of the business.

If capital is obtained by the use of bonds or mortgages, however, the holders usually have a lien (claim) on at least part of the assets of the company. This lien may impose limitations on the use of these assets, and the agreement under which the bonds or the mortgages were issued may limit the use of the income of the company.

If new stockholders or new partners contribute proprietary capital, they gain a voice in the management of the business. The original owners may not wish to give up any of their authority to outsiders. It is possible in most states to issue stock that does not have voting rights, but such stock may be harder to sell. Of course, if existing stockholders or partners provide the additional funds, the control of the company is not affected, provided they contribute in the proportion of their past holdings. New stockholders or partners also share in the earnings. For example, if the number of shares is doubled by selling new shares, there are twice as many shares among which earnings must be divided.

MARKETING SECURITIES

When bonds, stocks, or long-term notes are offered to the public, the procedure becomes complex. There are two methods by which these securities may be sold: (a) directly to investors, or (b) through investment banking channels.

ILLUS. 14–11

A company must supply its investors with detailed financial information.

Direct Sales To Investors

The corporation may wish to give existing stockholders the first opportunity to buy available securities. This may be accomplished by issuing **stock rights** which allow stockholders to buy one additional share of stock for each share owned at a price lower than the current market price. The lower price may attract more funds to the corporation without the additional expense of selling the securities through other investment channels. If stockholders do not wish to take advantage of their stock rights, these rights can usually be sold to others within a stated period at a small gain.

Seldom will the corporation attempt to sell its own securities to an unknown public since there is no assurance that the public will buy them, while the current stockholders can easily be asked if they wish to buy additional stock.

It may be advisable to appeal directly to investors in the following cases:

- When small issues are made. In such cases bankers will either refuse the issue or charge a proportionately large amount for its sale.
- When a company wants to obtain the influence as well as the investments of certain groups. For example, a business may sell its securities directly to employees, customers, and suppliers with the hope of enlisting their goodwill.
- When the business has a national reputation for financial success and the fair treatment of investors and, consequently, has a market for the securities that already exists.
- When the business wishes and can afford to create an investment clientele (persons who will look to the company for investment opportunity) for future financing. This situation may exist if a company issues large quantities of securities periodically and has a reputation for financial strength. Public utilities often follow this plan.

Investment Banking Channels

The process of selling securities through investment banking channels requires the corporation to contract with an investment company group to buy the securities and remarket them through their own channels. The advantage to the corporation is that the entire amount of cash becomes available immediately. The cost of such marketing is generally much higher than the sale of securities directly to shareholders.

Investment bankers are used by businesses for several reasons. For a firm that rarely raises capital by selling securities, it is much more convenient to turn the entire matter over to an investment banker. Also, many companies do not have the necessary expertise themselves to sell securities successfully.

NEW TERMS AND CONCEPTS

Define the following terms and concepts, which may be found in boldface type on the page shown in parentheses.

capital (262)
securities (262)
owned, or proprietary, capital (262)
retained earnings (263)
borrowed capital (263)
common stock (264)
preferred stock (264)
par value, or stated value (266)
market value (266)
book value (266)
no-par value stock (267)
short-term capital (268)
open line of credit (268)
promissory note (270)
maker (270)
payee (270)
factoring companies, or factors (271)
sales finance company (271)
long-term capital (271)
long-term notes, or term loans (271)
lease (271)
corporation bond (271)
mortgage bonds (271)
debenture bonds (272)
coupon bonds (272)
registered bonds (273)
convertible bonds (273)
warrant (273)
stock rights (276)

CHAPTER REVIEW

1. In financing a business, what is the meaning of capital?
2. List three sources of capital.
3. What is the difference between proprietary capital and borrowed capital?
4. Are holders of common stock the first investors to get dividends?
5. Are preferred stockholders guaranteed a fixed dividend?
6. Do preferred stockholders ordinarily have voting privileges in the management of the business?
7. When a corporation goes out of business, are both preferred and common stockholders likely to get much from the assets?
8. What is the relationship between the par value of stock and the market value?
9. How is the book value of a share of stock calculated?
10. Why is there no value stated on no-par value stock?
11. What are the types of questions that a borrower must be prepared to answer when obtaining a loan?
12. List three ways that a corporation obtains long-term capital.
13. What is the principal difference between mortgage bonds and debenture bonds?

14. What type of claim does a bondholder have against a corporation?
15. List three factors to consider in deciding the source from which capital should be obtained.

QUESTIONS FOR CLASS DISCUSSION

1. Discuss why a business should retain some of its profits as a reserve or surplus.
2. Why do you think that the preferred stock of a corporation would probably sell at a higher price than its common stock?
3. Why might a bank require a business to pledge its accounts receivable or merchandise inventory as security for a loan?
4. How can a warehouse receipt be used as security on a bank loan?
5. How does a sales finance company make a profit when it purchases installment sales contracts from businesses that need money?
6. When might a business lease, rather than purchase, equipment?
7. If a corporation cannot identify holders of coupon bonds, how do the bondholders collect interest?
8. What privilege does a warrant give an investor?
9. Why is it expensive to launch a new bond issue?
10. If a business needs long-term capital when interest rates are fluctuating, what are the risks involved?

PROBLEMS AND PROJECTS

1. In your school library, locate a copy of the *Statistical Abstract of the United States* and find a table with the help of your librarian entitled, "New Corporate Securities Offered for Sale, by Type of Security and Issuer." Prepare a report showing the following information for the most recent year that securities were offered for sale.
   a. Total dollar amount for securities, both publicly offered and privately placed.
   b. Total dollar amount for each type of publicly offered security: bonds and notes, preferred stock, and common stock.
   c. By combining the publicly offered and privately placed types of securities, list the following in order of largest to smallest, including total amount, for bonds and stocks, preferred stock, and common stock.
   d. List the three largest issuers of securities.
2. The assets of the Rosemont Corporation are $750,000; the accounts payable, $45,000; bonds payable, $100,000; common stock, $350,000; preferred stock, $150,000. Does the corporation have a surplus or a deficit? Of what amount?
3. Refer to the following balance sheet and answer these questions:
   a. If the par value of both common and preferred stock is $100 a

share, how many shares of each kind are outstanding?

b. If the preferred and common stock shares have equal claims, what is the book value of each share?

c. If the directors decide to distribute $4,800 as dividends, how much will be paid to preferred stockholders and how much to common stockholders?

d. If a stockholder owns 10 shares of preferred stock and 10 shares of common stock, how much of the dividends in (c) should the person receive?

The Barker-Trowe Corporation
BALANCE SHEET
December 31, 19—

Assets		**Liabilities and Capital**		
Cash	$ 18,500	Notes Payable		$ 1,000
Notes Receivable	500	Accounts Payable		3,500
Accounts Receivable	7,500	6% Bonds Payable		25,000
Merchandise	35,000	Common Stock:		
Equipment	8,000	Authorized	$50,000	
Real Estate	48,000	Unissued	10,000	
		Outstanding		40,000
		7% Preferred Stock:		
		Authorized	$50,000	
		Unissued	10,000	
		Outstanding		40,000
		Retained Earnings		8,000
Total Assets	$117,500	Total Liab. and Capital		$117,500

4. Dave Ambrose and Barb Miels each own 2,000 shares of stock, representing all of the common stock outstanding in a rural bottled gas company. They need $20,000 and have three choices of securing the funds: (a) borrowing $20,000 for a period of three months—April, May, and June—and again for a period of three months—October, November, and December—at a yearly interest rate of 12 percent; (b) selling 2,000 additional shares of common stock at $10 each to raise a total of $20,000 for permanent working capital; and (c) selling 2,000 shares of preferred stock at $10 a share with a dividend rate of 14 percent. In other words, these owners are faced with a need for cash to finance their operations, and they must decide whether to borrow the money, to sell common stock, or to sell preferred stock. Assume that the profit of the company is $36,000 a year without anticipating any interest charges.

a. How will the interest on the borrowed money affect Dave and Barb's profits if $20,000 is borrowed as indicated?
b. How will their profits be affected if 2,000 shares of common stock are sold?
c. How will Barb and Dave's profits be affected if 2,000 shares of preferred stock are sold?

5. The net profit of the Ajax Corporation has averaged $20,000 a year. There are 4,000 shares of common stock authorized, but only 2,000 are issued and outstanding. More capital is needed and the owners are considering selling the additional 2,000 shares at $100 a share. It is estimated that the new capital will make it possible to increase the net profit to $30,000.

a. What is the net profit per share now?
b. What is the expected net profit per share if 2,000 new shares are sold?
c. Does it appear to be a good action to take?

CASE 14–1

Donna Dickson is a member of a four-person car pool. Morning conversations on the way to work often deal with what people did the night before.

Donna started the discussion today because she had attended a lecture last evening on investing in stocks and bonds. Selected parts of the conversation by car pool members follow:

Carl: What did you learn that we do not already know, Donna?

Donna: I learned that there are all kinds of stocks and bonds. There is something to meet everyone's needs. But it is all quite confusing.

Pedro: My broker suggested I buy some new coupon debentures with warrants, but I did not understand what he was talking about. Did the lecturer explain these things?

Donna: Not really. The lecturer spent nearly all the time talking about stocks. Maybe next week's talk will cover bonds.

Susan: My uncle gave Larry and me a convertible bond for a wedding gift. We are going to keep it because the company has been doing great. I wish I had some stock in this company too, but we cannot afford it right now.

Donna: Susan, can you have lunch with me today? I did learn something about convertible bonds that might be helpful.

Required:

1. Explain coupon debentures with warrants to Pedro.

2. If you were having lunch with Susan, what would you tell her about the convertible bond she owns?

CASE 14–2

The manager of the Corner Appliance Store needs a new delivery truck. The desired truck has new technologically advanced features that will improve the delivery process and reduce operating costs. However, the truck costs nearly $30,000.

The manager is considering getting a loan or selling the accounts receivable. The store has $50,000 in accounts receivable, which it can either sell to a factoring firm for 70 percent of the total amount the customers owe, or it can get a six-month 20 percent loan for $30,000 from a bank if it pledges the accounts receivable as security.

Required:

1. How much would the company receive if the accounts receivable were sold?
2. How much will the company receive in cash from the bank loan? How much will the interest be?
3. Discuss the advantages and disadvantages of each plan.
4. Is there any other way for the company to acquire the new truck?

Have You Thought About Becoming . . .
. . . A STOCKBROKER?

If you think you would like working closely with securities such as stocks and bonds, consider becoming a stockbroker. Stockbrokers—often called brokers—sell securities to individuals, businesses, and other organizations. Brokers are called upon to give advice about various types of securities and to complete the detailed steps required to buy, sell, or trade securities through stock exchanges.

Stockbrokers need to be specially trained. Large stock brokerage companies train people who are interested in becoming stockbrokers for them. After such training, each trainee must pass an examination to become a stockbroker. Most stock brokerage firms also provide on-going training in order to keep brokers up to date on all financial services.

Stock brokerage companies usually prefer trainees who have some college background. Generally, they select people who have business experience, especially in sales or in management. College courses in economics, accounting, finance, computers, and math provide valuable background for brokers. A course or two in sales and marketing can help because all brokers are sales representatives.

Brokers spend a great deal of time selling securities to clients (customers). As a result, a broker should have ambition, a pleasant personality, a good appearance, and the desire to work independently. Of course, brokers should also be honest and ethical because they are responsible for handling large sums of money for clients.

It is not unusual for successful brokers to become managers within stock brokerage firms. Also, banks and large business firms which have huge sums of money to invest often hire experienced brokers to serve their needs.

Successful brokers earn relatively large incomes. However, there may be slow economic periods during which earnings would be less. Despite economic ups and downs, the demand for brokers is expected to be higher than that for most other jobs during the next ten years.

15

FINANCIAL SERVICES

After studying this chapter you will be able to:

- Identify differences among financial institutions.
- Discuss various features of checking accounts.
- Describe different kinds of secured and unsecured loans.
- Select the right financial institution for your needs.
- Present reasons for changes in the financial world.

All businesses rely upon the services of financial institutions such as banks. A business needs to deposit cash, make payments by check, invest excess funds, and borrrow money. Whether a business is small, large, new, or old, financial services are absolutely essential. A knowledge of the types of financial institutions available and the services they provide aids managers in operating business organizations.

FINANCIAL INSTITUTIONS

Financial institutions play a major role in the business world by handling transactions that deal primarily with money and securities. While banks provide many of the services required of a business, other financial institutions also provide useful services.

Commercial Bank

One of the earliest banks, the **commercial bank,** makes loans to businesses and individuals and handles regular passbook savings accounts. A **passbook savings account** is one that allows an individual to

ILLUS. 15–1
Commercial banks offer many financial services to individuals and businesses.

make deposits and withdrawals without financial penalties. This type of account also pays a small amount of interest. A passbook shows the deposits, the withdrawals, and the interest earned on the account.

In addition, a commercial bank offers certificates of deposit. A **certificate of deposit,** or **CD,** is a type of savings account for which an individual is required to deposit a specified minimum sum of money in the bank for a fixed period, such as six months or more. If that person withdraws funds before the stated period, the result is a penalty—a substantial loss of interest. By agreeing to deposit money in a CD for a specified time, the individual is offered higher interest rates than those on regular passbook savings accounts where funds can be deposited and withdrawn anytime without penalty. Most other financial organizations also offer CD's.

Among the many additional services offered by commercial banks are handling securities such as stocks and bonds, providing safe deposit boxes, and offering general financial advice. Still other services that commercial banks offer include payroll preparation, legal services, tax information and preparation, bill-paying services, collection of promissory notes, insurance planning, and vault service.

ILLUS. 15–2
Banks are selected on the basis of the needs of individual businesses.

Mutual Savings Bank

A **mutual savings bank,** often called a **savings bank,** specializes in handling passbook savings accounts and loans. While a commercial bank is more likely to offer short-term loans, a savings bank is more likely to offer long-term loans such as mortgages. Recent changes in banking laws allow savings banks to offer many of the services provided by commercial banks. Prior to 1981, for example, savings banks could not provide checking accounts. Savings banks can now offer savings accounts with check-writing privileges called **NOW accounts (Negotiable Orders of Withdrawal).** While there is a legal difference between regular checking accounts and NOW accounts, there is no practical difference to the customers.

Trust Company

A **trust company** may be a separate company or a department of a commercial bank or a savings bank. The trust company, or trust department, receives property from customers to manage as directed by the customers. Property may be real estate, marketable securities, or cash. Property is also managed for the benefit of a third person by trusts. For example, property can be put in a trust for a child or adult. Estates and pension funds are also managed by trust companies.

Savings and Loan Association

A **savings and loan association,** another type of financial institution, primarily provides savings accounts and makes loans to borrowers for real estate mortgages. Savings and loan associations also provide NOW accounts, certificates of deposit, and other services similar to the services of commercial and savings banks. Their primary purpose, however, is to use deposits of customers to issue mortgages on homes. The importance of savings and loan associations in relation to several other lending institutions is shown in Illus. 15–3.

Investment Company

An **investment company** specializes in buying securities from various sources to be sold later at a profit. Investors buy shares in investment companies with the hope of eventually selling the shares at a higher price.

Many types of investment companies exist that serve varied purposes. A **mutual fund** is a type of investment company that invests mostly in stocks and bonds which are held for relatively long periods of time. A **money market fund,** on the other hand, is a type of investment company that invests mostly in securities that tend to pay interest and which are likely to be held for very short periods of time.

ILLUS. 15–3

Loans outstanding by selected financial institutions in a recent year.

Type of Financial Institution	Loans Outstanding (in Billions of Dollars)
Commerical Banks	$259.1
Savings and Loan Associations	86.7
Life Insurance Companies	18.3
Mutual Savings Banks	8.2

During periods of abnormally high interest rates, many businesses and individuals invest in money market funds rather than in other lower yielding investments. Most money market funds permit checks to be written against deposits. In most cases, however, checks must be larger than a given amount, such as $500. Recently banks and savings and loan associations were also permitted to offer customers a type of money market account in order to compete successfully with the popular money market funds offered by investment companies.

U. S. Government

The United States government also serves as a financial institution. Many businesses invest funds in a variety of securities made available by the U.S. Treasury Department and other government agencies. A **treasury bill,** or **T-bill,** is a short-term security sold by the federal government to finance the cost of running the government. T-bills are purchased in $10,000 amounts and mature in 3 to 12 months. T-bills are considered one of the safest short-term investments. When a business has cash to invest for a short term, it will find that T-bills generate higher interest rates than regular passbook savings accounts.

The federal government also sells similar securities called **treasury notes** and **treasury bonds.** Treasury notes are available in $1,000 and $5,000 amounts and generally mature in 2 to 10 years. Treasury bonds are available in $1,000 amounts and generally mature in 10 to 30 years. Businesses frequently invest in these securities because they are practically risk free and are readily bought and sold. In addition, the interest earned on these securities is not taxed by some states.

Stock Brokerage Firm

Stock brokerage firms also offer financial services. In addition to buying and selling stocks and bonds for customers, a **stock brokerage firm** offers services similar to the services offered by banks such as checking privileges and certificates of deposit. Some stock brokerage firms combine the services offered by banks, credit card companies, and investment companies. A business may find such combined services of value in meeting most of its financial needs. As a result, stock brokerage firms have become strong competitors of banks and most other financial institutions.

Other Financial Institutions

The financial institutions discussed above handle the needs of most businesses. However, other organizations exist that are either smaller in size or offer only a single service.

Credit unions, which were discussed in Chapter 6, provide many of the services available from banks, but on a much smaller scale. Insurance companies have funds available in large amounts to loan to eligible businesses for long periods. Pension funds created by businesses to benefit employees provide yet another source of funds for long-term loans.

CHECKS AND OTHER NEGOTIABLE INSTRUMENTS

Because very few transactions involve cash, other devices are needed to conduct business operations. When a business borrows or lends money, negotiable instruments are usually used.

A **negotiable instrument** is written evidence of a contractual obligation and is normally transferable from one person to another. Negotiable instruments are frequently referred to as negotiable paper or commercial paper. Promissory notes, discussed in Chapter 14, are negotiable instruments that are frequently used. However, the most commonly used negotiable instruments are checks. Other forms of negotiable instruments include certified checks, bank drafts, cashier's checks, and bank money orders.

Regular Check

A vital service that financial institutions offer is a checking account service. Businesses make most payments by writing checks.

A **check** is a written order on a bank to pay previously deposited money to a third party on demand. The person who writes the check is the **drawer.** The person to whom the check is payable is the **payee.** The bank that is ordered to pay the check is the **drawee.**

In operating a checking account, certain practices and procedures recommended by the bank should be followed. Some of these are discussed in the following sections.

Deposits. Checks received by businesses should be deposited promptly. Most banks will refuse to accept a check for deposit that is more than six months old. A business that does not cash checks immediately gives up the use of valuable funds. Moreover, undeposited checks are subject to loss or theft.

Endorsements. When checks are deposited, they must be endorsed. An **endorsement** is the signature—usually on the back—that transfers a negotiable instrument. Endorsements should be prepared carefully and correctly. Different types of endorsements are shown in Illus. 15–4.

ILLUS. 15–4
Do you know when to use each of these endorsements?

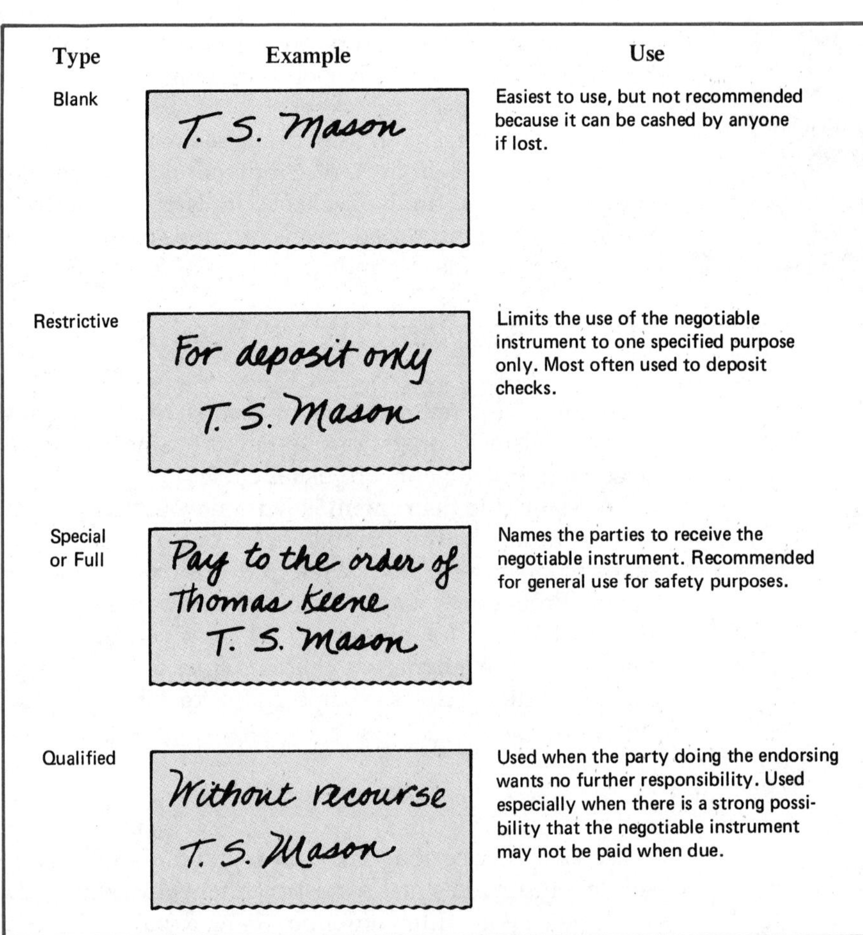

Bad Checks. A **bad check** is one that is not honored (paid) when it is presented to a bank for payment. It may not be paid because there are insufficient funds in the account on which it is drawn, or because it was written by a dishonest person. In either case, it is possible to sue the person who has written the check. However, unless fraud was clearly intended, suit is not generally brought. When a check is returned by the bank because of insufficient funds in a checking account, the depositor notifies the drawer, who arranges to correct the problem. Usually funds are added to the checking account and a new check is written.

Stopping Payment. After a check has been issued, the drawer can direct the bank to refuse payment when the check is presented. In most states, when a bank has been properly ordered to stop payment on a check, it is the bank's responsibility to do so. The bank is then liable if it fails to stop payment. Stopping payment on a check should be used only for protective purposes. For instance, if a business discovers fraud or deception, it may issue a stop-payment order directing the bank to refuse payment when the check is presented. Illus 15–5 gives an example of a stop-payment order.

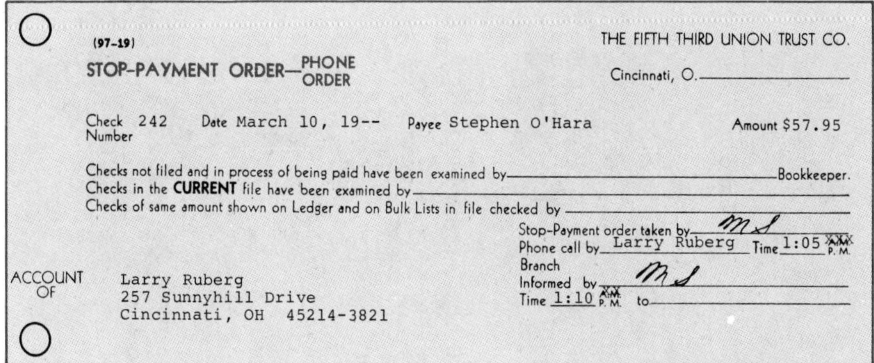
(97-19)
THE FIFTH THIRD UNION TRUST CO.
STOP-PAYMENT ORDER—PHONE ORDER
Cincinnati, O.

Check Number 242 Date March 10, 19-- Payee Stephen O'Hara Amount $57.95

Checks not filed and in process of being paid have been examined by ___ Bookkeeper.
Checks in the **CURRENT** file have been examined by ___
Checks of same amount shown on Ledger and on Bulk Lists in file checked by ___
Stop-Payment order taken by M.S.
Phone call by Larry Ruberg Time 1:05 P.M.
Branch
Informed by M.S.
Time 1:10 P.M. to ___

ACCOUNT OF
Larry Ruberg
257 Sunnyhill Drive
Cincinnati, OH 45214-3821

ILLUS. 15–5
A stop-payment order.

Preparation of a Reconciliation Statement. To maintain a checking account, it is necessary to keep a record of all transactions, such as deposits made and checks written. Each month the bank sends the customer a bank statement (see Illus. 15–6), which lists the monthly transactions. The ending bank statement balance, however, and the checkbook balance are usually different for many reasons. It is necessary, therefore, to determine why the balances are different so that any necessary changes or corrections can be made in the checkbook balance. A **reconciliation statement** is a summary that reveals the causes for the differences between the checkbook balance and the bank statement balance as shown in Illus. 15–7 on page 291. In order to prepare a reconciliation statement, it is necessary to take the following steps:

1. Verify the checks recorded on the bank statement by comparing them with the canceled checks accompanying the statement.
2. Verify all deposits by checking those listed on the bank statement with those recorded on the checkbook records.
3. Determine from the checkbook records which checks were outstanding on the date of the bank statement.
4. Subtract from the cash balance shown on the bank statement the total of the checks outstanding, and add the amount of any

ILLUS. 15–6
A bank statement.

The First-Mason Bank
MASON, OHIO 45040-0045

Elizabeth B. Gordon
1813 Baxter Street
Mason, Ohio 45040-0045

ACCOUNT NUMBER	PAGE	DATE
108325-41	1	June 2, 19--

BALANCE FROM PREVIOUS STATEMENT	NUMBER OF + CREDITS	AMOUNT OF DEPOSITS AND CREDITS	NUMBER OF DEBITS	AMOUNT OF WITHDRAWALS AND DEBITS	TOTAL ACTIVITY CHARGE	STATEMENT BALANCE
$350.72	2	$220.00	10	$312.78	$1.35	$256.59

DATE	TRANSACTION DESCRIPTION	TRANSACTION AMOUNT	ACCOUNT BALANCE
5-01	CHECK 932	9.21	341.51
5-01	CHECK 933	78.00	263.51
5-08	CHECK 929	22.80	240.71
5-10	DEPOSIT	125.00+	365.71
5-15	CHECK 931	16.20	349.51
5-15	CHECK 936	52.93	296.58
5-20	CHECK 934	65.45	231.13
5-23	CHECK 935	32.75	198.38
5-23	CHECK 937	12.25	186.13
5-25	DEPOSIT	95.00+	281.13
5-29	CHECK 938	23.19	257.94
5-31	SERVICE CHARGE FOR MAY	1.35	256.59

deposits made but not shown on the bank statement. This should give the adjusted, or correct, bank balance.

5. Subtract from the checkbook balance (on the date of reconciliation) any charges, such as a service charge, made by the bank and not recorded on the checkbook records. The balance is the adjusted checkbook balance, and it should be equal to the adjusted, or correct, bank balance.

The bank statement was reconciled as follows:

1. The checks and deposits were verified. The outstanding checks were found to be for $15.50 and $33.24, a total of $48.74. A deposit of $100 was made May 31 but does not appear on the bank statement.
2. The checkbook balance was found to be $309.20, but a bank

ILLUS. 15–7
A reconciliation statement.

Elizabeth B. Gordon
Bank Reconciliation Statement
May 31, 19_ _

1.	Write here the new balance as shown in the account summary	$	256.59
2.	Check the deposits you have made during the current period and enter in this space any which have not been credited on this statement	$	100.00
3.	Total of lines 1 and 2	$	356.59
4.	List in 4a below any withdrawals or checks you have issued which have not been shown or returned with this statement, and enter total here	$	48.74
5.	Subtract line 4 from line 3. This should be your present balance	$	307.85

NOTE:
If your statement does not balance, please check to be sure you have entered in your register all transactions shown on the front of your statement.

You should have added, if they occurred:
1. Any transfers from another account to cover any overdrafts.
2. Credit memos.
3. Any interest paid on your account. Not all accounts receive interest.

You should have subtracted, if they occurred:
1. Authorized deductions. (Such as Money Management).
2. Service Charges.
3. Debit memos. (Such as purchasing of checks).

4a. Check Number	Amount
930	$ 15.50
939	$ 33.24
	$
	$
	$
	$
	$
	$
	$
	$
	$
	$
	$
	$
	$
	$
	$
	$
	$
	$
	$
	$
	$
	$
TOTAL TO BE ENTERED IN 4 ABOVE	$ 48.74

service charge of $1.35 had not been recorded on the checkbook stubs.

3. The reconciliation was then recorded in the manner shown in Illus. 15–7.

Certified Check

It is sometimes preferable to transfer money by using a certified check. A **certified check** is one on which the bank certifies that money is being held specifically to pay the check when presented. An example of a certified check is shown in Illus. 15–8. A certified check is useful when the person receiving it must be assured that the drawer of the check has sufficient money in his or her bank for the payment of the check. Such a check certifies that it will be paid by the bank on presentation. As soon as the cashier of the bank certifies the check, the amount of the check is charged to the depositor's account.

For instance, Mr. Pippin must make a payment of $345.67 on a purchase. He writes his check and presents it to the cashier of his bank for

ILLUS. 15–8
A certified check.

certification. The bank immediately reserves this amount for payment of the check. Mr. Pippin then delivers the check to Home Suppliers.

Bank Draft

Sometimes a creditor may require the customer to make payment by a bank draft. A **bank draft** (see Illus. 15–9) is a check that a bank draws on funds deposited to its credit in another bank. A bank draft is a convenient means of transferring money when the individual who is making payment is not known by the person or firm to which the payment, or remittance, is to be sent.

ILLUS. 15–9
A bank draft.

For example, Miss Adams, who lives in Winchester, Indiana, wishes to make a payment of $500 to Hartford and Sons in Chicago, Illinois. Since Miss Adams is not known in Chicago, her personal check may not be accepted. Miss Adams, therefore, buys a draft that the Industrial Trust & Savings Bank in Muncie, Indiana, draws on its funds in the First National Bank of Chicago. When the draft is presented to the latter bank, it is paid as any other check would be paid.

Cashier's Check

One may buy a cashier's check in somewhat the same way that a person buys a bank draft. The **cashier's check** (see Illus. 15–10) is a check on the bank that issues it, payable to the person designated by the purchaser of the check.

ILLUS. 15–10
A cashier's check.

61319
A FULL SERVICE BANK
INDUSTRIAL TRUST & SAVINGS BANK 71-99/749
MUNCIE, INDIANA 47305-4821
PAY TO THE ORDER OF DAVID K. CARR $ 1000.00
EXACTLY $1000 AND 00 CTS
CASHIER'S CHECK
Richard P. Kelly
AUTHORIZED SIGNATURE
⑆074900990⑆ ⑈123 456 7⑈

For example, Mrs. Grant's personal check for $1,000 may not be an acceptable means of payment to her creditor, Mr. Carr. Mrs. Grant, therefore, purchases from the Industrial Trust & Savings Bank a cashier's check made out to Mr. Carr. Mrs. Grant pays the Industrial Trust & Savings Bank $1,000 plus a fee. Mrs. Grant presents the check to Mr. Carr, who in turn presents it to the Industrial Trust Bank for payment. Banks also use cashier's checks to pay their own debts and expenses.

Bank Money Order

A **bank money order** (see Illus. 15–11) serves essentially the same purpose as a cashier's check. The main difference is that the name of the

ILLUS. 15–11
A bank money order.

BANK MONEY ORDER
100024
REMITTER
Thomas Egan
DATE August 9, 19-- 71-99/749
PAY TO THE ORDER OF Duncan-Culman, Inc. $ 40.15
EXACTLY $40 AND 15 CTS DOLLARS
INDUSTRIAL TRUST & SAVINGS BANK
A FULL SERVICE BANK
MUNCIE · INDIANA 47305-4821
Charles Powell
⑆074900990⑆ 593⑈0662⑈

remitter (the sender) of the bank money order is written on the money order but usually is not written on a cashier's check.

LOANS

Bankers are usually eager to lend money, but they must lend it cautiously, even though at times they take reasonable risks. A business should not hesitate to borrow money if it will help the company make more money. That is the way most businesses are able to grow. However, the banker will expect complete facts to be given before the decision can be made as to whether the business will be able to repay the loan under the terms of the agreement.

Requirements for Obtaining a Loan

In addition to personal characteristics of business owners, such as honesty and integrity, most banks and other lending agencies want other information when making a loan. This information involves the business ability of the borrower, past business experience, chances of success in the future, personal investment in the business, the need and purpose of the loan, and the probability of its repayment on time and in full. The information that most lenders require of a borrower is shown in Illus. 15–12.

Kinds of Loans

Most regular bank loans are called **short-term loans** because they extend for 30, 60, or 90 days. These loans are often renewed, and are either unsecured or secured.

Unsecured Loans. Under normal conditions bank credit is widely extended on **unsecured loans** (nothing of value pledged to the bank) merely by the signing of a promissory note. However, bank practice varies in this respect, and the type of business will often determine whether a bank will give an unsecured loan.

Character, capacity, and capital (explained in Chapter 16) are factors considered by bankers in giving unsecured loans. Unsecured loans are generally made for a shorter period than secured loans. Unsecured loans are ordinarily granted only to an established, successful business or to individuals in business who are well known by the lender.

Secured Loans. A **secured loan** is also called a **collateral loan.** For this type of loan the borrower pledges something of value to the bank as security. Collateral loans are usually the easiest to obtain because they give the banker protection. Therefore, a collateral loan is usually made at a lower

ILLUS. 15–12

Information usually requested from borrowers.

1. Proper identification.
2. Nature of business.
3. How the business is organized, its ownership, and any special agreements.
4. Personal data on all principal owners as to connection with the business, connection with other companies, life insurance, banking connections, and civic activities.
5. Other financial information about the business, such as other bank connections and indebtedness.
6. The amount, the purpose, the need, and the plan for repaying the loan that is requested.
7. A detailed balance sheet showing the assets, liabilities, and ownership of the business.
8. A detailed income statement showing the income and expenses of the business.
9. Detailed information regarding liabilities and claims, such as unpaid taxes and other business debts that are due or will become due.
10. Proof as to future prospects and plans for operation of the business.

rate of interest than an unsecured loan. The following types of security or collateral are those most commonly used:

- Accounts receivable and notes receivable
- Merchandise
- Bonds, stocks, and other marketable securities
- Buildings and real estate
- Machinery and equipment
- Cash value of life insurance
- Warehouse receipts

A person may borrow money on real estate and grant a mortgage that gives the lender the right to take possession of the real estate if the loan is not paid. An example of a real estate mortgage is shown in Illus. 15–13.

Any stock or bond that has a value can usually be used as collateral. A bank will ordinarily lend about 50 percent of the value of a good stock or a good bond.

Sometimes a business person cannot obtain a loan without someone else to guarantee that the loan will be repaid. This person who signs the note is a **cosigner.** A cosigner is a form of security or collateral.

Interest Rates

Although interest rates are governed to some extent by law, bank rates are largely based on the supply of and the demand for money. The lowest rate of interest is called the **prime rate.** This is the rate at which large banks

ILLUS. 15–13
A real estate mortgage.

Know All Men by These Presents:

That James D. Graham of Montgomery County, Ohio, *in consideration of* the sum of Twenty Thousand ($20,000) Dollars *to* him *in hand paid by* Raymond E. Kelly *does hereby* ***Grant, Bargain, Sell and Convey*** *to the said* Raymond E. Kelly his *heirs and assigns forever, the following described* ***Real Estate,*** *situate in the* City *of* Miamisburg *in the County of* Montgomery *and State of Ohio.*

Lot No. 103 on Blanchard Road of the Far Hills subdivision.

and all the ***Estate, Right, Title and Interest*** *of the said grantor in and to said premises;* ***To have and to hold*** *the same, with all the privileges and appurtenances thereunto belonging, to said grantee,* his *heirs and assigns forever. And the said* James D. Graham *does hereby* ***Covenant and Warrant*** *that the title so conveyed is* ***Clear, Free and Unincumbered,*** *and that* he *will* ***Defend*** *the same against all lawful claims of all persons whomsoever.*

Provided Nevertheless, *That* if the said James D. Graham shall well and truly pay or cause to be paid, his certain promissory note of even date herewith, for Twenty Thousand ($20,000) Dollars drawn to the order of Raymond E. Kelly and payable in three years from date, with interest at fourteen (14) percent per annum

then these presents shall be void.

In Witness Whereof, *the said* James D. Graham who *hereby releases* his *right and expectancy of dower in said premises, has hereunto set* his *hand , this* seventh *day of* November *in the year of our Lord one thousand nine hundred and* -------

Signed and acknowledged in presence of us:

Dennis Gray

Howard Wright

James D. Graham

The State of Ohio **County of** Montgomery **ss.**

Be It Remembered, *That on the* seventh *day of* November *in the year of our Lord one thousand nine hundred and* ------ *before me, the subscriber, a* Notary Public *in and for said county, personally came* James D. Graham *the grantor in the foregoing Mortgage, and acknowledged the signing thereof to be* his *voluntary act, for the uses and purposes therein mentioned.*

In Testimony Whereof, *I have hereunto subscribed my name, and affixed my* official *seal, on the day and year last aforesaid.*

Warren J. Lasure

make large loans to the best qualified borrowers. Small loans and loans to less qualified customers are made at current, regular rates. All rates can vary from day to day and from month to month.

On short-term commercial loans it is common for the bank to deduct the interest in advance. Interest deducted from a loan in advance is called **discount.** Suppose, for example, that a loan of $10,000 is needed for three months and that the bank charges 12 percent interest per year. As shown, the borrower will receive $9,700. Goods, bonds, or stocks with a market value of approximately $20,000 may be required as security by the bank.

Amount to be paid to bank in three months	$10,000
12 percent interest deducted in advance.	300
Amount of cash given to borrower	$ 9,700

The formula for computing interest is:

$$\text{Interest} = \text{Principal} \times \text{Rate} \times \text{Time}$$

Thus,

$$\text{Interest} = \$10{,}000 \times 12\% \times 3/12$$

In this example, the actual interest charge is slightly more than 12 percent, for $300 is being charged for the use of $9,700 for three months. If the loan is not repaid in three months, the bank has the privilege of selling the securities to obtain the $10,000.

Repayment of a Loan

Some borrowers have a tendency to borrow money without giving specific thought as to when and how it can be repaid. They assume that if they cannot repay a loan when it becomes due, they may renew it and continue to pay the interest without making payments on the principal. Borrowing without a definite intention and specific plan of repaying the principal is a dangerous practice for both the borrower and the lender. The borrower may be forced into bankruptcy, and the lender may be unable to collect on the debt. Generally, lenders have found that borrowers will pay long-term obligations with less difficulty if a provision is made for repaying the loan at intervals instead of in one amount at the end of the loan.

A loan may be payable on demand (whenever requested by the lender), or it may be payable over a stated period of time, such as a month or year. The **maturity date** of a loan refers to the date on which it must be repaid. When borrowing money, it is important for an individual to set up a schedule of loan maturities based on a budget of cash as explained in Chapter 12. In estimating one's flow of cash, a reasonable margin of safety should be allowed so that funds will be available to pay a maturing loan.

THE CHANGING NATURE OF FINANCIAL INSTITUTIONS

The financial world has been undergoing a great deal of change during the last decade. Three factors have caused changes to occur: deregulation of banking, competition, and technology.

In 1980 Congress passed the Depository Institutions Deregulation and Monetary Act. A major aim of the law was to increase competition among financial institutions. Prior to this law, many state and federal laws controlled what financial institutions could and could not do. The amount of regulation was extensive.

The 1980 law gave savings banks, savings and loan associations, and credit unions the right to offer services previously reserved for commercial banks. It also gave more freedom to financial institutions regarding the interest rates they set, for example, on savings accounts, certificates of deposit, and mortgages. Further, the law allowed institutions to enlarge the geographic area they serve if the institutions obtained government approval.

These types of changes have increased the amount of competition among financial institutions. As a result, new types of financial services have been created and will continue to appear. Businesses have more choices to consider when a financial need arises.

While the various types of banks compete directly with one another, they must now also compete with investment companies and stock brokerage firms. Stock brokerage firms offer many of the services previously allowed only by banks, such as NOW accounts and certificates of deposit. Banks also provide services previously offered primarily by stock brokerage firms, such as money market funds.

Competition has caused financial institutions to seek new and better ways to serve customers. One way to accomplish this is by using electronic technology. As a result, automatic teller systems have become popular. By connecting electronic terminals, a store can transfer funds from a customer's bank account to the store's bank account when a sale is made. Computer technology may eventually eliminate the need for businesses and financial institutions to use cash and checks. Computer technology has already had a marked effect on how financial institutions operate.

ILLUS. 15–14
Banking services may be available at a variety of locations.

NEW TERMS AND CONCEPTS

Define the following terms and concepts, which may be found in boldface type on the page shown in parentheses.

commercial bank (283)
passbook savings account (283)
certificate of deposit, or CD (284)
mutual savings bank (285)
NOW accounts (285)
trust company (285)
savings and loan association (285)
investment company (285)
mutual fund (285)
money market fund (285)
treasury bill, or T-bill (286)
treasury notes (286)
treasury bonds (286)
stock brokerage firm (286)
negotiable instrument (287)
check (287)
drawer (287)
payee (287)
drawee (287)
endorsement (288)
bad check (288)
reconciliation statement (289)
certified check (291)
bank draft (292)
cashier's check (293)
bank money order (293)
short-term loans (294)
unsecured loans (294)
secured loan, or collateral loan (294)
cosigner (295)
prime rate (295)
discount (296)
maturity date (297)

CHAPTER REVIEW

1. What happens when funds from a certificate of deposit are withdrawn before the date stated on the certificate?
2. Are interest rates likely to be higher on regular passbook savings accounts or on certificates of deposit?
3. List ten services provided by commercial banks.
4. Is a commercial bank or a mutual savings bank more likely to offer long-term loans, such as mortgages?
5. Can savings banks offer savings accounts with check-writing privileges?
6. What type of financial institution specializes in managing property for the benefit of a third person?
7. What is the primary purpose served by savings and loan associations?
8. From Illus. 15–3, which type of financial institution loaned the most money in a recent year?
9. List three types of securities sold by the federal government which are practically risk free.
10. From Illus. 15–4, what type of endorsement do most businesses use when depositing checks received daily?

11. If you wrote a check but later wanted to prevent it from being cashed at your bank, what should you do?
12. Give at least three kinds of information or facts that a borrower will be expected to furnish when requesting a loan.
13. What three factors have caused changes to occur in the financial world?
14. What is a major aim of the Depository Institutions Deregulation and Monetary Act?
15. In addition to competition with one another, with what other types of financial institutions must banks compete?

QUESTIONS FOR CLASS DISCUSSION

1. How are mutual funds and money market funds alike and how are they different?
2. What does an investment company with a money market fund have in common with a commercial bank?
3. How are the following securities alike and how are they different: treasury bills, treasury notes, and treasury bonds?
4. Is there any difference in the methods of transferring a note and a check from one person to another?
5. If you received a paycheck and cashed it at the local food market, what type of endorsement would be best (a) by you, and (b) by the food market when the check is deposited in its checking account?
6. Explain what is meant by a reconciliation statement.
7. If you wish to transfer money to a person in another city who will probably not accept your personal check, what instruments mentioned in this chapter could be used to transfer the money?
8. If you are willing to accept a personal check from someone for a large, important payment and you want to be sure that it will be paid when deposited at your bank, what can you ask the drawer of the check to do?
9. How can the signature of a cosigner be used as security for a loan?

PROBLEMS AND PROJECTS

1. By using your library or by contacting a stock brokerage firm, obtain a list of money market funds. Select one of the funds and write to it requesting general information. Study the materials you receive and make a report indicating the kinds of securities the company invests in, the minimum initial deposit needed to become a shareholder, and whether checks can be written. If checks can be written, indicate the minimum size of the check.

2. The following information appeared on the bank statement of R. E. Matthews on December 1:

Checks			
No. 31	$24.50	Balance, November 1	$321.42
No. 32	2.36		
No. 33	26.00	Deposits	$ 49.30
No. 35	18.00		18.05
No. 36	11.25		26.50
No. 38	32.81		10.00
No. 39	14.30		19.55
Service Charge	$ 1.65	Balance, November 30	$313.95

Prepare a reconciliation statement taking the following into consideration:

Checks outstanding	No. 34	$ 12.60
	No. 37	47.35
Checkbook balance, November 30		$355.65
Deposit of December 1 not shown on bank statement		$100.00

3. As the financial manager for your company, you need to borrow $5,000 to purchase a new piece of equipment. The bank is willing to loan the money at 15 percent interest payable in 120 days, with the interest deducted in advance.
   a. What is the amount of the interest?
   b. How much money will you receive from the bank?
   c. How much must be paid to the bank at the end of 120 days?

4. Show Illus. 15–4 to five different people who have checking accounts, and ask them how they endorse checks when they (a) deposit them in their checking account, and (b) cash them at a store or someplace other than a bank. Make a report of your findings following your teacher's instructions.

5. Assume that you have an invoice for $1,153 on which the terms are 4 percent 10 days, net 30 days. You wish to take the discount but find it necessary to borrow money at 12 percent until the end of 30 days in order to pay the invoice. You will need to borrow $1,000. How much money will be saved by borrowing the money for 20 days in order to obtain the discount?

CASE 15–1

Jim Liu, owner of a delicatessen in a shopping center, often chats outside his business with Dan Hall, who owns the bakery next door. One weekday morning when business was slow, Jim mentioned that he needed to go to his bank in order to put some cash in his passbook savings account. Jim was not that familiar with the American financial system. Dan asked

Jim how much money he had in his savings account. Jim said he had a regular practice of putting 10 percent of his profits in the account each month. Jim was now concerned that perhaps he should start an account with another bank because the sum was getting quite large. The rest of the conversation follows:

Dan: You are losing money, Jim, by putting that much of your savings in a regular passbook account.

Jim: What do you mean? I came to this country ten years ago and opened this business. I have always believed that a savings bank was the best place to save money. Now you tell me I am losing money.

Dan: It is a place to save money, but the interest you are making right now is 8 percent less than what you could make at other places. In fact, you should buy CD's and T-bills, or even put some of your money in a money market fund.

Jim: Wait. I do not understand these words you are using. But I do know that I do not want to lose my hard-earned profits in any risky investments.

Required:

1. Could Jim invest his money in other savings instruments at his savings bank? Explain.
2. Are treasury bills and certificates of deposit considered risky investments? Explain your answer.
3. If Jim had $100,000 in his savings account, rather than in a money market fund earning 8 percent more interest, how much money would Jim lose in a given year?

CASE 15–2

The Home Furnishings Company has borrowed all it can borrow on unsecured credit from its bank. It owns its own building. Many of its sales are on the installment plan, and the company has $20,000 outstanding on accounts receivable. Orders have been placed for a substantial amount of furniture for a special sale, but it is not expected that sufficient money will be available to pay the bills promptly and to take advantage of special discounts. The company wishes to protect its credit standing but needs additional cash.

Required:

1. Can the Home Furnishings Company borrow on an unsecured loan from another bank?
2. What are some ways in which the Home Furnishings Company can probably obtain the cash needed?

Have You Thought About Becoming . . .

. . . A BANK OFFICER?

A bank officer is a manager who is in charge of a department or a bank service, such as credit, installment loans, mortgages, financial planning, and investments. Because of the many services offered by banks, various positions are available to people seeking banking careers.

An outstanding bank clerk or teller can become a bank officer. This person needs to have leadership qualities and a broad knowledge of business, in addition to having tact and good judgment. A bank officer often supervises other employees and works closely with customers. Needless to say, one should also have an interest in and an ability to work with numbers and to analyze information such as that found on financial statements and on loan applications.

Most bank officers have college degrees. Because of the numerous activities involving people and numbers, a college degree in business or social science is most desirable.

The American Bankers Association offers specialized training to aspiring bank officer trainees and to bank officers who want a promotion. With appropriate training, education, and successful work experience, promotions to senior bank officer, bank manager, or vice-president are within reach. As banking services continue to expand, opportunities exist for those with an interest in banking careers.

16

CREDIT AND COLLECTIONS

After studying this chapter you will be able to:

- Describe basic types of credit plans.
- Distinguish between business credit cards and bank credit cards.
- Identify how an applicant's credit rating is determined.
- Explain some of the major credit regulations provided by law.
- List some of the requirements of the Truth-in-Lending Act.
- State ways in which credit sales can be analyzed.

Your old jogging shoes are about worn out so you decide to buy a new pair in your favorite sporting goods store. After you find the right size and color, the salesperson asks: "Cash or charge?" You would probably be surprised if that question were not asked. Of course, not all businesses sell on credit. Most, however, do sell on either a cash or a credit basis.

If a business extends credit, the policies that determine how credit is extended and how collections are made will greatly affect the success of that business. Therefore, business owners must have an understanding of general principles and practices that apply to credit when establishing credit policies and collection procedures that they should follow.

CREDIT PRINCIPLES AND PRACTICES

Retail credit is credit that is extended by the retailer to the consumer, whereas **trade credit** is credit extended by one business to another business. While there are some differences between retail credit and trade credit, all forms of credit operate on the same general principles. Although some of the main differences between trade credit and retail credit are pointed out, the emphasis in this chapter is on retail credit.

Retail Credit Plans

A retail store owner may extend credit to customers under any one of a number of different types of credit plans. The factors which most commonly influence the selection of credit plans are the credit practices in the community and the credit practices of competitors.

Regular Credit. In a **regular credit,** or **open account** plan, a customer may charge a purchase at any time but must pay the amount owed in full by a specified date. When a customer buys merchandise, the sale is charged to the customer's account. At the end of each month the customer is expected to pay for purchases made during the month. A business usually sends a monthly statement to each customer, which lists the purchases made during that month.

Regular credit is a popular form of both retail and trade credit. The length of time allowed for payment, however, tends to be somewhat longer for trade credit than for retail credit. Discounts often accompany trade credit, but are seldom offered for retail credit.

Installment Credit. An **installment credit** plan is used when a customer makes a sizable purchase and agrees to make payments over an extended period of time. The principal difference between regular credit and installment credit is that an installment credit customer is given a longer time in which to pay. Also, the customer is usually required to pay an interest charge for the privilege of making monthly payments that may extend for as long as several years or more. Installment credit is granted by retail merchants who sell expensive items that have a long life, such as automobiles, furniture, and major home appliances.

Because installment credit extends for a long time and involves large sums of money, it is handled somewhat differently from regular credit plans. Usually a customer makes a down payment for the purchase and signs a formal contract for the balance. An **installment contract,** or **conditional sales contract,** is the agreement under which the buyer promises to make regular payments until the goods are fully paid. With regular credit, legal ownership **(title)** passes to the buyer at the time of purchase. But with installment credit, title does not pass to the buyer until all payments have been made. The merchandise can be **repossessed** (taken back) by the seller if the buyer does not pay as agreed. These special conditions should be included in the installment credit contract and explained to the customer.

Revolving Credit. Many retail stores have established what is called **revolving,** or **optional credit,** which combines the features of regular credit and installment credit. Under the revolving credit plan, the customer is permitted to make purchases on credit at any time, usually up to a specified amount. As with regular credit plans, the full amount may be paid by the end of the billing period without a finance charge. However, customers who do not wish to make full payment have the option of making partial payments each month. The minimum amount of a partial payment is dependent upon the amount of the unpaid balance in the account. A finance charge, stated as an interest rate, is added each month to the amount that is unpaid. An example of a revolving credit plan agreement is shown in Illus. 16-1.

ILLUS. 16-1
A revolving credit plan requires that the customer follow all of the requirements included in the agreement.

Dawn's Optional Charge Account Agreement

In consideration of **Dawn's** extending credit to me or to the person presenting my charge card identification, I agree:

1. To pay the amount billed on my monthly statement in full within 25 days from the billing date **or**

2. To pay at least one-sixth of the balance shown on my monthly statement, with a minimum payment of $10.00. If I elect not to pay my monthly statement in full I will pay a **Finance Charge** which will be the greater of 50 cents or an amount determined by applying a periodic rate of 1½% per month (an **Annual Percentage Rate** of 18%) to the first $700.00 of the **Average Daily Balance** and a periodic rate of 1% per month (an **Annual Percentage Rate** of 12%) to any part of the **Average Daily Balance** in excess of $700.00.

3. Failure to make a payment as prescribed in paragraph 1 or 2 above will permit **Dawn's**, at its option, to declare the entire balance of the account due **Dawn's**, and **Dawn's** may charge an attorney's fee not exceeding 20% on the first $500.00, and 10% on the excess of the amount due if, because of delinquency of payment, the account is referred to an attorney, not an employee of **Dawn's**, for collection.

4. **Dawn's** hereby waives and disclaims the rights to retain, acquire, or enforce any security interest in any real property which is used or expected to be used as the principal residence of the customer.

5. The charge card issued to me may be revoked or terminated at any time, and must be surrendered to **Dawn's** upon demand.

6. All purchases made on my account will be considered to have been made in the State of Pennsylvania, regardless of my State residence or the State to which I direct the purchase be delivered.

7. The information that I have given to **Dawn's** for the purpose of obtaining credit is warranted to be true and correct and **Dawn's** is authorized to investigate my credit record and to report to proper persons and Credit Bureaus my performance on this agreement.

8. **Dawn's** will send to me each month a statement which will show my previous balance (last month's new balance), new balance, **Finance Charge**, purchases, payments and credits, and the amount of my monthly payment due.

NOTICE TO THE BUYER

1. You may at any time pay your total indebtedness under this agreement.
2. Do not sign this credit agreement before you read it or if it contains any blank space.
3. You are entitled to a completely filled in copy of this credit agreement.

OPTIONAL CHARGE ACCOUNT AGREEMENT

Sheila Hill — Jan. 23 19--

Customer's Signature **Date**

Other Credit Plans. Layaway plans and budget plans, which are variations of regular, installment, and revolving credit plans are also offered by retail merchants. A **layaway plan** is one that permits a customer to make payments on an item until the item has been fully paid; however, the store holds the merchandise for the customer until the last payment has been made. The layaway plan is especially practical for customers who may not have sufficient cash readily available for a purchase or who do not wish to use other credit plans.

Still another credit plan is the **budget plan,** which is short-term credit usually covering a two- or three-month period. Department stores, furniture stores, and similar stores often allow customers to purchase major items on 60 or 90 days' credit without additional charge. For instance, a store may permit a customer who has a good credit record to buy furniture amounting to $500 and allow the customer 60 to 90 days to pay for it without a service charge.

Credit Cards

Over the last 20 years credit card purchases have grown rapidly. Credit cards are used to buy all kinds of goods and services. Most people who qualify for credit cards already have such cards. "Plastic money," as such cards are often called, is currently used by about 60 percent of all U.S. families. However, newer types of credit cards may create still larger numbers of credit card users in the years ahead.

Business Credit Cards. Large department stores and national chain businesses, such as oil companies, issue credit cards to customers who request them. These businesses operate their own credit departments. They seek credit card applicants, check whether the applicants qualify for credit, and issue cards. Most businesses that issue credit cards allow customers to purchase on regular or revolving credit plan terms. The major disadvantage of the business credit card is that each business must operate its own credit card system. The major disadvantage to the customer is that a separate credit card must be obtained from each business where credit purchases are made. Therefore, customers often must obtain a variety of credit cards.

Bank Credit Cards. The bank credit card overcomes the weaknesses of the business credit card. Rather than each company establishing and maintaining its own credit system, a bank operates the credit system. A customer obtains a credit card from a bank and uses it to purchase goods and services from any of thousands of participating retailers. In this way one credit card takes the place of many separate cards. Both the consumer and the retailer benefit. As a result, bank credit cards have become popular.

The two most used bank credit card systems are MasterCard and Visa. Both systems operate in very much the same manner. Banks that are a part of either credit system invite qualified customers and retailers to participate

ILLUS. 16–2
Can you identify which of these are business credit cards and which ones are bank credit cards?

in the system. Customers apply for credit through a bank, and each participating retailer sells on credit to customers who present a bank credit card. When a credit purchase is made, the retailer prepares a charge slip. Charge slips are then submitted to the bank for payment. After deducting a service charge, which is about 3 to 5 percent of the total charge sales, the bank pays the retailer and bills the customer who, in turn, pays the bank. The customer benefits by making one monthly payment even though purchases may have been made at many different stores. And the business benefits by selling on credit without operating its own credit system.

Bank Debit Cards. A recent development that is closely tied to bank credit cards is the bank debit card. A **debit card** allows a person to pay bills, make cash withdrawals from automatic teller machines, and pay bills by phone from a checking or savings account. Debit card users, however, do not actually write checks because computers are used extensively to handle debit card transactions.

A debit card operates much like a bank credit card from a retailer's point of view. The card is presented to the retailer when a customer makes a purchase. By using a special cash register (point-of-sale terminal), funds are electronically deducted from the customer's bank account and added to the retailer's bank account. Retailers no longer send sales slips to the bank and the bank no longer bills and collects from customers. The bank does, however, send monthly summaries of transactions to retailers and customers. Banks charge fees, of course, for debit card services.

Through the use of debit cards and credit cards, the amount of cash and the number of checks handled are greatly reduced. The amount of paperwork is also greatly reduced. In fact, it is predicted that a "cashless" and "checkless" society may eventually develop, though only time will determine the accuracy of this statement.

Other Credit Cards. In addition to bank credit cards, other types of credit cards are available, such as Carte Blanche, Diners Club, and American Express. The user usually pays an annual fee for these travel and entertainment credit cards, which are generally made available to users with excellent credit ratings. People who travel extensively or entertain often obtain this type of card.

Determining Credit Standing

A commonly recognized formula for determining the credit worthiness of a person or a business exists. The formula is the "three C's" and consists of character, capacity, and capital.

Character—a moral obligation to pay debts—is the first consideration. Many business people believe that an individual's character is more important than wealth. Wealth alone cannot determine one's credit; nor, of course, can one get unlimited credit on character alone.

Capacity is merely another term for earning power. An individual may have character and have perfectly good intentions of paying a debt. But if the individual lacks the ability or capacity to pay, collection may be impossible.

The third measuring standard, capital, applies only to people who have things of value that can be used as collateral. A person with a temporary lack of earning power may be entitled to receive credit if that person has good character and good capital resources, such as property, investments, or savings. Capacity and capital without character will, however, usually disqualify any credit applicant.

Illus. 16-3 shows the results of a survey to determine how retail and trade credit managers rate in importance various kinds of credit information. Notice that character ranks first. The payment record, which shows both ability and willingness to pay, ranks second. The financial statement (referred to as the balance sheet) ranks third and is important in determining credit extended to a merchant. Financial statements reveal how well a business is doing and whether it will be able to pay its bills when due.

Sources of Credit Information

Retail merchants may get credit information about their customers from (a) the customers and (b) credit agencies. These two sources of credit information are discussed in the following sections.

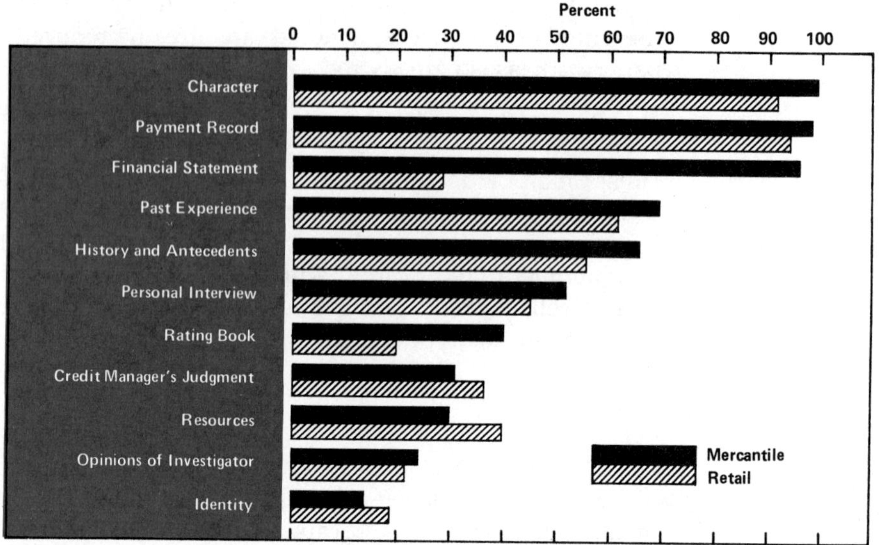

ILLUS. 16-3

Credit managers consider some types of credit information to be more valuable than other types.

Customers. Retail stores that operate credit departments obtain information directly from customers when they complete a credit application form such as the one shown in Illus. 16-4. The application provides information about the customer's family situation, housing, and annual income. This information is used when deciding whether to grant credit. Also, the names of the applicant's employer and bank are provided as well as the names of other companies from which the applicant has made credit purchases. The companies may be contacted for further information before deciding (a) whether to grant credit and (b) how much credit to grant. Many companies use the services of a credit agency to gather information about credit applicants and to check the credit standing of current credit customers.

Credit Agencies. In general there are two types of credit agencies: (a) agencies that provide credit information on individual purchasers and (b) agencies that provide credit information on business firms.

Private credit agencies collect information and publish confidential reports for the benefit of their subscribers, who are usually retailers. Many local credit agencies belong to either the National Retail Credit Association or the Associated Credit Bureaus of America. Each association shares credit information with member agencies. A business subscriber thus has access to credit information on millions of consumers whenever such information is needed for making a credit decision.

Each subscriber contributes to these credit reports by furnishing information and periodic ratings. Additional information is gathered from local newspapers, notices of change in address, death notices, and court records. Such information is valuable to the retailer as a protection against loss on accounts. If a customer moves, the retailer will want to know of the

Dawn's DEPARTMENT STORE

CHARGE ACCOUNT APPLICATION
FORM 1-4C

PLEASE WRITE CLEARLY

MR. ☐ MRS. ☐ MS. ☒ FIRST NAME Doris INITIAL S. LAST Bushey

SOCIAL SECURITY NO 081 — 325 — 6824

HOME TELEPHONE 737-1620

RESIDENCE ADDRESS STREET NO & NAME APT. NO CITY STATE ZIP CODE: 1400 Walnut Street, Philadelphia, PA 17054-3256 — HOW LONG MO | YRS 4

PREVIOUS ADDRESS - IF LESS THAN 3 YRS AT PRESENT ADDRESS — HOW LONG MO | YRS

ABOUT YOURSELF 1

AGE AT LAST BIRTHDAY 24 — NO OF DEPENDENT CHILDREN None

MARITAL STATUS ☐ SINGLE ☐ MARRIED ☒ UNMARRIED

RESIDENCE ☐ OWN ☐ RENT ☒ BOARD ☐ WITH PARENTS ☐ WITH RELATIVES

ANNUAL * INCOME ☐ UNDER \$5,000 ☐ \$5,000 TO \$7,500 ☐ \$7,500 TO \$10,000 ☒ \$10,000 TO \$15,000 ☐ \$15,000 TO \$20,000 ☐ \$20,000 TO \$30,000 ☐ OVER \$30,000

OCCUPATION Assistant Buyer — EMPLOYER OR SOURCE OF INCOME Wanamaker's — HOW LONG MO | YRS 1 — BUSINESS PHONE 734-1820

EMPLOYER'S ADDRESS Center City, Philadelphia — TYPE OF BUSINESS Department Store

PREVIOUS EMPLOYER — HOW LONG MO | YRS

IF YOU WISH A JOINT ACCOUNT, PLEASE COMPLETE ITEM 2

ABOUT YOUR SPOUSE 2

SPOUSE'S FIRST NAME — SOCIAL SECURITY NO — — — OCCUPATION

SPOUSE'S EMPLOYER — EMPLOYER'S ADDRESS — ANNUAL INCOME * \$

CREDIT EXPERIENCE 3

NAME AND ADDRESS OF BANK Philadelphia National Bank — CHECKING ☑ SAVING ☑ — ACCOUNT NO 031-782-461

DEPARTMENT STORES	ACCOUNT NO.	OIL COMPANIES, CREDIT CARDS, ETC.	ACCOUNT NO.
Gimbel's	73184	Gulf	821-61-43B

LOANS-AUTO, PERSONAL, ETC.	PURPOSE	ACCOUNT NO.
None		

* INFORMATION REGARDING INCOME FROM ALIMONY, CHILD SUPPORT OR MAINTENANCE PAYMENTS NEED NOT BE REVEALED.

PLEASE SIGN AND INDICATE BELOW

I AGREE TO THE TERMS AND CONDITIONS ON THE REVERSE SIDE

AMOUNT OF CREDIT REQUESTED \$ 300

X Doris S. Bushey SIGNATURE 4/1/-- DATE

NUMBER OF CARDS REQUESTED 1

X SPOUSE'S SIGNATURE DATE

NOTICE TO THE APPLICANT

1. Do not sign this credit agreement before you read it or if it contains any blank space.
2. You are entitled to a completely filled in copy of this credit agreement.

THIS AREA FOR OFFICE USE ONLY

EMPLOYEE'S NAME ______ CLERK NO. ______ DEPT. NO. ______ DATE ______

ILLUS. 16-4

To receive credit, you must fill out an application form.

change of address. If a customer dies, the retailer will want to be sure that any existing claim is presented to the estate. If there is court action of any kind against a customer, the retailer will want to protect the company's claim.

When businesses deal with each other, problems differ from those encountered by retail merchants who transact business with individuals. An important source of information on the credit standing of retailers, wholesalers, and manufacturers is Dun & Bradstreet, Inc. A book of credit ratings is published regularly by this credit agency and is sold as a service to subscribers. The service covers the entire United States. In addition, a subscriber can obtain a special report on any business person or professional person in any part of the country. The reliability of this agency has been established through many years of effective service to all types of business and professional people.

Credit Law

Credit is governed to a great extent by state and federal laws. Some of the laws that relate directly to credit are examined next.

State Credit Laws. All 50 states have laws that regulate credit transactions. The legal profession created the Uniform Commercial Code and the Uniform Commercial Credit Code which have been adopted by the majority of states. These model laws cover credit conditions relating to credit terms, negotiable instruments, and installment sales contracts. Companies with credit departments often obtain the advice of an attorney on credit matters and usually hire credit managers who have a knowledge of the appropriate state and federal laws.

Federal Credit Laws. Federal credit laws have been passed that affect credit relationships between retailers and consumers. These laws apply to such areas as fair and equal credit rights, the cost of credit, and the process for correcting errors on credit transactions.

Equal Credit Opportunity Act. The Equal Credit Opportunity Act of 1974 makes it illegal to deny an applicant credit because of age, sex, marital status, race, and national origin. The age of the applicant, however, may be used to deny credit if it affects the financial soundness of a business transaction. Legally credit may be denied a person too young to sign contracts or too old to carry out a long-term credit request. For example, a person aged 65 who requests a 25-year credit plan to buy a home may be denied credit because the person may die before the debt is completely paid. However, a person aged 65 with a good credit history who requests credit terms for six months, for instance, should not be denied credit solely on the basis of age.

Women are entitled to the same credit rights as men. At one time, single women were often denied credit. Today the law prevents unfair credit treatment of single women or men. In the past, when a husband and wife obtained credit, only the husband's name appeared in credit records even though both spouses could make credit purchases. This situation became especially unfair under certain conditions. If the husband died, for example, the wife was often refused credit because she had no established credit record. No longer is it legal in such situations for only the husband's name to appear on shared credit accounts and in credit records. Both husband and wife have the right to open separate accounts with the same creditor if both are creditworthy.

Still another provision of the Equal Credit Opportunity Act is that an applicant must be notified by the creditor within thirty days of the decision made on the application for credit. If credit is refused, the applicant must be notified in writing. Furthermore, the applicant has the right to know why credit was refused. A specific reason, such as not being employed at a job long enough, is acceptable; but a vague reason, such as stating that the applicant is not worthy of credit, is not valid.

Truth-in-Lending Act. The Consumer Credit Protection Act, passed in 1968 and better known as the Truth-in-Lending Act, has had a major impact on credit practices. The law and its later amendments contain many provisions protecting consumers who buy on credit. Some of the major features of the law are shown in Illus. 16-5. In addition, a Truth-in-Leasing Act was passed to help consumers more readily compare the cost and terms of one lease with another, and with the cost and terms of buying for cash or on credit.

Fair Credit Reporting Act. Credit agency files contain a great deal of information about consumers. This information is usually obtained from retailers, employers, banks, and other sources and is used as a basis for giving or refusing credit. Due to the large amounts of information credit agencies process, occasional errors occur. To protect consumers from inaccurate or out-of-date information appearing in credit agency files, the Fair Credit Reporting Act was passed in 1970. Under this law, a person has a right to see information in credit agency files and to have any errors in the files corrected.

CREDIT POLICIES AND COLLECTION PROCEDURES

Any business that extends credit to customers is concerned about losses from uncollectible accounts. In some businesses there are practically no bad-debt losses; in others the losses run rather high. Surveys show that the losses from uncollected debts usually are less than 1 percent of net sales. However, when economic conditions are bad countrywide, bad-debt losses can increase greatly. During such times large numbers of uncollectible accounts can lead businesses to bankruptcy. If bad-debt losses are to be kept to a minimum, it is necessary that credit policies and collection procedures be established.

ILLUS. 16–5
Consumer credit requirements for business firms under the Truth-in-Lending Act.

Truth-in-Lending Act Requirements

1. The total dollar cost of obtaining credit must be shown on forms and statements as the finance charge.
2. The finance charge must be shown on forms and statements as an annual percentage rate.
3. The total cost of credit and the finance charge must be displayed prominently on credit forms and statements.
4. If a credit card is lost or stolen and is used by an unauthorized person, the maximum credit loss to the customer is $50. The customer is subject to no loss if the business is notified of the missing card before unauthorized purchases are made.
5. A business cannot send a credit card to a person unless that person has requested or applied for it.
6. If a business advertises credit terms, it must include all information that might be needed by a buyer who wished to compare similar terms among competitors. These terms generally include the down payment and the number, amount, and date of payments.
7. Business firms must allow a customer three business days to cancel credit purchases on which the buyer's home is used as security.
8. Business firms must notify customers in writing about the required procedure for challenging possible errors on forms and statements. The customer, who must submit the challenge in writing, must receive a response from the business within 30 days; and within 90 days the challenged amount must either be corrected or the customer must be provided with an explanation as to why the business believes there is no error.

Credit Policies

Whether a business operates on a credit basis depends more on competition than on cost factors. If competing firms extend credit, it is almost necessary that a similar business also extend credit. The chief disadvantage of offering credit is higher operating costs because of increased record keeping and bad-debt losses. The chief advantage is that credit increases the volume of sales. With proper attention given to credit sales, the increase in sales volume should lead to increased profits. In order to profit from credit sales, credit policies must be created.

If a business decides to sell on credit, a number of important policy decisions must be made to create an effective credit system. The simplest credit system for a small retailer to use is to participate in a bank credit card service, such as Visa or MasterCard. However, if the business chooses to start its own credit department, one of the first decisions to be made is the selection of the type of credit plans to offer, such as regular credit, revolving credit, or installment credit. A credit application form must be designed that meets state and federal requirements. Also, the business should decide whether to use the services of a credit agency for help in making credit decisions about each applicant.

While making these policy decisions, a business must also establish specific credit terms, finance charges, and a billing schedule. For example, a department store that uses revolving credit may allow customers 30 days in which to pay accounts in full, and charge 1½ percent a month interest on account balances that are not paid within the billing period. It may further decide that the maximum amount of credit will be $500 for new customers and $1,000 for customers who have established good credit records.

A business should also consider establishing a billing policy. Retailers with many charge account customers find it convenient to use cycle billing. In **cycle billing,** monthly statements are sent to some customers on one day of the month and to other customers on other days of the month. The billing cycle is usually determined by the alphabetical arrangement of customers' names. For example, customers whose last names begin with *A* through *H* are sent their statements on the 10th of the month, *I* through *R* on the 20th of the month, and *S* through *Z* on the last day of the month. In cycle billing, a customer is usually required to pay the account balance within 10 to 15 days after the date shown on the statement. The major advantage of cycle billing is that all charge accounts do not become due on the same day of the month.

Management also must decide how to collect from customers. This is an extremely important decision, especially when it involves overdue accounts.

Collection Procedures

The person who is in charge of making collections should bear in mind the two major objectives of the collection procedure: first, to get the money, and second, to retain the goodwill of the customer. When one considers the second objective, it is evident that much tact is necessary in making collections.

The usual collection procedures include the sending of a statement each month followed by impersonal reminders, first reminding the customer that the amount is past due and then asking why payment has not been made. Eventually a letter must be written indicating that no further credit can be extended until the account has been paid or other arrangements have been made. At this stage it is important to talk with the customer to find out what the problem is.

Honest people who cannot pay debts when they are due are embarrassed and worried about their failure to pay the bill. As long as there is a desire and a willingness to pay, there should be a frank discussion to work out a payment plan. Part of the reason for the overdue bill may be that too much credit was extended too easily. This is as much the fault of the seller as it is of the buyer.

ILLUS. 16–6
Consumers who rely too heavily on credit may find they are unable to pay bills when due.

A fundamental fact that affects the procedures followed in collecting past due accounts is that the longer the account is overdue, the less are the chances for collecting the money owed. Illus. 16-7 indicates the likelihood of collection for unpaid accounts of varying lengths of time. The data given are based on the experiences of retail stores.

ILLUS. 16–7
Possibility of collecting accounts that are overdue.

Age of Account	Possibility of Collecting
60 days or more	90%
6 months or more	50%
12 months or more	30%
24 months or more	25%
36 months or more	15%
5 years	almost none

Steps in Collecting from Customers. Most credit managers find that establishing a rather precise plan to collect from customers is extremely worthwhile. A carefully developed plan that encourages customers to pay on or ahead of schedule not only aids in reducing bad debt losses, but improves cash flow by keeping the amount of accounts receivable as low as possible.

While the following plan is generally workable for most small businesses, managers must remember that special cases call for individual handling. The type of business and type of customer will determine, in part, whether changes might be desirable in the following credit collection plan.

1. Issue an invoice or a charge slip at the time the order is filled. This document serves as a record and as a reminder to the customer that money is owed. Some businesses offer a cash discount, as described in Chapter 10, to encourage customers to pay quickly.
2. Mail a statement at the end of the month during which the sale was made or at the end of the cycle-billing period. By the end of this second step, most customers will have paid.
3. Mail a copy of the statement 15 days after the date the account should have been paid. A sticker, such as Sticker 1 shown on Illus. 16-8, is placed on the front of the statement.
4. Mail another copy of the statement within 30 days of the date that the amount should have been paid; use something similar to Sticker 2 in Illus. 16-8. Some businesses will continue to send copies of statements at 15-day intervals and add stickers, such as Stickers 3 and 4.
5. Make a telephone call to the customer if there is no response within 30 to 60 days after the account should have been paid. If the call does not bring results, send a letter to the customer stating that unless payment is received within the next 10 days, legal action will be taken.

ILLUS. 16-8
Collection stickers, which are placed on copies of monthly statements, can be purchased in office supply stores.

Sticker 1

Sticker 3

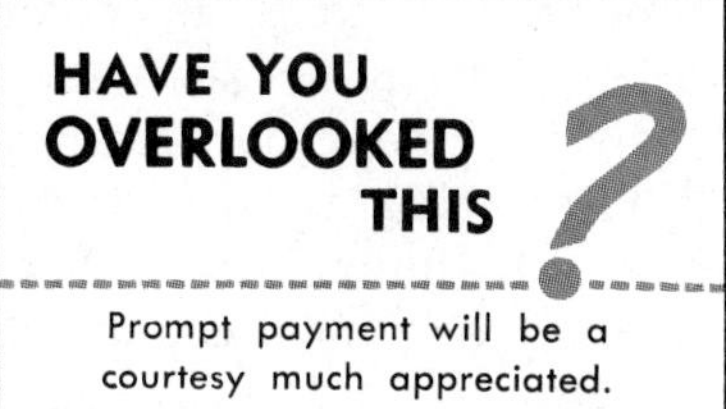

Sticker 2

Sticker 4

The collection steps for a large business are very much like those of a small business, except that large companies send a series of three to five letters to past due accounts rather than depending mostly on stickers. The tone of each letter is slightly stronger than the previous letter until an ultimatum is given in the last letter.

Final Collection Step. A credit manager must decide how to handle the last step in the collection process. One way is to have an attorney begin legal action to collect. Another alternative is to sell the account to a factoring company that buys overdue accounts. Factors, which were described in Chapter 14, often purchase accounts for less than half the amount of the account. Yet another choice the credit manager has is to hire a credit agency to collect the account. The credit agency charges a substantial fee for this service.

In a limited number of situations, the credit manager may decide to take no final collection action at all. This decision may be made when the cost to collect the overdue account is greater than the account balance or when the business is informed that the customer is financially unable to pay. In such situations the amount is written off as a loss. However, with installment credit plans, the last recourse is to repossess the merchandise.

These final collection steps are used as a last resort. The legal rights of the consumer must not be violated during the collection process. Because some collection agencies in the past used unfair methods to collect overdue accounts, the federal government passed the Fair Debt Collection Practices Act in 1977. Under this law, collection agencies cannot use abusive, deceptive, or unfair collection methods such as threatening to harm the reputation of the person, making late night phone calls, or telling the debtor's employer or friends about the overdue account. Under most state laws, if an account has not been paid within a specified number of years, collection is no longer legally possible.

ANALYZING CREDIT SALES

In every business it is important to watch accounts receivable (the debts or money owed to the business) in order that their total does not get out of proportion to the amount of credit sales. For example, if credit sales are not increasing but accounts receivable are gradually growing larger each month, an effort should be made to collect the accounts more efficiently.

The total accounts receivable may not show the true picture of conditions. For instance, an analysis of the accounts receivable record may show that most of the accounts receivable are only 30 or 60 days old, while only a few are 90 days old or older. The situation may, therefore, not be unusual. On the other hand, if an analysis of the accounts receivable record shows that most of the accounts receivable are 90 days old or older, it may prove necessary to have some of the customers sign notes, to place some accounts with a collection agency, to start lawsuits for collection of some accounts, and to strengthen and speed up the collection procedure so that accounts in the future will not become so old.

The most common method of studying accounts receivable is often referred to as **aging the accounts.** The form in Illus. 16-9 is an example of the type of analysis that can be used.

ILLUS. 16-9
An analysis of accounts receivable shows the status of each account.

ANALYSIS OF ACCOUNTS RECEIVABLE

DATE January 2, 19--

NAME AND ADDRESS	1 TO 30 DAYS	30 TO 60 DAYS	60 TO 90 DAYS	OVER 90 DAYS	TOTAL	EXPLANATION
Adams-Jones Company, Cincinnati, Ohio...	$235.00				$235.00	
Artwell Company, Chicago, Illinois..	$426.51				$426.51	
Brown and Brown, Gary, Indiana......	$ 52.50	$40.00	$27.41		$119.91	They wrote "will clear up account this month."
A. Davis, Inc. Detroit, Michigan..				$175.00	$175.00	Account in hands of attorney.
Custer Stores, Granville, Ohio....			$76.06		$ 76.06	Now on COD basis.

The amounts owed by the Adams-Jones Company and the Artwell Company have not been due 31 days. However, in the case of Brown and Brown, $27.41 has been due for more than 60 days but less than 90 days; an amount of $40 has been due for more than 30 days but less than 60 days; and an amount of $52.50 has been due less than 30 days. The amount due from A. Davis, Inc. has been due more than 90 days. The amount owed by Custer Stores has been due more than 60 days but less than 90 days.

A second method of analyzing accounts receivable is to determine what percentage of the accounts outstanding is collected each month. For example, if the total amount outstanding is $10,000 and collections are $8,000, 80 percent of the accounts receivable have been collected. Each business must decide for itself what percentage collected is acceptable.

A third method of measuring the efficiency of collections is to compute the percentage of delinquent accounts in relation to the total outstanding accounts. For example, if 10 percent of the accounts in January are delinquent, 15 percent are delinquent in February, and 20 percent are delinquent in March, this is an unfavorable trend.

A fourth method of determining the efficiency of collecting accounts is to compute the bad-debt losses. If a business had $200,000 in net sales and $4,000 of uncollectible accounts, then the bad-debt loss is 2 percent ($4,000 ÷ $200,000). Even though most bad-debt losses are generally less than 1 percent of net sales, a business must compare its loss rate with those of similar businesses. Industry averages are available from credit agencies such as Dun & Bradstreet, Inc.

By a careful analysis of credit sales, a business can learn which policies and procedures are most effective for increasing total sales and for keeping uncollectible account losses to a minimum, while increasing net profits.

NEW TERMS AND CONCEPTS

Define the following terms and concepts, which may be found in boldface type on the page shown in parentheses.

retail credit (304)
trade credit (304)
regular credit, or open account (305)
installment credit (305)
installment contract, or conditional sales contract (305)
title (305)
repossessed (305)
revolving credit, or optional credit (305)
layaway plan (307)
budget plan (307)
debit card (308)
character (309)
capacity (309)
cycle billing (315)
aging the accounts (319)

CHAPTER REVIEW

1. Which type of credit is a popular form of both retail and trade credit?
2. Installment credit is granted by retailers who sell which types of goods?
3. Which type of customer would use a layaway credit plan?
4. What is the major disadvantage of business credit cards to (a) retailers and (b) customers?
5. Give the names of the two most used bank credit card systems.
6. What kind of credit information is ranked first in importance by credit managers who extend trade and retail credit?
7. From what two sources do retailers obtain information about their credit customers?
8. How can a subscribing retail business benefit when its credit agency belongs to either the National Retail Credit Association or the Associated Credit Bureaus of America?
9. Under what condition could a senior citizen be denied credit solely on the basis of age?
10. Has the Truth-in-Lending Act had much of an impact on credit practices?
11. Name three decisions that a retail business will have to make related

to the establishment of credit policies.

12. What are the two major objectives of the person who is placed in charge of collection procedures?
13. List the five steps in a collection sequence.
14. List four ways the credit manager can handle the last step in the collection process.
15. What percentage of net sales is usually lost from uncollected debts?

QUESTIONS FOR CLASS DISCUSSION

1. How does installment credit differ from regular credit?
2. Discuss whether a budget plan is more like a revolving credit plan or a regular credit plan.
3. Why could it be better for a small retail store to use a bank credit card system for selling on credit than to establish its own business credit card system?
4. Discuss the importance of character, capital, and capacity in a decision to grant credit to a young person who has just graduated from college and who has just started a full-time job but has never had credit before.
5. If a large producer of stereo sets sold only to retail shops around the country, how could the producer check on the trade credit of each new credit applicant?
6. Under the requirements of the Truth-in-Lending Act, as shown in Illus. 16-5, discuss how it could be possible for a consumer to lose no money if a thief stole a credit card and bought merchandise with it.
7. Although the use of credit usually leads to increased sales for retailers, when could credit sales actually lead to decreased profits?
8. What would you do as a retail store owner if a customer paid very slowly and you found that the person's credit rating and credit reputation ranked very high?
9. Why would a business use a factoring company to collect an overdue account if the cost to collect is so high as to be prohibitive?
10. Both Business *A* and Business *B* have $10,000 in accounts receivable; yet *A* has more trouble than *B* in collecting accounts. Discuss how Business *A* can find out more about the nature of its overdue accounts in order to improve its condition.

PROBLEMS AND PROJECTS

1. Take a survey of three stores that offer credit and determine which of the following types of credit plans they offer customers: regular (or open), installment, revolving (or optional), layaway, or budget. Report on which type of plan is the most popular and which one is the least popular.

2. Obtain a copy of a revolving credit plan from a large department store and compare its terms with the revolving credit plan in Illus. 16-1. Make a report to your class on the terms that are the same or somewhat the same, and those that are different.
3. Talk to five people who carry credit cards. Make a list of the cards they have and indicate whether each card is (a) a bank credit card, (b) a bank debit card, (c) a retail department store card, (d) an oil company card, (e) a travel and entertainment card, or (f) any other type of card. Make a report of your findings.
4. Use the following information to prepare a credit report dated November 30 on the accounts receivable for a business that offers only 30-day open credit terms. The report should contain (a) an analysis of accounts receivable similar to the one shown in Illus. 16-9, and (b) the percentage of delinquent accounts in relation to the total outstanding accounts receivable.

   Sykes purchased $200 of goods on November 15.
   Sanford purchased $500 of goods on November 19.
   Jenkins purchased $700 of goods on November 12.
   Lancaster purchased $300 of goods on October 17.
   Godowski purchased $200 of goods on October 10.
   Tomaino purchased $100 of goods on September 25.

5. Assume that you have been hired as the credit and collection manager of the Midwest Wholesale Hardware Company. You have been hired because the former credit manager retired and the owners of the business have discovered that there are many overdue accounts due to a poor collection system. Prepare a detailed plan and schedule for the mailing of monthly statements and overdue collection notices. Indicate when the final collection step will be taken and how the final collection step will be handled.

CASE 16–1

Marla Benitez was just hired as credit manager for a new branch of a well-known department store that has an excellent reputation for selling top-quality merchandise. She was told to use a credit bureau to gather information about credit applicants as well as to obtain information from each customer through the store's standard credit application form. On her first day on the job, she received three applications for revolving credit plans on which decisions had to be made immediately. Here is a sketch of the main points about each person:

Jessica Abbot: Age 15; baby-sits evenings while going to high school; lives with her parents; no prior credit record.

George Lorenz: Age 40; employed as a lawyer for a large real estate firm; married and owns his own home; has credit with three other business firms and pays his bills on time.

Kurt Demarest: Age 66; retired early from his job as a dishwasher for a local restaurant because of a heart problem; married and rents an apartment; has credit with two other department stores; credit record is quite uneven, although he eventually pays his bills.

Required:

1. State whether you would grant credit to each person if you were Marla Benitez and give your reasons.
2. If one person had to be denied credit, which one would you select and why?
3. Should Marla Benitez consider the Equal Credit Opportunity Act when making her decisions to grant credit? Explain.

CASE 16–2

Toni, a recent college graduate, has just been promoted from her part-time clerk's position to work in the credit department of a popular fashion-oriented clothing store. Toni feels that even though most customers can pay for their merchandise immediately by cash or check, credit is very convenient. Toni's friend, Sandy, works in the collection department of the same store. He has been involved in collections for some years and believes that a fashionable store with well-to-do customers does not need credit. Further, too many of the store's customers are always late in paying bills. They never give a reason for being late other than the typical: "Oh, I just forgot."

Toni always purchases items over $50 on credit herself, and Sandy has never purchased anything on credit. In fact, he does not have a single credit card. Sandy and Toni usually avoid discussing credit, knowing they disagree. However, Sandy approached Toni one day and told her that her uncle was now 30 days late in paying his bill for an expensive suit. Toni, not being aware of the situation, was embarrassed and shocked.

"I am sure it was just an oversight," she said.

"Not so," said Sandy. "We have sent him two notices 15 days apart by certified mail. It is no oversight." Sandy could not resist adding, "Now, do you still believe credit is so great for everyone? If the well-to-do cannot pay on time, I bet half of the poor people are always in debt and unable to pay their bills. Credit should be outlawed. It encourages people to buy over their heads. Without credit, everyone would be better off. Stores would not have to worry about collecting debts, and customers would only buy what they need."

By now Toni was really angry. "And you and I would not have a job. Credit is good for the country and the people. Many customers would not shop here without credit. Furthermore, anyone who does not like credit does not have to use it. Did it ever occur to you that my Uncle Henry might be away on a month's ocean cruise?" With that, Toni left the room and slammed the door.

Required:

1. What are possible advantages to credit?
2. What are possible disadvantages to credit?
3. Do you agree with Toni or with Sandy? Explain.

Have You Thought About Becoming . . .

. . . A CREDIT MANAGER?

Because many individuals and organizations purchase on credit, the credit manager fills a vital role in business. Before credit is issued, someone must determine whether the credit applicant can and will pay when bills are due. The credit manager has the responsibility for determining whether an individual—or a business—is a good credit risk. Many skills are needed to make credit decisions that directly affect the success of any business.

Not only must credit managers excel in making decisions, but they must also excel in creating and applying credit policies and procedures. They need to know how to analyze credit reports and how to gather relevant information. Further, they must be able to collect from customers with overdue accounts by using good human relations skills. Good communication skills are especially valuable.

Because much knowledge is required of credit managers, a college education, or at least course work in business administration, is desired. Credit managers often work with higher level managers in establishing company-wide credit policies; therefore, they must be knowledgeable about sales, finance, and general business matters. Those without a college education may work in the credit office of a company by performing such specialized tasks as processing credit applications and gathering credit information for review by the credit manager.

Generally, special training is available from credit associations or colleges for those interested in advancement. Because of the important role played by credit managers, large companies may promote credit managers to higher level management positions. However, in small businesses, opportunities for advancement are limited.

There will always be a need for credit managers. But the number of positions available will not grow rapidly because of the extensive use of computer technology in processing credit information. Nevertheless, many jobs will become available each year to replace people who leave the occupation and to handle the expected increase in the numbers of people and businesses buying on credit.

17

BUSINESS RISKS AND INSURANCE

After studying this chapter you will be able to:

- Explain commonly used insurance terms and insurance contract clauses.
- List points to consider when selecting an insurance company, agent, and policy.
- Identify types of insurance of particular value to business owners.
- Discuss the types of risks that business firms face for which insurance cannot be purchased.

If you have $5 in your pocket, there is a risk that you might lose it. While you might not want to lose the money, its loss would not be a serious problem. However, if you own a $300 bicycle, you may not be able to afford to replace it if it is stolen. You may choose to buy insurance to protect against the larger loss.

Businesses are often faced with uncontrollable events that could result in financial loss. A fire could destroy buildings; burglars could steal property and money; a customer or employee could get hurt at the business and sue; the owner or manager could die. These events may never occur for a specific business. If they do, however, the loss could be so great that the business would fail.

To protect against the possibility of loss, a business can purchase insurance. Insurance enables a business to trade a large, but uncertain, loss for a smaller, affordable loss (the cost of the insurance).

INSURABLE LOSSES

Not every loss can or should be insured. Businesses will have some types of losses that will not be very costly even if they do occur. Those losses should not be insured. The business should purchase insurance on losses that would be difficult to overcome. Some types of losses can be expected in businesses on a somewhat regular basis and so insurance is not necessary. For example, most retailers know that a certain amount of shoplifting will occur. While they will attempt to reduce shoplifting, they will also recover some of the loss by marking up the prices on all products sold. Businesses can lose money if employees do not show up for work. Because it can be expected that some employees will be absent, businesses may have part-time workers available or actually hire more people than needed. This additional cost helps to reduce the larger loss that could occur if the business could not operate.

INSURANCE OPERATIONS

To understand a discussion of insurance operations, one must first become acquainted with common insurance terms. Those terms are defined in Illus. 17-1.

ILLUS. 17–1
Common insurance terms.

Insurer	A company that sells insurance.
Policyholder	The person or business purchasing insurance.
Policy	The written agreement, or contract, between the insurer and the policyholder.
Insured	The persons or organization covered by the insurance policy.
Peril	The cause of a loss for a person or organization. Common perils are fire, accidents, sickness, death, and theft.
Risk	The uncertainty that a loss may occur.
Premium	A payment by a policyholder to the insurer for protection against risk.

It would be difficult for one business to predict the probability that certain losses will occur or the amount of those losses. However, many businesses face the same types of perils. When many businesses are grouped together, the probability of a certain type of loss and the amount of the loss can be reasonably estimated. For example, it is easier to estimate the amount of fire damage to be suffered among 10,000 businesses during a year than to estimate the amount of loss that any one firm will have.

Insurance companies are formed to spread losses across many firms or people. They will only insure against losses that are reasonably predictable. Each policyholder pays a premium to the insurance company. By paying a premium, the policyholder is paying a smaller amount of money for protection against a possible large loss.

The funds collected from policyholders are used by the company in somewhat the same manner as deposits are used by banks. With the funds paid by policyholders, insurance companies make investments that earn an income. Insurance companies must, of course, keep a reasonable amount of cash available to pay the claims of policyholders. In order to make a profit, the insurance company must earn more from premiums and investments than is paid out in claims by policyholders.

Insurance Rates

An **insurance rate** is the amount charged for a certain value (such as $1,000) of insurance. Rates vary according to the risk that is involved. For instance, if a particular community has a large number of robberies, theft insurance rates are high in that community. If fire protection is poor, buildings are not fireproof, and fires are frequent in a certain community, the fire insurance rates are high in that community. Rates charged for insurance are based on the past experience of the insurance company with losses for the type of property that is to be insured. Therefore, the rates established for any particular year anticipate that the losses for that year will be essentially the same as those of previous years.

Rates for various kinds of insurance in each state are determined by the experiences of insurance companies. The same basic rates are usually charged by insurance companies for the same kinds of risks in the same locations within a state.

Regardless of the basic rates, the charge made to any policyholder may be lower or higher than the basic rate depending on certain circumstances. For example, a modern fireproof building that has an automatic sprinkler system and is located where there is good fire protection can be insured at a lower rate than a frame building that does not have a sprinkler system and is located where there is poor fire protection. In many states, automobile rates vary from the basic rate depending on whether the driver has a good or bad accident record, the age of the person who drives the car, and the make of the car.

Cancellation

The insurance policy contains information about how contracts may be terminated. Most property or liability insurance contracts may be canceled by the insurer or may not be renewed when they expire. If they are canceled, enough notice must be given to policyholders to allow them to find another insurer. Generally life insurance contracts may not be canceled by the insurer except for nonpayment of premiums.

Insurable Interest in Property

The policyholder must have an insurable interest in the property. An **insurable interest** is generally defined as the possible financial loss that the policyholder will suffer if the property is damaged or destroyed. A person who has purchased a piece of property but has not paid for it has an insurable interest. A person who uses a building as a warehouse has an insurable interest in the building, even though that person does not own the building. A person who has a mortgage on a piece of property has an insurable interest in the property. The interest in property to be insured must be specifically indicated in the policy.

Deductibles

Many insurance contracts include deductibles. Generally a **deductible** is an arrangement that permits the insured to bear part of the loss in return for a lower premium. Most deductibles are expressed as a dollar amount of any given loss that will not be covered by the insurer in the case of a loss. For example, if an insured driver has a $100 deductible collision insurance policy and a $500 loss occurs, the insurer pays $400 and the insured bears the $100 loss. If the loss is only $100, the insurer pays nothing.

Often it is worthwhile for the insured to include a higher deductible in the policy. For example, the premium for a $100 deductible collision insurance policy on your auto may be $250 a year; the premium for a $200 deductible policy may be $220. Having the $200 deductible policy saves you $30 a year. Of course, if there is a loss you must pay $200 of it rather than just $100. In general, if you typically can afford to pay the deductible amount if a loss occurs, you should include it in the insurance policy.

HOW TO BUY INSURANCE

Most insurance contracts are written by insurance agents. **Insurance agents** represent the insurance company and sell insurance to individuals and businesses. Some agents represent several different insurance companies and can provide many types of insurance for a business. Other agents represent only one company or may sell only one type of insurance, such as life or auto insurance.

In most communities there are reputable agents offering all types of insurance. There are often many differences in the policies and services offered by insurance companies and agents. A business person should discuss insurance needs with two or three insurance agents before selecting a company and the type and amount of insurance. Points to consider when choosing an insurance company and an agent are given in Illus. 17-2.

ILLUS. 17–2
Points to consider in selecting an insurance company and agent.

1. Can the company that the insurance agent represents furnish the right kind of insurance?
2. Does the insurance agent have a proper knowledge of insurance?
3. Are the policies understandable?
4. Are the company's rates reasonable?
5. What kind of service does the agent furnish?
6. What kind of reputation does the agent have for helping when losses occur?
7. What reputation does the company have for settling claims?
8. Can the company help in reducing risks?

In buying insurance the primary objectives are: (a) to get the proper coverage of risks, and (b) to make certain that the claim will be paid in the event of loss. For example, a person who needs fire insurance wants to be sure that the insurance company that issues the policy will make a fair adjustment promptly so that business activities will not be interrupted. A person who buys liability insurance wants to be sure that if a person is injured, the insurance company will determine the responsibility of the insured and make a fair settlement with the injured person.

A business person should consider the areas where major losses could occur when planning the purchase of insurance. Protection is needed for both property and people. The remainder of this chapter examines the major types of insurance as well as noninsurable risks.

PROPERTY INSURANCE

A business may obtain various types of insurance to fit its needs in protecting its property. The major types of property insurance which a business might have are: (1) fire insurance, (2) business interruption insurance, (3) transportation insurance, (4) automobile insurance, and (5) burglary and robbery insurance.

Fire Insurance

Fire insurance usually provides funds to replace such items as buildings, furniture, machinery, raw materials, and finished products destroyed by fire. Fire insurance on a building may not cover the equipment, machinery, and stock in the building. Separate policies may be required to

ILLUS. 17-3
A business should not underestimate the damage that can be caused by a fire.

give a business full protection from fire loss. The owner of a building should be interested in insurance to protect his or her investment. The occupant of a rented building should be interested in insurance to protect personal contents in the building. You should know exactly what is covered by the policy when buying fire insurance.

Features of Fire Insurance Policies. When business people buy fire insurance they should know what they are buying and how they will be protected. They should give careful consideration to the amount of protection, the kind of protection, and special clauses in the policy. Illus. 17-4 shows a typical insurance policy.

There is no advantage in a business firm being overinsured. Insurance companies will pay no more than the actual value of the loss even if more insurance is carried. However, a business must be careful that it carries enough insurance. The value of some property increases from year to year. When an insurance policy is renewed, it should be revised in amount so that it covers the real value of whatever is being insured. It is, therefore, important to check the policy carefully before it is renewed.

In every fire insurance policy the property that is covered should be clearly identified as to description and location. The property included in the policy and the property excluded should be clearly understood.

The standard insurance policy usually will not cover such items as accounts, bills, money, and notes. This fact emphasizes the need for

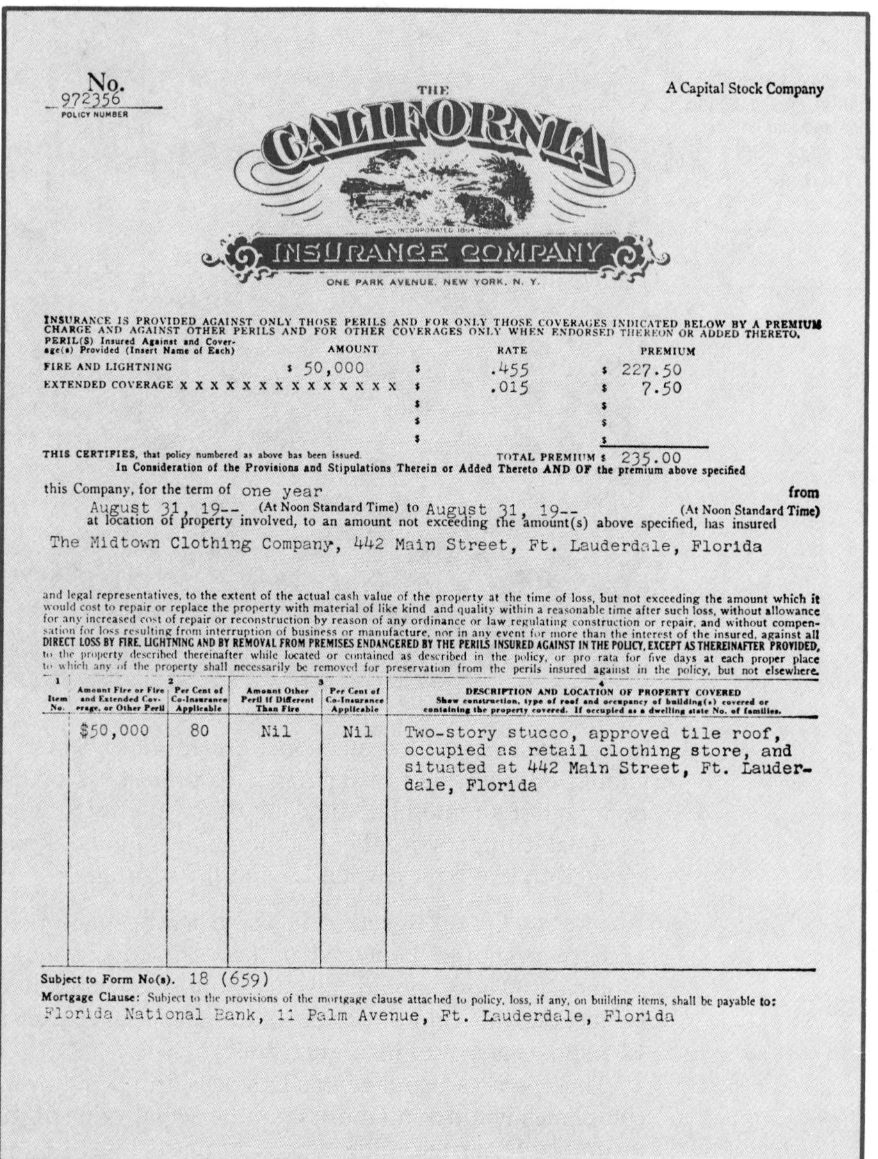

No. 972356
POLICY NUMBER

A Capital Stock Company

THE CALIFORNIA INSURANCE COMPANY

ONE PARK AVENUE, NEW YORK, N. Y.

INSURANCE IS PROVIDED AGAINST ONLY THOSE PERILS AND FOR ONLY THOSE COVERAGES INDICATED BELOW BY A PREMIUM CHARGE AND AGAINST OTHER PERILS AND FOR OTHER COVERAGES ONLY WHEN ENDORSED THEREON OR ADDED THERETO.

PERIL(S) Insured Against and Coverage(s) Provided (Insert Name of Each)	AMOUNT	RATE	PREMIUM
FIRE AND LIGHTNING	$ 50,000	$ .455	$ 227.50
EXTENDED COVERAGE X X X X X X X X X X X X X X		$ .015	$ 7.50
		$	$
		$	$
		$	$

THIS CERTIFIES, that policy numbered as above has been issued. TOTAL PREMIUM $ 235.00

In Consideration of the Provisions and Stipulations Therein or Added Thereto AND OF the premium above specified this Company, for the term of one year from August 31, 19-- (At Noon Standard Time) to August 31, 19-- (At Noon Standard Time) at location of property involved, to an amount not exceeding the amount(s) above specified, has insured

The Midtown Clothing Company, 442 Main Street, Ft. Lauderdale, Florida

and legal representatives, to the extent of the actual cash value of the property at the time of loss, but not exceeding the amount which it would cost to repair or replace the property with material of like kind and quality within a reasonable time after such loss, without allowance for any increased cost of repair or reconstruction by reason of any ordinance or law regulating construction or repair, and without compensation for loss resulting from interruption of business or manufacture, nor in any event for more than the interest of the insured, against all DIRECT LOSS BY FIRE, LIGHTNING AND BY REMOVAL FROM PREMISES ENDANGERED BY THE PERILS INSURED AGAINST IN THE POLICY, EXCEPT AS THEREINAFTER PROVIDED, to the property described thereinafter while located or contained as described in the policy, or pro rata for five days at each proper place to which any of the property shall necessarily be removed for preservation from the perils insured against in the policy, but not elsewhere.

Item No.	1 Amount Fire or Fire and Extended Coverage, or Other Peril	2 Per Cent of Co-Insurance Applicable	Amount Other Peril if Different Than Fire	3 Per Cent of Co-Insurance Applicable	4 DESCRIPTION AND LOCATION OF PROPERTY COVERED Show construction, type of roof and occupancy of building(s) covered or containing the property covered. If occupied as a dwelling state No. of families.
	$50,000	80	Nil	Nil	Two-story stucco, approved tile roof, occupied as retail clothing store, and situated at 442 Main Street, Ft. Lauderdale, Florida

Subject to Form No(s). 18 (659)

Mortgage Clause: Subject to the provisions of the mortgage clause attached to policy, loss, if any, on building items, shall be payable to:
Florida National Bank, 11 Palm Avenue, Ft. Lauderdale, Florida

ILLUS. 17-4
A fire insurance policy.

keeping such items in fireproof filing cabinets, safes, or banks, as discussed in Chapter 12. It is difficult to establish a value for most records if they are lost in a fire. Since records are not covered by an ordinary policy, extreme care should be exercised in protecting them. Even if such items are insured and their value is known, the difficulty of replacing them is a good reason for their protection. Special clauses in an insurance policy or special policies may protect the items mentioned. A reduced premium rate can be obtained on this type of insurance if the insured person or business agrees to keep records in a safe place.

Extended Coverage. Some basic fire insurance policies may be extended to cover additional risks such as wind, hail, explosion, aircraft or auto damage, and smoke damage. Additional protection beyond the major peril is called **extended coverage.** It is obtained by paying an additional premium and by adding a special clause to the contract.

Coinsurance Clauses. **Coinsurance** is a term applied to a fire insurance policy in which the insurer and the insured share the risks. Coinsurance clauses are included in policies to encourage business organizations to purchase an adequate amount of insurance. Seldom does a fire completely destroy a property. If business people decided that the average destruction to a building was 40 percent, they might choose to insure their properties for that amount rather than the full valuc of the property. Insurance companies would lose a great deal of premium income but would still have to pay the full amount of the policy. Insurance companies protect themselves by including coinsurance clauses which require the insured to buy insurance up to a certain portion of the total value of the property. If a business carries less insurance on the property and a loss occurs, the insured must bear a portion of the loss. Thus, coinsurance means that the insured must take some of the risk of loss from fire if it has failed to insure for the required amount.

Coinsurance clauses are normally written for 80 or 90 percent of the property value. For example, if the insured and the insurance company place a value of $50,000 on a building, under an 80 percent coinsurance clause the insured is required to carry at least $40,000 of insurance (80 percent of $50,000). If a loss occurs, the insured can recover any amount of the loss up to $40,000. However, if the insured carries only $30,000 of insurance, it can collect only 75 percent of any loss since it is carrying only 75 percent of the required $40,000 of insurance. Illus. 17-5 contains examples of how 80 percent coinsurance clauses operate.

Value of Property	Percentage Required by Policy	Amount Required by Policy	Actual Percentage Carried	Amount Carried	Loss	Amount Paid by Insurance Company	Loss Borne by Insured
$100,000	80	$80,000	90	$90,000	$90,000	$90,000	$ 0
100,000	80	80,000	80	80,000	80,000	80,000	0
100,000	80	80,000	80	80,000	50,000	50,000	0
100,000	80	80,000	80	80,000	90,000	80,000	10,000
100,000	80	80,000	60	60,000	60,000	45,000	15,000
100,000	80	80,000	60	60,000	90,000	60,000	30,000

ILLUS. 17-5

How 80 percent coinsurance clauses operate.

All examples of coinsurance can be determined by using one formula:

$$\frac{\text{Amount of insurance carried}}{\text{Amount of insurance required}} \times \text{Loss} =$$ Amount recoverable from the insurance company (may never exceed the value of the loss or the property).

It is important for the policyholder to reappraise the value of property from time to time. This ensures that the value carried on the insurance policy is enough to meet the coinsurance requirement.

Coverage for Large Fire Risks. In many communities it is impossible for any particular business to obtain all the insurance it desires through one insurance company. Insurance companies operating in high-risk areas will insure only a certain percentage of the value of the property in that area. There are two ways, however, in which a business may obtain complete coverage. One is for the business to obtain policies from two or more companies that together cover the entire value of the property. The other way is for the business to purchase complete coverage from one insurance company, which in turn will insure part of the value of the property with one or more other insurance companies. The practice of an insurance company selling part of a large risk to other insurance companies is known as **reinsurance.** This practice shows good management on the part of the insurance company because it distributes the large risk among a number of companies. Any particularly large loss might cause serious financial harm to a single company; but when it is distributed over several companies, it is not so significant. In other words, several insurance companies bear the loss instead of one company.

Business Interruption Insurance

Business interruption insurance (formerly called use and occupancy insurance) is designed to compensate firms for loss of income during the time required to restore property damaged by an insured peril. For instance, after a fire in an office, a factory, or a store, the business suffers an additional loss because it cannot carry on its operations in the normal manner. Some of its expenses continue in spite of the fire. These are such expenses as interest on notes, taxes, rent, certain insurance, advertising, telephone service, and some salaries. The business may lose not only the normal income from sales but also could lose its customers, who may go to other sources and never come back. On the other hand, during the period that the business is shut down because of the fire, it may save the salaries of certain employees and a few other miscellaneous expenses.

In determining the amount of business interruption insurance to carry, the business person should consult an insurance agent. It is advisable to prepare a list of items that are customarily considered fixed charges and to make an estimate of the firm's normal profit, based on past experience and future expectations. When such an estimate has been made, a record should be kept of the method of computing the estimate so that these figures can be submitted in justifying a claim if a loss occurs.

Transportation Insurance

Protection against damage, theft, or complete loss of goods while they are being shipped is obtained by purchasing **transportation insurance.** While the transportation company may be responsible for many losses during the shipment of goods, some losses may be the responsibility of the seller or buyer. The owner of the goods may purchase insurance, or the company that transports them may provide it as a part of the cost of transportation. Most transportation companies insure all of their shipments through an insurance company. However, they may choose to assume risks themselves and pay for any losses rather than to carry insurance. Any time products are shipped, businesses should understand if insurance is provided for the goods and who is paying the cost of the insurance.

Automobile Insurance

An individual or business may purchase several different kinds of automobile insurance for protection against such losses as theft, property damage, or personal injury. Several parts of a typical automobile insurance policy are described next.

Collision Insurance. **Collision insurance** provides protection against damage to one's own car when it is in a collision with another car or object. This type of insurance is costly because of the number of accidents and the high cost of repairs. A way to reduce the cost of collision insurance is to buy it with as large a deductible as possible (described earlier in the chapter). For example, a policy with a $100 deductible clause means that the owner of the insured car must pay all losses up to $100. The insurance company will then pay on losses above $100. By increasing the deductible portion to $200 or more, an individual or business can get an even lower premium. For businesses insuring a fleet of cars, higher deductibles can result in considerable savings.

Comprehensive Coverage. Most basic automobile insurance policies include a coverage called **comprehensive insurance.** Insurance paid for under this clause usually includes loss caused by flying objects (but not collision), fire, theft, explosion, windstorm, hail, water, and vandalism.

In the case of insurance covering fire and theft, the most common practice is to issue policies which state that the insurance company will pay the market value of the automobile at the time of the loss. For instance, a new car may be insured on January 1 for its actual value, or cost, of $9,200. If it is stolen six months later, the amount that the insurance company is

ILLUS. 17-6

How many risks can you identify in this photo? Are they insurable?

obligated to pay is only the market value of a used car of that particular age and model. That amount will be somewhat less than $9,200. Most policies are worded in such a manner that if the automobile is destroyed, the insurance company will only pay the market value at the time of the loss. When there is only a partial loss, the insurance company pays for the amount of repairs.

Liability Insurance. **Liability insurance** provides coverage for the costs of injury to other people in an accident that was the fault of the insured. **Automobile liability insurance** is a specific type of liability insurance that provides protection against damage caused by the insured's automobile to other people or their property.

Property damage insurance and bodily injury insurance are usually sold together in the same policy. They are both important because the risks are unknown and the claims for damages may be very extensive.

The liability insurance section of a policy will state the maximum amount of damage that will be paid in case of an accident. Most states have a minimum amount of liability insurance that must be carried. For example, one state requires $10,000 of property damage insurance, $25,000 of bodily injury insurance if one person is injured, and $50,000 of bodily injury insurance if more than one person is injured. Often, the amount of insurance carried is much higher than the minimum required amounts. Liability claims against companies and individuals can amount to large sums of money.

Medical Payments Insurance. For an extra fee, a clause can be inserted into an automobile insurance policy which will cover the medical, surgical, hospital, and nursing expenses caused by accidental injuries to any occupant of the automobile, including the insured. These payments will be made regardless of the legal liability of the policyholder. This type of insurance is called **medical payments insurance.**

No-Fault Insurance. Normally the insurance company of the person responsible for an accident must pay the costs of damages. However, some states have passed no-fault insurance laws. Under **no-fault insurance,** each insurance company is required to pay the losses of its insured when an accident occurs regardless of who might have been responsible for the accident. The laws governing such policies vary in different states. No-fault insurance was developed to eliminate the need for the victim to have a costly lawsuit or a long-delayed trial to recover for losses suffered in an automobile accident. The intent of no-fault insurance is to reduce the costs of automobile insurance.

Burglary and Robbery Insurance

Burglary and robbery insurance provides protection from loss due to robbery of money, goods, and various other business assets. Because of the differences in types of businesses and methods of operating them, the risks vary considerably as do premium rates. Burglary and robbery insurance does not cover losses of goods taken by employees or merchandise that is shoplifted. Separate insurance is available to cover these losses, but it is often very expensive. Businesses are taking special security efforts to prevent these types of losses from occurring.

INSURING PEOPLE

Many business risks involve people. People can do things that damage a business, and people can be injured by a business. Many types of insurance are available to protect businesses from risks involving people. They are discussed next.

Fidelity Bonds

Fidelity bonds are often used by businesses to protect against losses caused by the dishonesty of employees or other people representing the business. For instance, when a person employed by a bank is required to handle money, that employee must be bonded. Then, if the employee steals money from the bank, the bonding company must pay the loss if the employee is not able to return the money. Bonds on individuals are issued only after a careful review of the employee's background. The rate of the bond is dependent upon the risk involved. For instance, the bond required for a person handling a small amount of money will not be very large, and the rates will probably be reasonably low. On the other hand, if the person handles a large amount of money, the bond will probably be rather large and the rate will be high.

Performance or Surety Bonds

Performance bonds, or **surety bonds,** protect against losses that could occur if a contract is not completed as agreed upon. For instance, if a contract is signed to construct a building, it may be necessary for the contractor to furnish a bond. If the contract is not carried out according to its terms, the company that issued the bond must pay damages to the business for whom the building was being constructed.

Liability Insurance

Personal liability insurance covers claims for damages resulting from injuries to customers or employees. A person may receive injuries from slipping on a floor or on ice, falling down steps, or any other kind of accident in or around the business. Failure of a business to recognize the possibility of these types of claims can be a very serious error in business management. One large liability judgment by a court can easily cause the failure of a business. Judgments running into hundreds of thousands of dollars are common.

Another type of liability can be from injuries to customers caused by the products of a business. For instance, the dye in some clothing may cause a skin infection; spoiled food may cause illness; defective machines may

ILLUS. 17-7

Many products contain a warning label to protect the manufacturer and the customer.

cause injury. Insurance covering such claims is known as **product liability insurance.** Businesses should test products to make sure they are safe. Even though businesses believe they are selling safe products, they usually have product liability insurance.

Life Insurance on Owners or Executives

Life insurance plays an important function in business. In the case of a sole proprietorship, the owner will usually find it easier to borrow money if adequate life insurance is carried. An owner may carry life insurance so that in the event of death the proceeds from the insurance will pay any debts of the business, thereby permitting the business to be turned over free of debt to the owner's family. Some sole proprietorships are so dependent on the owner of the business that when he or she dies, it is difficult for the business to continue successfully. If the owner provides proper insurance, funds will be available to carry on the business until it can be sold or until someone can be found to manage it.

Life insurance has an especially important place in partnerships. Generally a partnership is dissolved at the death of one partner. Usually each partner carries life insurance on the other partner so that when one partner dies the other will receive, as beneficiary of the insurance policy, sufficient money to buy the share of the partnership owned by the deceased partner.

Important executives of corporations are also usually insured. The theory behind this plan is that if a key executive dies, the progress of the corporation may be damaged; but the proceeds from the insurance will help the corporation make any adjustments that are necessary until a new executive can be found.

In a small corporation owned by just a few stockholders, there is also a practice of stockholders carrying insurance on each other so that if one stockholder dies it is possible for the remaining stockholders to purchase the stock of the deceased stockholder and maintain ownership of the business within the small group.

Insurance for Employees

Group insurance (usually life or health insurance for the members of an organization) is provided as an employee benefit by many businesses. The business and the employees may share in the payment of the premiums. Under this plan, insurance is provided for many employees who could not individually obtain insurance because of their health, or pay for the insurance because of its cost. Usually no medical examination is required and the insurance is usually available at a lower rate than employees could buy it individually. Most employers are required by law to carry workers' compensation insurance to cover accidents or illness caused by the work.

Most employers and employees are also taxed by the federal government to provide social security in the forms of pensions, unemployment compensation, and medical care. These kinds of protection are discussed in Chapter 22.

SPECIAL TYPES OF INSURANCE

In addition to the types of insurance already discussed, a business may sometimes need certain special types of insurance; the special insurance is based on specific business activities. Some of the more common types include credit insurance, credit life insurance, forgery insurance, and title insurance.

Credit Insurance

A company may purchase **credit insurance** to protect itself against losses on credit that is extended to customers. If the business cannot collect an amount due, the insurance company will pay the loss. However, the insurance company still has the right to try to collect from the customer.

Credit Life Insurance

Credit insurance should not be confused with credit life insurance. **Credit life insurance** is used by small loan companies, banks, and dealers who provide installment credit loans. The borrower or installment purchaser must buy sufficient life insurance to pay the balance of his or her debt in the event of death.

Forgery Insurance

Forgery insurance may be obtained by business people, individuals, banks, and other institutions to provide protection against loss caused by forged or altered checks and securities. Losses may occur as a result of a person altering a signature, altering an amount on a check, or the wrong person cashing a check. Business people are constantly exposed to these risks. Any business that regularly cashes a number of checks should carry this kind of insurance for protection from loss.

Title Insurance

When land or buildings are purchased, they may have been owned by several other persons or businesses in the past. **Title insurance** is purchased to protect against losses that could occur if title to the property had not been legally transferred sometime in the past. A company could suffer a large loss if it were forced, because of a problem with the title, to give up buildings or land it had purchased. While title insurance will not guarantee that the company can keep the property, the insurance company must pay for the losses that result from giving up the property.

NONINSURABLE RISKS

Businesses are also concerned with certain special types of risks for which there is no insurance. For instance, anyone who has operated a business has discovered that the needs and wants of people change. These changes cause serious business risks. Products are produced in anticipation of their sale. If the needs and wants of consumers change, however, the business is likely to suffer a loss on unsold goods.

Fashions, particularly in clothing, change frequently. Consequently, clothing manufacturers and retailers are sometimes overstocked at a time when styles change or customers look for new fashions. A company that is stocked with old merchandise, therefore, suffers a loss and probably has to sell the goods at a low price. A company should be careful to avoid overstocking.

Old equipment and lighting can also cause customers to avoid a business. A store with a modern interior and new lighting may attract customers away from an old, established store. Improved methods of transportation may give one type of business an advantage over another. For instance, private parcel services have injured the parcel business of the post office. Change is a constant factor in business.

ILLUS. 17-8
Builders cannot insure against a slump in the sales of new homes.

Changes in the weather can cause serious business risks. For example, a long winter season may prevent manufacturers and retailers from selling spring clothing. A rainy summer may slow the business of resorts if people stay at home. A lack of snow may reduce sales of skis and snowmobiles.

Changes in economic conditions present another serious risk. Increased unemployment rates cause people to be more careful when spending their money. This risk can be overcome to some extent by studying business forecasts and by planning carefully in anticipation of changes in the economy. Therefore, a knowledge of economics and business trends is valuable to business people.

Within any business community there are numerous local risks, such as the relocation of highways, which may cause customers to change their shopping behavior. The development of new highways may take customers to larger communities to do their shopping; street improvements may make one location better than another and, therefore, draw customers away from an old location; street repairs or the establishment of no-parking zones may have a bad effect on certain types of businesses; population changes and shifts in a community may make it necessary to move business firms. Against these and similar risks there is no insurance. Unless business people recognize trends and take action, they may find their businesses totally or partially destroyed. Noninsurable risks pose a great challenge to business managers.

NEW TERMS AND CONCEPTS

Define the following terms and concepts, which may be found on the pages shown in parentheses.

insurer (327)
policyholder (327)
policy (327)
insured (327)
peril (327)
risk (327)
premium (327)
insurance rate (328)
insurable interest (329)
deductible (329)
insurance agents (329)
fire insurance (330)
extended coverage (333)
coinsurance (333)
reinsurance (334)
business interruption insurance (334)
transportation insurance (335)
collision insurance (335)
comprehensive insurance (335)
liability insurance (336)
automobile liability insurance (336)
medical payments insurance (337)
no-fault insurance (337)
burglary and robbery insurance (337)
fidelity bonds (337)
performance bonds, or surety bonds (338)
personal liability insurance (338)
product liability insurance (339)
credit insurance (340)
credit life insurance (340)
forgery insurance (340)
title insurance (340)

CHAPTER REVIEW

1. How are insurance rates established?
2. Describe what may be considered an insurable interest in property.
3. Name five losses that can be covered by insurance.
4. Does a fire insurance policy on a building usually cover the equipment, the machinery, and stock in the building?
5. Is there any advantage in carrying fire insurance for a greater amount than the actual value of property?
6. Under a fire insurance policy with a coinsurance clause, why are the rates per thousand dollars of insurance lower than they are under an ordinary fire insurance policy?
7. If you carry collision insurance on an automobile, what kind of protection is provided?
8. Under an automobile insurance policy, on what basis is the value of the car determined when the insurance company pays for the loss?
9. Why is bodily injury insurance important?
10. In what way can a business obtain protection against possible loss due to theft by an employee?
11. How does a performance bond provide protection on a contract?
12. What types of losses are covered by product liability insurance?
13. What is the main reason that group insurance is so important to many people?
14. Name some business risks for which it is impossible to buy insurance protection.
15. How can businesses protect themselves against noninsurable risks?

QUESTIONS FOR CLASS DISCUSSION

1. A manufacturing plant is located in a very modern fireproof building, but there is poor local fire protection. How will the fire insurance rates be affected?
2. How does the nature of the product being manufactured in a factory determine fire insurance rates?
3. Does a person who rents a building have an insurable interest in the building?
4. What would be your opinion of a fire insurance company that would insist that you correct certain defects in your building before insuring the building for you?
5. Is it possible to carry too much insurance? Explain.
6. Why is business interruption insurance so important to some companies?
7. Many large corporations operating large fleets of cars driven by sales representatives do not carry collision insurance but

maintain their own auto repair business. Why do these corporations believe that collision insurance is not a good value?

8. Assume that you are able to make what appears to be a very favorable contract with a new construction company. The contractor does not have much money with which to operate and asks that you pay part of the cost of the construction in advance. Explain how you can protect yourself if the contractor does not perform the work.
9. If you operate a store, what are some of the possible claims for damages that might be brought by your customers?
10. Why is it important for companies offering credit on large purchases to ask customers to purchase credit life insurance?

PROBLEMS AND PROJECTS

1. From the information in the following table indicate for each of the examples A, B, C, and D how much of the loss will be paid by the insurance company.

Example	Value of Property	Coinsurance Clause	Amount of Policy	Amount of Loss
A	$100,000	80%	$80,000	$80,000
B	40,000	80%	25,000	30,000
C	60,000	80%	48,000	30,000
D	20,000	80%	16,000	5,000

2. A business has fire insurance policies on its building as follows: Insurance Company A, $50,000; Insurance Company B, $30,000; Insurance Company C, $20,000. There are no deductibles. If there is a fire loss of $96,000 how much will each company pay?
3. Obtain an automobile insurance policy and make a report on the different kinds of losses covered by the policy, the obligations of the policyholder, and the kinds of liabilities or losses that are not covered.
4. Determine the minimum amount of automobile insurance coverage required by your state for (a) property damage and (b) medical payments.
5. Using either library research or an interview with an insurance agent, prepare a report on no-fault automobile insurance.

CASE 17–1

Carl and Judy Lockhart are making final plans to open a small antique shop. Most of their capital is tied up in inventory, display equipment, advertising, and a six-month advance payment on the rental of the store building. They plan to operate the shop themselves and thus, save the cost of employees. Judy has suggested that they consider buying a few insurance policies to protect themselves from various risks. Carl believes that, because their capital is so limited, they can do without insurance. "After all," he reasons, "we are renting the building so we do not need fire insurance on it or on our inventory. If there is a fire, the landlord's policy will cover us. And we do not have any employees, so why should we waste money on unnecessary insurance?"

Required:

1. If the landlord has a standard basic insurance policy, is it likely that the inventory will be covered in case of fire loss? Explain.
2. What minimum types of insurance policies should the Lockharts seriously consider? Give reasons for your answers.

CASE 17–2

Jorden Grover purchased a delivery truck two years ago that cost $9,500. Its present value is $7,800. He purchased an auto insurance policy from the Justright Insurance Company. Coverage included comprehensive insurance, $250 deductible collision insurance, $25,000 of property damage insurance, and $10,000/$20,000 of bodily injury insurance.

Jorden was involved in an accident in which he was at fault. As a result of the accident, the delivery van had $1,500 damage and the other driver's car received $3,000 damage. Jorden had $500 of medical bills. The driver of the other car was more seriously injured and had $12,000 of medical bills.

Required:

1. Determine how much the Justright Insurance Company would pay as a result of the accident for:
   a. comprehensive insurance
   b. collision insurance
   c. property damage
   d. medical payments
2. Would Jorden be responsible for paying any damages resulting from the accident? If so, how much?
3. If Jorden lived in a state with no-fault insurance, how much would the Justright Insurance Company pay?

Have You Thought About Becoming . . .

. . . AN ACTUARY?

Do you know how many houses in a city of 100,000 people are likely to burn during the year? What are the chances that a 30-year-old person will live to be 80 years old? These are the types of questions that actuaries must be able to answer.

Actuaries are responsible for determining the rates charged by insurance companies. Insurance companies must know how much to charge for each insurance policy in order to collect enough money to pay for all claims and to give the company a reasonable profit.

Actuaries are very skilled in mathematics. They must predict how many policyholders are likely to have claims during a certain period of time. They must also estimate how much it will cost the insurance company to pay for the losses of the policyholders.

Actuaries work for insurance companies, professional insurance associations, and state and federal governments. Actuaries need a good education. You will need at least a bachelor's degree in mathematics. The Society of Actuaries has developed a series of tests that must be passed before you can get a job with most insurance companies. Courses that prepare you for actuarial work include probability, calculus, statistics, and analysis. You will want to take several business courses as well, such as accounting, finance, and insurance.

UNIT 5

Communications

Phone calls, letters, memos, reports . . . words, words, words. Business hums each day putting facts and ideas into some form that can be used by others. The information is spoken, written, and graphically displayed. Computers help in gobbling up, sorting, storing, and sending vast amounts of information to those who need it. This world of words is wrapped up in one word—communications.

In Unit 5, the process of communication is presented along with suggestions for communicating clearly and effectively. Successful methods and techniques for communication are also included. In addition, computerized data and word processing systems, which assist in the handling and communicating of data, are presented.

Automating office operations has greatly influenced how companies communicate. Amy D. Wohl is one expert who is able to give advice on how to automate the office for improving output through effective electronic means. Her biographical profile appears on the next page.

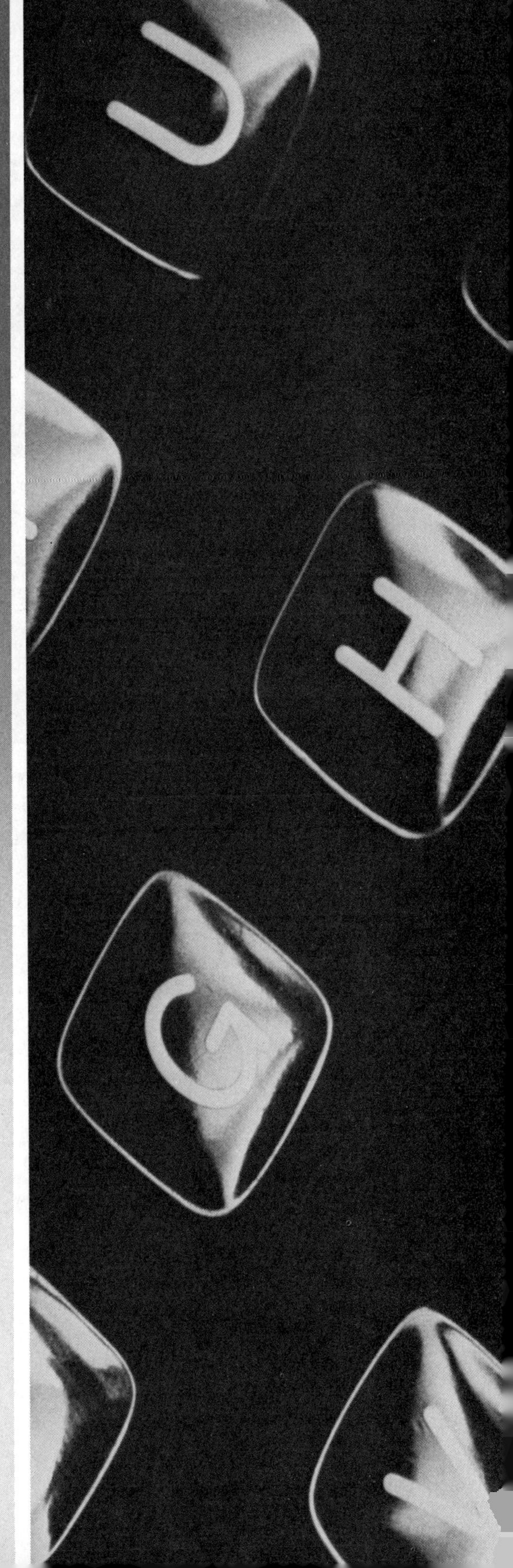

AMY D. WOHL

How will we communicate in the electronic office of the future? Will computer-like equipment replace office personnel? What will the modern office look like ten years from now? These are the kinds of questions Amy D. Wohl is asked nearly every day in her role as an office automation consultant. She is president of Advanced Office Concepts Corporation, a firm she started in the suburbs of Philadelphia a few years ago.

In her consulting business, most of her time is devoted to advising executives on how to automate office operations. As a nationally recognized leader, she is frequently asked to speak at business meetings and at national conventions of office management and computer associations. Ms. Wohl has also served in various leadership roles in many office automation organizations such as the International Word/Information Processing Association and the Office Systems Research Association.

Amy Wohl's interest in the field of office automation grew, in part, out of her interest in writing about analytical topics. Her undergraduate and graduate degrees were in economics, where she used computers to prepare college term papers. Prior to forming her own company, she gained valuable experience by managing four monthly technical newsletters and a complicated reference service for the Office Systems Groups of Datapro Research Corporation.

Ms. Wohl's finely tuned communication skills enable her to write and discuss reports dealing with ways clients might improve productivity through office automation. In addition, she is editor and publisher of her own "Advanced Office Concepts" newsletter, a contributing editor to *Datamation* magazine, and an editorial adviser of *Output* magazine. No wonder she can chat for hours about the office of today and the potential paperless, pencil-less office of the future.

18

BUSINESS COMMUNICATIONS

After studying this chapter you will be able to:

- Describe the communication process.
- Identify barriers to good communications.
- List basic guides for improving communications.
- Compare various types of communication channels.
- Discuss how the use of committees and the brainstorming technique can help solve business problems.

Joan sat at her desk in a busy office preparing a memo to go along with the monthly sales report she was completing. While she was in the middle of a sentence, Steve waved as he moved from his desk to the supervisor's office for a ten o'clock meeting. As Joan waved and smiled in return, the phone rang. After a short conversation, she jotted a message and placed it on Sara's nearby desk. No sooner had she returned to her memo, when the day's mail was dropped on her desk. She read some of the incoming letters and muttered, "Here are more letters that must be answered at once, and my memo and report have to be in the sales manager's hands by noon tomorrow."

This type of office scene is common. During these few minutes, Joan's entire time was spent communicating. She spoke on the phone and she listened; she wrote a message and delivered it; someone waved to her and she waved back. She read some of the incoming mail, and worked on writing a memo and a report. The kinds of communications differed, but each contributed in some way to the successful operation of the business.

Communications are vital in operating any business or organization. Communication provides a link between employees and customers, between employees and employers, and between employees and other employees. People working in business spend a major portion of each day communicating by speaking, listening, writing, and reading. It has been estimated that executives spend as much as two thirds of each work day communicating. The time spent communicating during a regular working day for such executives is shown in Illus. 18-1.

ILLUS. 18–1
Much of an executive's time is spent communicating, especially listening and speaking.

How Executives Communicate

	Hours
Listening—to employees, suppliers, customers, community people	2½
Speaking—to employees, suppliers, customers, community people	1½
Reading—letters, reports, memos, business publications	1
Writing—letters, reports, memos, speeches	½
Other activities	2½
Total Time	8 hours

In this chapter you will learn about the process of communication. You will also find out why messages oftentimes are misunderstood and what can be done to improve the communication process. Some basic guides are provided, which will help to improve your communication skills. In addition, you will discover that the method for delivering a message must be carefully selected because it too affects communications.

THE PROCESS OF COMMUNICATING

There are many definitions for communications. One meaning, for example, states that communications is the sending of information, but such a meaning is limited and gives little consideration to the person receiving the information. In this chapter, therefore, **communications** means the sharing of information or an idea which results in a high degree of understanding between the sender and the receiver of a message. This meaning includes more than the passing along of factual data; it includes the sharing of ideas, beliefs, and opinions. The meaning further suggests that communications must involve more than one person; it is a *two-way process* between the sender and the receiver.

Communications is referred to as a process because it involves a sender who has information or an idea that must be put into words, and a receiver who must see, hear, or read it. The process of communicating involves symbols as well as words. **Symbols** include figures, marks, signs, and other ways to communicate. The receiver must interpret the words or symbols used by the sender in order to understand the message. If the receiver does not fully understand the message or if more information is needed, the receiver may request more information or clarification. Illus. 18-2 shows the communication process in simple form.

ILLUS. 18-2
The communication process involves a sender, a message, and a receiver.

CAUSES OF COMMUNICATION BREAKDOWNS

The communication process seems rather simple, yet there are many obstacles in getting the desired message from the sender to the receiver. The use of a wrong word or the faulty delivery of a message can cause messages to be misunderstood, delayed, or lost. Some of the main causes of communication breakdowns include incorrect words, distractions, and distortions.

Incorrect Words

A message must be expressed correctly for it to be received and understood correctly. When we speak or write, we select words and sentences to express our thoughts. One of the main causes of communication breakdowns occurs when we do a poor job of selecting the words and putting them into sentences. The receiver can get the wrong message when the words used are wrong. If a message is clear and complete, breakdowns in communication are reduced or eliminated. All too often, however, the intended message is misunderstood because the words used by the sender did not correctly express the message intended. To further complicate matters many words have several meanings, and the sender can never be perfectly certain that the receiver will apply the intended meaning.

Whenever possible the sender of a message should use specific, or concrete, words rather than vague, general words. For example, the italicized statements in the first column on page 352 are general and should be avoided, whereas the italicized statements on the right are preferred because they are specific.

General	Specific
Sales increased *a little.*	Sales increased by *10 percent.*
Many people attended the meeting.	*Five hundred* people attended the meeting.
A *small* shipment came in today.	Only *thirty* items arrived today.

Effective speakers and writers carefully select the best combination of words to express ideas. They know that proper word selection is an important key to eliminating one of the communication barriers.

Distractions

Interruptions occur all too often during the communication process. Anything that interferes with the sender creating and delivering a message and the receiver getting and interpreting a message is a **distraction.** Distractions are potential causes of communication breakdowns.

Communications can break down in various ways through distractions. When an individual is writing a letter, for example, a ringing telephone or an unexpected visitor to the office may affect the message. The receiver will be confused and may be required to request the missing information. Because distractions can affect messages, some managers learn to work with various interruptions while others try to keep interruptions to a

ILLUS. 18-3
Noise and distractions often cause breakdowns in communications.

minimum. For example, some managers place telephone calls or write messages during specific times of the day when interruptions are less likely to occur. Receivers as well as senders of messages are affected by distractions. Receiving a message at an inconvenient time affects the attention or action the receiver gives to that message. Startling news, such as an announcement of a promotion, affects how other messages are received.

The physical elements of messages may also affect the receiver. A poor connection during a telephone call, a badly typed letter, and poor grammar are all examples of distractions. A misspelled word, for instance, can distract the receiver's attention and affect the intended message. Messages that are well prepared, well written, and attractively presented reduce breakdowns and promote understanding.

Distortions

When messages are created, the sender must select the information to be included in each message. For efficiency in communicating, it is usually not necessary or desirable to provide the receiver with every bit of information surrounding an idea, an event, or a situation. The sender attempts to select only that information that the reader needs in order to understand the desired message. Depending upon what information is selected, though, the message can become distorted. **Distortion** refers to how people consciously or unconsciously change messages. The information that is selected is especially influenced by (a) the personal background of the sender, and (b) the sender's purpose or goal for the message.

Sender's Background. Information or ideas to be communicated can be influenced to a great extent by one's background. A person's background is the sum of the individual's personality, education, experience, and friends. If, for example, two employees see a shoplifter steal merchandise, their reports to the store manager will probably vary. The background of each employee will influence what is reported. For example, one employee may say, "I know the person wore a blue jacket because my friend has one just like it." The other may add, "The person had to be a man because he was six feet tall." Although both employees saw the same incident, each reported different facts and observations.

Sender's Purpose or Goal. Everyone who communicates has a goal, and the goal is often based on the relationship between the sender and the receiver. One is likely to communicate more detailed information to a close friend than to a stranger. An employee is likely to discuss a job-related problem one way with a co-worker but another way with a supervisor. In some cases, the goal of the sender may be self-enhancement or self-protection. In either case, information selected for the message is likely to be distorted.

Problems at the lower organizational level of a business that are communicated to a higher level are subject to distortion. Assume that a group of workers became upset about a particular situation and, as a group, agreed to work at half speed if the problem was not corrected by the end of the month. One worker, a friend of the supervisor, was selected to deliver the message. The worker said to the supervisor, "The group will take serious action if the situation is not soon corrected." The worker distorted the message somewhat in order to protect the existing friendly relationship with the supervisor.

The supervisor realized that the problem was of a sufficiently serious nature that it had to be reported to a higher level manager. The supervisor distorted the message by reporting as follows: "A minor problem is upsetting the workers, but it does not appear to be overly serious." The problem was then reported to the president of the company and again the message was distorted. By the time the message reached the president, the problem no longer appeared serious; and the president may have wondered why the situation was even mentioned. But, having experienced previous distortions, the president investigated. By so doing, the president recognized the seriousness of the situation, and corrected the problem.

Although most messages are distorted somewhat, serious problems are not likely to arise from minor distortions. However, managers must be alert to conditions that give rise to serious distortions. Knowing the people with whom one works and understanding the nature of the problems that arise help to control distortion as a communication barrier.

GUIDES TO IMPROVING COMMUNICATIONS

One can learn to be a good communicator. Books have been written on how to write and speak effectively, and communication courses are available at schools. You will be able to improve your communication effectiveness by following a few basic guides.

Plan the Message

One of the easiest ways to improve communications is to think through an idea before saying or writing it. When this step is omitted, a slightly different message from the one intended is often delivered. The planning phase of communicating requires that the message sender first clarify ideas. To clarify ideas it is desirable to make certain that each message (a) has a specific purpose, (b) provides all needed information, and (c) is organized in a logical way. If these steps are followed, messages are likely to be clear and specific rather than vague and confusing.

Keep the Message Receiver in Mind

Ineffective messages are all too often *I*-centered rather than *you*-centered. An **I-centered message** is a message that focuses on the sender, whereas a **you-centered message** focuses on the receiver. The *I*-centered message may read, "I shipped the goods today and I think you will have them by Friday"; whereas the *you*-centered message may read, "Your goods were shipped today and you should have them by Friday, in time for your special weekend sale." Effective communicators try to understand the receiver in terms of background, interests, needs, and problems. In this way, messages can be created that are more likely to be tailored to fit the receiver.

Use the *C's* of Communications

Whether written or spoken, a message must have certain basic elements to be effective. These elements, often called the **C's of Communications,** are as follows:

1. ***Correctness.*** Check carefully all facts and figures before delivering a message.
2. ***Completeness.*** Give the receiver all required information to avoid delays or confusion.
3. ***Conciseness.*** Keep each message as short as possible by omitting unnecessary details.
4. ***Clearness.*** Word each message as clearly as possible to avoid being misunderstood.
5. ***Courtesy.*** Build or retain goodwill by treating the receiver with courtesy and respect.

All five elements should be included in every message, whether written or spoken. Messages that contain all five elements will go a long way toward improving the communications process and reducing communication breakdowns.

Use Psychology When Communicating

To create effective messages, communicators should be concerned about how each message is likely to be received and accepted. Few messages are of a completely neutral nature, that is, free of feelings. Most messages contain news that will make either a positive or negative impression on the receiver. Certain psychology should be used, therefore, when messages contain either favorable or unfavorable news or the need for persuasion exists.

Favorable News. Favorable news consists of any message that pleases the receiver. A customer is pleased to hear that the merchandise ordered has been sent. Even when an order cannot be filled immediately, it should be acknowledged quickly, since the customer wants to know that the order was received and will be processed. Good psychology suggests that a business can make an excellent impression on a customer by delivering favorable news as quickly as possible. If a business decides to send a refund in response to a customer's request, the letter should begin with "Your refund is enclosed" rather than delaying it with "Thank you for your letter." An example of delivering good news quickly is shown in Illus. 18-4.

ILLUS. 18-4
Good news should be presented early in a letter.

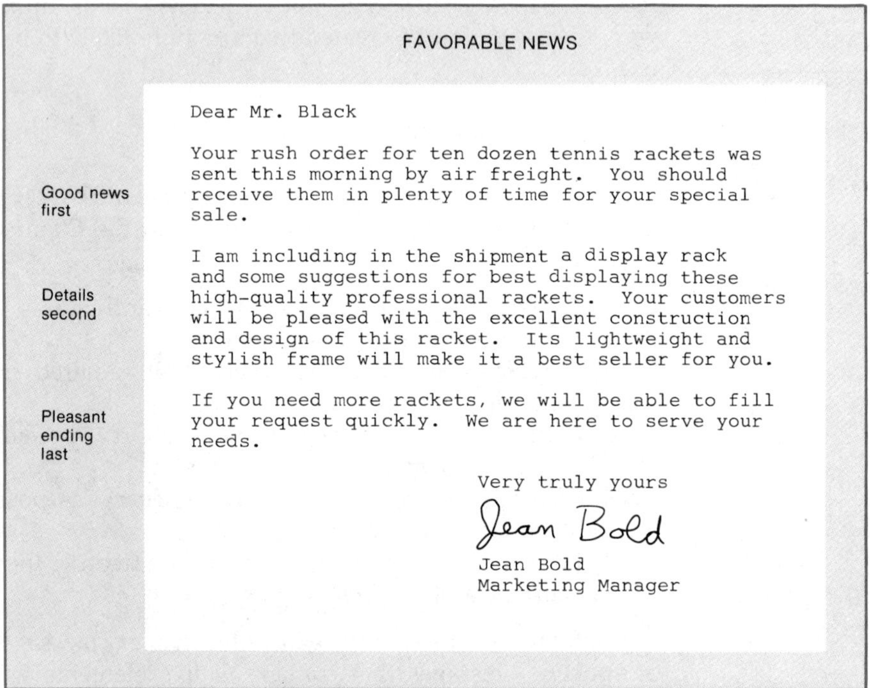
FAVORABLE NEWS

Dear Mr. Black

Your rush order for ten dozen tennis rackets was sent this morning by air freight. You should receive them in plenty of time for your special sale.

I am including in the shipment a display rack and some suggestions for best displaying these high-quality professional rackets. Your customers will be pleased with the excellent construction and design of this racket. Its lightweight and stylish frame will make it a best seller for you.

If you need more rackets, we will be able to fill your request quickly. We are here to serve your needs.

Very truly yours

Jean Bold

Jean Bold
Marketing Manager

Unfavorable News. Although unfavorable news must be given at times, it should be handled somewhat differently from favorable news. Communication experts suggest that messages containing unfavorable news best begin with a pleasant or neutral note followed by a discussion of the reason or reasons for the unfavorable news. This approach prepares the reader for the unpleasant message. Whenever possible, end the message with positive or neutral news. Note how this is accomplished in the example shown in Illus. 18-5.

Persuasive News. Quite often messages contain requests that require more than ordinary effort or cost to fulfill. People must be persuaded to take action that they normally might not take. For example, one may need to be persuaded to accept a new idea, or a customer may need to be persuaded that an overdue account should be paid immediately. A great deal of psychology must be applied when dealing with persuasive messages. Persuasion is most often used in business to sell goods and services. Effective persuasion techniques for personal selling were provided in Chapter 11.

ILLUS. 18-5
A letter that contains unpleasant news should begin with a pleasant opening.

UNFAVORABLE NEWS

Dear Mrs. Pearson

Pleasant opening

Thank you for the preference you have shown us by your application for a charge account.

Reason for refusal of credit

As you know, the usual custom before opening a new account is to get information which will serve as a basis for credit. The information we received from our credit bureau shows your payment record to be somewhat inconsistent, with some bills becoming quite old before they are eventually paid. While we cannot now fulfill your credit request, you may wish to reapply in the near future once you have had an opportunity to improve your credit record.

Offer to reconsider

Of course, if you have information that would reflect positively on your credit record now, call on us so that we can consider all of the facts.

Pleasant ending

In the meantime, please let us supply your needs on a cash basis. We will make every effort to serve you well with high-quality merchandise and friendly service.

Very truly yours

John R. Rifken

John R. Rifken
Credit Manager

COMMUNICATION CHANNELS

In simple terms, a **communication channel** is a device or means for delivering a message from a sender to a receiver. A business letter, a telephone call, and a meeting are examples of channels. Other channels include reports and telegrams. Each channel has certain special features that make it appropriate to use under different circumstances. Radio and television advertising, and the use of other sales promotion media that may also be considered public communication channels were discussed in Chapter 11.

Selecting the right channel depends upon a number of factors. One such factor is the need for feedback. **Feedback** occurs when the sender and the receiver discuss the message. Some type of oral communication channel, such as a meeting or a telephone call, is best when messages deal with general ideas and information requiring immediate discussion or clarification. Managers need to remember that breakdowns occur less frequently when there is opportunity for feedback.

The need for a permanent record is another factor that often influences the channel selection. When messages are numerous, require little feedback, and involve mostly factual data, it is efficient to use a written communication channel. For accounting and legal purposes, a written record is usually required. Misunderstandings often occur when one tries to remember what was said in a conversation. Thus, for any message that one does not wish to forget, a written communication channel, such as a letter, a memorandum, or a report should be used.

Cost, convenience, speed, and other factors also influence the selection of a communication channel. Some of these factors are considered in the following discussion of specific channels.

Letters

The letter is a frequently used channel in business, especially when communicating over a long distance. Generally letters cost less than other devices such as telegrams and long-distance telephone calls. Letters are suitable for many purposes and situations, some of which are shown in Illus. 18-6.

A letter can be used to deal with a special problem related to one person or as an efficient way to deliver a message to many people. When the same

Some Uses for Business Letters

- request credit from a supplier
- give credit to a customer
- refuse credit to a customer
- collect overdue accounts from a customer
- request product catalogs from a supplier
- order merchandise from a supplier
- send customers requested information
- acknowledge orders from customers
- fill a customer's order
- ask for an adjustment in a customer's order
- make an adjustment in a customer's order
- refuse an adjustment in a customer's order
- persuade others to take action
- convince others about an idea
- sell goods and services
- congratulate others
- thank someone
- request information about a job applicant
- request an interview with a job applicant
- reject a job applicant
- hire a job applicant

ILLUS. 18–6
Business letters can be used for many types of messages.

message is sent to many people or is used repeatedly in a commonly occurring situation, it is called a **form letter.** Most business firms use form letters for many purposes, such as to sell goods and services, grant credit to new customers, and answer requests. As a result, form letters are usually prepared in quantity, which lowers the cost of each letter. An example of a form letter used to build goodwill for a business is shown in Illus. 18-7.

The ability to prepare effective letters is important. Not only must a message give complete information, but it must also make a good impression on the reader. A letter can promote or discourage further communication. Moreover, goodwill can be lost easily if a letter does not sound friendly and businesslike. Since all letters represent the writer and the business, messages should be well written and neatly typed on good-quality paper.

Telephone

The telephone is widely used as a communication channel. Visit any business establishment and you will find a telephone at or near most work

ILLUS. 18-7
Form letters are used for many purposes, such as building goodwill.

TAYLOR'S SERVICE STATION
Washington Crossing Avenue
Taylorsville, PA 08560-8912

Dear Customer

Enclosed is a complimentary window scraper for your car. It will come in handy during the upcoming winter months.

Notice the wide edge that will cut your scraping time and the short handle that will give you an excellent grip for removing the stubborn ice that sometimes collects on windows overnight. Its size will also make for easy year-round storing in the dash of your car.

This gift is our way of saying thanks for letting us serve your automotive needs for four seasons of the year.

Sincerely

John W. Taylor

Your local dealer

stations. No employee is likely to be more than a few feet away from a phone. For some businesses, the phone is the primary means of communicating both inside and outside the business.

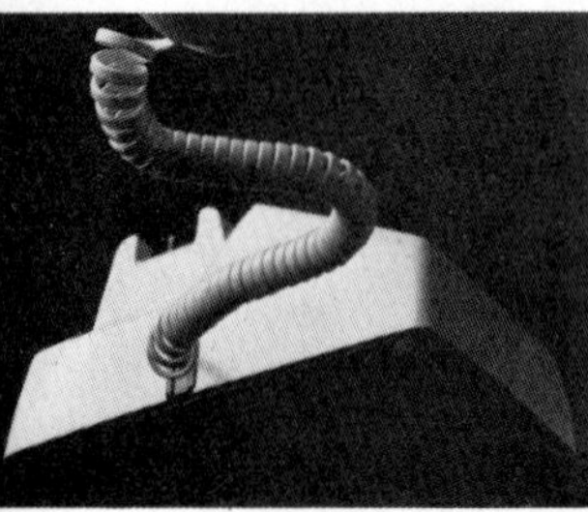

The telephone has several distinct features that set it apart from other channels. Though it may be generally more expensive than a letter, the telephone provides a faster means of communicating and allows for immediate feedback from the receiver of the call. It is also more personal than a letter because it permits voice contact. However, the value of voice contact can be lost if proper telephone techniques are not followed when talking with customers, suppliers, and others. Outgoing calls should be carefully planned so that time is not wasted and cost is kept to a minimum.

Telegrams and Mailgrams

Messages may be sent electronically by telephone lines, special cables, and air waves. Such electronic devices enable messages to be delivered quickly in written form, thereby combining the features of two communication channels—the letter and the telephone. While many devices have been created by which messages can be delivered electronically, the telegram and mailgram are still frequently used. In the next chapter, you will learn about a new means for sending messages electronically.

For years businesses have used the **telegram,** a means by which a short message is sent by wire and delivered in hours. Western Union provides a variety of telegram services. A recent variation of the telegram is the mailgram. A **mailgram** is a means by which a letter-length message is wired to a United States Post Office located near the receiver. The Post Office delivers the message the next morning. While somewhat slower than a telegram, the mailgram is less expensive. Though the mailgram is more expensive than a regular letter, it is faster. Both telegrams and mailgrams are used when written messages are needed quickly.

Reports

A **report** is a device used to deliver messages about a special topic or problem. Although reports can be delivered orally, the majority of business reports are in written form. There are basically two types of reports: informational and analytical. A report that summarizes facts, events, or conditions is an **informational report.** Sales reports, inventory reports, and financial reports are common examples. A progress report, such as the description of the work completed as a new building goes up, is also an informational report. An **analytical report,** on the other hand, deals with a special problem and usually includes recommended solutions. A report on the probable causes and possible solutions to a problem created by a sudden and rapid increase in merchandise being returned by customers is an example of an analytical report.

Reports serve many purposes and possess different characteristics. A report may be a short letter or memo, or it may consist of hundreds of bound pages. Informational reports may be prepared daily, weekly, monthly, or yearly to provide routine information such as personnel reports. Analytical reports are prepared whenever special problems arise. Regardless of form or purpose, the information should be presented so that those who receive the reports can use the information to make sound decisions.

Meetings

Within business firms, communicating is often done through meetings. Meetings may be scheduled on a regular basis or called whenever a need arises. Meetings may involve only two people, such as a supervisor meeting with an employee to review past performance; or meetings may involve a large number of people, such as the top managers and directors of a corporation meeting with the stockholders. Supervisors often meet with employees to discuss work problems, and managers often meet with each other to plan budgets and to set goals.

Meetings have distinct advantages as a communications channel. They allow for discussion and provide opportunity for everyone to express opinions or to provide information. These opportunities lead to a clarification of problems and concerns which, in turn, can lead to decisions that will most benefit the business. Two successful approaches used to discuss and solve problems that involve meetings are committees and brainstorming.

Committees. In business, committees are often formed to deal with special problems or tasks. Depending on the problems or tasks, committees may be temporary or permanent. A temporary committee dissolves after completing its assignment; whereas a permanent committee continues for an indefinite period. Whether temporary or permanent, committee members are usually appointed by a high-level manager. Committees usually fulfill their assignments by meeting regularly to complete an assigned task or to solve a problem.

The advantages to committees are that (a) the combined judgment of a group of people is often better than the judgment of a single person; (b) they encourage cooperation, especially in carrying out the decision recommended by the committee; and (c) they encourage better coordination between groups or departments such as marketing, production, and finance. A principal disadvantage to committees is the cost in time spent by committee members discussing problems rather than performing tasks. Also, it may be difficult for committee members to agree, especially when there are wide differences in opinion as to how best to solve a problem. Not only might a final decision take much time to reach, but it may also represent a compromise. While a solution reached by compromise may be good, it may not necessarily be the best solution. Despite these disadvantages, however, business firms frequently use committees to deal with problems.

Brainstorming. Problems arise in business for which prior solutions do not exist or are no longer acceptable. One technique for handling such situations is by brainstorming. **Brainstorming** is a group discussion technique that is used to generate as many ideas as possible for solving a problem. A group leader presents a problem and asks group members to offer any solution that comes to mind no matter how ridiculous it may sound. No attempt is made to judge the soundness of an idea when it is presented. Only after all possible ideas have been shared are they examined for usefulness. Often an idea that appeared to be ridiculous when first presented becomes the solution to the problem. Brainstorming is often used to deal with special types of problems in which many solutions are desired, such as generating new product ideas.

Grapevine

The communication channels thus far discussed are official channels through which an organization conducts most of its business. But an extensive amount of communicating occurs in an unofficial way that deals

ILLUS. 18-8
The grapevine—an unofficial and informal communication system.

with interpersonal relationships. Employees working side by side, for example, generally talk about their jobs and about personal matters. These conversations are normal and usually do not interfere with work. Often these conversations deal with attitudes and opinions about the work itself, about other employees, and about supervisors. Interpersonal conversations also occur during rest breaks, meals, and while sharing rides to and from work.

The informal communication system that develops among workers is called the **grapevine.** Informal messages travel quickly through a grapevine and are often subject to much distortion because they are based on unofficial and often partial or incorrect information. That is why grapevine messages are often labeled rumors.

Since grapevine communications do occur, managers need to know about them and to take corrective action when messages are incorrect or when messages interfere with company goals. There is usually little reason for managers to interfere with grapevine messages that do not affect business operations.

OTHER COMMUNICATION CHANNELS

Managers use other devices to communicate with employees. Employee handbooks and policy and procedures manuals are often used to inform employees about work rules and employment conditions. Even signs and posters are communication channels when they contain important messages and are posted in appropriate places, such as on bulletin boards. Businesses often use newsletters to inform employees about important matters affecting the company as well as to report personal news about individual employees, such as marriages, awards, and promotions. These and other communication devices help to keep employees informed about job and company matters.

NEW TERMS AND CONCEPTS

Define the following terms and concepts, which may be found in boldface type on the page shown in parentheses.

communications (350)
symbols (350)
distraction (352)
distortion (353)
I-centered message (354)
you-centered message (355)
C's of Communications (355)
communication channel (357)
feedback (357)
form letter (359)
telegram (360)
mailgram (360)
report (360)
informational report (360)
analytical report (360)
brainstorming (362)
grapevine (363)

CHAPTER REVIEW

1. How much time do executives spend each day in communicating?
2. Does communications refer to only the sending of messages?
3. Why is communications referred to as a process?
4. Name three things that cause communication breakdowns.
5. Does the fact that many words have many different meanings help to cause communication breakdowns?
6. What do some managers do to keep interruptions to a minimum?
7. Give three examples of how the physical elements of messages can affect the receiver.
8. What two factors cause messages to be distorted?
9. What is one of the easiest ways to improve communications?
10. Why are *you*-centered, rather than *I*-centered, messages preferred by message receivers?
11. Do most messages contain news that leaves neither a positive nor a negative impression on the receiver?
12. List seven common business communication channels.
13. What are the advantages and disadvantages of communicating through committees?
14. Why do grapevines often result in distorted messages?
15. Under what conditions should managers not interfere with the grapevine that exists in an organization?

QUESTIONS FOR CLASS DISCUSSION

1. Why are vague, general words less effective than specific, concrete words?
2. How do badly typed, untidy letters that are filled with errors in grammar affect receivers?
3. Two people saw an expensive calculator drop to the floor as it was being carried from one desk to another by a co-worker. One of the two observers who reported to the supervisor said, "It was an accident." The other observer said, "It was dropped on purpose." Explain how two different statements could result from observing one event.
4. Explain how someone who is planning to send a message can help to make certain the message will be clear.
5. What does psychology suggest about communicating good news as opposed to bad news?
6. What factors help a business decide which channels of communication to use when sending messages?

7. Compare the advantages and disadvantages of using the telephone rather than letters to communicate.
8. When is brainstorming an effective communications device?
9. If you were manager in a company and you heard a false rumor that several people were going to be fired, what action would you take?

PROBLEMS AND PROJECTS

1. Calculate how much time you spend communicating each day by placing the following information on a sheet of paper and keeping a record. Every 15 minutes record what you are doing by placing a check mark (√) in the column by the time shown for the main activity. If, for example, from 8:00 a.m. to 8:15 a.m. you spent most of your time telling a friend about something that happened to you yesterday, place a check mark under the column head "Speaking." Keep a record for the day, from 8:00 a.m. to 5:00 p.m. Add the number of check marks in each category and report the totals to your class.

Time	Listening	Speaking	Reading	Writing	Other Activities
8:00–8:15		√			
8:15–8:30					
8:30–8:45					

2. From Illus. 18-1, determine the percentage of time some executives spend each work day (a) listening, (b) speaking, (c) reading, and (d) writing. Also determine the total percentage of time that is spent in communicating and in other activities.
3. The communication process involves the use of symbols as well as words. Make a list of different kinds of symbols and devices that are used to communicate messages. For example, numbers are used to communicate amounts and traffic lights are used to communicate stop, go, and caution messages.
4. As an employee of the Smoke Alarm Company, you have been asked to write a letter to a person who just won a smoke alarm device in a contest that your company conducted. The alarm sells for about $30 and is an excellent warning device for alerting people during the day or night should a fire start in their home or apartment. Be sure to follow good psychology in the letter.
5. With the help of your teacher, complete the following activities which show how communications break down. Find a picture from a magazine that shows action, such as someone running, dancing, or playing a musical instrument. Then, ask for three, four, or five volunteers. Tell one volunteer to stay at the front of the class and ask the other volunteers to go beyond hearing and viewing distance. Now follow these steps:

a. Explain to the first volunteer that you will allow one minute to study the action picture, which must then be described to the second volunteer. (Show the picture for one minute to the volunteer.)
b. Call in the second volunteer and ask the first volunteer to describe the picture in as much detail as possible.
c. Call the third volunteer and ask the second volunteer to relay the description just received. Continue this process until all volunteers have had a chance to listen to the description and repeat what they heard.
d. Show the picture to everyone and ask if the scene is what they thought was being described.
e. Summarize by a discussion or written report what you learned about the communication process and how communications can break down.

CASE 18-1

Don Lincoln is a wholesaler of greeting cards, which he sells to small retailers. Many retailers write their orders on a special order form on Saturday morning so that Don will have them on Monday morning. The goods ordered are then delivered by Wednesday or Thursday that same week.

On Monday morning Don received the following request from a retailer: "Dear Don: Rush three dozen Danmark *Thank-You* cards. I need them fast." There was no name, only initials that could not be read. In addition, the customer had used note paper and an envelope without a return address rather than the order form so that the name of the retail store could not be identified. Furthermore, Danmark does not make *Thank-You* cards; the company specializes in birthday cards.

On Thursday Don received a call from the retail customer. The customer was greatly upset that the three dozen cards had not yet arrived.

Required:

1. Which of the C's of Communications did the retailer violate in the note to the wholesaler?
2. If the customer had used the telephone rather than a letter to order the goods, would this situation have been avoided?
3. If, on the phone, Don annoyingly tells the customer that he was not provided enough information, which one of the C's of Communication would he be violating?

CASE 18-2

Fanfare, Inc., is a specialty shop that sells electric fans of all kinds. Janis Zellner, who is assistant manager, was asked by the owner to prepare a form letter that could be sent to customers who had applied for credit but who had to be refused because of poor credit ratings. She prepared the following two letters so that the owner could select the better one.

Letter A

Dear Customer:

We cannot give you credit because our credit bureau informs us that your credit rating is too poor.

However, when you improve your record, we can then reconsider your credit application.

We hate to say no to a customer but in your case we have to; otherwise, we would not stay in business long. We hope you will understand.

Yours very truly,

Letter B

Dear Customer:

A request for credit from a customer is a vote of confidence in the way we do business. We appreciate your vote.

Your request for credit has been carefully studied. Our credit bureau informs us that, while your credit standing is now somewhat low, there is every indication that you can improve it greatly in the near future. Though we must refuse you credit now, we do hope to review your application as soon as your rating improves.

In the meantime, why don't you consider buying your next fan on our layaway plan. It's our way of helping you get the fan you want. Stop by and I'll personally show you how the plan works.

Yours very truly,

Required:

1. What are the strengths and weaknesses of Letter A?

2. What are the strengths and weaknesses of Letter B?

3. If you were the owner of the store, which letter would you select?

CASE 18-3

Linda Harley is the promotion manager for the First Commercial Bank of Indiana, a bank that is rapidly expanding. Because the bank is planning to open four new branch offices during the next three months, Linda needs new ideas to consider for promoting the bank and its services. She is especially concerned about doing a good job with the next branch, which will open in the city of Bedford.

In order to obtain new ideas, Linda called a meeting to be held before opening hours at the bank's main branch. She invited all of the bank tellers. At the meeting she told the tellers that she needed two kinds of suggestions. One type of suggestion was for a catchy slogan, such as "The first bank in Bedford is the First Commerical Bank." The second type of suggestion was for a promotional activity to use during the first week of the bank's opening. She said to the tellers, "Let's work on suggestions for a promotional activity first. For the last branch we opened, we gave each new customer a beautiful rose. While that worked very well, we need other ideas to attract customers to our Bedford branch. What ideas do you have?"

Linda waited a few minutes for suggestions, but none were offered. However, one bank teller said, "Linda, we should brainstorm these ideas. We did it at another bank I worked for and it was fun. Not only that, but it really worked. Let's try it."

Required:

1. Assume that you are one of the bank tellers. Offer as many ideas as you can for a promotional activity to use to open the bank.
2. Use brainstorming to come up with a slogan for the new branch bank.

Have You Thought About Becoming . . .

. . . A COMMUNICATION SPECIALIST?

People with communication skills are needed in all walks of life. Good communicators are especially needed in the business world. Of course, every manager needs to speak and write well, but so do many other employees. Because the need for good speakers and writers is great but the number is limited, businesses often hire communication specialists. Speech writers often help top executives prepare their talks. Even the President of the United States has speech writers. Frequently, people who write well are hired to train others who need to improve their writing skills. These specialists may also be called upon to review key messages and reports, create form letters, write press releases and advertising copy, or prepare the firm's monthly employee newsletter.

If you have good English skills and you enjoy speaking or writing, you may wish to become a communications specialist. Usually some college education is necessary. Liberal arts courses are highly desirable and you should take courses in general business administration and in oral, written, and visual communications. If you also obtain a master's degree, you may wish to become a communications consultant. As a consultant, you would help organizations identify and solve many types of communication problems. People with communication skills and interests also become business reporters for radio, television, magazines, and newspapers.

19

THE AUTOMATED OFFICE

After studying this chapter you will be able to:

- Discuss how computers can be used for data processing tasks.
- Discuss how computers can be used for word processing tasks.
- Describe the need for a management information system.
- Explain how modern office equipment can be used effectively by records managers.
- Compare the traditional office of today with the automated office of tomorrow.

Imagine two managers—Manager A and Manager B—who work for corporations of the same size. On Monday, both managers prepared a short report that was sent to a regional manager located in another state who needed the information to make an important decision. In the first firm, Manager A called in a secretary who took dictation and typed the report. Several hours later, the typewritten report was given to the manager who made some changes and returned it to the secretary, who then retyped it. A copy was made of the report, and the original was mailed to the regional manager, who received it several days later. Upon reading the report, the regional manager called Manager A to ask a few questions about the material in the report before making a decision. Manager A, however, was away from the office but returned the call the next morning. Five days had elapsed before the regional manager could make a decision.

Now consider Manager B, who faced the same situation. Rather than call a secretary, Manager B dictated the report directly into an automatic voice converter that changed the manager's spoken words to recorded words. The report was automatically displayed on a TV-like screen. By using special equipment, Manager B was able to make several changes in the report. After all corrections were made, the manager depressed a few keys, making it possible to automatically file the report, and transferred a copy of the report to identical equipment located on the regional manager's desk. The regional manager read the report from the TV-like screen and dictated two questions. These questions appeared on Manager B's screen. Manager B responded immediately using the same electronic devices. The total time involved was five hours.

These two situations represent the office of the past or present, and the office of the future. It took Manager A five days to complete what Manager B accomplished in five hours. In one situation the information was handled electronically and in the other situation, manually; that is, by hand or by other types of equipment. Because of available office technology, long time lags no longer need to exist between the creation and the distribution of information.

In most organizations, one of the roles of the office is that of support service. The service provided is essentially one of collecting, processing, storing, retrieving, and distributing data. **Data** are the original facts and figures that businesses generate, while **information** is data put into some usable form after having been summarized. The reason for summarizing data is to provide information when it is needed.

For efficiency, the right information must not only be made available to decision makers, but it must also be made available at the lowest possible cost. Two principal costs are people and equipment. Employees are much more productive if they have the appropriate equipment. In recent years, new office equipment has become available that helps keep costs under control while processing large amounts of data. By using computers and computer-related equipment, businesses can be run more efficiently and people can be freed to perform more important tasks.

COMPUTERS AND TECHNOLOGY

A **computer** is a piece of equipment that electronically receives, processes, and stores data, and then makes the information readily available. Computers have revolutionized the world—producers, wholesalers, retailers, and consumers have benefited from them. Computers are used on assembly lines, in offices, in classrooms, and in homes. They are used to calculate paychecks, telephone bills, and income tax returns. Computers are also used to play space-age games on our television screens and to send satellites into orbit. For over 30 years, the processing of data has gradually shifted from a manual to an electronic system through computers. Because data can be processed rapidly and accurately with computers, they have become very popular.

Computer Systems

A computer can be used in numerous ways to perform varied functions. How it is used revolves around the computer's equipment and the instructions necessary to operate the equipment.

As shown in Illus. 19–1, all computer systems include three elements: input, the central processing unit, and output. **Input** refers to data that are fed into the computer, such as the names of customers to be alphabetized or a math problem to be solved. The second element of a computer system is a **central processing unit (CPU),** which both stores and processes data. **Output**, the third element of a computer system, is information that has been processed. Output may take different forms, but often it is a printed document.

Generally data are entered into a computer by keyboarding. **Keyboarding** is the process of entering data by striking keys on a typewriter-like piece of equipment; however, unlike a typewriter, additional keys are provided to run the computer. Although many operations in the modern office are done electronically, keyboarding is usually done manually. As a result, businesses hire many data entry operators whose main function is keyboarding.

An added device for data entry operators is a television-like screen called a **cathode-ray tube** or **CRT**. A CRT immediately displays information on a screen as it is keyboarded. Errors can be easily identified and corrected before storing data magnetically and making printed copies. Data are most commonly stored on tapes and disks, though other storage devices are also used. Some examples of common storage devices are shown in Illus. 19–2.

A typewriter-like keyboard that inputs and outputs data is called a **terminal**. Many terminals also include a CRT and are usually connected to CPUs. With a terminal, data can be entered into and received from a CPU.

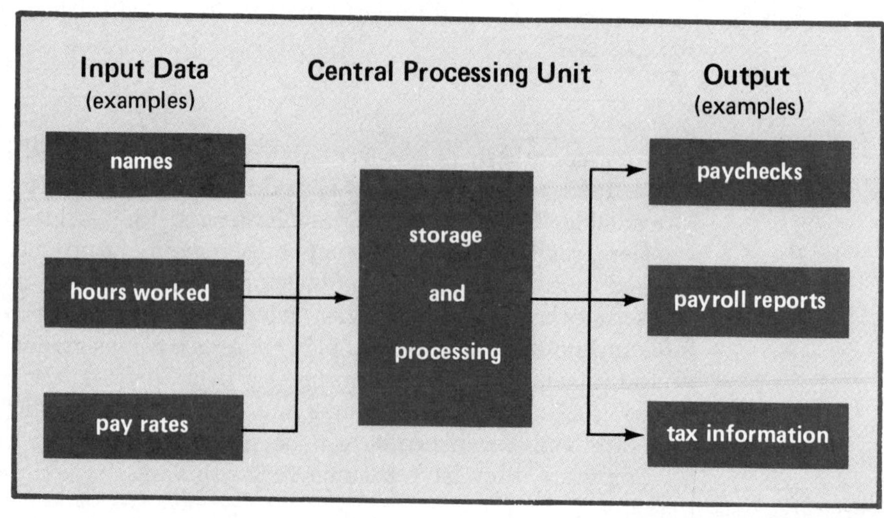

ILLUS. 19-1
Computers have three basic elements—input, the central processing unit, and output.

ILLUS. 19-2
Commonly used storage devices include floppy disks, magnetic tapes, disk packs, and cassette tapes.

The CPU may be located near the terminal, in another building, or even in another part of the country. One large CPU accommodates numerous terminals for data input and output.

Computer equipment is called **hardware**, whereas **software** is anything other than the equipment itself that is needed to operate a computer. Examples of software include training manuals and computer programs. A computer **software program** is a detailed set of instructions that directs the equipment to perform tasks in a specified manner. **Programmers**—persons trained to prepare programs—need great skill in writing detailed step-by-step instructions.

Most organizations that use computers purchase software programs for fairly standard functions. Many tasks, such as handling inventory records, are basically performed in the same way by many businesses. As a result, software programs are available through companies that specialize in preparing and selling software.

Computer Uses

With continual improvements in computer design and operation, more and more offices are using computers. Further, new and expanding uses for computers continue to be created. Of particular importance is the application of the computer to data processing and word processing.

Data Processing.

One of the main uses of computers is for **data processing**—electronically handling data that include numbers, alphabetic characters, and symbols. The need for electronic data processing has been evident since 1946 when the first large-scale computer was built.

The Past. Before the invention of computers, data were processed manually or by certain types of nonelectronic equipment, such as calculators and bookkeeping machines. When computers were introduced in 1946, the equipment was bulky and difficult to use. Early equipment was found only in large organizations and was used primarily by engineers and scientists to perform mathematical calculations. By the late 1950s, the equipment was also used for billing, payroll, sales reports, and other common business tasks.

Over the next several decades, the equipment was refined. It became smaller and easier to operate. Software also improved and the rate of change from manual to computerized data processing systems increased accordingly.

The Present. Today's computers perform many functions—some simultaneously—in fractions of seconds and store information in less space. While early computers filled an entire room, today the same computer can fit inside an object the size of a blackboard eraser with plenty of room to spare. This was made possible with the introduction of small electronic circuits called **chips**, which are smaller than the size of a thumbnail. As a result, today's computers take up little space as compared to previous models. But computer size varies with the amount of data a business needs to input, process, and store at one time. Generally **microcomputers** are very small; **minicomputers** are of medium size; and **mainframes** are large.

The use of computers for data-processing purposes today is widespread. Accounting departments use computers to handle all types of financial transactions, such as providing account balances and payroll information, and maintaining accounts receivable and accounts payable records. Banks, of course, process millions of checks and deposits for customers. Credit card companies handle purchases and payments for those who buy on credit. Hotel and airline reservations are also processed by computers, and schools prepare computerized student class schedules and grade sheets. Cash registers serve as terminals for processing retail sales transactions and for keeping track of merchandise turnover. Libraries use computers to loan books and to keep track of borrowed books; in addition, articles and books in the library related to a specific topic can be quickly located by a computer. Hospitals use computers to check on the progress of patients and to maintain medical services. Factories use computers in many ways to help produce goods more efficiently. Many organizations are using computers to convert data to information.

The Future. The use of computers for data processing will continue to expand. Microcomputers will grow more rapidly in number than minicomputers or mainframe computers. While mainframes will grow in number at a slower rate, most will be used for specialized purposes and will serve as a host to microcomputers. For example, microcomputers will be able to obtain data from mainframes or transfer data for storage in mainframes. Data processing equipment will continue to improve, and more and better software programs will become available to fit the specialized needs of businesses and individuals. While computers continue to become more powerful by performing additional functions, they will also become easier to use. Nearly all employees will be required to have a knowledge of computers and the ability to use terminals.

Word Processing. While computer systems are designed for data processing purposes, they are also specially designed to process primarily alphabetic data. Because alphabetic characters are used primarily to form words, the term *word processing* came into being. Since **word processing** deals with more than creating messages on computerized equipment, however, it is defined here as a system of processing communications by coordinating specialized people, modern equipment, and efficient procedures.

The Nature of Word Processing. Fundamental to a word processing system is the equipment and the tasks that can be accomplished with the equipment. Word processing equipment is available in many different forms. A typical word processing setup is shown in Illus. 19–3 on page 376. Generally the equipment is called a **word processor** or a **text editor**. Text-editing systems like the one shown include a keyboard, CRT, CPU, and a disk unit, which stores words magnetically on disks. A printer is also part of a complete word processing system. With modern equipment, more than one terminal can be connected to a single CPU.

Text-editing equipment is becoming widely used in offices because of its distinct advantages over standard typewriters. Unlike typewriters, for example, a text editor can electronically store, move, correct, and change material that is keyboarded into it. Even grammar and spelling errors can be detected. Additional keyboarding or re-keyboarding is needed only when words are added, replaced, removed, or corrected. Re-keyboarding of most material is eliminated. This not only saves time, but reduces the likelihood of the data entry operator making additional errors. In short, word processing leads to increased productivity, lower costs, and better quality documents.

ILLUS. 19-3
A typical word processing system includes a keyboard, a CRT, a printer, tape drives, and a CPU.

With text editing equipment, it is possible to store information compactly in electronic form. A variety of storage devices exist, such as disks, magnetic cards, tapes, and cassettes. A disk, which looks like a 45-RPM phonograph record, holds over 100 pages of material. Storage devices can be filed away from the equipment for later use. Any information on a storage device can be found electronically in seconds and a copy made if needed.

The wonder of word processing technology is not just in what the equipment can do, but in how fast it is changing the way offices operate. Work flow, for example, is improved, and new job titles and duties have been created. The office of the future will operate much differently from the office of the past. Major changes have occurred in word processing over the past two decades, with still more changes to come as the capabilities of the equipment expand and offices adapt to the changes.

The Past. Prior to word processors, most businesses processed words on paper with a typewriter. The first workable typewriter was invented in 1868. Many offices still use the typewriter to handle paperwork. In 1964, however, firms that employed hundreds of office workers to process all types of communications at a slow, costly pace underwent a tremendous change when IBM introduced the magnetic tape selectric typewriter (MT/ST). Although this first machine could store and recall information, it lacked many of the refinements found in today's equipment. New and improved equipment quickly followed, however. For example, CRTs and disk storage devices were soon introduced.

One of the effects on the office was the need to train people to operate the equipment. Various tasks normally performed by typists and secretaries were subdivided, with some of the employees becoming word processing specialists. Generally duties were separated into typing and non-typing functions. Further, new procedures had to be established. Attention was directed to all elements of a word processing system. Many offices were reorganized around the basic cycle of a word processing system: input, output, revision, distribution, and storage of information.

The Present. The major differences between the past and present are difficult to identify because numerous changes occurred and are occurring, frequently and rapidly. Businesses that process vast amounts of information, such as insurance companies and law offices, use word processing equipment extensively. While many small- and medium-sized firms still have not found the need to use word processing equipment to any extent, other firms that do not now have equipment are planning to install word processing systems in the very near future.

Not only can text editing machines automatically do in moments what once took hours, but this equipment is capable of handling a multitude of tasks. It is especially useful where repetitive work is involved. Mailing labels can be prepared and used over and over again. Form letters are automatically merged with mailing lists so that a personalized letter can be sent to each person on a list. Routine letters, memos, and business forms are prepared, edited, and distributed quickly. Long formal reports, proposals, and similar documents are often prepared on word processing equipment. Even employee manuals that are revised from time to time can be stored and updated readily.

The equipment is still relatively costly. A business cannot justify purchase of the equipment unless the volume of work is sufficiently large or the nature of the tasks warrants it. Typewriters with very limited word processing features, called **electronic typewriters**, are now available at a lower cost and can be incorporated into a more sophisticated system later. The number of manufacturers of text editing equipment has increased markedly in the last few years. As refinements evolve and equipment costs drop, it is likely that more and more businesses will be able to justify new or additional word processors.

The Future. Projections by manufacturers and experts indicate a rapid increase in the use of word processing equipment to handle mounting correspondence and other paperwork. With the increased use of text editors, the office will continue to be modified. New policies and procedures will be developed to maximize office productivity. The training and retraining of workers will become an ongoing process as new positions continue to open. The differences between word and data processing equipment will be reduced. Machines that easily shift from data processing to word processing tasks, and word processing to data processing tasks already exist and will continually be refined. The office of the future, however, will be most shaped by the extent to which word processing and related equipment can be adapted to meet the work needs of the office and the personal needs of the employees.

Management Information Systems

All business transactions involve data, and data are converted to information for the purpose of making decisions. Most organizations generate huge amounts of data, yet decision makers often have complaints. For example, there may be too much of the wrong kind of data, or requested information may arrive too late to be useful. In some cases, information may be available in another department and not readily available where needed, or not in the form needed.

Ideally, once data are collected, they should be processed quickly and the resulting information should be made available immediately to all who need it. Because businesses generally gather large amounts of data, some systematic way to manage information is demanded. A **management information system (MIS)** is an organized way to capture, process, store, retrieve, and distribute information throughout an entire organization.

Planning is at the center of creating an efficient MIS. Usually a firm conducts a careful study of its information needs as a first step in establishing a management information system. Once these needs have been established, the means for collecting and processing the data are agreed upon. Each department, of course, needs different kinds of information so the kinds of equipment may differ. For example, the accounting department usually needs data processing equipment, whereas the office manager will need word processing equipment.

Once the necessary equipment has been decided upon, procedures and policies are determined and control devices are agreed upon for the entire business. Once put into operation, the system is reviewed on a regular basis to determine whether to maintain or to revise the system. Employees who make day-to-day operating decisions must be as satisfied with the system, as must top managers who make long-range plans for the organization.

Managers have learned that when a MIS is introduced, there are natural fears and resistance to change. As a result, the human factor must be considered. Otherwise, productivity may actually decline rather than improve. All employees should be informed well in advance of system changes, invited to ask questions and to make suggestions, and shown how the new system will improve their work. If the planning has been thorough, fears will soon lessen or disappear. Frequently employees are happy with the changes, which usually leads to increased productivity.

RECORDS MANAGEMENT

A record is created every time a report is prepared, a letter is written, or an invoice is sent to a customer. Because records have increased so rapidly in volume in recent years, offices find it difficult to efficiently handle them all. An example of the paperwork explosion and the need to control it is

ILLUS. 19-4
A records management system allows a business to store a great deal of information in a small area.

reflected in the passage of the Paperwork Reduction Act of 1980. The purpose of this law is to limit and better manage the increased amount of paperwork handled in government offices. **Records management** is all of the activities dealing with the creation, maintenance, use, storage, and destruction of records. Effective records management is desirable in business as well as in government and in nonprofit organizations such as hospitals and universities.

With increased paperwork and the arrival of computer-based equipment that generates still more records, the job of the records manager has become critically important. In fact, the records manager is often in charge of a firm's management information system. Computer technology has provided the records manager with new and more efficient ways to create, store, and retrieve records.

Records Creation

Records are created in a number of ways. Handwriting, for example, is a basic method of creating records. To a limited extent, computer-based equipment can read, store, and process handwritten data. For example, computer-based equipment can be used to read handwritten orders that have been carefully prepared by salespeople.

Records are also created by typewriting. Often original drafts of documents are typed or dictated directly to a secretary or into a dictation machine for typing later. Typewritten material can also be handled by computer-like equipment. A secretary may type a rough draft of a report for an executive. This draft is then read by a machine and placed into the storage memory of a text editor. The document will not have to be re-keyboarded even though changes might be made before a final message is prepared for distribution. All unchanged material can be merged with all new or revised material.

The device used to read handwritten and typewritten material is called an **optical character reader (OCR)**. An OCR makes it possible for material to be read, stored, and processed by data and/or word processing equipment. If workers involved in creating records do not have direct access to a data processing or word processing terminal, OCR devices can be used to transfer material to computer-based equipment.

Records can also be created by voice dictation. A secretary may take shorthand and transcribe the material into a text editor, or a manager may dictate material into a machine which records the spoken voice. This dictation equipment is practical to use when secretaries are not immediately available or when managers are away from an office setting.

Sales representatives and engineers often use portable dictating equipment when they are away from an office. Material dictated into equipment can also be transmitted over telephone lines to further speed the process of getting it into print and/or electronic form. Also, equipment exists that allows messages to be dictated directly through telephone lines into dictation equipment.

A more recent means for converting voice-created documents into a form that can be entered, processed, and stored electronically is voice recognition equipment. A voice-activated typewriter, for example, permits an employee to dictate directly into equipment that then produces a printed message. Printed messages can also be converted to voice. While it may take a few more years for this kind of equipment to be used extensively in business, it has great potential. For example, errors could readily be found by blind or nearly blind keyboarders. Also, the number of employees needed to transcribe messages taken in shorthand or by transcribing machines would be greatly reduced. Uses outside the office setting also exist for voice recognition equipment, such as electronically placing orders by phone and taking inventory.

Document Storage and Retrieval

Records managers are not only concerned about record creation but also about record storage and retrieval. New office technology is having a strong impact on how information is handled. The output from computer-based equipment appears in any one of three forms: paper, digital, and microform.

Paper. Paper documents, no matter how prepared, are very costly to store and retrieve. Yet, such records are produced in quantity. In the automated office, still more paper documents are created by high-speed computers connected to printers. These printers provide **hard copy**, a term used to describe a printed copy of machine output. Printers attached to computer-based equipment can print copy in many forms. Hard copy, for example, can be printed in different type styles and sizes in seconds.

Machines used to make multiple copies of a single document have also become very versatile. Many new copiers contain the electronic circuitry found in computers. They are called **intelligent copiers**. Intelligent copiers produce print-like quality, graphics, and color; print copies directly from magnetic disks or tapes; and send copies over telephone lines. Because intelligent copiers store information, they can also be directly connected to data and word processing equipment for making many copies of reports or other documents.

Digital. Records stored on magnetic tapes, disks, and other devices are called **digital records**. Digital refers to the means by which processors operate electronically. Much information stored in digital form may never be put in paper form. Desired information can be read from a terminal on a CRT. Of course, information no longer needed can be easily eliminated. Hard copy can be obtained through printers or copiers. Obviously, digital records are often a real cost savings.

Microform. **Micrographics** is used to put documents on film in miniature form for filing purposes. Documents put in miniature form by using cameras and photographic film are called **microform**. There are two types of microform—microfilm and microfiche. Records placed on a roll of film are called **microfilm**; whereas, records placed on a flat sheet of film are called **microfiche**. Because the storage space required is greatly reduced, both types of microform are commonly used. Hundreds of pages can appear on a microfiche sheet, for example, that is smaller than a page in this book. Small projectors are used to enlarge and read microform material; hard copies can also be prepared.

As shown in Illus. 19–5, it is possible for digital records to be converted directly to microfilm from computers in lightning-like speed by a process called **computer output microfilm (COM)**. Moreover, a computer system can readily find any page on the microfilm almost instantly. The advantages of micrographics are that:

- Records will last much longer than in digital form.
- Storage and retrieval are more efficient than with paper records.

ELECTRONIC COMMUNICATIONS

Information is prepared to be used. But it must be readily available. Often, information is needed on short notice. Fortunately word processors

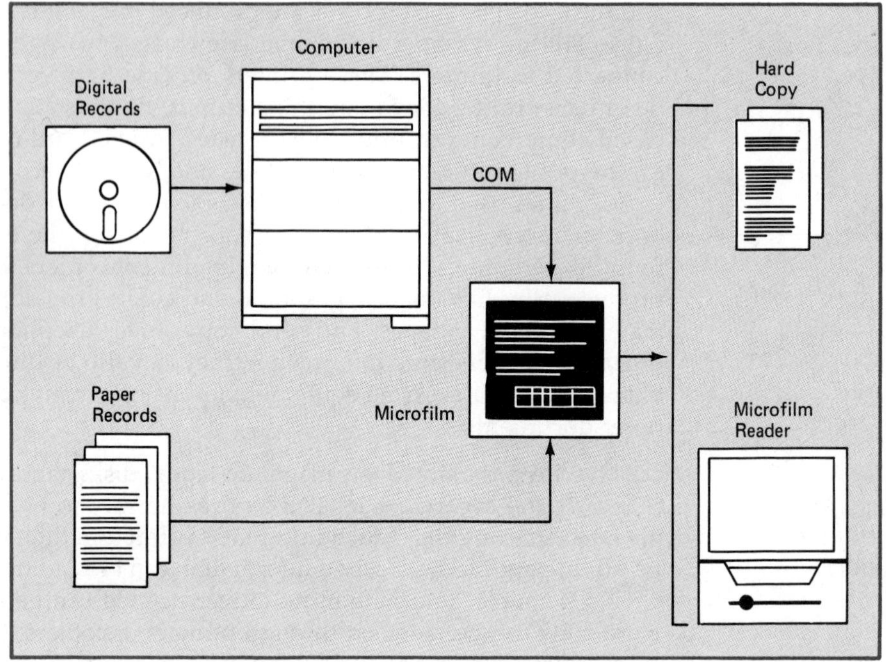

ILLUS. 19-5
Digital and paper records can be preserved and stored efficiently on microfilm.

can communicate with each other; that is, send and receive data from one terminal to another. Data processors also have this capability. In fact, data processors can also communicate with word processors and other computer-based equipment, such as printers and copiers. Managers in modern offices, therefore, have available all magnetically stored data in their businesses. A special network of cables connects all electronic equipment within a business in order to expedite information sharing.

Terminals are also used to send messages that would normally be telephoned, telegrammed, or mailed. The term **electronic mail** refers to sending computerized information electronically using such means as satellites, cables, and telephone lines. The time delay caused by mailing messages disappears. Also, the problem of a message being forgotten or misplaced is practically eliminated, because the message is stored in the sending and receiving terminals. Messages can be sent and received at any time of day or night. Managers usually check their terminals on a regular basis each day. The advantages of using electronic mail are significant, especially when managers are separated by miles and by time zones. Communications, in general, are improved by the ease and speed with which messages are exchanged by the use of electronic equipment.

Information from other businesses can also be obtained instantly through electronic communications. Organizations exist that sell information that others might want. For example, many firms obtain information through terminals about current stock prices on Wall Street, weather reports, airline schedules, and important news stories. Such up-to-the-minute information is often helpful in running an efficient business.

THE OFFICE OF THE FUTURE

Most changes in the office are brought about gradually. While numerous large firms have automated many office tasks, few are yet fully automated, even though the technology for doing so exists. The office of the future will make use of the computer-based technology described in this chapter, and all equipment, procedures, and personnel will be an integral part of a management information system. Each office employee's work station is likely to have a terminal for entering and receiving data. As little information as possible will be in the form of hard copy—most will be on tape, disk, or storage media not yet created.

Executives will also have work stations with terminals that serve many functions. Most information needed for decision making will be readily available through the terminals. Executives will be able to input and output data via terminals, and to monitor operations at their work stations. In addition, they will have the convenience of electronic mail. Messages will be exchanged and meetings held without leaving the office. Although geographically separated, those in conference will be able to see and hear each other, and have access to the same information on their CRTs. Decisions reached at sessions of this nature can then be communicated instantly throughout an organization.

In part, the technology for the office of tomorrow is actually available today. Any anxiety or fears related to operating terminals will disappear as

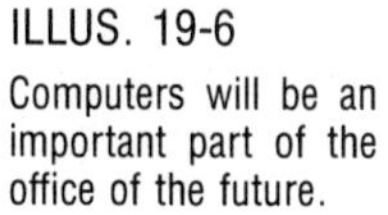
ILLUS. 19-6
Computers will be an important part of the office of the future.

computers become more popular in homes, schools, and offices. Employees will become as comfortable working at terminals as they are today with typewriters and telephones. Of particular importance, however, is that what now takes 40 hours to accomplish will be completed in 40 minutes. While the age of the paperless office may not arrive during the twentieth century, modern offices are aiming in that direction.

NEW TERMS AND CONCEPTS

Define the following terms and concepts, which may be found in boldface type on the page shown in parentheses.

data (371)
information (371)
computer (371)
input (372)
central processing unit, or CPU (372)
output (372)
keyboarding (372)
cathode-ray tube, or CRT (372)
terminal (372)
hardware (373)
software (373)
software program (373)
programmer (373)
data processing (374)
chips (374)
microcomputers (374)
minicomputers (374)
mainframes (374)
word processing (375)
word processor, or text editor (375)
electronic typewriters (377)
management information sysyem, or MIS (378)
records management (379)
optical character reader, or OCR (380)
hard copy (381)
intelligent copiers (381)
digital records (381)
micrographics (381)
microform (381)
microfilm (381)
microfiche (381)
computer output microfilm, or COM (381)
electronic mail (382)

CHAPTER REVIEW

1. Why have computers become popular?
2. What are the three elements included in a computer system?
3. What are the two most common computer storage devices?
4. What made it possible for computers to be made small in size?
5. Give five examples of how computers are used for data processing purposes.
6. What does a typical word processing setup include?
7. What is significant about the MT/ST word processor that IBM introduced in 1964?
8. What type of work is best handled by word processing equipment?

9. Why are data converted to information?
10. What is the first step in establishing a management information system?
11. Why was the Paperwork Reduction Act of 1980 passed?
12. What is a voice-activated typewriter?
13. In what three forms can the output from computer-based equipment appear?
14. What are the advantages of micrographics?
15. What are two advantages of electronic mail?

QUESTIONS FOR CLASS DISCUSSION

1. What are the most expensive factors involved in getting information to decision makers?
2. Should a small company that is planning to buy a small computer to handle fairly routine tasks also hire a programmer?
3. How does data processing equipment differ from word processing equipment?
4. What are the advantages of text-editing equipment?
5. How has word processing affected the way offices are run?
6. What will cause word processing equipment to become more extensively used in the future?
7. Discuss the steps involved in creating a management information system.
8. Why are records managers so important to many businesses?
9. Identify the ways in which records can be created and then put into printed form.
10. Describe an executive work station in the office of the future.

PROBLEMS AND PROJECTS

1. Use your library to prepare a list of important events or inventions in the history of data processing. List these items by dates, starting with the oldest date.
2. Visit a local store that sells personal computers. Select one brand and model of a personal computer, and ask for a demonstration of how it can be used for word processing purposes. Prepare a report. Be certain to:
   a. describe the equipment.
   b. give the name of the software program.
   c. describe how changes can be made and errors can be corrected.

3. Visit your local post office and obtain information about its use of electronic mail. Request a booklet and ask questions about how the system works. Then prepare a report for your class.
4. Use magazine articles and books to prepare a 200–300 word essay on the use of management information systems in a particular business or industry.
5. An office manager has five office workers. The total annual labor cost is $40,000. If the office manager spends $10,000 to buy a word processor, only three secretaries would be needed. If the equipment lasts five years, at which time it will have no trade-in value, will it be worth buying the new equipment from a cost point of view? And how much will the manager save the business each year by the decision that is made?

CASE 19–1

Carol Crawford and Francis Weeks are both employed at the Binford Company, a small life insurance firm. Both Carol and Fran have been with the business for over ten years but are now quite upset by recent events. The office manager announced yesterday that all employees must attend several all-day training sessions on how to input and output data on customers' policies using computer terminals. The company will install a computerized system over the weekend. They have just returned from the first day's training session. The following conversation took place:

Fran: I don't know about you, Carol, but this change is just like coming to an entirely new job. I am very unsure about how all of this is going to work out.

Carol: We should have at least been told about this in advance, rather than have it come as a complete surprise. We could easily get a job at another insurance company. Maybe we should quit. The company is not willing to give us more money to learn all this new-fangled computer stuff. With our experience, we should not have any trouble finding a new job.

Fran: Hold on, Carol. We should not be too hasty. We make good money here. I agree, however, that they should have told us about this so we could have been doing some reading and getting ourselves ready for the change.

Carol: From what we learned today, we could certainly make the company sorry that they did not get our opinions before deciding to computerize this operation.

Required:

1. Describe what mistake the management of the Binford Company made in moving to a computerized system. Explain.

2. In what ways could Carol make the company regret not involving the employees in the decision? Explain.

CASE 19–2

Phil Landow is the records manager for a paper mill that employs 20 managers and 450 workers. There are three different plants, each located in a different state. Each plant processes its own paperwork. All records are then delivered (usually weekly) to the main plant for storage purposes. However, the two smaller plants keep a copy of all records also.

Five workers are needed at the main plant just for filing the records and retrieving any that might be needed later. Less than 10 percent of the documents are ever used again.

These records contain payroll information, production schedules, inventory sheets, financial data, etc. The main office is now so crowded with file cabinets that something must be done. An addition can be added to the plant to handle the records, but Phil Landow favors some type of system that would require less space and decrease the time it takes to retrieve records.

Required:

1. List and discuss two possible plans that Phil Landow might consider.
2. If Phil decides to automate as much of the firm's operation as possible, how should he proceed?

CASE 19–3

Two administrative secretaries were overheard in the employee lunch room discussing matters related to their office operations. Part of the discussion was recorded and it appears below:

Anthony: If we had an OCR, we could save a great deal of time getting this material into our only text editor.

Thelma: Maybe, but I think if we replaced our five electronic typewriters with terminals connected to the word processor's CPU, we would be better off.

Anthony: As long as we are wishing, I would like to get a disk drive for the word processor and get rid of the slow cassettes we are presently using.

Thelma: I wonder when this office will become automated. We are still working in the dark ages.

Required:

1. In terms of the typical office today, do you think the office is in the dark ages? Explain your answer.
2. Discuss the following that were included in the conversation: OCR, electronic typewriter, disk drive and cassette, text editor, and CPU.

Have You Thought About Becoming . . .

. . . A WORD PROCESSING SUPERVISOR?

As a result of the impact of new technology on office operations, newly created career opportunities are now available for office workers. One challenging new position is that of a word processing supervisor. This first-level manager is responsible for the smooth flow of work within a word processing center in a business. The word processing supervisor coordinates the work of those who create documents that need to be keyboarded, schedules the tasks to be performed, orders supplies, trains and directs employees, and checks the quality of work produced within the center. Good management and communication skills are needed together with a thorough knowledge of equipment.

Many word processing supervisors have worked their way up in their organizations through some of the newly created specialized positions. For example, word processing operators are those who operate text-editing equipment. These employees may also be called correspondence secretaries or data entry specialists, depending upon individual firms and the size of word processing departments.

In particular, large firms often have a career ladder that provides pay raises for increased responsibilities as one moves to higher level positions. A possible ladder might include: word processing trainee, word processing specialist I, word processing specialist II, and word processing supervisor. If there is more than one word processing department in an organization, there may be a word processing manager to whom word processing supervisors report.

If a word processing managerial position appeals to you, you should begin your specialized education at the high school level, and build upon your knowledge of equipment, systems, and procedures at the two- and four-year college levels. Advanced degrees that focus on information systems are desirable if you wish to climb to higher level positions in the automated office.

UNIT 6

Human Resources

The most important asset to any business is not the amount of money it has in land, buildings, modern computers, or other equipment. Rather, a firm's most prized resources are the people working for it. Human resources—employees—are what make businesses successful or unsuccessful. For that reason, business firms find it worthwhile to devote a great deal of attention to developing productive workers.

In Unit 6 you will learn how managers effectively work with and motivate employees. In addition, you will be provided with information of procedures and techniques often used by firms to select, train, promote, and compensate workers. Moreover, you will be introduced to the role of labor unions in contributing to labor-management relations.

The success of a business depends in part on how well executives treat their employees. Dr. An Wang is an accomplished business leader who practices effective labor-management relations. His biographical profile appears on the next page.

AN WANG

In 1945 An Wang came to the United States from China to begin graduate studies. Six years later he not only had a doctoral degree in physics, but he had also started a computer manufacturing company in Boston. Today Dr. Wang is chief executive officer and chairman of the board of that company, Wang Laboratories, Inc. It is one of the leading producers of computers and word processing equipment. The company employs over 19,000 people world-wide and is one of the 500 largest companies in the country.

Dr. Wang developed an interest in technology when he was an undergraduate student at Chiao Tung University in Shanghai, China. Soon after earning his Ph.D. degree at Harvard University, he invented a computer memory device, which has been in most computers for over 20 years. Dr. Wang also created an early version of a desktop computer that was popular for some time.

In recognition of his many contributions to computer technology, Dr. Wang has been awarded honorary degrees by several universities and has served on the boards of others. Because of his deep interest in technology and education, he formed the Wang Institute of Graduate Studies of which he is president.

Dr. Wang's keen mind, strong managerial and technical abilities, and market instincts are special attributes. Because of his highly personal managerial style, his employees fondly call him "the doctor." The doctor's style includes adapting his own philosophy to managing the entire company. He believes in giving employees, stockholders, and customers a fair return on their investments in Wang Laboratories, Inc. In addition to country club and day-care privileges, his employees may buy stock in the firm at reduced prices. Dr. Wang predicts that by 1990 his company will be one of the top five producers of electronic office equipment.

20

LEADERSHIP AND HUMAN RELATIONS

After studying this chapter you will be able to:

- Identify characteristics of effective leaders.
- Compare different types of leadership styles.
- Identify important human-relations skills needed by managers.
- Discuss how personality and basic needs are related to work satisfaction.
- Describe some ways in which job satisfaction can be improved through job design.
- Present three strategies for dealing with conflict.

What happens when employees are dissatisfied with their jobs or their supervisors? For a short time, there may be no noticeable problems. However, after some time employees will get less work done and the quality of their work will suffer. If the dissatisfied employees deal with customers, customer complaints will increase. Employee absenteeism will increase and employees will look for better jobs or will be fired for poor performance. As you can see, failure to give attention to the needs of workers can have very negative effects on a business.

In order to make a profit, a firm's management will attempt to operate the business in the most efficient manner possible. During the early history of business, management tried to increase efficiency by improving both machines and manufacturing methods. Limited attention was given to the needs of the workers. However, management slowly began to realize that employees can greatly affect the success or failure of a business.

As management became aware of the importance of employees to business success, a different approach was taken. Today, business firms spend millions of dollars yearly to improve working conditions and to train managers who are able to develop good working relationships among employees. Effective managers must be good leaders, and they must understand what motivates employees to do their best work. In addition, effective managers are able to deal with many types of human-relations problems that arise among employees. In this chapter you will learn about the leadership characteristics and human-relations skills needed by managers.

LEADERSHIP CHARACTERISTICS

While managers are involved in many activities, one of the most important is to create an atmosphere that will encourage employees to do their best work in order to make the business successful. Individual workers, however, have their own goals and needs. The closer the work done for the business meets the needs of individual workers, the greater the satisfaction will be for both. Managers must work to satisfy the needs of each employee while also meeting the goals of the business. Success in this task requires leadership. **Leadership** is the ability to direct or influence others to achieve organizational goals. Leadership includes the ability to apply human-relations skills. **Human relations** refers to how well people get along together. Good human relations exist in a group of people that get along well together in contrast to a group in which there are arguments, misunderstandings, hostility, and suspicion.

Because the quality of leadership is directly related to the success of an organization, it is important that managers possess certain leadership characteristics. Leadership will be examined by studying leadership traits, leaders' views about workers, and leadership styles.

Leadership Traits

Managers help employees get work done correctly and willingly. A poor supervisor may be able to get workers to perform the necessary tasks, but the work may be done poorly and grudgingly or reluctantly. A good supervisor, on the other hand, is able to influence workers so that they will enjoy their work and will take pride in doing a good job. To get others to perform well requires certain leadership traits. Some of the common traits that effective leaders possess are shown in Illus. 20–1.

Having the traits described in Illus. 20–1 does not insure that a person will be a good leader. Leaders must also have an understanding of the work that must be done, and the business in which they work must be well organized. Each leadership situation differs, with each situation calling for more or less of a certain trait. Thus, two managers who possess most of the

ILLUS. 20–1
Effective leaders possess most of these traits.

Basic Leadership Traits

Intelligence	A certain amount of intelligence is needed to direct others. However, a leader does not need to be a genius.
Judgment	Leaders must make many decisions. They must consider all facts carefully to make good decisions. Using good judgment is essential to making good decisions.
Objectivity	Leaders must be able to look at all sides of a problem and not make biased judgments or statements.
Initiative	Leaders have ambition and persistence in reaching goals. They are self-starters who plan what they want to do and then do it. They have drive and are highly motivated.
Dependability	Those who lead are consistent in their actions, and others can rely on them. They are where they should be when needed.
Cooperation	Leaders understand the importance of other people and enjoy being with them. Thus, they work well with others.
Honesty	Leaders are honest and have high standards of personal integrity.
Courage	Leaders possess the courage to make unpopular decisions and the courage to try new approaches in solving problems.
Confidence	Leaders have a great deal of self-confidence. They attempt to make the best decisions possible and trust their own judgment.
Stability	Leaders for the most part are not highly emotional. You can depend on their reactions in various situations.
Understanding	Leaders recognize that the feelings and ideas of others are important. They try to understand the people they work with.

leadership traits will probably perform differently in any given leadership situation.

Leadership traits are important in the business world. Managers are often hired and evaluated on the basis of such traits. Many leadership training programs are related to the basic leadership traits. Through training and personal effort, individuals can improve upon each of the traits. People can learn to be dependable, to have initiative, to cooperate with others, and so on. Training and experience can improve a manager's judgment in making business decisions. For the most part, people are not born with specific leadership traits; but these traits can be developed to improve the performance of managers.

Viewpoints About Workers

While leadership traits are quite common among good managers, the way individual managers deal with employees may be very different. Each manager has attitudes about people and work. Those attitudes will help determine how the manager makes decisions, relates to other people, and treats employees. Studies have found that many managers have very different views of their employees. Some managers believe employees dislike work, while other managers have the opposite view.

Belief That Employees Dislike Work. Some managers assume that employees dislike work and will avoid it whenever possible. This type of manager is likely to further assume that workers are often lazy and try to avoid responsibility if possible. Workers will need to be forced to put forth the effort needed for the organization to achieve its goals. As a result of these beliefs, this kind of manager closely supervises and controls workers and makes all important decisions.

Belief That Employees Like Work. A manager who believes workers generally like to work handles workers in a much different manner. This manager is likely to assume that employees like responsibility and try to meet the goals of the organization as well as their own goals. The manager believes that employees obtain satisfaction from doing a job well. Workers do not need close supervision and control if they like their work. The manager with this set of beliefs will ask workers for their suggestions and ideas on how to complete the work.

A Changing View of Employees. Studies have found that neither of the views just discussed is correct for all workers and all jobs. Although each manager tends to favor one viewpoint over the other, the manager who can change from one viewpoint to the other as circumstances change is likely to be the more effective manager. For example, a supervisor knows that for some jobs which workers strongly dislike, closer supervision and control are needed. When workers are eager to perform their tasks, less supervision and control are needed. Flexibility in a manager's viewpoint toward workers permits flexibility in the treatment of workers.

Leadership Style

The general way in which a manager treats and directs employees is called **leadership style**. It includes the way in which a manager gives directions, handles problems, and makes decisions. Leadership style is influenced by many factors, including the manager's background, personality, and beliefs about whether employees like or dislike work. Because leadership style is influenced by numerous factors, each manager has a slightly different style from all other managers. However, leadership styles can be placed in general categories.

Autocratic Style. The **autocratic leader** is one who gives direct, clear, and precise orders with detailed instructions as to what, when, and how work is to be done. Employees do not make decisions about the work being performed because when questions or problems arise the leader will be there to handle them. Those who work for autocratic managers routinely perform tasks with little or no personal involvement in the work itself.

One of the reasons for using the autocratic style is that it is efficient. The work is completed in exactly the way the manager expects it to be done. Each worker generally has a clear idea of what is expected, but when there is doubt about how to perform, the manager is consulted. The autocratic leader believes that managers know what must be done and how it should be done to best reach the goals of the organization. It is also assumed that workers do not have the skills necessary to plan and carry out the work.

While some workers prefer leaders with autocratic styles, many others do not. A major disadvantage of the autocratic style is that it discourages employees from thinking about better ways of doing their work. As a

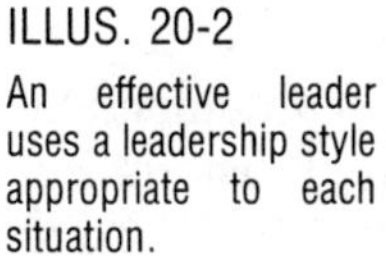
ILLUS. 20-2

An effective leader uses a leadership style appropriate to each situation.

result, some employees become bored and tend to lose interest in their work. This type of leadership may lead to a decline in the quality and quantity of work. Human-relations problems can occur when supervisors use only an autocratic style, because certain employees are unsatisfied when they have limited opportunities to participate in decisions affecting their work. They may begin to resent their supervisor and the company they work for.

The autocratic style is effective in some situations. For example, it is often the best style to use in emergency-type situations. Getting out a large rush order, for example, does not allow time for a supervisor to discuss the order with employees. It is much more efficient for a supervisor to give specific orders and to expect a rapid response. An autocratic style is often needed with temporary employees, such as part-time workers hired for rush periods. The effective leader is one who knows when a situation calls for an autocratic style of leadership and uses it until that situation is over.

Democratic Style. The **democratic leader** is one who encourages workers to share in the making of decisions about work-related problems. When using the democratic style, managers discuss solutions with employees rather than merely announcing decisions. The manager may still make the final decision but only after discussing possible solutions with employees. Even when a decision is not involved, the democratic manager will provide workers with assistance or encouragement and offer reasons why certain work changes must occur. The principal characteristic of the democratic style, however, is that it gives workers an opportunity to be involved with the supervisor in the decision-making process.

Many workers prefer a manager who generally practices a democratic style of leadership. Workers who are permitted to influence decisions feel important and are more likely to carry out the decisions willingly. Workers who participate in the decision-making process are often highly motivated and, as a result, need not be as closely controlled and supervised.

As good as the democratic style may sound, however, it also has shortcomings. Not all workers like to participate in decision making; some prefer to be told when and how to work. Also, the democratic style is time-consuming in that time must be taken from work to discuss problems. Furthermore, many jobs are fairly routine with little or no opportunity available for sharing in decision making. Workers may become upset if they are asked to help make decisions on unimportant matters only.

The democratic leadership style is effective in many situations, especially when employees are interested in their work and are looking for more responsibility. It is also effective when workers have the knowledge needed to determine how best to perform their jobs. That is usually true for experienced or well-trained employees. When special problems arise and the manager wants to gather as many helpful ideas as possible, the democratic style is effective. Managers who assume that employees enjoy work are usually comfortable with this leadership style.

Open Style. The **open style** of leadership is one in which the manager gives little or no direction to workers. Employees are given general instructions on the work to be done, but methods, details, and decisions are left to each individual. In the open style, any employee may become the leader when certain decisions must be made. Generally, each worker concentrates on specific tasks and is not often involved in the tasks of others.

The open style works best with experienced workers and in businesses where few major changes occur. If people have their own specialized jobs to do and are experts in their jobs, the manager may use this style of leadership. However, because it can lead to confusion and lack of direction, it is not useful in many business situations.

Effective Leadership

The most effective manager is the one who selects a leadership style that best fits a particular situation. Whichever style is used, there are certain characteristics that employees prefer in all managers. Those characteristics are shown in Illus. 20–3.

ILLUS. 20–3
Employees prefer managers who possess these leadership characteristics.

Characteristics that Employees Think Managers Should Have

1. Encourages employees to share in the decision-making process.
2. Informs employees honestly, whether circumstances are favorable or unfavorable.
3. Does everything possible to keep morale high.
4. Is easy to talk to.
5. Counsels, trains, and develops employees.
6. Communicates effectively with employees.
7. Shows thoughtfulness and consideration.
8. Is willing to make changes in methods of doing things.
9. Is willing to support employees even when mistakes are made.
10. Expresses appreciation when an employee does a good job.

Source: Adapted from Larry E. Greiner, "What Managers Think of Participative Leadership," *Harvard Business Review,* Vol. 51, No. 2 (March-April, 1973).

HUMAN RELATIONS

Managers are continually in contact with people: employees, other managers, customers, and people from outside the business. Because of these contacts, the need for human-relations skills is great. Earlier in the chapter, human relations was defined as how well people get along together. It is the manager's responsibility to help employees get along as well as possible with each other.

Several skills are involved in effective human relations. Those skills may be just as important to the success of a business as the skill to make decisions or the skill to operate a complicated piece of equipment. Human-relations skills may be as difficult to develop as the other business skills listed. The important human-relations skills needed by managers are: (1) self-understanding, (2) understanding of others, (3) communication, (4) group building, (5) developing job satisfaction, and (6) dealing with conflict.

Self-Understanding

In order to work well with others, managers must have self-understanding. Self-understanding involves an awareness of your attitudes and opinions, your leadership style, your decision-making style, and your relationships with other people.

Employees look to managers for information and directions. They want managers to be able to make decisions, solve problems, and communicate expectations. If managers understand themselves and what other people expect of them, they can decide on the best way to work with people and the leadership style to use. They can use the understanding of their strengths, weaknesses, and appearances to others to improve their skills as managers.

Understanding Others

Every individual is different. Each person has a different background as well as different attitudes, skills, and needs. A manager cannot treat everyone in the same way. Some people need a great deal of supervision; others do not. Some employees want to help make decisions, while others do not care to be involved in the decision-making process. Some people work harder when praised; others need to be criticized occasionally.

Managers need to know the best way to work with each employee. They need to be able to satisfy individual worker's needs and, at the same time, accomplish the goals of the company. The manager who understands the needs of employees will be a better manager.

Communication

In Chapter 18 we discussed the importance of communication in business. Managers spend much of their time communicating. When breakdowns in communication occur, human-relations problems are likely to develop.

ILLUS. 20-4
A good manager understands the needs of workers.

Managers must understand what information needs to be communicated and what methods to use. They need to know when too much communication is occurring and when there is not enough. Managers must have skill in using official communications channels and in understanding informal channels.

Group Building

When people in a company work well together, the company is able to produce more and be more profitable. When problems exist among people, it is difficult for a business to be successful.

People need to feel that they are a part of a group, that they are important, and that they can count on other group members for help. Managers that have group building skills are able to get people to work well together to accomplish the goals of the company.

Developing Job Satisfaction

Most workers are not totally satisfied or dissatisfied with their jobs. Some people enjoy their work most of the time, while others enjoy their work some of the time. On certain days work may be enjoyable; on other days it may be unenjoyable. The causes of differences in job satisfaction are many. Each work situation is influenced by such factors as the personalities of the employee and the manager, the needs of employees, the goals of the business, and the nature of the work itself.

Personality. Even though there are several billion people living in the world today, each person is unique. One reason why no two people are alike is personality. **Personality** pertains to a person's attitudes, habits, and traits. Personality is influenced by family, childhood, friends, physical features, age, and intelligence. These and other influences result in wide differences in personalities.

Managers must be aware of personality differences if they are to deal effectively with employees. For example, when two people with entirely different personalities are asked to work together, human-relations problems may arise. Human-relations problems are not as likely to arise if both employees have similar personalities.

Personality should be suited to the kind of work to be performed, because personality characteristics can affect job performance. A shy person who enjoys working alone, for example, might perform better as a bookkeeper than as a salesperson. Thus, effective managers should make every effort to match job characteristics with personality characteristics. Personnel managers often give tests to new workers in order to better match the job and the individual.

Needs of People. Managers must be very concerned about worker motivation. **Motivation** can be defined as the reason (or reasons) that cause a person to act or to do something in a certain way. People are motivated by their individual needs. For example, when a person is hungry, the need to find food motivates the person to take the necessary action to obtain food. While at any one time the needs of individuals are quite varied, experts have grouped needs into five categories: physical needs, safety needs, social needs, self-respect needs, and self-realization needs. These needs are shown in Illus. 20–5.

People's needs change, and more than one need can be at work at any one time. Moreover, once a need is substantially met, it no longer serves as a strong motivating force; however, another need is likely to replace it. For example, if an employee is working with a faulty piece of equipment, the greatest need may be protection from being hurt. Once the employee has been provided with a safe piece of equipment, the need for safety is reduced in importance.

The five basic human needs shown in Illus. 20–5 are listed in order of importance. The first basic concern is for physical needs, which are more important than safety needs. Safety needs are usually more important than social needs, and so on. In the United States today, most employees' physical, safety, and social needs are satisfied. Because these needs are met in large part, the self-respect and self-realization needs have grown in importance as motivating forces for many workers. However, they will continue to have some basic needs that must be satisfied. Therefore, it is important for managers to realize that those needs cannot be ignored.

Nature of Work. To better understand how workers may gain increased satisfaction from their jobs, experts have studied those factors which employees like most about their work. From those studies, efforts have been made to design jobs to better meet workers' needs.

ILLUS. 20-5

The basic needs of people are much like a set of stairs, with each step, or need, having to be somewhat satisfied or reached before the next need serves as a strong motivating force.

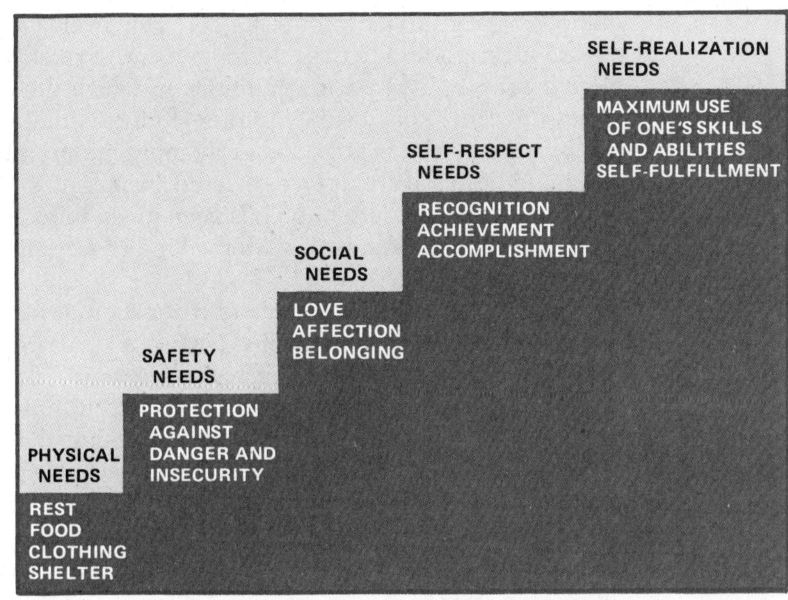

Source: Adapted from A.H. Maslow, "A Theory of Human Motivation," *Psychological Review*, Vol. L, (July, 1943), pp. 370-396.

Studies have found that the most satisfaction from work occurs when the average worker: (a) performs interesting tasks, (b) has a feeling of responsibility, (c) gains recognition, and (d) has a feeling of achievement. This shows that workers are more concerned with self-respect needs than with the amount of the weekly paycheck or related benefits, such as the

ILLUS. 20-6

Recognition is especially important to some employees.

number of paid holidays or sick days. However, pay is definitely considered more important than such things as work rules, number and length of work breaks, and physical conditions in which the employee works. The most surprising conclusion in these studies is that, while the amount of pay is important, it is not necessarily more important than the work itself.

Since the typical employee has an increased need to get satisfaction from the work itself, attention has been given in recent years to improving job design. **Job design** deals with the kind of work to be done and the way the work is organized.

To help overcome boredom and frustration of workers, managers have tried to get more variety into jobs. Making a job more interesting by adding variety to the task is called **job enlargement**. For example, picture an assembly line requiring three separate steps to finish a product; namely, drilling a hole, installing a bolt, and checking the finished product for quality. If the work is highly specialized, each of three workers performs one task only. Job enlargement allows each worker to do all three steps, or permits the employees to rotate the three jobs periodically. It must be remembered that job enlargement gives the employee more variety, not more work to do.

Another managerial technique to improve worker satisfaction is to get employees personally involved in their work through participation in decision making. The practice of allowing workers to assume some of the decision making previously done by managers is called **job enrichment**. For example, managers may request workers' opinions on matters affecting them, or may involve employees in setting job goals. Job enlargement, job enrichment, and similar techniques tend to increase work satisfaction which, in turn, encourages employees to do their best. As a result, improving employee satisfaction contributes to attaining the goals of a business.

Dealing With Conflict

At times people disagree with each other. Most job-related disagreements are likely to be temporary and are easily settled. Disagreements become a concern to a business when they lead to conflict. **Conflict** is a situation that develops when one person interferes with the achievement of another person's goals. Conflicts usually occur between two people, but they may also occur between an individual and a group, or between groups. Because conflict is usually an obstacle to job performance, managers need to be concerned about it.

Beneficial Conflict. A small amount of conflict is sometimes beneficial because it may challenge employees and may stimulate new ideas. For example, the advertising manager may decide to budget as little as possible to advertise a particular product, while the sales manager may have decided to try to boost sales for that particular product through increased advertising. At this point conflict exists because of a disagreement between

ILLUS. 20-7
Conflict sometimes can be beneficial and productive.

the goals set by each manager. However, this type of conflict can lead to a healthy discussion of how much to spend on advertising and how best to advertise to produce the highest sales at the lowest advertising cost. The result can lead to the achievement of a goal that is best for the business. When conflicting goals are discussed and resolved, the organization can benefit. However, when conflicting goals are not changed, long-term problems often result. If the sales and advertising managers went ahead with their individual plans, money would be wasted and sales would be lost.

Undesirable Conflict. While some conflict in organizations may be healthy, too much conflict can be harmful. Undesirable conflict results when the actions of any person or group interfere with the goals of the organization. If, in the preceding example, the sales manager became resentful of the advertising manager and undermined the company's budget goals by deliberately overspending the amount agreed upon for the product, undesirable conflict would result. Employees that dislike others and carry grudges often cause larger problems for the organization. Therefore, most conflicts should be resolved as soon as possible.

Resolving Conflict. Conflicts can be resolved in various ways. Since each situation differs, it is necessary for the manager to decide which type of strategy will best resolve each conflict.

Avoidance Strategy. One strategy used to resolve conflict is to take a neutral position or to agree with another person's position even though it differs from your personal belief. This approach avoids the conflict. One manager may decide to accept the goal of another manager, or to avoid expressing an opposing opinion about the goal. When a conflict is relatively unimportant, the avoidance strategy may best resolve the conflict. However, if a disagreement involves extremely important issues, an avoidance strategy may not be advisable. It will often lead to resentment.

Compromise Strategy. A second way to resolve conflict is to seek a compromise. Everyone involved in a conflict agrees to a mutually acceptable solution. Often a compromise grows out of a thorough discussion of the goals and the best way to achieve those goals. This strategy is preferred because it usually leads to a workable solution, since everyone involved personally contributes to the decision. Also, people are more likely to support a compromise strategy that they have helped to develop.

Win/Lose Strategy. The most dangerous approach used to resolve conflict is a win/lose strategy. A win/lose strategy is one in which no one compromises, thereby resulting in one person winning and one losing. A win/lose strategy is never acceptable to everyone, although people often engage in such a strategy. Win/lose strategies interfere with the achievement of organizational goals because they often: (a) take time and energy away from the main problems and issues; (b) delay decisions; (c) arouse anger that hurts human relationships; and (d) cause personal resentment, which can lead to other problems.

Because win/lose situations are destructive, managers attempt to prevent them. Setting clear objectives that are understood and agreed upon, stressing the need for cooperation in reaching objectives, and working for group decisions when special problems or disagreements arise are ways managers can avoid win/lose strategies.

Other Human-Relations Problems

In addition to dealing with conflict, managers face other types of human-relations problems daily. One problem is that of dealing with the personal problems of workers. Most personal problems are simple situations that require little or no action by managers. For instance, sometimes all a supervisor need do for the employee who has a flooded basement or a child with a temporary illness is to listen thoughtfully. Occasionally personal problems are very serious and may affect an employee's work. For example, an employee who is addicted to drugs or alcohol will probably be unable to perform on the job satisfactorily. Today, many business firms try to offer counseling and other help rather than simply discharging employees who have major personal problems. Managers must be able to identify problems and be ready to provide assistance when important problems occur.

Another human-relations problem is that of disciplining workers who violate work rules. **Work rules** are regulations that are created for the purpose of enabling an organization to meet its goals. The rules are developed so that work is done more efficiently. Work rules, for example, might deal with smoking, hours of work, care of equipment, and employee safety. Some firms specify penalties for work rule violations. For instance, employees who punch a time clock usually receive a paycheck deduction for arriving late or leaving before quitting time. Usually penalties vary based on the type of rule and the number of times a rule is violated. A supervisor who establishes and follows a fair set of guides in disciplining workers, such as those found in Illus. 20–8, soon earns the respect of employees.

ILLUS. 20–8
Employers must be fair and reasonable when enforcing established work rules.

Management Guidelines for Enforcing Work Rules

1. Explain work rules to all employees.
2. Acquaint employees with penalties for work rule violations.
3. Investigate each violation thoroughly before taking any action.
4. Act as soon as possible after investigating a violation and deciding on the action to be taken.
5. Inform the employee of the penalty and the reason for the penalty.
6. Treat similar violations with consistency.
7. Adjust a penalty, if necessary, to fit any special circumstances surrounding a violation.
8. Punish in private and praise in public.
9. Encourage employees to follow work rules by rewarding those who excel at doing so.

Effective leaders are those who are able to handle all types of human-relations problems. The successful leader understands human behavior and applies good human-relations principles in working with people. Conflicts are not created by the manager, but they are also not ignored. The effective manager tries at all times to help employees satisfy their own needs while also accomplishing the goals of the business.

NEW TERMS AND CONCEPTS

Define the following terms and concepts, which may be found in boldface type on the page shown in parentheses.

leadership (392)
human relations (392)
leadership style (394)
autocratic leader (395)
democratic leader (396)
open style (397)
personality (400)
motivation (400)
job design (402)
job enlargement (402)
job enrichment (402)
conflict (402)
work rules (404)

CHAPTER REVIEW

1. In the early history of business, were managers concerned more about machines and technology, or about the needs of employees?
2. List 11 common traits that effective leaders possess.
3. How can a person improve the traits and abilities needed to be a good leader?
4. If a manager believes that employees like work, what type of supervision and control will likely be used?
5. When should effective managers change the way they supervise employees?
6. What factors influence a manager's leadership style?
7. When should an autocratic leadership style be used?
8. How are decisions made under a democratic style of leadership?
9. What are the disadvantages of an open style of leadership?
10. List six important human-relations skills needed by managers.
11. What categories of needs are increasing in importance for most workers today?
12. Is the amount of pay the most important factor in job satisfaction for most workers?
13. What are two ways that managers can get more variety into employees' jobs?
14. How can a modest amount of conflict sometimes be beneficial?
15. What type of strategy works best when resolving a conflict that is relatively unimportant?

QUESTIONS FOR CLASS DISCUSSION

1. How does a weak supervisor differ from a strong supervisor in terms of getting employees to perform necessary tasks?
2. Discuss why it would be possible for a person to possess all the traits shown in Illus. 20–1, yet not be a good leader.
3. Do you believe that all good leaders are born leaders?
4. What would a manager who exercises general rather than close supervision and control over workers most likely believe about whether employees like to work?
5. Which type of worker would prefer a manager with an autocratic leadership style rather than a democratic style?
6. When the physical and safety needs of workers have been met, which set of needs then serves as the strongest motivating force?
7. Discuss four job preferences that the average worker ranks higher in importance than salary.
8. Discuss ways in which managers can redesign jobs in order to make work more satisfying.

9. In coping with conflict, why is a compromise strategy better than a win/lose strategy?

10. Why does a manager need to have a specific set of work rules?

PROBLEMS AND PROJECTS

1. Contact three managers to find out how they rank leadership traits in importance. List the 11 traits found in Illus. 20–1 on the left side of the paper. Across the top make three columns and head them: Most Importance, Average Importance, and Least Importance. Ask each manager to place a checkmark in one of the three columns for each trait.
2. Place each of the following job qualities on separate slips of paper or cards: (a) pleasant work area; (b) interesting tasks; (c) fair work rules; (d) good pay; and (e) responsibility. Ask five adults who have been working full time for at least one year to arrange the slips in order of importance to them. Place the most important item on the far left. Next to it on the right should be the item of second importance. Continue until the least important item is on the far right. Make a record of which item was first, second, third, fourth, and fifth. After five people have responded, summarize the results and compare your results with the results found in the text. Prepare a report for your class.
3. For each of the five categories of needs listed in Illus. 20–5, list things managers can do for employees to satisfy the need. Then list things that managers do that dissatisfy employees.
4. Identify someone you think is a good manager. Write a report that includes that person's (a) best leadership traits, (b) beliefs about whether people like or dislike work, and (c) leadership style.
5. Show three teachers or administrators in your school the list of ten management guidelines for enforcing work rules in Illus. 20–8. Ask the teachers or administrators which of these rules are used with students for enforcing school rules.

CASE 20–1

Marie Prant is a cashier in a grocery store, and Chuck Hill is a stock clerk who puts merchandise on the shelves after price-stamping it. Occasionally Chuck forgets to price-stamp an item. When this happens, the cashier must ring for Chuck to ask him the price. Marie takes great pride in being considered the fastest and best cashier in the store. Thus, she becomes irritated whenever she is slowed down to get a price check. She is especially annoyed on Fridays and Saturdays when items are not marked and there are long lines of customers.

One Saturday, Marie had to call Chuck to price two items within several minutes. A few minutes later, Marie had to call Chuck again. Chuck was slightly delayed in getting to the register, and when he arrived Marie snapped at him, "If you are not going to do your job, you should quit. You are holding up all of my customers. I am serious, Chuck; if you are still working here on Monday, I will quit."

Chuck said nothing other than to give the price of the requested item and went back to work stamping prices and stocking shelves. The manager, Janice Lumis, heard what had happened. Not wanting to lose either employee, she had to decide what to do before Monday morning.

Required:

1. Can this be called a conflict situation? Explain.
2. Which conflict strategy did Chuck Hill use? Explain.
3. Which conflict strategy did Marie Prant use? Explain.
4. If you were Janice Lumis, what action would you take?

CASE 20–2

Sally Bensen had been supervisor for ten stenographers in the marketing department for nearly two years. The workers thought a great deal of Sally. In fact, many of them said she was the best supervisor they had ever had. Sally's manager, Juanita Sanchez, was most impressed with the good human relations among the stenographers, and with the excellent work her department did. The manager was so impressed that Sally was transferred to manage 20 typists and clerks in the accounting department. Since Sally had prior accounting training and experience working as a bookkeeper, Juanita Sanchez thought she would be perfect in the new job.

After only two months, human relations in the accounting department had gone down and work output had declined. "What is happening, Sally?" Juanita asked. "Why isn't it working out?"

Sally responded, "I do not know. In the marketing department, I always discussed problems with the workers, and as a group, we worked out solutions acceptable to everyone. In the accounting department, no one wants to discuss problems and solutions. They want me to solve all of the problems for them. That is just not my style."

Required:

1. Is it possible that a person might be an effective leader in one situation but not in another? Explain.
2. What type of leadership style does Sally practice?

3. Do you think that Sally would be more successful if she changed her leadership style to fit the situation in the accounting department? Explain.

Have You Thought About Becoming . . .

. . . A JOB ANALYST?

You may not have heard of the career of job analyst, but in large companies it is an important job. The job analyst is a specialist in the personnel department and is responsible for preparing job descriptions and job specifications.

In order to hire the best people, the personnel department must have accurate and detailed descriptions of all jobs in the company. Those descriptions are also used to plan training programs and to prepare for employee evaluations.

Information for job descriptions and specifications is collected three ways: (1) experienced workers and their supervisors complete questionnaires about specific jobs; (2) job analysts conduct interviews with employees and supervisors about job duties; or (3) the analyst observes several workers performing a job and lists the duties being performed. When information about the job has been collected, the job analyst prepares a written job description and a job specification card. The analyst may also prepare a number of other reports for use by managers regarding working conditions, training needs, personnel policies, and the organization of work.

Job analysts usually need to have a college degree in personnel management. They must have excellent interviewing, observation, and writing skills. The ability to manage large amounts of information is also important. A job analyst has the opportunity to learn about many jobs and activities in a company, so it is a very good way to prepare for a career in personnel management.

21

SELECTION, TRAINING, AND PROMOTION

After studying this chapter you will be able to:

- List the functions of a personnel department.
- Identify steps and procedures in recruiting employees.
- Compare the different ways in which employees can be trained.
- Discuss reasons for promoting and transferring employees.
- Calculate the labor turnover rate for a business.

The success of any business firm, large or small, depends on people. It is said that employees are one of the most important assets of a business. Therefore, the management of employees helps to determine how successful a business will be. If a business is to make a profit, management must recruit good employees, help them to be as productive as possible, and work to meet the personal needs of the employees.

PERSONNEL MANAGEMENT

The aspect of management which is concerned with obtaining and effectively utilizing human resources is called **personnel management.** Not so many years ago, the functions of personnel management were thought to have been performed well if all of the jobs in the business were filled. Today, however, it is recognized that much more is involved in effective personnel management.

Functions of Personnel Management

There are many functions of personnel management performed by business today. The extent to which these functions are performed depends on many factors, such as the size of the business and the importance placed on personnel programs by management.

Selecting New Employees. Hiring well-qualified employees is an important function of personnel management. It is necessary for management to recruit applicants, determine their qualifications, hire those whose qualifications best match the job to be filled, and prepare employees for their new jobs.

Training Employees. Personnel management needs to follow up selection procedures with effective training programs. New employees and employees transferred to new jobs must be trained. Changes in jobs, machines, processes, and policies are constantly occurring, which require additional training for workers. Employees also need training to prepare them for promotion.

Illus. 21-1
New employees should be informed of company policies and procedures.

Promoting and Transferring Employees. Another function of personnel management is to develop policies and procedures for promoting and transferring personnel. Some employees find that a new job in the same company is more challenging and exciting than their old job. Employees not performing well may do better if transferred to a different job. Without opportunities for promotion, personnel who have been selected and trained by a business will look for employment elsewhere.

Determining Wages and Benefits. The amount of compensation received in the form of wages and other benefits is of vital concern to all workers. Administration of the wage and benefits programs of a company is another function of personnel management.

Maintaining Health and Safety Programs. To be efficient, employees must be healthy; they must also be protected from accidents. Personnel management is very concerned with providing health and safety programs.

Maintaining Labor-Management Relationships. If the workers in a business are members of a union, a function of personnel management is to assist in negotiating labor contracts with the union and to discuss and resolve differences between management and the union. If the company does not have a union to represent employees, the same activities will occur but on a less formal basis.

Establishing a Good Working Environment. An unhappy, dissatisfied worker is not an efficient worker. Assisting in the establishment of a work environment in which the morale of the workers is high and in which workers have cooperative working relationships is an important function of all managers, but of personnel managers in particular.

Organizing for the Management of Personnel

In a company that has only a few employees, the owner or general manager performs the personnel functions. The manager that works side by side with employees should attempt to understand them and appreciate their viewpoints. Likewise, the employees should learn something about the problems of running the company. As a result, the employees would have a better attitude about the job and would feel free to discuss problems with their employer. Such conditions make for good employer-employee relationships.

Much of today's business, however, is conducted on a large scale. It is not unusual to find companies with thousands of employees. Naturally, it is impossible to have a close relationship between the owners and the employees in a company of this size. Since large business firms need employees for many different kinds of highly specialized jobs, the job of selecting qualified employees, training them for their jobs, providing for their health and safety, and helping them work efficiently is complex and important. Large businesses, therefore, require personnel departments which are often organized into divisions representing the major functions of personnel management. The dotted lines in Illus. 21–2 indicate that the chief function of a personnel department is to give advice and service to other departments. Department managers will use the services of the personnel department regularly as they work with the employees in their departments.

In the remaining sections of this chapter we will examine procedures for

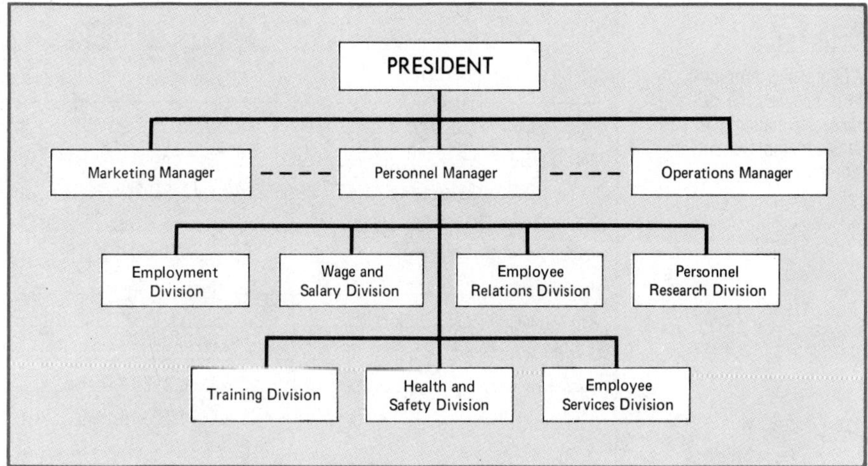

ILLUS. 21–2
The personnel department provides advice and services to other departments within the company.

selecting, training, and promoting employees. Chapter 22 discusses employee compensation and benefits, and Chapter 23 describes the process of developing effective labor relations.

SELECTING PERSONNEL

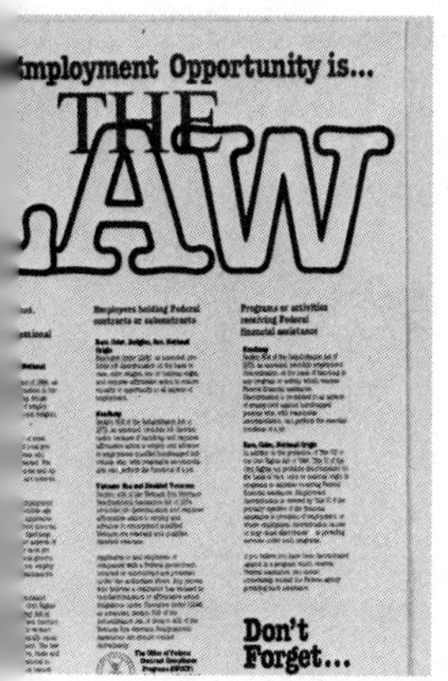

Hiring new employees is an important management activity. If selection procedures are effective and the right employees are hired for each job, many problems will be avoided. If poor selection procedures are used, many people will be hired who are not appropriate for the job. This will result in higher training costs, dissatisfied employees, and many other personnel problems.

While it is illegal to discriminate in hiring employees, it is good business practice to search for the most qualified applicants. Firms that automatically exclude women and persons from minority races will often lose effective employees who can contribute to the success of the business.

A business must take the necessary time to find and hire the right people. This section discusses some of the essential procedures which should be followed in selecting personnel.

Employment Requisition

As a first step in the process of hiring a new employee, it is necessary to establish that a new employee is needed. In many business firms this is accomplished by issuing an **employment requisition** (a request for a worker). An example of an employment requisition is shown in Illus. 21–3 on page 414.

Employment requisitions are filled out by the manager of the department needing a new employee and then sent to the personnel department.

ILLUS. 21–3

When a new employee is needed, the department manager issues an employment requisition.

The Sheffield Company

Employment Requisition

Number needed 1 Date needed 7/12/-- Date of request 5/2/--

Job title Receptionist Department Office

Duties Greet visitors, operate switchboard, light typing

Addition to force No Permanent ____ Temporary ____

Replacement For Maxine Wood Permanent X Temporary ____

Rate of pay $180 a week to start Hours of work 8:30 a.m.--5 p.m., M-F

Education High school graduate

Experience Experience as a receptionist desirable but not necessary

Charge to Acct. No. ____ Signed John Hendricke Dept. Chief

Approved Nancy Kent Dept. Manager

Employment Department Record	Department Manager's Acceptance
Name ____	Name ____
Address ____	Address ____
Was employed ☐ Transferred ☐ To fill this requisition	Started work on
To begin work on ____ Rate ____	____ at ____
Reg. No. ____ Acct. No. ____ Signed ____ Emp. Dept.	Signed ____ Dept. Manager

The need for an employee should be anticipated as far in advance as possible so that the personnel department will have time to find a suitable employee.

Job Specification

The employment requisition does not contain complete information about the job for which a worker is needed. The personnel department must have complete and accurate knowledge of the job to be filled before it can properly screen applicants. One of the best ways to obtain this information is to have detailed specifications prepared for each kind of job. A **job specification** includes information as to the nature of the work done in the particular job, the necessary qualifications needed by the employee to do that work, and the opportunities that the job offers to the employee. This information is usually printed on cards, which are known as **job specification cards** (see Illus. 21–4). These cards are kept on file in the personnel department or specifications for all jobs in a company may be maintained by the computer. The information is used in deciding how to find qualified applicants for the job, and, after applicants are recruited, the information is used to determine which applicant is best qualified for the job.

Cordes and Hughes, Inc.

Job Specification

Job Title Stock clerk Department Stock room

DUTIES

Responsible for filling all orders, maintenance of stock records as prescribed by management, appearance of stock room

EMPLOYEE QUALIFICATIONS

Education: College ______ High School X Technical ______

Experience Must have some experience and knowledge of electrical trade

Physical requirements Good health

Mental requirements Accurate, honest, conscientious, systematic

EMPLOYEE INFORMATION

Hours of work 8 a.m. to 4:30 p.m., Monday to Friday

Wages $160 to start; annual raise; maximum wage $210

Vacation One year, two weeks

Promotions To assistant purchasing agent

ADDITIONAL REMARKS

Illus. 21-4

A job specification card outlines employee duties and qualifications.

Recruiting Applicants

After the personnel department has received an employment requisition, it must then recruit applicants for the job. It is desirable that there be enough applicants from which a well-qualified person can be selected. Many sources of prospective employees exist; the personnel department will determine which source or sources to use for each job vacancy.

Employees of the Company. Often a vacancy can be filled by transferring a present employee from another job. Such a transfer may give an employee a chance to use abilities better than was the case in the previous job. The policy of transfer or promotion from within the company provides a strong incentive for employees to be efficient and to prepare themselves for advancement. Filling a vacancy from within the firm usually creates another vacancy that must be filled from an outside source or by another transfer. Many companies have a policy of posting all vacancies and allowing current employees to apply for any vacancy.

Friends of Present Employees. Employees of a business may recommend friends for employment. This is most likely to happen if current employees are happy with their jobs. Again, procedures need to be developed to inform employees of job openings and allow them to recommend people for the job.

Applications on File. A business that has earned a reputation as a good employer is likely to have many applications on file at all times. A company that has many job openings may choose to take applications continually and use them when openings occur. Usually, with this procedure, applications are maintained for a period of time (say six months). Applicants not hired in that time must then reapply to keep their applications active.

Placement Bureaus. Colleges and universities, technical and vocational schools, and some large high schools maintain placement bureaus to aid their graduates in obtaining jobs. These bureaus can furnish lists of suitable candidates for open job positions. Also, the offices of many trade unions maintain lists of unemployed members and can furnish applicants for job vacancies.

State Employment Service. All states maintain an employment service known as Job Service. Local offices throughout a state are staffed by people trained to locate and select workers in all types of occupations and to refer these workers to potential employers. A state's Job Service can be particularly helpful to small- and medium-sized companies which do not maintain personnel departments.

Private Employment Agencies. Another source a business can use to look for prospective employees is the private employment agency. Individuals looking for employment register with and provide personal data to these agencies. Payment for the agency's services is generally made by the individuals for whom the agencies find employment. Private employment agencies usually specialize in supplying personnel of a particular kind, such as office or factory workers. They provide a preliminary screening of possible applicants for the job openings.

Advertising. Advertising in newspapers or magazines is a popular and effective method of obtaining job applicants. This source is frequently used

when a business needs large numbers of workers or when the workers are needed immediately. Classified newspaper ads and ads in trade publications often get results. They can be either open ads, which give the name of the company, or blind ads, which give a box number at the newspaper office to which an applicant may write. Open ads usually yield more applicants than blind ads.

When the right kinds of employees are difficult to find and when they are needed in rather large numbers, some businesses use radio and television advertising to recruit job applicants. This type of advertising is expensive and is ordinarily used only by large companies.

Processing Applicants

Most business firms require applicants to fill out an application form. The company must be careful that the form does not ask for information that can be considered discriminatory and contrary to state and federal labor laws. Questions should be asked that obtain information necessary to make the best selection for the job. The application form can be used to screen out those people who do not meet the basic job requirements.

The following procedures are typically followed by personnel departments after applicants for a job have been obtained:

1. Applicants are interviewed to determine whether they have the general qualifications called for by the job specification card. During the interview, applicants should be given detailed facts about the company and the job so that they will understand what is expected. This also helps avoid disappointment or misunderstanding on the part of the applicant. A good interviewer keeps careful notes about the qualifications of each applicant and the level of interest each applicant has in obtaining the job.
2. For the applicants who pass the preliminary interview, tests are administered to determine their level of knowledge and skill.
3. Applicants are usually given a physical examination. It is wise for a business to require an examination since it will reveal whether the applicant is physically able to do the work expected. It may also protect the business in a lawsuit if the employee later claims disability as a result of the work. The medical report becomes a part of the permanent record of the employee. In many cases, the physical examination is not given until an applicant is ready to be hired.
4. References (persons who know the applicant) are contacted to see if the applicant's previous experience has been satisfactory. The company also checks other facts on the application for accuracy. Some employers believe that references are of no value because an applicant will not list a reference who is likely to give

a poor recommendation. However, careful questioning during the interview can often reveal important information. Schools attended and former employment should be checked even though these are not given as references.

5. In many cases, the applicants who have thus far proved satisfactory to the personnel department are sent to the head of the department that has the opening. The department head can then interview those applicants, describe the job in more detail, and answer questions the applicant may have.
6. When an applicant is hired, the records for the personnel department are then prepared.

Orientation to the Job

After an applicant has been hired, an orientation (introduction) to the new job and to co-workers is very important. The first hours on a new job are trying ones for most people. Statistics show that a large number of new employees leave their positions during the first week and sometimes, even on the first day. If a new employee is placed behind a desk or a machine with scarcely a word of explanation or advice from anyone, that person may develop an immediate dislike for the place, the position, and for co-workers.

The new worker should be taken on a tour of the company, which should include the location of the lunchroom, of lockers for clothes, and the like. The department head should have another talk with the new employee about the company in general and the employee's new job. The department head or the new employee's immediate supervisor should then introduce the new employee to co-workers, and a particularly friendly person in the department should be asked to take the new employee to lunch. If the company has a manual which states the policies and regulations of the business, a copy should be given to the new employee. Finally, the supervisor of the new employee should provide detailed information and directions about the job. Illus. 21–5 gives recommendations on effective orientation procedures.

Follow-up of New Employees

The personnel department should perform a follow-up of each new employee to see whether the right person has been selected. This practice will aid the department in the future selection of employees. By consulting the department head or supervisor, the personnel department can determine how well the new employee is working. By consulting the new employee, the personnel department can determine whether he or she is satisfied. The follow-up can be used to determine if orientation was effective and what training will be needed.

ILLUS. 21–5

A good orientation program is important for new employees.

New Employee Orientation Guidelines

1. Set aside adequate time for the orientation. Do not rush through a great deal of information.
2. Do not use business language that a new employee is not likely to understand.
3. As you show the employee around the business, explain the importance of what the new employee is seeing.
4. If there is a lot to be learned, break the orientation into several sessions.
5. Whenever possible, provide materials for the employee to keep and study. Be sure to explain the materials, and be careful that the materials are not too difficult to read and understand.
6. Make sure the new employee understands the information. Ask questions and give plenty of opportunity for the employee to ask questions. Some things may need to be explained more than once.
7. Show the employee where to go with problems and questions. Reassure the individual that it is alright to ask questions at any time.

TRAINING PERSONNEL

Selection methods, which result in the employment of qualified workers, should be followed by effective training programs. The difference between the average worker in any occupation and the expert worker is largely a matter of training, and the difference in their output is usually very noticeable.

If a company has no plan for training its workers, the new employee and the employee who is transferred to a new job usually learn their jobs by a trial-and-error method. They work as well as they can and are corrected by the supervisor when a major error is made. The substitution of formal training programs for trial-and-error methods costs money, but it is a cost which can be easily justified in most businesses. The simplest argument in favor of a formal training program is that a company pays for a training program whether it has one or not. In a company which has no formal training program, employees must do a great deal of learning on the company's time. This learning, which is sometimes accompanied by costly errors, is done at company expense. It follows that if money is being spent, it should be spent for training and the training should be well planned.

Numerous reasons exist to justify training all employees. Changes are constantly occurring in the business which require additional training for workers—changes in jobs, in machines, in processes, and in policies. Employees also need training which will prepare them for promotion. A business may use various types of training methods.

On-the-Job Training

The most common type of training is **on-the-job training.** The employee is placed in the new job and, in effect, learns it under close supervision until skilled enough to do the job with a normal amount of supervision. The intensive supervision is usually given by the new employee's supervisor, who usually has received training in how to teach others effectively. The major disadvantage of on-the-job training is that during the training period, the production of the unit in which the job is located slows down.

Vestibule Training

Vestibule training is conducted by company instructors in classrooms away from the work area. The objective of vestibule training is to simulate the job for which the trainee is being prepared. As contrasted to on-the-job training, where learning and actual work are being accomplished at the same time, vestibule training concentrates the attention of trainees on learning the job. Because the trainees can concentrate on learning the job without the pressure of actual production, vestibule training is often more effective than on-the-job training. Also, vestibule training is superior to on-the-job training in that it does not slow production in the regular work area.

A procedures manual is a valuable aid during on-the-job and vestibule training, and it is also useful to workers after the training has been completed. A procedures manual gives definite instructions for the performance of certain operations and tasks. For example, a correspondence manual describes the various styles of business letters used by the company and often includes capitalization, punctuation, and grammar rules. A sales manual describes effective sales procedures, shows examples of forms to be completed with customers, and gives detailed product knowledge.

Apprenticeship Training

In **apprenticeship training,** a trainee becomes an assistant to a skilled worker for a period of time, usually from two to six years. During the apprenticeship, the trainee learns by watching and assisting the skilled worker. Often the learning which the apprentice obtains from the worker is supplemented by formal classroom instruction. Apprenticeships are most often used in the skilled trades such as printing, plumbing, and electrical work.

Supervisory Training

Business now recognizes that the supervisor occupies a key position in the business organization. Supervisors are the first line of management;

that is, they are the ones who are in direct contact with the workers. To most workers, the supervisor represents the company; therefore, the attitude of most workers toward the company is based on their reaction to their immediate supervisor. The increasing recognition of the need for good supervisors has led to the development of training programs which are designed to assist supervisors in improving their performance. Most supervisors are selected for their positions because they have demonstrated excellent technical skills. Therefore, programs for **supervisory training** usually are designed to improve the leadership and management skills of supervisors. Since most on-the-job training is conducted by supervisors, training programs are also set up to teach supervisors how to train their workers. Most often supervisory training is conducted in formal classes taught by training experts.

Executive Development

Executive development (preparing persons for careers in top management) is vital to the long-run success of a business. Training for management positions is accomplished in many different ways. Formalized courses, which are quite similar to business courses offered in colleges and universities, are provided by some companies. At times, management trainees are sent to universities to participate in executive development seminars, and some are sent to universities to obtain advanced degrees. Much on-the-job training is also given to management trainees. Often management trainees act as assistants for the executives whose jobs it is anticipated they will eventually hold. Some companies also rotate management trainees from job to job so that they will understand the total operations of the company.

An effective training program serves more than the new employee. It can help to identify employees who are not able to perform the job as required, even after training. Those people will need to be transferred to less demanding positions, or be terminated. Effective training also prepares people for transfers to new jobs and for promotion.

PROMOTING, TRANSFERRING, AND DISCHARGING PERSONNEL

The selection and training process can be quite expensive. Once a good employee is found, the company should attempt to keep the employee as long as possible. Good policies and procedures for promoting and transferring personnel will help keep employees and reduce the need to hire and train new workers.

Promotions

Promotion is the advancement of an employee to a position in which the employee has more authority and responsibility. Usually a promotion also includes an increase in pay and results in more prestige and privileges. Promotion opportunities occur when jobs are vacated as the result of retirement, resignation, death, or dismissal, and when a new position is created.

As much as possible, a business should follow the policy of filling vacancies in high-level positions by promoting its own employees. Assuming that the company's selection program has been successful in securing well-qualified employees, these employees will be ambitious and will look for opportunities for advancement. If employees find that there are few opportunities for advancement, they may not work as hard at their jobs, and they will not be as motivated to take advantage of the company's training programs.

Promotion policies must be carefully prepared, and it is very important that all employees understand these policies. Employees must, first of all, know the possible positions to which they might advance. To accomplish this, as is discussed in Chapter 24, many companies provide employees with an organization chart which shows lines of authority and promotion.

Employees will want to know the factors that are considered in promotion. The two basic factors that most companies consider are ability and **seniority** (the length of time a person has worked for the company). The task of evaluating the abilities of employees being considered for promotion is difficult. Generally the decision as to which employee most deserves the promotion should be made by the immediate supervisor of the workers involved, who is most aware of their abilities. If two or more workers have about the same abilities, the one with the most seniority should receive the promotion.

Transfers

Transfer is the assignment of an employee to another job in the company which, in general, involves the same kinds of skills and responsibilities. At times transfers are made at the request of the employee, but more often they are initiated by the employee's supervisor.

Some of the reasons for transfers are as follows: (1) employees being trained for management positions are transferred from one position to another to give them more experiences; (2) capable employees are transferred to jobs which give them a better chance for promotion; (3) workers are transferred to a new department which has been established because of the growth of the company; (4) workers choose to transfer to jobs that better meet their interests or skills; (5) employees are transferred when it is discovered that they are not well suited to their present positions; and (6) workers are transferred when they are unable to get along with their fellow workers or supervisors.

Transfer policies and procedures must be carefully established and must be understood by employees. If the reason for a transfer is not thoroughly explained, the employee being transferred may feel unfairly treated.

Discharges

A **discharge** involves a permanent separation of an employee from the company. In ordinary language, this means that the employee is fired. Discharge of an employee usually is caused by failure to do the job, failure to get along with the supervisor, or failure to get along with other employees. More people are discharged for human-relations reasons than for lack of ability. Discharges are unfortunate for both the employer and the employee.

A layoff is similar to a discharge. A **layoff** is a temporary reduction in the number of employees. It may arise because the job is eliminated due to a decline in business, changes in products or procedures, or the adoption of more efficient processes or equipment. Discharges are caused by the employee, whereas layoffs are caused by changes affecting the company. After a layoff, an employee may be recalled when a new job is available. Discharges and layoffs are expensive for a company and result in an employee morale problem. Therefore, managers should consider them carefully and use them only when absolutely necessary.

Frequently the discharge of an employee is not left entirely in the hands of the department head. A department head wishing to discharge an employee must consult the personnel department. Such a consultation may result in transferring the employee to another department. In this way a low rate of labor turnover can be maintained.

Labor turnover is a term used to describe the extent to which employees come and go in a business. Turnover affects the efficiency of a business because the loss of an experienced employee necessitates hiring and training a new employee. Consequently, business firms make every effort to keep their turnover rate low.

Two of the most common formulas for computing turnover are:

Number of employees who have terminated their employment with the business ÷ Average number of employees = Percentage of labor turnover

Number of employee replacements ÷ Average number of employees = Percentage of labor turnover

Let us suppose that during one year 15 employees left their jobs in a company. Twelve new employees were hired to replace those who had left, and the average number of employees on the payroll was 100. According to the first formula, the labor turnover was 15 percent (15 ÷ 100). According to the second formula, it was 12 percent (12 ÷ 100).

ILLUS. 21-6
Exit interviews may give managers insight into problems which exist within the company.

Exit Interviews

When an employee is discharged or resigns, it is desirable that the employee be given an **exit interview** (an interview with an employee who is leaving). This interview is often conducted by someone in the company other than the employee's immediate supervisor. The exit interview offers the company an opportunity to learn the views of the employee. In the case of resignations, the reasons for leaving often provide clues to problems or help identify conditions management needs to know about. These interviews may lead to an improvement in company policies and procedures.

NEW TERMS AND CONCEPTS

Define the following terms and concepts, which may be found in boldface type on the page shown in parentheses.

- personnel management (410)
- employment requisition (413)
- job specification (414)
- job specification cards (414)
- on-the-job training (420)
- vestibule training (420)
- apprenticeship training (420)
- supervisory training (421)
- executive development (421)
- promotion (421)
- seniority (422)
- transfer (422)
- discharge (423)
- layoff (423)
- labor turnover (423)
- exit interview (424)

CHAPTER REVIEW

1. In the past, what was an indication that personnel management activities had been performed well?
2. List the seven functions of personnel management.
3. What conditions exist in a small business that encourage good personnel management?
4. What is the meaning of the dotted lines in the organizational chart shown in Illustration 21–2?
5. What can happen to firms that automatically exclude certain groups of people when they are hiring new employees?
6. Who is responsible for completing an employment requisition?
7. Why is a job specification card necessary?
8. What are the major sources of applicants for a company?
9. Which type of advertisements usually yield more applicants for a job—open ads or blind ads?
10. Why do some employers consider references given by an applicant to be of little value?
11. Why is orientation for new employees so important?
12. What is the most common type of training?
13. What skills are usually emphasized in a supervisory training program?

14. Why should a business attempt to promote its own employees whenever possible?
15. What is the value of an exit interview?

QUESTIONS FOR CLASS DISCUSSION

1. In what ways can personnel management help improve the health and safety of employees?
2. Which of the functions of personnel management do you think are the most important? the least important? Why?
3. How can a manager of a small business become a better personnel manager?
4. What should the interviewer accomplish in the first job interview?
5. Why do some employees leave their job soon after they are hired?
6. What are some ways that a supervisor can help a new employee adjust to the job?
7. Do you agree that a company pays for a training program whether it has one or not?
8. How should seniority be used in deciding on a promotion?
9. Why are more people discharged for human-relations reasons than for lack of ability?
10. Why should a transfer, rather than a discharge, be considered for an employee that is not performing well?

PROBLEMS AND PROJECTS

1. Obtain an application blank from a business and fill it out. Which of the questions on the application do you think would be most helpful to the company in deciding whether it should hire you? Are there any questions that do not seem to be useful?
2. Prepare an employment guide to be used by students from your school when they graduate. Gather information that will help them apply for jobs. It should include such areas as sources of jobs, application blanks, job interviews, and the first day on the job.
3. Interview a person from a local company who is responsible for training employees. Learn what types of training are provided, who is responsible for training, and what training materials are used. Prepare a report on the interview for your class.
4. As the manager of a supermarket, you are responsible for hiring a new checker/cashier. Answer the following questions.
   a. What sources would you use to find applicants?
   b. What procedures would you follow to select a new checker/cashier?
   c. What type of training would you provide for the new employee?
5. The Jonesville Company had an average of 300 employees this year. The number of employees who left the company during the year was 20; the number of employee replacements was 15. During the prior year the average number of employees was 280 with 15 leaving and 10 replacements. Using both methods shown in this chapter, calculate the labor turnover rate for each of the two years.

CASE 21–1

The Midsouth Textiles Company employs a large number of factory workers and has a specific procedure for selecting and training employees. Upon passing a preliminary interview, the successful applicants are hired to work for the firm. New employees go through the following program:

a. They are given two days of orientation to acquaint them with company policies and rules and to introduce them to work areas and equipment.
b. They are then assigned to an experienced worker to learn the routine tasks of equipment operation. If they are not able to operate the equipment well at the end of six weeks, they are discharged.
c. New assignments to more difficult jobs with higher pay are made at the end of six months. Employee ratings submitted by supervisors determine who gets the new assignments. Those

employees not chosen stay at the more routine job and do not get pay increases.

d. Every six months, employees can apply for transfers and promotions. Only those who have demonstrated outstanding performance will be allowed to change jobs.
e. After five years with the company, an employee can be selected for the company's executive training program. To be selected, an employee must have been promoted at least three times and must pass a management aptitude test.
f. All executives are selected from the executive training program, and promotions are made whenever openings exist.

Required:

1. What are the strengths of Midsouth's selection and training procedure?

2. Can you identify any weaknesses?

CASE 21–2

Charles Morgan had been hired in the mail room of the Teletron Trading Corporation five weeks ago. His job was to collect mail twice daily from each office in the building, sort and process the outgoing mail, deliver outgoing mail to the local post office, and pick up incoming mail from the post office. He learned the job in one day by working with the outgoing employee, Tom Williams. Tom Williams had been hired by another company.

After one month, Morgan thought that he was doing rather well with such little supervision. In fact, the supervisor was seldom around. A week later he received notice that he was to be discharged effective next week. Since no explanation accompanied the announcement, he went to the personnel office immediately. The personnel manager pulled a folder from the file and began reading notes that had been placed there during the past month. Morgan responded truthfully to each of the items presented:

a. An hour late to work on May 15: "My car would not start, but I called to say that I would be in as soon as possible."
b. Two offices complained that the mail had not been picked up on the second of the month: "It was my second day on the job and I could not remember all the stops. After the second day, I made a schedule and I have not missed an office since."
c. The Research Department complained that an important document had been sent by regular mail that should have been sent special delivery: "I did not know the policy for deciding when and how to send items until I found and asked the supervisor. The supervisor gave me a procedures manual to study. Tom Williams did not tell me there was such a manual."

Several other similar complaints were included in the personnel file, each readily explained by Morgan. According to the personnel manager, Morgan was discharged in keeping with company policy. The discharge policy was that five or more complaints a month about an employee during the first year of employment were grounds for discharge.

Required:

1. What is your opinion of the company's discharge policy in Morgan's case?
2. Are there any personnel training problems that exist with the Teletron Trading Corporation?
3. What recommendations can you make to improve the training program?

Have You Thought About Becoming . . .

. . . A TRAINING DIRECTOR?

Have you considered combining a career in business with a career as a teacher? You can do that if you become a training director. A training director is responsible for preparing employees to be successful on their jobs. That usually includes orientation and training for new employees, as well as training experienced employees for promotions or transfers.

The training director may actually conduct the training programs in smaller companies. In larger companies, however, the director will usually work with instructors and supervisory personnel who conduct the training.

A training director needs to be able to identify training needs, organize training sessions, prepare materials to be used in the sessions, and evaluate the effectiveness of the training. It is important that the director understand and use the best training methods for each employee and each job.

Businesses are beginning to recognize the value of training. They are investing many thousands of dollars in training programs for employees, supervisors and executives. Positions in training departments are becoming more important each year. A position as a training director can be very satisfying as you watch employees who have been through your training programs use the skills that you have taught them.

If you are considering a career in training, you will need a college degree. Courses in personnel management and education are valuable. Courses in oral and written communications are also important. Some colleges now have specialized programs to prepare people for careers in training.

22

COMPENSATION AND BENEFITS

After studying this chapter you will be able to:

- Distinguish among the various types of wage and salary plans.
- Identify reasons why different wages and salaries are paid for different jobs.
- Describe the most common kinds of fringe benefits.
- Suggest ways in which the modified workweek can be used in business.
- Explain major provisions of both the Occupational Safety and Health Act and the Social Security Act.

The money people receive for the work they do is called **compensation.** One of the important reasons people work is for the compensation they receive for that work.

The amount of compensation for a job is affected by many factors: the degree of skill required, the conditions within which the job is performed, the amount of experience the worker has, the supply and demand for labor, economic conditions, and many other factors.

The satisfaction that people have with their jobs and the amount of work that they accomplish is certainly affected by the amount they are paid. An important responsibility of management is to insure that the compensation system used by the company satisfies employees and encourages them to do a good job.

In this chapter we discuss the types of compensation systems most often used by companies to pay employees. The policies and procedures used to manage compensation are described as well as other benefits provided to employees.

WAGES AND SALARIES

Two terms are often used to describe compensation systems. **Wages** is used to describe compensation paid on an hourly basis, and **salaries** is used to describe compensation of executives, supervisors, sales personnel, and other employees paid on a basis other than an hourly rate.

Wage and Salary Plans

Because businesses vary so greatly in the types of work they do and in the qualifications required of their employees, many methods are used in determining employee compensation. Under some wage plans two workers doing the same kind of work are paid the same rate of pay regardless of whether one produces more than the other. There are other systems in which a good worker can earn more than a worker who produces less. In the following sections, we will examine the major types of compensation plans.

Time Wages. The payment of salaries or wages on the basis of a specific period of time (a year, a month, a week, a day, or an hour) is probably the most common method of compensation. Under a **time wage plan,** an employee is paid a specific amount of money for each period of time worked. The most common kind of time wage is the hourly wage, but **straight salary,** (a flat rate per week or month) is also frequently used. Major advantages and disadvantages of time wages are shown in Illus. 22-1

ILLUS. 22-1
There are advantages and disadvantages of the time wage compensation plan.

Advantages	Disadvantages
• Only a small amount of clerical work is required to determine the wages to be paid.	• It offers no immediate incentive for extra effort and good work.
• Employees can budget personal expenses better since they know what pay they will receive.	• A conscientious worker may feel it is unfair to receive the same salary as someone who does not work as hard.
• This is the only satisfactory way of paying employees who do a variety of work, such as the employee who answers the telephone, serves as information clerk, and does some filing or record work.	

Commission. Under the **commission plan** of compensation, employees—usually salespeople—are paid a percentage of the volume of business done by them. For example, a salesperson may be paid a 5-percent commission on total net sales made each week. Thus, if sales for one week were $5,000, the commission earned was $250. The advantages and disadvantages of the commission plan are shown in Illus. 22-2.

ILLUS 22-2

Commission compensation plans appeal to some workers but not to others.

Advantages	Disadvantages
• It provides a direct incentive to employees to do as much work as possible. • It enables management to control costs. For example, the sales representatives of a wholesaler are paid a commission. Thus, the costs of sales representatives' salaries are a predetermined percentage of the selling price and vary directly with the sales volume of each person.	• Management may not have much control over the activities of employees on commission. For example, sales representatives are likely to do what they believe will ensure themselves a reasonable salary. • Employees are likely to be most interested in doing only those things that will directly increase their earnings. • Salespeople working on a commission are likely to concentrate on customers who place large orders and to neglect those who do not. • The amount an employee earns is likely to vary a great deal when there are seasonal fluctuations in sales volume.

Salary and Commission. The **salary and commission plan** combines a salary with a certain commission. For instance, a salesperson may be paid a salary of $200 a week plus a 2-percent commission on total sales for the week. Such a method eliminates most of the disadvantages of the straight salary and straight commission plans used alone. This plan is used chiefly for salespeople and managers.

Salary and Bonus. With a **salary and bonus plan** employees are paid a regular salary. In addition to their salary, they are paid a bonus if they do better than expected in a certain time period. For example, each salesperson may receive a salary of $400 a week. At the end of six months, each salesperson whose sales are more than $20,000 receives a bonus of 1 percent on his or her total sales. Sometimes the bonus is increased so that a higher percentage is received with even better performance. In the example just mentioned, the bonus might be 1 percent on all sales up to $20,000; 2 percent on all sales of $20,001 to $25,000; 3 percent on all sales of $25,001 to $30,000; and 4 percent on all sales of over $30,000. The bonus, however, is not always a percentage; sometimes it is a definite sum of money. If a group of employees does excellent work for six months, it may be rewarded with a $300 bonus.

The major advantage of the salary and bonus plan is that it keeps employees working harder over a longer period than they would if they were paid a salary plus a commission. This plan is a good way to pay salespeople, and bonuses are often used for production jobs in both factories and offices. The bonus is provided when production is greater than a predetermined level.

Piece-Rate Plans. A common type of incentive wage in businesses using mass production is the piece-rate plan. Under a **piece-rate plan,** the employee is paid a fixed rate for each unit of production. For example, if an employee gets 20 cents for each unit and produces 250 units a day, he or she receives $50. Although piece-rate plans are usually found in factories, certain office employees may also be paid on the basis of units of work completed. For examples, billing clerks may be paid according to the number of invoices they complete, and the wages of some typists and data entry personnel may be determined by the number of lines of material typed or entered.

ILLUS. 22-3

Piece-rate plans are often found in mass production businesses.

Piece rates for each job are usually established by a careful study of each job. If the studies have been properly made, a piece-rate plan can work well. Some advantages and disadvantages of this plan are given in Illus. 22-4.

ILLUS. 22-4
There are also some advantages and disadvantages of the piece-rate compensation plan.

Advantages	Disadvantages
• Workers are paid based on what they produce. • It encourages workers to improve their skills. • The plan is easily understood. • Labor costs can be determined with a small amount of clerical effort.	• The plan does not protect employees against loss of earnings due to causes beyond their control, such as equipment breakdown. • Employees may tend to sacrifice quality for quantity, although proper inspection can keep the quality up to standard. • The rates of compensation are difficult to establish. • The plan is discouraging to beginning workers who cannot produce as much as experienced workers.

There are many types of piece-rate plans used in business, and many of the variations have been made in order to avoid some of the disadvantages listed above. For example, in many plans the piece rates are used as an incentive for workers to improve their production, but the workers are guaranteed a minimum hourly wage.

In some cases individual workers and labor unions have objected to piece-rate plans. When such a plan is used, it may result in more production as employees try to increase their salaries. If the piece-rate is then lowered, the plan proves quite objectionable to workers. If, however, the piece-rate plan is operated fairly, it usually benefits workers as well as the employer.

Group Incentive Plan. Some business firms have adopted **group incentives** for certain types of work. Production levels are set for the department. The earnings are then divided among the workers. The system encourages team spirit in working together. It is used best in small departments.

Profit Sharing. **Profit sharing** divides some of the firm's profits among the employees. This payment is in addition to the normal wage received by the employees. In a very small business the owner may share profits by granting a bonus of a flat sum, such as $25 to $1,000, to employees each year—the amount depending on the success of the business activities of the past year. Some companies share profits by giving their employees either a lump sum of cash or shares of stock in the company. The amount depends on the financial success of the company and the length of service of the employee.

Here are some examples of profit-sharing systems used in businesses:

- The profit-sharing system of a large mail-order company is designed to encourage employee savings. The employees contribute 5 percent of their wages to a fund, and the company contributes 5½ to 7½ percent of its profits to the same fund. After contributing for ten years, employees are entitled to make withdrawals from their accounts.
- The plan of a large soap manufacturer is to encourage employees to purchase shares of stock in the company. Employees may have 5 percent deducted from their paychecks to apply to the purchase of stock. The company contributes an additional amount. In less than two years, the lowest paid employee will have contributed enough to be issued a share of stock. In addition to getting any regular dividends paid by the company to its stockholders, each employee owning a share of stock is given a yearly cash profit-sharing dividend.
- A manufacturer of photographic supplies makes an annual cash payment to employees, the size of which is determined by the amount of the regularly declared dividend on the company's stock and the earnings of the employee for the five preceding years.
- A manufacturer of meat products puts into a profit-sharing retirement fund each year a sum of money that varies with the length of service of the employee and the earnings of the company that particular year.

Profit-sharing systems have been developed to encourage employees to be interested in the success of the business. If employees know they will share in the profits, they will usually work to help the company be more profitable.

Factors Affecting the Amount of Wages or Salaries Paid

The determination of the amount of wages and salaries to be paid by a company is an important management decision. In addition to the compensation plan used, other factors to consider in determining the amount of money which an individual should receive include: the abilities of the employee; the relative importance of the job as compared to other jobs; the number of years the individual has worked for the company; the number of employees available with certain skills compared to the demand for that kind of labor; the prevailing wage rates in the community and in the industry; the current economic conditions; and certain federal and state labor laws (these wage and hour laws are discussed in Chapter 23). Additional attention is given here to the difficult task of establishing the relative importance of one job as compared to other jobs, and to the influence of the cost of living on wages.

Establishing the Relative Importance of Jobs. Great differences exist between the receptionist's and the president's skills, duties, responsibilities, authority, and contribution to the success of the company. There is also quite a difference in the receptionist's wage as compared with the president's salary. In between these extremes are numerous other jobs which require varying degrees of skill and ability, which have quite different duties and responsibilities, and which contribute in greater or lesser amounts to the company's success.

Employees are quite naturally concerned about how much money they earn compared to other employees. If Joan is earning less than Kathy and believes that her work is of greater value to the company than Kathy's, Joan may be quite upset. Thus, it is important for a business to determine the relative value of each type of job to the company and to use this information in establishing a wage structure.

Job evaluation is the term used to refer to the process of ranking jobs in the order of their importance. Job evaluation should not be confused with **employee evaluation** which is the rating of workers' performance. In job evaluation, the jobs must first be analyzed to determine such things as the tasks performed, the skills needed, the responsibility required, and the nature of the working conditions. This information is then used as a basis for arranging jobs in the order of their importance.

Several different methods are used by business for ranking jobs in the order of their importance. A commonly used method is the point system. An example of the point system is shown in Illus. 22-5 on page 436. In this example the job has a value of 420 points. Thus, the rate of pay for the job is lower than that for a job with a point value of 600.

Impact of Cost of Living on Wages. Employees evaluate how good their wages or salaries are by what their real money earned will purchase. **Real wages** represent the amount of goods and services that the money will buy. For example, let us assume that the monthly cost of living for Mr. Martin and his family in 1982 was $1,000. If the same things which made up this $1,000 cost in 1982 now cost $1,200, Mr. Martin would have to be earning $200 more a month in order to have the same standard of living as he and his family had in 1982. From this example, it is easy to see that the amount of money that one earns is important in relation to the cost of living. There is no real increase in wages if the cost of living rises at the same rate or faster than wages. Employees may not be happy if they are producing more for the company than they did one year ago but their wages will not buy as much as they did last year.

ILLUS. 22-5
Some firms use the point system of job evaluation.

Abilities Required	Points	
Skill		
1. training needed	60	
2. experience required	70	
3. versatility	40	
4. human relations	20	190
Responsibility		
5. for details	35	
6. for quality	35	
7. for other people	10	80
Effort		
8. physical	25	
9. mental	50	75
Conditions		
10. working environment	50	
11. exposure to danger	25	75
Total Points		420

FRINGE BENEFITS

In addition to the regular wages and salaries that are paid employees, most workers today receive other types of compensation which are called **fringe benefits.** Illus. 22-6 shows that fringe benefits represent a sizable portion of employees' total compensation—nearly 40 percent for the average worker in a recent year. If an employer's payroll for a year amounts to $2,000,000, the extra cost to the employer for the fringe benefits is about $800,000. Some of the most common types of fringe benefits are described here.

Insurance

Many business firms have made it possible for their employees to obtain insurance at lower rates through group insurance. In many cases the company pays part of the insurance premium. Insurance is provided for all workers in the company.

This often includes people who might not be able to pay the regular rates. With group insurance plans, no physical examination is usually required. Some employees would be unable to pass the physical examination required when insurance is obtained individually. Life, health, and dental insurance are the common types of insurance programs provided by businesses.

ILLUS. 22-6

Fringe benefits are an added cost of compensation for employers.

The Cost of Fringe Benefits

If a worker received an annual wage of $20,000 in a recent year, the employer would have paid an additional $7,500 in fringe benefits. The cost of fringe benefits is a 37.5 percent added payroll cost to the employer for each employee. The average $7,500 in fringe benefits is divided as follows:

	Percentage	**Amount**
pay for time not worked (vacations, holidays, sick leave)	28.5	$2,137.50
social security benefits	16.4	1,230.00
pensions, profit sharing	15.2	1,140.00
health insurance	12.5	937.50
rest periods and breaks	10.1	757.50
unemployment compensation	4.3	322.50
life insurance	2.0	150.00
workers' compensation for job-related injuries	.6	45.00
all other benefits	10.4	780.00
Totals	100.0	$7,500.00

Basic Data: United States Department of Commerce estimates.

Pensions

Many companies have pension plans. **Pensions** provide money to be paid to the employee after retirement. A percentage of an employee's salary is put into a pension fund during the years the employee is working. The funds are invested by the company or by an investment business. Companies sometimes pay the entire cost of the pension, but in many cases the employee makes a contribution as well.

The length of service required before an employee is eligible for full benefits is usually from 20 to 35 years. Employees who retire sooner will receive a smaller pension.

There is great variation in the amounts of the pension payments and the method of payments. Pension plans usually provide a minimum and a maximum monthly pension based on the salary of the employee and length of service.

The Employee Retirement Income Security Act (ERISA), a federal law that was passed in 1974, protects most employees from losing contributions made into pension funds. Prior to this law, many employees lost all pension rights whenever they left an employer. The provisions of ERISA also apply to profit-sharing plans.

ILLUS. 22–7
Potential employees should consider the fringe benefits as well as the salary.

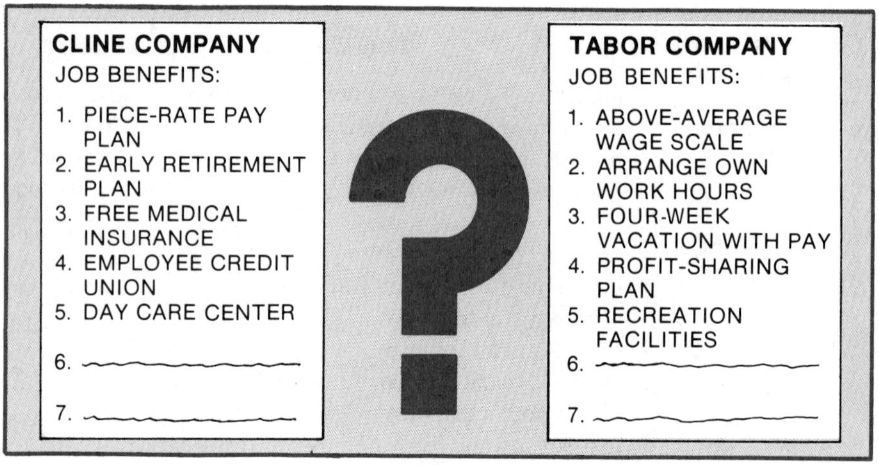

CLINE COMPANY JOB BENEFITS:	TABOR COMPANY JOB BENEFITS:
1. PIECE-RATE PAY PLAN	1. ABOVE-AVERAGE WAGE SCALE
2. EARLY RETIREMENT PLAN	2. ARRANGE OWN WORK HOURS
3. FREE MEDICAL INSURANCE	3. FOUR-WEEK VACATION WITH PAY
4. EMPLOYEE CREDIT UNION	4. PROFIT-SHARING PLAN
5. DAY CARE CENTER	5. RECREATION FACILITIES
6. ______	6. ______
7. ______	7. ______

Pay for Time Off

It is common practice to pay workers for a certain amount of vacation. In addition to regular vacations, many employers pay workers for certain holidays even though no work is performed. Many companies give employees a certain number of paid absences because of sickness, sickness in the family, or death in the family. These benefits are usually provided only after the employee has worked for the company for a period of time.

Other Programs Which Benefit and Protect Personnel

Many companies provide various services and programs which benefit or protect their employees, such as cafeterias, health services, and recreation facilities. Three benefits of particular importance to employees and employers are modified workweeks, health programs, and safety programs.

The Modified Workweek. In recent years some firms have experimented with a variety of plans to modify the standard 40-hour five-day workweek. The four-day week has gained popularity. By working longer hours for fewer days each week, employees are provided an extra day away from work. Forty hours of work can be completed during a ten-hour four-day week. Another variation of the four-day week is an eight- or nine-hour day with shorter coffee and meal breaks. This variation may produce a workweek of slightly less than 40 hours.

To better respond to employee needs, some firms have introduced other modifications to the standard workweek. Some companies allow employees a choice in the hours they work during the day. Some employees come to work earlier than normal, allowing the workday to begin and end earlier while others choose to start and finish later in the day. A bank in Boston,

Illus. 22-8
Some companies provide health and recreation facilities for their employees.

which has approximately 800 employees on such a plan, finds that the plan improves employee morale. This is especially true for those with young children. Absenteeism and tardiness have been reduced. A four-day week may also be staggered by having some employees start on days other than Monday. This plan enables a business firm to operate as many days a week as it likes without requiring employees to work more than forty hours a week, or four days each week. As a result, overtime labor costs may be reduced or eliminated.

Another interesting work modification is known as **job sharing.** In this plan one full-time job is shared by two people each working one half of the time. They may each work half of a day or alternate days or weeks. In this way, people who cannot work full time can still be employed and the business has two skilled employees to use. It is particularly useful when one of the employees is sick or is on vacation.

Choices in work schedules enable employees to adjust individual life styles to the world of work. Working parents, for example, find advantages to adjusting work hours to accommodate family needs. Business benefits too, by attracting employees who otherwise might not be available and by obtaining maximum use of expensive equipment and other resources. Absenteeism declines and worker morale and productivity increase under many of the plans for modifying the workweek.

The Health Program. If employees are to do their best work, they must be healthy. A person who is ill will not work as effectively and is more likely to have accidents. Illness may also mean absence from work, which is costly to the business. An example of a company health program is described in Illus. 22-9.

ILLUS. 22-9
There are many parts to a good health program.

1. A physical examination is required at the time of employment and at periodic intervals thereafter.
2. Health education is carried on by means of posters on bulletin boards, booklets, and talks. Employees are taught how to prevent certain kinds of illnesses and how to maintain their health.
3. The business provides healthful surroundings for the employees. This includes proper ventilation, heating, and lighting, as well as care of restrooms, cafeterias, and lounges.
4. A first aid room and a medical staff are provided.
5. The operation of a cafeteria, in which wholesome food is provided at reasonable prices, is a part of the health program.
6. Studies of fatigue and accidents are made and used as the basis for a more efficient planning of employee work. As a result of these studies, the business has established rest periods and breaks throughout the workday.
7. Programs are operated where employees are encouraged to exercise, practice good nutrition, and prevent health problems. Facilities are provided in which employees can exercise during meal breaks and after work.

The Safety Program. If it were possible to determine all costs of industrial accidents during one year, the sum would be enormous. Because thousands of workers are injured and some are killed every year, the primary purpose of safety programs is to reduce the number of accidents.

Accidents are due to mechanical, physiological, or psychological causes. Mechanical causes of accidents include unguarded machinery, defective machinery, slippery floors, and obstructed work areas. Such causes usually can be eliminated if proper care is exercised by employees and management. Physiological causes of accidents are long hours of work, inadequate lighting, tasks that are dull and monotonous, and the like. These causes cannot always be eliminated, but they can be reduced somewhat by the maintenance of proper working conditions. Psychological causes of accidents include stress, carelessness, and lack of training. To eliminate these causes, both workers and management must cooperate on improving safety.

In large organizations, specialists devote their entire time to the promotion of safety. One of the first steps in a safety program is regular inspection of buildings, equipment and working conditions. Regular inspection will lead to better planning and arrangement of equipment and to better safeguards of machinery. Inspection will also disclose bad housekeeping practices, poor handling of materials, or faulty electric wiring. Regular inspections will call attention to the need for proper maintenance of the plant and equipment.

One of the important sources of safety suggestions is the employees themselves. Many organizations have formed safety committees made up of employees. When employees realize that they have a part in a safety program that will protect them, they are more inclined to cooperate. Unless employees do cooperate, there cannot be a successful safety program.

Many states have enacted safety regulations covering business. In addition, a federal law on health and safety exists and is discussed in the next section.

Other Benefits. Increasingly, businesses are providing other types of fringe benefits for employees. While they may not be as common as those already described, they are important benefits to the employees of the company. Such benefits include free parking, use of company automobiles, services of lawyers and accountants, and financial and personal counseling. Other employee services that are now being provided are child care services, payment of educational expenses, and assistance with moving costs if the employee is transferred.

BENEFITS PROVIDED BY LAWS

Due to the passage of several federal laws, business firms must contribute to employee benefits. The laws discussed in this section include the Occupational Safety and Health Act, the Social Security Act, and workers' compensation laws.

Occupational Safety and Health Act

When the people of the United States became concerned about the social and physical environment of society in recent years, they also became concerned about the environment of the work place. Prior to the passage of federal safety legislation, there were almost 14,000 job-related deaths and over 2,000,000 disabling injuries annually.

The federal Occupational Safety and Health Act was passed in 1970. This law provides for the establishment and enforcement of occupational safety and health standards. Responsibility is placed on both employers and employees. Employers must provide a work place that is free of health and safety hazards and meet safety standards set by the United States Department of Labor. Employers must inform all employees of job hazards and federal standards. For their protection, of course, employees are required under the law to observe the standards. Since the passage of the act, the number of job-related deaths and disabling injuries has declined.

Federal inspections and investigations are made from time to time at small and large firms which transact business in more than one state. Employees, however, may request additional plant inspections and may report violations directly to the United States Department of Labor. Major industrial accidents are investigated to try to prevent such accidents from occurring in the future.

Social Security Act

The Social Security Act was passed by Congress in 1935, and it has been changed many times since then. Approximately nine out of ten persons who are employed are covered under the provisions of this Act. The most important programs provided by the Act are (1) old-age, survivors, and disability insurance, (2) health insurance, and (3) unemployment insurance.

Old-Age, Survivors, and Disability Insurance (OASDI). The OASDI portion of the Social Security Act provides pensions to retired workers and their families, death benefits to the survivors of workers, and benefits to disabled workers and their families. The process of figuring benefits is somewhat complicated, but the amount received is based on the amount of the taxes credited to the worker's social security account.

Health Insurance. The 1965 amendments to the Social Security Act established a broad program of health insurance for people who have reached retirement age. This program, known as Medicare, provides both hospital insurance and other medical insurance. Social security taxes are used to pay for this program.

Social Security Taxes. The money to pay retirement, survivors, disability, and hospital (Medicare) benefits comes from social security taxes paid by employers, employees, and self-employed persons. Therefore, the share paid by the employer is a fringe benefit for the employee. People who are self-employed pay a slightly higher social security tax than do regular employees. Illus. 22-10 indicates how the contributions of both employers and employees have greatly increased over the years as Congress has frequently increased the tax to meet the payments needed as increasing numbers of people receive benefits. Social security taxes are increasing, but the amount of benefits paid is also increasing rapidly. Congress has spent a great deal of time studying the social security system to insure the benefits will be available to those who paid into the system.

Unemployment Insurance

The unemployment insurance program is administered by each state. Under federal law, each state collects taxes from businesses. These taxes are the source of funds which are paid to certain people who are unemployed.

Unemployment Benefits. Unemployment insurance gives many workers some income when they are out of work. Unemployment compensation

ILLUS. 22-10
Payroll taxes for social security have increased over the years.

SOCIAL SECURITY TAX Paid each year by employer and by employee			
Year	Rate	Maximum income taxed	Maximum annual tax
1937	1.00%	$ 3,000	$ 30.00
1950	1.50%	$ 3,000	$ 45.00
1960	3.00%	$ 4,800	$ 144.00
1970	4.80%	$ 7,800	$ 374.40
1975	5.85%	$14,100	$ 824.85
1980	6.13%	$25,900	$1,587.67
1985	7.05%	$43,500	$3,066.75

laws vary from state to state, but workers usually receive about one half of their regular wage for a period of from three to nine months. Before unemployment benefits are received, the worker must meet certain requirements. To be eligible for benefits under most state laws, a worker must qualify as follows:

1. Must be unemployed through no fault of his or her own.
2. Must register at a state employment office for a job.
3. Must be able and available for work.
4. Must be totally unemployed for the amount of time specified in the state law.

ILLUS. 22-11
Unemployment was so high during the Great Depression years that soup lines were a common sight.

Unemployment Insurance Taxes. The money to pay unemployment benefits comes from taxes paid by the employer (in a few states employees are also taxed). The tax varies among the states, with lower tax rates being applied to states having little unemployment and high rates to those states with greater unemployment. The employer is taxed a percentage of the wages and salaries paid to employees.

Workers' Compensation Laws

All states have workers' compensation laws which require employers to provide insurance for a worker's death, injury, or sickness arising from the worker's employment. Some types of workers are exempt, such as those in agriculture, but almost all employees in business are covered by this type of protection.

In some states the law requires that payments by the employer be made directly to the state, which will then pay the claims according to law. Business owners must be aware of records to be maintained and forms that must be completed for the government. In other states the laws merely require that the employer must provide this kind of protection. The employer may pay the claims directly or purchase insurance which will pay the claims.

THE NEED TO KEEP UP TO DATE

Because the various states and the federal government are frequently changing laws and regulations on the benefits discussed in this chapter, it is necessary that business keep informed on such matters. Each state has a Department of Labor which is a good source of information on state laws. The authoritative source on federal regulations is the Wage and Hour Section of the United States Department of Labor.

NEW TERMS AND CONCEPTS

Define the following terms and concepts, which may be found in boldface type on the page shown in parentheses.

compensation (429)
wages (430)
salaries (430)
time wage plan (430)
straight salary (430)
commission plan (431)
salary and commission plan (431)
salary and bonus plan (431)
piece-rate plan (432)
group incentives (433)
profit sharing (433)
job evaluation (435)
employee evaluation (435)
real wages (435)
fringe benefits (436)
pensions (437)
job sharing (439)

CHAPTER REVIEW

1. What are some of the factors that affect the amount of compensation paid for a job?
2. Why is a straight salary a poor compensation system for a very productive employee?
3. Why is a commission plan often used to compensate salespeople?
4. Identify the major difference between a commission and a bonus.
5. How are piece rates established?
6. How does a profit-sharing system benefit a business?
7. In what way does job evaluation influence the wage structure of a company?
8. Are real wages affected by the cost of living?
9. Approximately what percentage of the average employee's total compensation is paid in fringe benefits?
10. What are the advantages to an employee of participating in a group insurance plan?
11. How are pensions protected by federal law?
12. Describe how a job-sharing plan works.
13. What is the purpose of the Occupational Safety and Health Act?
14. List the three most important programs provided under the Social Security Act.
15. In most states, do employers or employees pay the tax for unemployment?

QUESTIONS FOR CLASS DISCUSSION

1. Why are some jobs compensated with wages while others use a salary?
2. If a salesperson receives a much larger commission for selling one product than another, what is likely to happen? Why would a company use different commission rates for different products?
3. List some jobs for which a piece-rate compensation plan would be appropriate.
4. How should a business determine the best compensation plan to use?
5. Offer some examples of jobs for which the salaries have been affected by the supply of and demand for labor.
6. Explain what real wages are.
7. Are there situations where fringe benefits offered are more important to an employee than the wage or salary earned?
8. In what ways can a company benefit from implementing a modified work week?

9. How can the high costs of a health and safety program be recovered by a company?

10. Why do self-employed persons pay a higher social security tax than do regular employees?

PROBLEMS AND PROJECTS

1. A wholesaler has developed a complex pay structure. Each salesperson is given a base salary and a quota. Salespeople are paid a commission on all sales using the following chart:

   4 percent for all sales up to $40,000
   5 percent for sales between $40,001 and $100,000
   6 percent for any sales above $100,000

   A bonus of $1,000 is paid to each salesperson who exceeds the quota established. Calculate the earnings of three salespeople by completing the following table using the information given.

Salesperson	Base Salary	Commission	Bonus	Total Salary
Edwards				
Vajesh				
Sing				

   Edwards has a base salary of $16,000, sales of $65,000, and a quota of $60,000.

   Vajesh has a base salary of $25,000, sales of $120,000, and a quota of $140,000.

   Sing has a base salary of $28,000, sales of $220,000, and a quota of $200,000.

2. Jones and Jackson are about to open a used-car partnership. They are not sure whether the best plan for paying salespeople would be to (a) offer an attractive commission only for each car sold, (b) offer an attractive hourly wage rate, or (c) offer a small hourly wage rate and a reasonable commission. Discuss with several other students the various plans and decide which compensation plan might be best for this type of business. In your report to the class, give reasons for your answer.

3. Interview an employee or the personnel manager of the following three types of businesses: a factory, a retail store, and an office. Determine the types of fringe benefits provided by each of the businesses. Make a chart comparing the benefits. Discuss the differences.

4. The Superthrift Supermarket has a weekly payroll of $18,000. The payroll figure does not include fringe benefits. Assume that Superthrift has the same percentages of fringe benefit costs as shown in Illus. 22-6.

Determine the amount that the company pays each week for each of the fringe benefit categories listed and then calculate the total amount paid for employee fringe benefits.

5. Interview an employee of the Social Security Office to determine (a) the current social security tax rate, and (b) employee benefits provided by social security.

CASE 22–1

The Farney Company, which manufactures metal folding chairs, has 12 workers and 1 supervisor in one of its small assembly plants. Each employee is responsible for the total assembly of each chair so that the work of each employee is independent. A piece-rate wage plan is used.

The employees recently expressed a desire for a change in the standard 40-hour, five-day week. Yesterday, management informed all employees that a plan for a modified workweek would be considered as long as (1) each employee worked at least 36 hours a week; (2) weekly output for the plant did not drop; (3) the plant operated at least during the hours of 8:00 a.m. to 5:00 p.m., Monday through Friday; and (4) at least three employees were on the job at any one time except during meal hours.

The plant supervisor called a meeting of all employees to arrange a plan that would satisfy both the employees and management. Before the meeting began, however, the supervisor knew that there would be problems. A few workers were against any changes. Many had already decided the days and hours they preferred, and it seemed that no preferences were the same.

Required:

1. What type of modified workweek seems most likely to be effective?
2. How could the modified workweek affect morale, absenteeism, and production?

CASE 22–2

Maryanne Watchung had just finished reading the current issue of the company newsletter when Ray Fasula, another employee, walked into the employees' lounge. The following conversation took place.

Maryanne: Just look at this, Ray. In this newsletter, management says that the average employee in this company makes $12,000 a year. That is what you and I make.

Ray: That's right, but does the newsletter tell you that we also have about $3,000 deducted for taxes, the pension plan, and union dues?

Maryanne: No, it says quite the opposite. What the newsletter does say is that the company pays another $3,000 in fringe benefits for people like us in addition to the $12,000 salary. What do you think of that?

Ray: I think something is wrong, Maryanne. We get about $9,000 in take-home pay, and the company says they shell out $15,000 for us. That is a $6,000 difference.

Maryanne: I agree. I never see any of those fringe benefits in my pay envelope. Let's go to the payroll office and ask for an explanation of what is going on. I think we are being taken advantage of.

Required:

1. Do you agree that Maryanne never sees any of those fringe benefits? Explain.
2. How should the payroll clerk explain the $6,000 difference between the total compensation for each employee and the employee's take-home pay?
3. What percentage of each employee's annual gross pay goes to fringe benefits?

Have You Thought About Becoming . . .

. . . A PERSONNEL RECORDS MANAGER?

In every company there is a need to maintain information about the employees of the company. In a very small company, personnel records may be handled by the owner or a secretary/bookkeeper. Those records may be very simple and will require very little attention. However, in a large organization with hundreds or thousands of employees, the task of managing all of the personnel information is a very complicated task.

The personnel records manager is responsible for keeping a complete file of information on each employee. That file could include personal and health information, date of employment, job changes (transfers and promotions), pay records, performance evaluation, and records of fringe benefits. Records must be complete, accurate, and updated whenever changes occur.

Many companies still maintain personnel records through a manual filing system and the manager must be able to organize and maintain those files. Other businesses have developed computerized records systems. In those systems, the manager must understand how to operate and maintain computer records.

To be an effective records manager you must be accurate and willing to work with details. Since personnel records are confidential, you must use good judgment about the use of the information in the records.

The minimum educational requirement for this job is usually a high school diploma with additional clerical training in records management. In companies with large personnel departments, the person responsible for records may need a two- or four-year college degree with course work in personnel, records management, and computer operations. The position of personnel records manager is an important one in large companies, and only highly skilled people will be hired.

23

LABOR RELATIONS

After studying this chapter you will be able to:

- Describe the nature of unions in the United States today.
- Identify the major objectives and tactics of labor unions.
- Identify the major objectives and tactics of management.
- Explain the basic purposes of important federal labor laws.
- Discuss equal employment opportunity legislation and affirmative action programs.

As defined in Chapter 3, profit is the reward received by the owners of a business for producing goods and services. The management of a business directs many of its efforts toward increasing profits. These efforts involve controlling costs and increasing the efficiency of the business. The efforts of management to reduce costs and improve efficiency are, at times, in conflict with the desires of workers for higher wages and other benefits. Often these differences can be resolved by discussions between management and workers, but sometimes no common ground for agreement can be found.

As business developed in the United States and elsewhere, some employers did not provide good working conditions or pay fair wages; and workers found that as individuals they had little power to negotiate with management for pay increases and better working conditions. To obtain the economic power that would enable them to gain concessions from management, many workers joined labor unions. As labor unions grew larger and more powerful, labor-management conflicts occurred which were detrimental to management, to workers, and to the general public. These conflicts led to the passage of legislation concerning the rights and responsibilities of labor unions and management.

This chapter discusses the union-management relationship and the labor laws which influence this relationship. In addition, laws and regulations dealing with equal employment opportunities are examined.

LABOR UNIONS AND LABOR RELATIONS

About one out of five workers in nonagricultural businesses is a labor union member. The extent to which workers belong to unions varies by industry, by occupation, and by geographical area. Unions have been successful in organizing workers in mining, construction, manufacturing, transportation, and public utilities. About half of all factory production workers are organized. Certain basic industries such as steel, transportation, automobile, aircraft, and electrical manufacturing are highly organized.

While union membership in white-collar and professional occupations has been relatively small, growth has occurred. In recent years the number of bargaining units among state and federal employees and teachers has increased rapidly. A continued increase in the unionization of service workers is expected.

National Unions

Although there are many single-firm unions, the strength of the labor movement resides in unions which draw their membership from workers located throughout the country. The largest and most powerful union organization in the United States is the American Federation of Labor and Congress of Industrial Organizations (AFL-CIO). About 80 percent of the workers who are organized are members of national unions affiliated with the AFL-CIO.

The American Federation of Labor (AFL) was formed in 1886, and originally the membership was organized according to occupations or

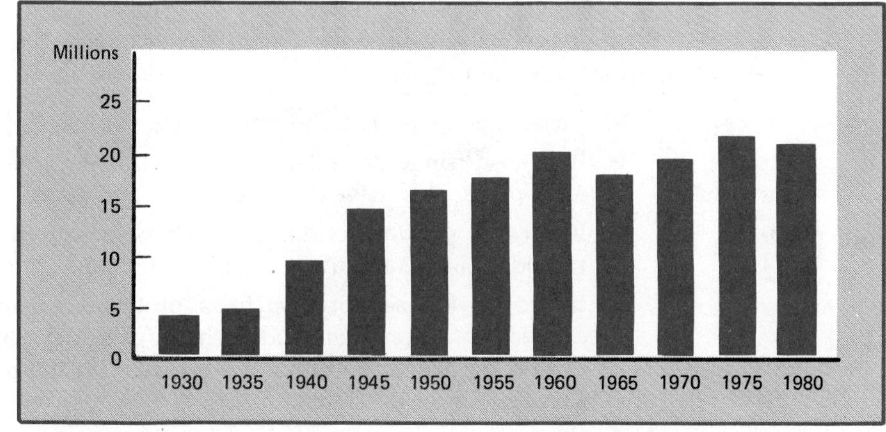

ILLUS. 23–1
The most rapid growth of union membership was in the 1930s and 1940s.

crafts. In 1936 eight unions, some of which had belonged to the AFL, formed a separate federation which became known as the Congress of Industrial Organizations (CIO). The formation of the CIO was the result of opposition to the emphasis in the AFL on **craft unionism;** that is, the organization of workers by occupations, such as machinists, carpenters, and plumbers. Those who formed the CIO were proponents of **industrial unionism;** that is, they wanted to organize unions for skilled, semiskilled, and unskilled workers employed by the same large industry, such as the steel industry.

The difficulties between the AFL and CIO did not prevent the growth of unionism; and, with the passage of time, both the AFL and CIO became mixtures of craft and industrial unions. Many efforts to merge the two federations were made over the years, and finally in 1955 the AFL and the CIO merged to form the AFL-CIO.

Several strong national unions are not affiliated with the AFL-CIO. Two of the largest independent unions, for example, are the Teamsters and the United Automobile Workers.

ILLUS. 23-2
Over 200 unions exist in the United States, with certain occupations being more highly unionized than others.

Unionized Occupational Groups in the United States

Teamsters	Meat Cutters
Automobile Workers	Communications Workers
Steelworkers	Hotel and Restaurant Workers
Electrical Workers	Teachers
Machinists	Operating Engineers
Carpenters	Ladies' Garment Workers
Retail Clerks	U.S. Government Workers
State, County, and Municipal Workers	Musicians

Union Objectives

Labor unions have established many objectives. The principal objectives include the following:

- Increased wages and shorter working hours.
- Increased fringe benefits, such as health, hospital, and insurance plans; sick leave; welfare funds; and pension plans.
- Improved working conditions, such as safety regulations, rest periods, fair treatment, and job satisfaction.
- Improved job security, such as protection against job loss caused by automation and technological developments and protection against job loss of workers with the most years of service—**seniority rights.**

- Increased acceptance of unions by employers as the bargaining agent of employees.
- Increased union membership. Management is at liberty to hire union and nonunion members. To increase union strength, however, unions prefer a union shop. In a **union shop** an employer may hire nonunion workers but the workers must join the union within a stated period and usually must remain a union member for continued employment. In early efforts to require union membership, unions tried to obtain the closed shop and preferential shop, both of which were later outlawed. The **closed shop** required employers to hire only union members, and the **preferential shop** required employers to give preference to union members in hiring and in layoffs. Management prefers an **open shop** in which employees may choose not to join a union.

Union Tactics

In order to meet their objectives, unions attempt to bargain with employers. When bargaining does not yield desired results, unions may resort to the following tactics:

- A strike. A **strike,** or **walkout,** occurs when employees refuse to work until their demands are met. There are different types of strikes. Some are lawful and some are unlawful. A **slowdown strike,** for example, is a lawful strike in which workers perform at a much slower than normal pace. A **sitdown strike,** which is unlawful, is one in which workers show up at their jobs but refuse to perform their tasks. Also unlawful is a **wildcat strike,** which occurs when workers walk off their jobs in violation of the labor-management agreement or without approval from union leaders.
- Picketing. **Picketing** is the placing of union members at the entrance to a business to persuade others not to enter. It is common practice during a strike to picket the employer in order to discourage other employees from working, to discourage customers and suppliers from transacting business with the company, and to inform the public that a strike is in progress.
- A product boycott. A **product boycott** is the practice of union members refusing to purchase products from a company whose employees are on strike or when conditions exist to which the union is opposed. The product boycott has been a reasonably successful labor union tactic. Other groups, such as consumers and members of minority groups, have also used the product boycott successfully.

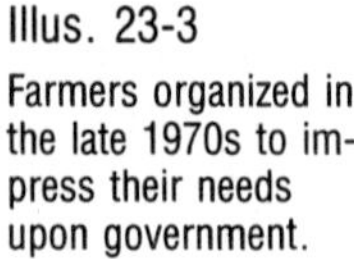

Illus. 23-3
Farmers organized in the late 1970s to impress their needs upon government.

- Lobbying. Unions engage in many activities that publicize their objectives and their desire to increase the strength of unions. The principal means used to promote the strength of unions is **lobbying** (influencing legislators regarding proposed legislation and other policy decisions). Major state and federal laws favorable to unions have been passed as a result of successful lobbying efforts.

Management Objectives

The major management objectives regarding the use of labor are to:

- Reduce labor costs and improve worker efficiency. The responsibility of management is to make a profit for the business. To fulfill its responsibility in the competitive business world, management must attempt to keep labor costs low and to improve worker efficiency. Because some of the objectives of unions result in increased labor costs, management's objectives often conflict with union objectives.
- Retain managerial authority. For an organization to function effectively, management needs authority to require workers to perform assigned tasks. Management does not like its authority infringed upon by unions; for example, having to consult a union before transferring, disciplining, or discharging a worker.
- Reduce union activity. In general, management prefers a **nonunion shop;** that is, it prefers not to have its workers represented by a union. If workers are organized, management prefers an open shop. While employers cannot discriminate

against employees who are interested in unions, they may attempt to persuade employees not to join a union. Some employers try to show how employees benefit without a union.

Management Tactics

If management cannot achieve its objectives through bargaining, the following tactics may be used:

- Injunction. An **injunction** is a court order directing a person or group to do or to stop doing a specific act. For example, an employer may request an injunction against a union from striking if the employer believes the strike violates the labor contract. Because injunctions against union activities were used unfairly in the past, restrictions were placed on their use. For instance, injunctions cannot be used to prevent unions from peacefully picketing a company or fairly boycotting its products. Even with restrictions, however, an injunction can be used effectively to prevent illegal union activities, such as acts of violence or damage to the employer's property.
- Lockout. A **lockout** is a temporary work stoppage by an employer in an attempt to win a dispute with the employees. In a sense, a lockout is a strike by the employer against the employees because management refuses to let workers enter the business. The lockout cannot be used as a device to discourage employees from joining or forming a union, although it was used extensively for that purpose prior to the passage of certain laws. Today employers seldom close their businesses in order to pressure employees to negotiate, even though they have the right to do so.
- Hiring new employees. In an effort to force regular employees who are out on strike to return to their jobs because of fear that they might lose them, management has sometimes hired new employees to operate the business. After the strike, however, the employer is usually required to discharge the new workers in order to rehire the employees who had been on strike.
- Strike insurance. To protect themselves against a long and damaging strike, some companies purchase strike insurance. While strike insurance is expensive, its purpose is to cover the basic expenses of the business that occur while a union is on strike. The insurance allows management to hold out longer during a strike.
- Lobbying. Employers, like unions, spend a great deal of time and effort promoting their viewpoints and lobbying for favorable legislation and against unfavorable legislation regarding

employer-employee relations. Lobbying occurs at all levels of government, and is conducted by individual businesses, trade associations, Chambers of Commerce, and other business groups. Legislation has allowed union members and company executives to form **political action committees (PACs)**. The committees can collect funds that are then contributed to political candidates that support the goals of the union or the company. PACs have become an important lobbying tool since unions and corporations are not allowed to use their own money for political purposes.

Collective Bargaining

The basic characteristic of a labor union is that the members agree to bargain as a group with the employer for higher pay and other benefits rather than to bargain with the employer as individuals. This process is known as **collective bargaining**. Collective bargaining involves representatives from management and labor meeting together to discuss and to resolve their differences. If management and labor are able to resolve their differences, which is often the case, they state their agreement in a contract which is called the **labor contract**. Labor contracts are usually quite lengthy and specify wages, hours, fringe benefits, seniority, disciplinary procedures, grievance procedures, and the length of time the contract will remain in force. Both management and labor are bound by the terms of the labor contract.

Illus. 23-4
Management and unions often settle their differences through collective bargaining.

The negotiations between representatives of management and labor do not always result in agreement on all issues. If the negotiations reach a point where neither party is willing to compromise further, both parties may agree to resolve their differences by means of mediation or arbitration.

Mediation. At times, management and labor attempt to resolve their differences by securing the help of a disinterested third party. In **mediation**, the third party (mediator) listens to the arguments of both sides and suggests ways in which labor and management may compromise in arriving at a solution to the existing problem. Labor and management are not obligated to accept the mediator's suggestions.

Arbitration. Management and labor also attempt to resolve their differences by means of **arbitration**. When this means of settling disputes is used, management and labor agree in advance that they will be bound by the decision of the arbitrator. Thus, in contrast to the mediator, the arbitrator has the power to make a decision which will settle the dispute. Although arbitration may be settled by one individual, often an arbitration board is used. Generally the arbitration board consists of three persons—one chosen by labor, one chosen by management, and a third person agreeable to both management and labor.

LABOR LEGISLATION

Conflicts between labor and management led to the passage of federal legislation. The three important laws that currently define the rights and responsibilities of unions and management are the Wagner Act, the Taft-Hartley Act, and the Landrum-Griffin Act. In addition to these laws, this section also discusses labor legislation which regulates wages and hours and discriminatory practices.

Wagner Act

In 1935 Congress passed the National Labor Relations Act, known as the Wagner Act. This act is our basic labor law. The Wagner Act guaranteed the right of workers to organize unions and the right of these unions to bargain collectively with employers. The act also created the National Labor Relations Board to administer the provisions of the act. The National Labor Relations Board was given the power to conduct elections in companies so that employees could decide which union, if any, they wanted as their representative for bargaining purposes. The Board was also given the authority to prevent employers from engaging in the following activities which were designated as unfair labor practices:

1. Interference in any way with the right of employees to organize unions and bargain collectively.

2. Domination of or interference with the formation or administration of a labor union.
3. Financial contribution to or other support of a union.
4. Discrimination of any kind against employees which would tend to encourage or discourage joining any labor union.
5. Discharge of or any discrimination against an employee who has given testimony under the act.
6. Refusal to bargain collectively with the union chosen by the majority of the employees as its representative.

Taft-Hartley Act

Employers believed and, after a time, other groups came to believe that the Wagner Act favored unions; and in 1947 Congress passed the Labor-Management Relations Act (Taft-Hartley Act). The effort in the Taft-Hartley Act was to restore a balance of power between management and labor. Except as it is amended by the Taft-Hartley Act, the provisions of the Wagner Act remain in force.

The basic unfair labor practices which were designated by the Wagner Act were not changed by the Taft-Hartley Act, but it added the following unfair union practices:

1. Threats by unions that employees will lose their jobs unless they support the union's activities.
2. Causing an employer to discriminate against employees because of antiunion activities.
3. Refusal to bargain collectively with an employer.
4. Engaging in a **secondary boycott** (a boycott of a person or a firm not engaged in a dispute) or engaging in **jurisdictional strikes** (stopping work because of a dispute between different unions).
5. Charging excessive initiation fees to keep new members out of a union.
6. Requiring employers to pay for work employees have not done.

Other important provisions of the Taft-Hartley Act are:

1. Unions may be sued for breach of contract.
2. The closed shop is outlawed.
3. If in the judgment of the President of the United States a strike exists which imperils the national health or safety, the President may obtain a court injunction delaying the strike for a period of 80 days. During this cooling-off period, further efforts to settle the dispute are to be made.
4. The act allows states to adopt more restrictive legislation against union membership requirements. Many states have passed so-called **right-to-work laws** which provide that an individual does not have to join a union in order to obtain and hold a job.

Landrum-Griffin Act

In 1959, as a result of investigations of union activities which revealed corrupt and irresponsible practices, Congress passed the Labor-Management Reporting and Disclosure Act (Landrum-Griffin Act). The law deals with internal union affairs by providing safeguards for union members and by placing additional restrictions on the activities of unions and their officers.

The first part of the act is a bill of rights for members which is designed to insure their rights to participate in union affairs, to be informed of union agreements, and to have fair hearings in disciplinary actions. Other parts of the act provide for reporting procedures which have as their purpose the prevention of and detection of illegal or unfair practices.

Wage and Hour Laws

Federal and state laws dealing with wages and hours have been passed which affect labor and management. The Fair Labor Standards Act (FLSA), which was enacted by the federal government in 1938 and has since been amended several times, is often referred to as the Wage and Hour Law. In general, the provisions of this act cover workers employed in industries engaged in interstate commerce or in the manufacture of goods shipped in interstate commerce. The act also covers employees of certain retail and service establishments whose sales volumes exceed a prescribed amount.

The major provisions of the FLSA deal with overtime payments and minimum wage rates. For most employees covered by the act, employers must pay a minimum hourly wage for the first 40 hours of work during a week and 1½ times the regular hourly rate for all work in excess of 40 hours.

In addition to the FLSA just discussed, many states have laws which set minimum wages for regular and overtime work, and which ensure that men and women will receive equal pay if they are performing the same work. Many other state laws exist which relate to wages. The Department of Labor in the state should be contacted if a business has any doubts as to whether or not it is complying with all state laws.

UNION-MANAGEMENT RELATIONSHIPS

While strikes and other union-management conflicts are often highly publicized, there are also many examples of good relationships between unions and management. The objectives of each group can be accomplished through cooperation. It has been found that conflicts between unions and management in some companies have been so expensive that everyone suffered. In some cases, employees had to be terminated and businesses closed. Many companies and unions are now attempting to cooperate even more to meet the needs of the company and its employees.

In the early 1980s, a new tactic in labor-management negotiation was attempted by some companies. Because the economy was in a long recession, many companies were unable to make a profit. Companies involved in contract negotiations asked unions to reduce wage scales and benefits that had been agreed upon in earlier contracts. These requests were referred to as **give-backs.**

Labor unions had not given up pay and benefits in the past. However, they were faced with very high unemployment rates and the chance that even more workers would lose their jobs if businesses were not able to make a profit. While some unions resisted the give-backs, other unions agreed to reductions. In return for the give-backs, management was asked to provide more job security for employees and to give unions a greater voice in company operations.

EQUAL OPPORTUNITY LEGISLATION

Throughout the history of the United States, it has been difficult for some groups to have the same opportunities as other groups. A major obstacle to equal opportunities has been discrimination. Women and people of various national origins and religions have experienced discrimination. To correct these injustices, laws have been passed to help promote equal opportunities and to eliminate inequalities. In particular, laws prohibiting various forms of discrimination in employment have been enacted to promote the fair treatment of every worker.

Almost all employers, unions, and employment agencies are affected by current federal legislation that guarantees equal employment opportunities. These laws prevent many types of unfair employment practices, and federal guidelines have been created that have prompted many individual firms to take positive steps toward correcting injustices that still exist.

Laws Prohibiting Discrimination

A series of federal laws was passed during the 1960s and 1970s prohibiting discriminatory employment practices based on sex, race, color, religion, national origin, age, and mental or physical handicaps. A summary of the most important laws is shown in Illus. 23-5. The legislation prohibits discriminatory actions by employers that relate to hiring, paying, promoting, training, and firing employees, or to the setting of terms, conditions, and privileges of employment that could be considered discriminatory. Much of the U.S. work force is protected under one or more of these laws. In addition, the states have passed similar, and sometimes stronger, laws that support federal legislation.

In addition to specific forms of discrimination prohibited by law, court rulings and interpretations of the laws by enforcement agencies have found a number of specific employment practices to be unlawful. A few of these unlawful practices include the following:

ILLUS. 23-5
Unfair employment practices are prohibited by federal legislation.

Equal Employment Opportunity Laws

Law	Provision
Equal Pay Act, 1963	Prohibits a company from paying different wages to men and women doing substantially equal work for the same employer.
Civil Rights Act, 1964 (amended, 1972)	Prohibits discrimination based on race, color, sex, religion, or national origin; applies to employers of 15 or more persons including business firms, labor organizations, state and local governments, and educational institutions.
Age Discrimination in Employment Act, 1968 (amended, 1978)	Prohibits discrimination against individuals between the ages of 40 and 70; applies to employers of 25 or more persons as well as to union and employment agencies.
Vocational Rehabilitation Act, 1973	Prohibits discrimination against mentally or physically handicapped persons by business firms that sell under contract to the federal government.

- Requiring job applicants to take tests that are not directly related to the job to be performed.
- Setting minimum height and weight requirements, especially if the purpose is to discriminate and the employer is not able to show that these standards are essential to the performance of the job in question.
- Using the marital status of a woman, her age, number of children, and child-care arrangements as a basis for employment.
- Requiring that all applicants have a minimum education if the requirement is not related to job performance.
- Testing or scoring an individual for English language proficiency when English language skills are not required in the work to be performed.

- Using arrest records to disqualify job applicants, particularly if there are no convictions.
- Requiring an honorable discharge for applicants who are military veterans if the purpose is to discriminate for any reason.
- Refusing to hire any job applicant who is not a citizen of the United States.
- Rejecting applicants because of poor credit ratings.

Affirmative Action

The most important equal opportunity law was the Civil Rights Act of 1964, which was later amended in 1972. In addition to prohibiting discrimination based on race, color, religion, sex, and national origin, the Act also created the Equal Employment Opportunity Commission (EEOC). The EEOC was established to ensure that all applicants are considered on the basis of their abilities and qualifications when a business is hiring or promoting employees. The EEOC enforces the law by bringing action against violators and by assisting employers in eliminating discrimination.

Several other federal agencies and the EEOC were given the power to not only administer the appropriate laws, but also to assist employers in establishing affirmative action programs. An **affirmative action program** is a planned effort by employers not only to obey the laws, but to correct any existing forms of employment discrimination, with particular attention to the hiring, training, and promoting of women and minorities. While employers under certain conditions are required to have affirmative action programs, most employers have made voluntary efforts to follow the recommended affirmative action guidelines provided by the federal agencies. Those employers who are required to have affirmative action programs prepare detailed yearly plans and keep careful records on actions taken and progress made in achieving affirmative action goals.

NEW TERMS AND CONCEPTS

Define the following terms and concepts, which can be found in boldface type on the page shown in parentheses.

craft unionism (452)
industrial unionism (452)
seniority rights (452)
union shop (453)
closed shop (453)
preferential shop (453)
open shop (453)
strike, or walkout (453)
slowdown strike (453)
sitdown strike (453)
wildcat strike (453)
picketing (453)
product boycott (453)
lobbying (454)

nonunion shop (454)
injunction (455)
lockout (455)
political action committees, or PACs (456)
collective bargaining (456)
labor contract (456)
mediation (457)
arbitration (457)
secondary boycott (458)
jurisdictional strikes (458)
right-to-work laws (458)
give-backs (460)
affirmative action program (462)

CHAPTER REVIEW

1. Why were labor unions formed in the United States?
2. What percentage of factory production workers belong to unions?
3. Identify the largest union organization in the United States.
4. List several objectives of labor unions.
5. What types of strikes are illegal?
6. List the major objectives of management in the use of labor.
7. What are the major items that are typically included in a labor contract?
8. How can a union and management reach an agreement if they are not willing to compromise?
9. What are three federal laws that define the rights and responsibilities of unions and management?
10. Can a company refuse to bargain with unions that have been chosen by the employees?
11. Which law contains a bill of rights for union members?
12. What types of workers are covered by the Fair Labor Standards Act?
13. Under what conditions are tests given to job applicants considered illegal?
14. Describe the purpose of the Equal Employment Opportunity Commission (EEOC).
15. What should a business include in an affirmative action program?

QUESTIONS FOR CLASS DISCUSSION

1. Why do most local unions choose to affiliate with national unions?
2. What management objectives conflict with the objectives of labor unions?
3. Why do unions use product boycotts as a tactic to achieve their objectives?
4. What benefits would you identify if you were an employer attempting to persuade employees not to join a union?
5. Why would management and labor choose arbitration rather than mediation to settle contract differences?

6. Discuss the value of using a federal board to conduct elections in which employees decide if they want to be represented by a union.
7. Why were some unions willing to accept give-backs in contract negotiations?
8. List some of the inequalities in employment that resulted in federal legislation.
9. Describe some tests that could be useful for job applicants and would not unfairly discriminate.
10. Why have many employers established their own affirmative action programs even though they have not been legally required to have a program?

PROBLEMS AND PROJECTS

1. The R.J. Dean Company is a unionized firm that does business nationally. Joe Speck, an employee, belonged to the union but was fired for giving testimony against the company in a court case. Could he be fired legally? Explain.
2. Make a list of companies in your community which have employees who are members of unions. For each company, indicate the union or unions to which their workers belong.
3. Interview a local business person and a local labor leader with respect to their views concerning organized labor. Report the results of your interviews, and make a statement which identifies your point of view about the value of labor unions.
4. Pauline Watson is a driver for the Overland Trucking Company, which operates across state lines. She is paid $6 an hour. Last week Watson worked ten hours a day for six days and received $360 for this work. Does her work and her payment of wages meet the requirements of the Fair Labor Standards Act? Explain your answer.
5. Review newspapers for several weeks. Find and read reports of employment discrimination. Summarize the types of discrimination reported.

CASE 23–1

Ted Jawarski joined several other workers in the coffee line during the afternoon break at his job with the Model Toy Company. Ted and several of his friends were actively talking to employees about unionizing the workers. They were so successful that a vote on unionization was to take place within the next several days. As several employees sat down with their coffee, the following conversation took place:

Judy: Ted, you know I have been one of your supporters for the union, so I think you should know this. Yesterday I got a letter at my home from the president of this company saying how good the company has been to us. The letter explained that our wages are just as good as those of companies like ours that have unions. I wonder what we would gain by joining a union.

Gil: I think it is legal for the president to try to influence us not to join a union. What bothers me, Ted, is that whatever extra wages the union might get us will have to be paid in union dues. I think I am going to vote against the union just for that reason.

Jennie: I would like to join our company union, but I do not want to join a big union that is going to strike every time some little disagreement comes up. Can we form a local union?

Required:

1. Is it against the law for the company president to try to persuade the workers not to form a union?
2. If you were Ted Jawarski, how would you answer Gil's concern for the high cost of union dues in relation to what one gets?
3. Would the management of the company prefer a national union or the company union as suggested by Jennie? Explain.

CASE 23–2

Helen Thomson and Maria Garcia are employed by the Dickens Company. Helen Thomson has been an extremely efficient, friendly, and cooperative worker. To increase the number of women in high-level jobs, management has offered her a supervisory position; but she is upset about management's point of view toward pay. The salary offered her is only two thirds of that for equal positions held by men in the company. She has been told that all of the supervisors are men, most of whom have large families and who need the high salary. Further, management claims that the workers might not produce as much under a woman supervisor; so they prefer to pay her less.

Maria Garcia, on the other hand, has been employed by the firm for 35 years. She had been asked to consider early retirement but has refused. The reason management has requested an early retirement is to get a young person to learn a new but complicated method for performing her duties. Maria is willing to learn the new method but management believes that due to her age she will not learn as well as a young person will. In addition, they believe that the training will be lost when she retires in only a few years. Because of her refusal to retire early, Maria feels that management has made the job uncomfortable. "I have been given odd working hours from week to week, and my duties have been increased; they are trying to drive me away from working here," says Maria.

Required:

1. What do these situations have in common?
2. Is the Dickens Company violating any laws? If so, which ones?
3. What action can Helen Thomson and Maria Garcia take to correct the situation?
4. Do you agree with management's reasons for offering Helen Thomson less salary and for asking Maria Garcia to retire early?

Have You Thought About Becoming . . .
. . . A LABOR RELATIONS WORKER?

In this chapter you learned about the importance of the union-management relationship. Careers in labor relations may be found within the personnel department of a business or within a separate department, often called the industrial relations department. A separate department for labor relations is most likely to be found in a large company.

A business firm is not the only place in which one may pursue a career in labor relations. Labor unions hire lawyers, economists, and statisticians who perform the same jobs for the union as are performed by labor relations employees in private business. There are also positions in labor relations in various government agencies, particularly in the areas of arbitration and mediation.

Even though there is a demand for experts in labor relations, it is a difficult field for a beginner to enter. Most companies want to hire persons who have a college degree and several years' experience in various aspects of employee relations and business administration.

A new employee in a company's labor relations department may receive training by first helping to conduct studies of union demands concerning seniority practices, overtime pay, and rehiring policies. As the trainee becomes more experienced, he or she may be assigned to help handle grievance cases. The top position in the department is that of labor relations director, whose responsibility is to negotiate labor contracts, handle collective bargaining cases, and help top executives set labor-relations policies for the company.

To become successful in labor relations, a person must study labor legislation and labor economics. Personnel management and business administration and organization are also required.

UNIT 7

Management Functions

You learned in Unit 1 that to produce goods and services a business needs natural resources, labor, and capital. In addition, there is a critical fourth factor of production—management. Managers make things happen. They set goals, acquire facilities, employ workers, and put money to work in useful ways. Managerial efforts result in the production of goods and services for customers to buy.

In this last unit, you will learn about the various tools and techniques that managers use to perform the planning, organizing, leading, and controlling functions of management. You will also learn how managers make decisions and how managers use information and research to assist in solving business problems.

Steven P. Jobs, whose biographical profile appears on the next page, is a manager who has had to make many important decisions. He represents top-level executives of large corporations.

24. Planning and Organizing
25. Controlling and Decision Making

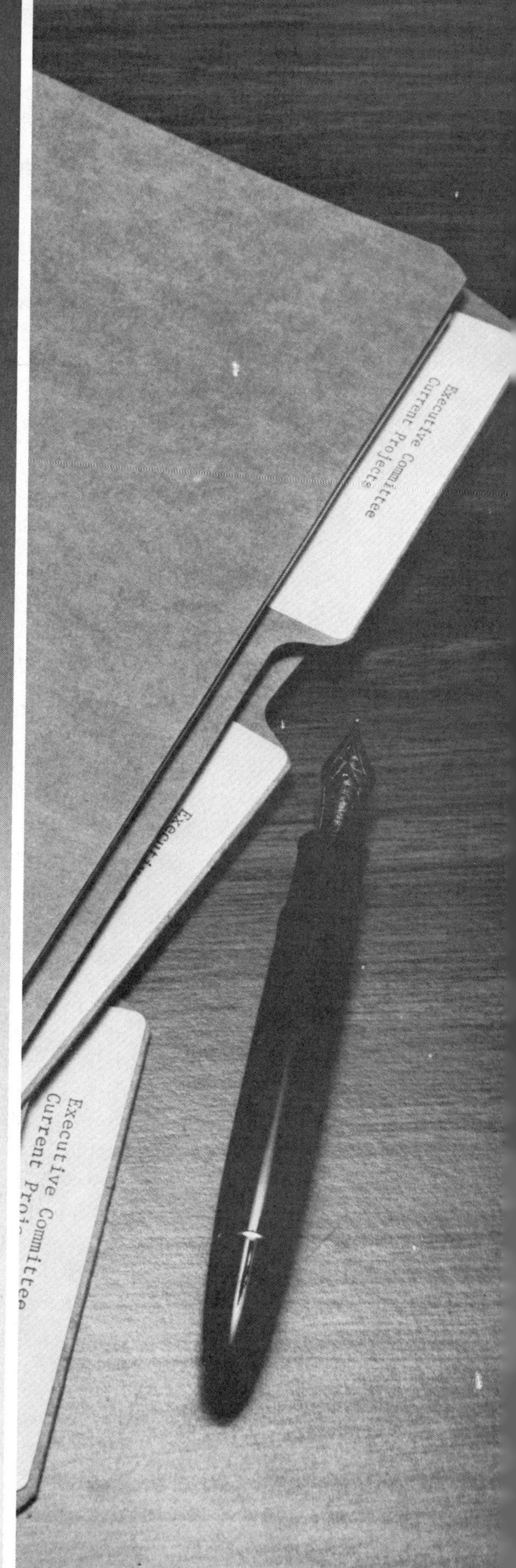

STEVEN P. JOBS

Apples! A simple, tasty fruit and a simple, handy computer. The concept of simplicity represents the Apple personal computer and the Apple ®[1] company philosophy. The Apple—named by Steven P. Jobs, the company's chairman of the board of directors—has become one of the most popular modern inventions.

In 1975 Steven Jobs, then 21, and Steve Wozniak, 26, formed a partnership to manufacture a small computer that Wozniak had developed. Apple I was produced in a garage, but sales increased so rapidly that the new business had to reorganize. By 1976 the partners met Mike Markkula, a marketing person with business experience. The three formed Apple Computer, Inc. in California in 1977 and began mass producing a machine that was soon to become a powerful force in America—the Apple II. By 1980, a more powerful and versatile Apple III appeared, and assured the company a lion's share of the explosive personal computer market.

The success of Apple computers is in large part due to the creative genius of Steven Jobs, a college dropout who frequently lectures on college campuses. Mr. Jobs envisioned the widespread use of the personal computer long before most other computer experts, and was cited by *Time* magazine as the driving force behind the creation of the personal computer industry. He compares the impact of the personal computer on society to the gasoline engine. He insists that the design of the Apple resemble the automobile—practical, attractive and easy to operate.

Even though many companies now make personal computers, Apple Computer is expected to retain its strong market position under Steven Jobs' leadership. The introduction of new types of computers, such as Lisa and MacIntosh, should assure the company's success in a highly competitive field.

[1]Apple is a registered trademark of The Apple Computer Corporation. Any references to Apple refer to this footnote.

24

PLANNING AND ORGANIZING

After studying this chapter you will be able to:

- Describe how the work of managers is different from that of other employees.
- List the tools that managers use for planning purposes.
- Identify the basic elements to be considered in organizing work.
- Describe the importance of assigning duties, delegating authority, and evaluating the work completed.
- Explain the importance of the organization chart.

NATURE OF MANAGEMENT

Managers are responsible for the success of a company. The decisions made by managers determine what a company will do and how well it will perform. There are a number of activities that must be performed by all managers no matter what type or size of company they work for. In this chapter we will examine what managers do and the tools managers use to help them operate a company successfully.

Management Functions

Because there are so many types of managers it is difficult to identify exactly what managers do. The president of a large company is a manager, but so is the owner of a small company. The people who are responsible for personnel departments and purchasing departments, a company's sales force, or its word processing center are all managers. So are supervisors of people working on an assembly line or in a warehouse. While each of these jobs involves many unique activities, each is also concerned with management.

Management is the process of accomplishing the goals of an organization through the effective use of people and other resources. Other resources include money, buildings, equipment, and materials. Studies of all types of managers have shown that their activities can be grouped within four functions: (1) planning, (2) organizing, (3) leading, and (4) controlling. These are shown in Illus. 24–1.

Planning means deciding what needs to be done and how it is to be done. **Organizing** involves obtaining and arranging resources so that work can be accomplished. A manager is **leading** when helping employees to complete their work, and **controlling** when checking to see that the company's objectives have been accomplished as planned. In addition to those four functions, many managers are often involved in other nonmanagement activities that are a part of their jobs.

ILLUS. 24–1
A manager performs all four functions of management.

Management and Nonmanagement Employees

Many employees of a business complete activities that appear to be management functions. They may have responsibility for planning and organizing their own work on a daily basis. For example, a secretary given a report to type will spend time planning how the report should be typed and organizing the materials and equipment that must be used. However, the secretary can only make decisions for one job and has no authority over other people. Most of a secretary's time is spent on nonmanagerial tasks.

A manager spends much of the time completing management functions and is responsible for the work of other people. An employee must perform all four of the functions in order to be considered a manager. However, not all managers spend equal amounts of time on each of the four functions.

One way to distinguish between top-level managers and lower-level managers is the time spent on each function. Top-level managers spend most of their time planning and organizing. Low-level managers in a company usually spend most of their time leading other employees and controlling their performance.

Managers whose main job is to direct the work of other people are called supervisors. **Supervisors** are typically the first (or lowest) level of management in a company and often have several nonmanagerial activities to perform as well. **Executives** are top-level managers who spend almost all of their time on management functions.

THE PLANNING FUNCTION

The first and probably the most important step in management is planning. Planning means looking ahead, setting goals, and considering ways of meeting those goals. A business will have many goals—some as simple as changing the advertising being used and some as difficult as opening a new business in a foreign country.

Setting Goals

Whether a firm is new, old, large, or small, it must set goals or objectives. Goals that are clearly established and properly communicated

Illus. 24-2
Opening a business in a foreign country can be especially challenging and requires much planning.

to employees stand the best chance of being reached. Well-defined goals or objectives provide a basis on which managers can organize, lead, and control their departments or companies successfully. Goals must be developed to determine what the company should do in the future.

Precise Goals. Goals must be specific and meaningful. The goal "to make a profit" is vague; however, the goal "to increase sales by $25,000 in the next six months" is much more specific. Managers must be very careful in setting goals and must consider such factors as (1) the general economic conditions of the country and local area, (2) past sales records, (3) the demand for products or services, (4) the role of competitors, (5) the financial resources of the firm, and (6) for some businesses, the season of the year. Many firms do a great deal of research before they set goals.

Clear and Coordinated Goals. Goals should be clear and should be coordinated with each other. For a small business, goals must be clearly established in the mind of the owner and easily stated orally to the few employees. Once a firm employs two or more managers, goals require more attention. Although each department within a business has separate goals, all goals must be coordinated. Assume, for example, that the sales manager of a firm decides to increase sales and that the advertising manager chooses to reduce advertising costs during a certain year. To boost sales, the firm may need to increase advertising. It is evident that the sales manager and the advertising manager have good intentions but conflicting goals. Managers must work together so that goals become consistent and complementary. If that happens, there is a better chance that goals will be accomplished.

Long- and Short-Term Goals. Successful business firms develop long- and short-term goals. Long-term goals cover a period beyond one year, and short-term goals are for one year or less. The planning process moves from long-term general goals to short-term specific goals. Long-term goals are stated in more general terms because they point the general direction and provide a basis for establishing short-term goals. Once long-term goals are developed, short-term goals for the upcoming year can be planned in detail. Each manager then considers what must be done next week, next month, and next quarter to reach the one-year goals and the long-term goals. Once specific plans are developed, it is much easier to organize and operate the company and to evaluate whether the firm is doing an effective job.

Planning Tools

There are several tools that help managers plan. These tools not only make planning easier, but if used correctly, should result in better plans for the company.

Budgets. The most popular planning tool is the budget. As you learned in

Chapter 12, financial budgets assist managers in determining the best way to use available money to reach goals. Financial budgets, such as sales and advertising budgets, are especially helpful in planning ways to achieve short-term goals.

Schedules. While budgets help in financial planning, schedules are of value in planning for the most effective use of time. For most business purposes, a **schedule** is a time plan for reaching objectives. Schedules identify the tasks to be completed by a department or individual and the approximate time required to complete each task. A supervisor may develop a schedule to organize the work to be done by each employee for a day or a week (see Illus. 24-3). Schedules are usually used by production managers to plan the completion and shipment of orders. Schedules are also used by traveling salespeople to determine which customers they will contact each day. Word processing employees need to schedule letters and reports to make sure they are completed on time.

ILLUS. 24-3
Schedules are used by managers as planning devices.

WORK SCHEDULE FOR JULY 23

Special Order Department

Employee	Order 532	Order 533	Order 534
Shenker, M.	X		
Duffy, P.	X		
Gaston, S.		X	
Robinson, J.		X	
Kingston, C.			X

Standards. Another planning tool for managers is the use of standards. A **standard** is a yardstick or a measure by which something is judged. In business, standards are set to insure that the quality of work completed is always acceptable. Standards may set the number of defective products allowed on an assembly line or the number of calls a salesperson must make during a day. Because standards are used to control as well as to plan, the different types of standards are presented in Chapter 25, Controlling and Decision Making. Managers are responsible for setting standards and for using those standards to judge performance. They also must know when to revise outdated standards.

Policies. As part of planning, managers frequently establish policies. **Policies** are guidelines used in making decisions regarding specific, recurring situations. A policy is often a general rule to be followed by the entire business or by specific departments. A broad policy may state that the work of all employees must be evaluated by supervisors at least twice a year. Thus, even an employee who has been with the company for ten years must be evaluated. Policies help to reduce misunderstandings and encourage consistent decisions for similar conditions.

Procedures. A **procedure** is a list of steps to be followed for performing certain work. In order to implement the policy described in the previous paragraph, specific evaluation procedures must be developed. For routine tasks, procedures improve business efficiency and are of special help to employees who are learning a new job. The procedure shown in flowchart form in Illus. 24–4 would be of great help to a new employee in the catalog order department for the Johnson Company. Experienced employees can help managers design new procedures and improve old ones.

ILLUS. 24–4

Procedures may be placed in flowchart form.

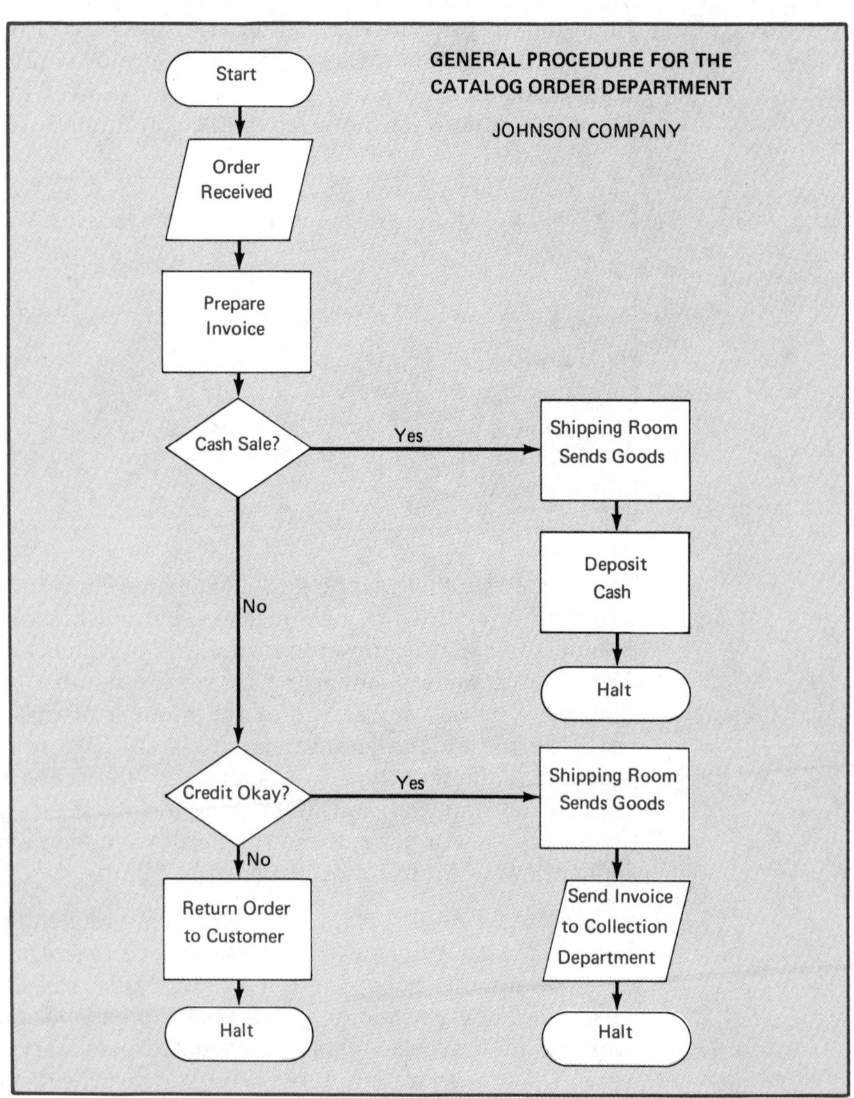

Research. In order to do a good job of planning, managers need to have a great deal of information available. To develop budgets, it helps to know how money was spent in past years, what certain tasks will cost, and how competitors are spending their money. Schedules will be improved if the manager knows how long it takes to complete certain jobs. Better standards and procedures can be established by carefully collecting information on the way jobs are performed. Research is used to collect data for managers and to provide the information needed to improve their planning decisions.

THE ORGANIZING FUNCTION

Planning is an extremely important function of management. However, before a plan can be put into operation, the company must be organized to best carry out the plan. Organizing involves arranging resources and relationships between departments and employees, and defining the responsibility each has for accomplishing the job. For example, when the plan is to start manufacturing a new product, it must be determined who is to be involved in accomplishing each part of the job. The following departments of the business probably need to be involved: manufacturing, personnel, sales, advertising, and finance. Each department will have specific responsibilities. To better understand the organization function, one should become familiar with an organization chart and how it is used.

Role of Organization Charts

A common device used in establishing a business is the organization chart, an example of which is shown in Illus. 24–5. An **organization chart** is a visual device which shows the structure of an organization and the relationships among workers and divisions of work. The importance of the organization chart is to (1) indicate each employee's area of responsibility and to whom each reports, (2) coordinate the division of work and to make those divisions clear, (3) show the types of work done by the business, and (4) indicate lines of promotion.

Large organizations usually give new employees a booklet which explains the organization of the business and shows an organization chart. By understanding an organization chart, employees have some idea of where and how they fit into the company and what types of jobs are available.

Elements of Organization

The manager of a new firm has the complicated task of organizing the entire structure of the business. A manager for an ongoing firm cannot risk ignoring the organization function either. Organization may need to

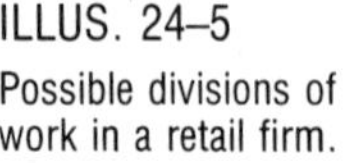
ILLUS. 24–5
Possible divisions of work in a retail firm.

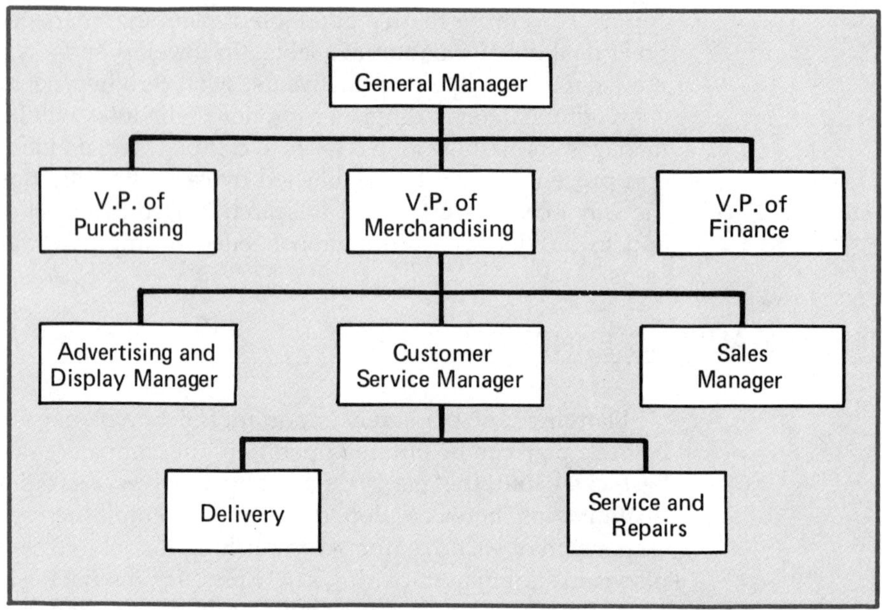

change, for example, when goals are revised or when the business expands. Whether one is a manager of a new or existing department, division, or firm, the process of organizing involves three elements: the division of work, the facilities, and the workers.

Division of Work. In establishing an organization structure, the total work to be done must be divided into units, such as departments. The first consideration is the grouping of activities into broad, natural divisions, such as buying and selling. For firms with few employees, this may be all that is needed to divide the work into manageable units. For large firms, the major divisions may need to be further divided into units before departments of reasonable size can be formed. In a company with an effective division of work, departments are composed of related tasks, work flows well within and among departments, and all responsibilities are assigned to employees.

Major divisions of work vary with the type of firm. Use of at least three divisions, however, is rather common. A retail store may be divided into purchasing, merchandising, and operations. A manufacturing firm's divisions may include production, marketing, and finance. Most firms have an administrative unit and a personnel unit.

As a business grows, the number of major divisions must be increased or new units must be added to existing divisions. When a retail store expands, the basic divisions of buying and selling may be subdivided. Selling may be subdivided into advertising, personal selling, and customer service. Buying, on the other hand, may include purchasing and receiving. Determining how to divide work into efficient units is based on (1) the type of work to be done in each business and (2) the amount of work to be done.

Organization is necessary in a small business as well as in a large business. For example, the owner of a retail store that sells television sets, radios, and stereos has two employees—A and B. Employee A is placed in charge of television sets by the owner but is to call the owner if there is a problem. Employee A is also in charge of the store when the owner is absent. Employee B is in charge of radios and stereos but is to bring any problem to the owner. Employee B is told that Employee A is in charge of the store when the owner is absent. This example illustrates how organizations assign responsibility and delegate authority.

Facilities. While divisions of work are being established, the physical aspects of organizing must also be considered. These aspects include providing necessary equipment and materials for performing tasks and arranging the layout of the facilities so that all work flows smoothly.

Work should move through the business as efficiently as possible. Employees should not have to waste time or motions, and work should not be delayed. An office clerk, for example, who files records frequently not only needs appropriate file cabinets but the cabinets should be located close to the clerk's desk in order to save steps.

Physical working conditions also have an effect on the morale of workers. Job satisfaction is influenced by lighting, temperature control, ventilation, color of walls, cleanliness of the building, quality of tools and equipment, and such added conveniences as parking facilities and lunchrooms.

ILLUS. 24-6
Productivity is strongly affected by the physical environment in which employees work.

Workers. Dividing the work into manageable units and providing adequate equipment and facilities must be done with the workers in mind. In fact, organizing involves establishing good relationships between the employees, the work to be performed, and the facilities needed so that productivity will be high. In part, organization is a successful matching of the employee and the employee's materials and work.

Characteristics of Good Organization

When a business is operated by one person, there is little need for an organization chart—all of the work is performed by one person. The need for organization increases when two or more persons work together. When two or more persons engage in any kind of cooperative activity, be they members of a football team or construction workers building a house, they can accomplish better results if the overall task is divided so that each member has certain specific duties to perform. Thus, as soon as one employee is hired by a businessperson, problems of organization develop because responsibility must be divided. We will now examine basic characteristics of good organization that apply to the management of workers.

Responsibilities Are Assigned and Authority is Delegated. **Responsibility** is the obligation to do an assigned task. In a good organization, the assigned tasks are clearly identified so that all employees know exactly the tasks for which they are responsible.

Authority is the right to make decisions about work assignments and to require other employees to perform assigned tasks. Authority is delegated from the top of the organization down through the lowest levels. One of the greatest mistakes in business is to assign responsibilities to employees without giving them sufficient authority to carry out those responsibilities. Each employee and each supervisor should know specifically (1) what each job is to accomplish, (2) what the duties are, (3) what authority accompanies the job, (4) who the manager in charge is, (5) who reports to the manager, and (6) what is considered satisfactory performance.

There are all sorts of handicaps that may arise if there is not definite organization for a business. Unless employees specifically know their responsibilities, duties, and authority, they are not likely to do their best work. Furthermore, there is likely to be confusion existing most of the time. For instance, the person handling credits and the person handling sales may get into disputes through misunderstandings.

An organization chart showing personnel and departments definitely places responsibility for major duties and shows authority. When responsibility and authority are understood, overlapping duties can be eliminated easily. By pointing out authority, such a chart can also be helpful in eliminating conflicts between individuals and between departments.

The organization charts shown in Illustrations 24–7, 24–8, and 24–9 show how a business may grow from a one-person enterprise into a partnership with specialized duties, and then expand as additional employees assume certain responsibilities.

Illus. 24–10 on page 480 shows in more detail how the authority is delegated and the tasks are performed in a small retail store operated by an owner and two employers.

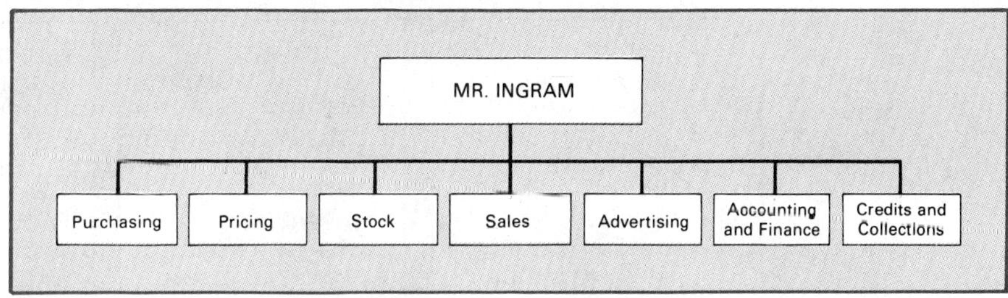

ILLUS. 24–7
The owner of a proprietorship performs all of the work.

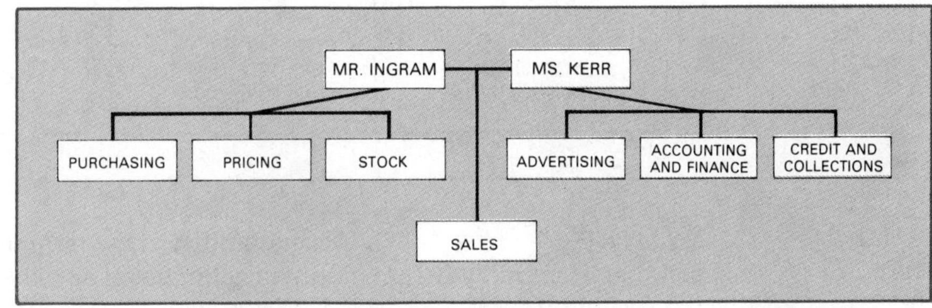

ILLUS. 24–8
There is a division of work in a partnership.

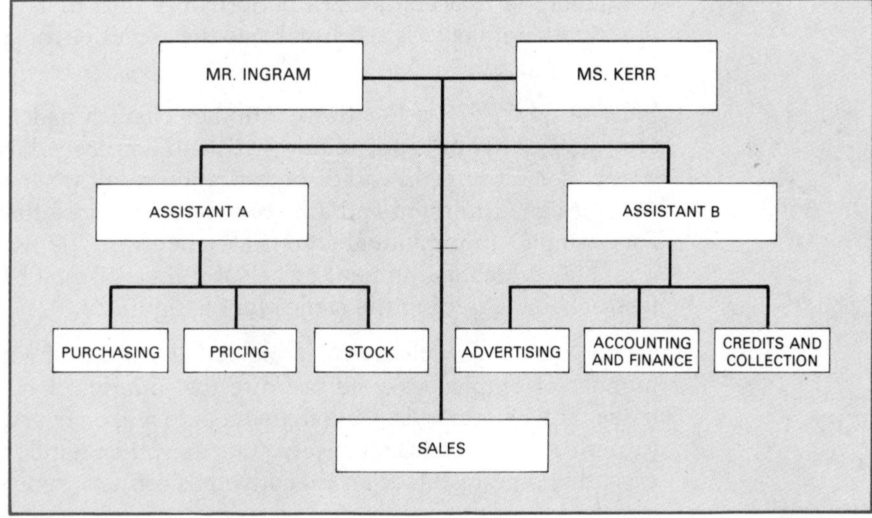

ILLUS. 24–9
In an expanded partnership, there is a division of work and a delegation of authority.

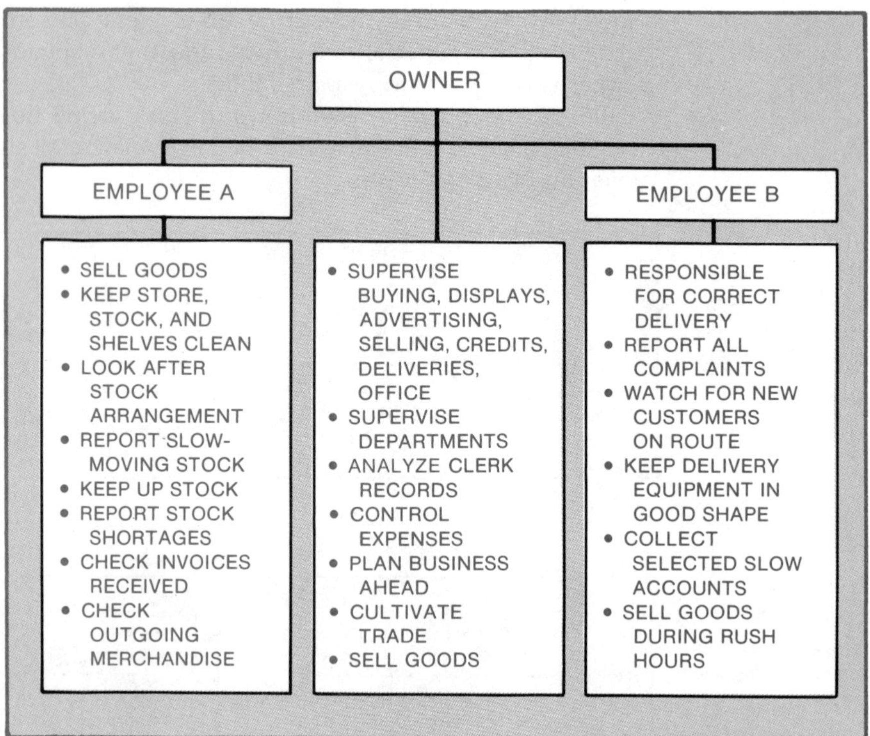

ILLUS. 24–10
Possible organization for a retail store.

Quality of Work is Evaluated. **Accountability** is the term used to refer to the fact that each individual in an organization is responsible to a superior for the quality of work performed. When an executive assigns responsibility and delegates authority to a certain employee, that executive assumes the responsibility for insuring that the work is completed and for evaluating the quality of that employee's performance. Or, to say this another way, the chosen employee is accountable to the executive for effectively performing the assigned work.

Unity of Command is Practiced. Another characteristic of good organization, **unity of command,** requires that no employee have more than one supervisor. Confusion and disorganization result when subordinates have work assigned to them and are accountable to more than one supervisor. For example, an individual who is assigned work by two supervisors may not know which assignment to perform first, or may be given conflicting instructions regarding the same work assignment.

A Reasonable Span of Control is Maintained. **Span of control** refers to the number of employees who are directly supervised by one person. The manager who supervises too many people will be overworked and unable to perform all duties effectively. On the other hand, waste of valuable executive time results if an executive has too few people to supervise. In general, the span of control can be larger at the lower levels of an organization than at the upper levels. For example, the manager of a unit in a department store may supervise 15 or more workers, while the president may find it difficult to supervise the work of 4 or 5 vice-presidents.

Types of Organization Structures

The two principal types of organization structures that are used in business are (1) the line and (2) the line-and-staff organization.

Line Organization. In a **line organization,** all authority and responsibility may be traced in a direct line from the president down to the lowest administrative unit in the organization. A line organization is shown in Illus. 24–11 (sales is the only area for which the complete organization is shown). The lines joining the individual boxes indicate the lines of authority. The lines show, for example, that the president has authority over the sales manager, that the sales manager has authority over the assistant sales manager, that the assistant sales manager has authority over the branch manager, and the branch managers have authority over the sales representatives.

ILLUS. 24–11
Direct lines of authority and responsibility exist in a line organization.

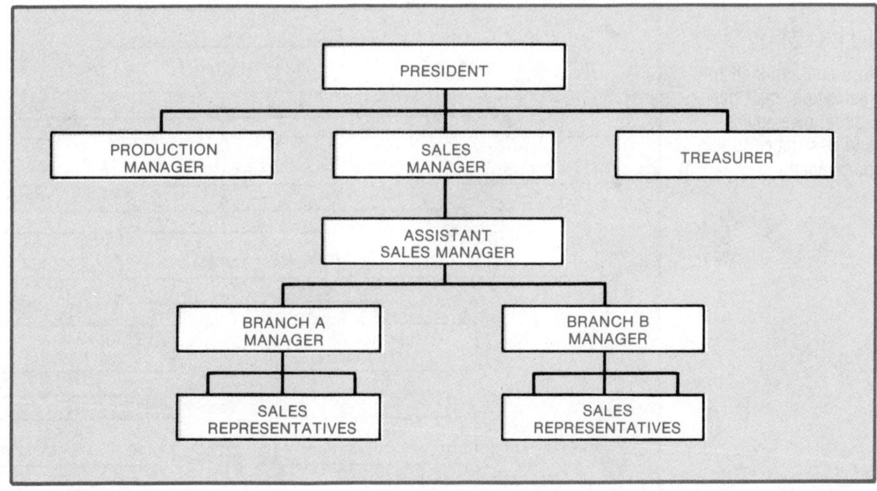

In a line organization the president has direct control over all units of the business, but responsibilities and authority are passed along from one person to another down to the lowest level of the organization. Under this form of organization, each person is responsible to only one manager who in turn is responsible to someone else. This type of organization can be very efficient, since new plans and ideas can be put into effect immediately. It is most often used by small businesses or businesses that are very specialized.

Line-and-Staff Organization. Most large businesses use the **line-and-staff organization,** which adds staff specialists to a line organization. As a business grows larger, the work increases in amount and in complexity. The result is that line personnel have more and more difficulty in developing the skills needed in all of the areas for which they are responsible. To solve this problem and still retain the advantages of direct and definite lines of authority, staff specialists are added to the line organization to give advice and assistance to line personnel. Staff personnel have no authority over line personnel—that is, staff personnel cannot require anyone in the line organization to perform any task. They are there to help with specialized jobs. Thus, line personnel are still responsible to only one supervisor.

The line-and-staff organization in Illus. 24-12 is like the line organization in Illus. 24-11 except for the addition of two staff specialists—the advertising specialist and the marketing research specialist. The fact that their responsibility is to give specialized advice and assistance to the sales organization of the business is indicated in the organization chart by the broken lines. The type of organization will determine whether a manager must have expertise in a number of areas only generally related to the unit being managed, or whether specialists will be available to help.

ILLUS. 24–12

In a line-and-staff organization, staff personnel give advice and assistance to line personnel.

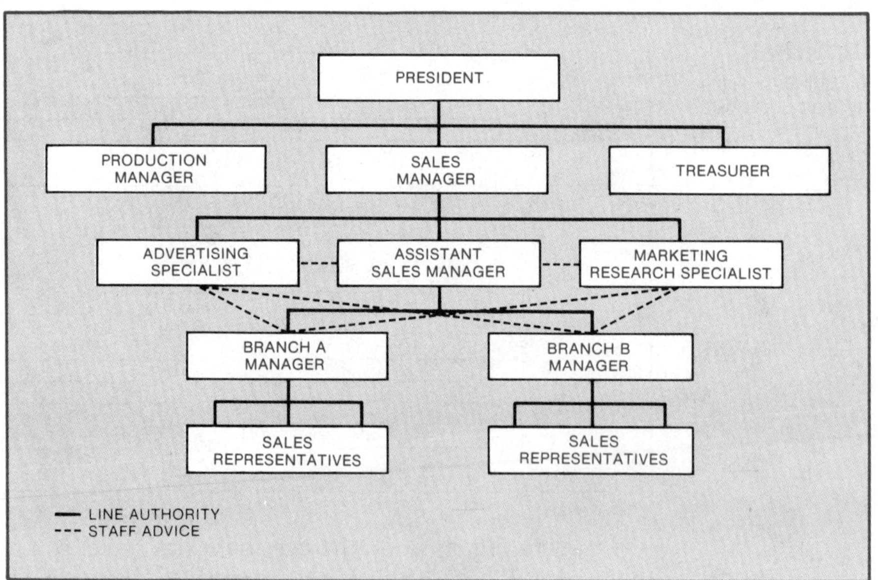

NEW TERMS AND CONCEPTS

Define the following terms and concepts, which can be found in boldface type on the page shown in parentheses.

management (470)
planning (470)
organizing (470)
leading (470)
controlling (470)
supervisors (471)
executives (471)
schedule (473)
standard (473)
policies (473)
procedure (474)
organization chart (475)
responsibility (478)
authority (478)
accountability (480)
unity of command (480)
span of control (480)
line organization (481)
line-and-staff organization (482)

CHAPTER REVIEW

1. What are the four functions of management?
2. How can you identify if an employee is a manager?
3. What makes a supervisor different from an executive?
4. Identify the difference between a general goal and a specific goal.
5. How do coordinated goals benefit a company?
6. What is the period of time covered by a short-term goal?
7. Explain how a schedule is used to help a manager plan.
8. Develop a standard that could be used in a word processing center.
9. Why are written procedures valuable for new employees?
10. List four purposes of an organization chart.
11. What factors should be used when establishing divisions of work within a company?
12. How can you determine if authority and responsibility have been assigned properly?
13. Why should an employee report to only one supervisor?
14. How is the span of control different at lower and upper levels of an organization?
15. What do broken lines in an organization chart mean?

QUESTIONS FOR CLASS DISCUSSION

1. Why should the supervisor of a warehouse be considered a manager?
2. Discuss why executives spend more time planning and organizing than do supervisors.
3. Why are long-term general goals developed before short-term specific goals?
4. How is your schedule of classes related to a business schedule?

5. Explain how the flowchart in Illus. 24-4 can help a new employee in the catalog order department.
6. Why should all employees in a company be familiar with the company's organization chart?
7. What problems are likely to result when responsibilities are assigned to an employee, but that employee is given no authority to carry out the assigned responsibilities?
8. Identify the result if a manager fails to assign duties and responsibilities to others.
9. Why do most small business firms use a line organization rather than a line-and-staff organization?
10. If the sales manager of a nationwide organization and an office manager of a district office both have jurisdiction over salespeople working out of the district office, what can be done to avoid misunderstandings?

PROBLEMS AND PROJECTS

1. You and a friend plan to open a laundromat with 12 washing machines and 4 dryers. Write several policies that will help you plan the running of the business.
2. Draw an organization chart for an automobile dealer and service station based on the following facts:
   a. The owner of the business is J.M. Gray.
   b. The business consists of a service station, a used-car sales department, a repair department, and a parts department.
   c. Gray's son, John, acts as his assistant but also manages the parts department and supervises to a certain extent all of the other functions.
   d. B.L. O'Hara and three assistants have charge of the repair department.
   e. O.P. Thompson has charge of the used-car sales department, but a young woman by the name of Linda Williams spends most of her time selling the used cars.
   f. Gray's nephew, Jim Blake, takes care of the service station with the assistance of two part-time employees.
3. Interview a manager and list all of the major activities he or she completes on the job. Then decide with your classmates to which management function, if any, each activity best relates.
4. With the help of your teacher, identify five activities that must be completed by your class during the next three weeks. Then develop a schedule that shows how you plan to complete the activities.
5. Jane Findley has just developed a new game that she plans to sell by mail order for $10.50 during the next Christmas season. Write two long-term general goals and three short-term specific goals that would be appropriate as guides for Ms. Findley's new business.

CASE 24–1

Christine Jordan started a business 20 years ago as a one-person operation. It grew slowly for a while because Jordan did all of the work. As the business expanded, she hired more people. The business now employs 100 people. She is the president and manages the business personally. She has an open-door policy, and all employees are permitted and expected to come to her for answers to their problems. She has given responsibility to her sales manager, her producution manager, and a purchasing agent; but she makes all of the decisions or approves the decisions before they are made. She thinks that an organization chart is unnecessary because everybody knows how the organization operates, and they understand that she is the boss.

Required:

1. What do you think about the efficiency of an organization of this type?
2. How do you think the department heads and the employees feel about the present type of organization and management?
3. Do you have any suggestions for the improvement of this business?

CASE 24–2

The Toyline Company makes and sells a line of children's toys. In six months, retail stores will begin buying the firm's products in large quantities in preparation for the Christmas shopping season. The marketing manager is confident that sales will be higher this year than last. Thus, several new salespeople have been hired and are being trained for the upcoming rush period. Increased advertising has also been planned.

The production manager, on the other hand, has been running into difficulties getting raw materials from the firm's only supplier. Production has been cut by 20 percent during the last two months, and the inventory of finished goods is less than planned. The production manager, not having received word to the contrary, has planned to keep the finished goods inventory at last year's level. There is no indication as to when the raw material problem will be solved. In addition, the union contract expires in three months and there has been discussion of a possible strike.

Required:

1. What management problems are apparent in the Toyline Company?
2. Why have these problems occurred?
3. Using the management tools discussed in the chapter, give examples of how each of the problems could be solved.

Have You Thought About Becoming . . .
. . . A STRATEGIC PLANNER?

You have learned that planning is one of the most important management activities. However, as companies grow, managers have to spend more time on other activities. This means less time is available for planning, which results in problems for the company.

To help solve this problem, some companies have developed a staff position of strategic planner. Managers are still responsible for planning in these companies, but they can get help from the strategic planners.

Duties of strategic planners involve scheduling decisions and developing materials and guides to assist managers. They often conduct research, gather information, and communicate with many people as a part of their planning duties. Strategic planners must be familiar with all types of business information that can be helpful to managers. They must be able to summarize large amounts of information into meaningful reports. Often they will be asked to evaluate the plans of managers or help coordinate the plans of several departments.

Strategic planners are found only in very large companies today. You probably have not heard of this career before. However, it shows that new types of jobs are being developed in businesses. Just as the strategic planner was developed to help managers do a better job of planning, other jobs are sure to be created in the future to improve business operations and management.

Most strategic planners have a Master's degree in Business Administration with course work in all of the major areas of business operations. They also will have completed several courses in statistics and research.

25

CONTROLLING AND DECISION MAKING

After studying this chapter you will be able to:

- Identify four general types of business controls.
- Discuss four areas needing special types of controls to reduce losses.
- Discuss the need for management information.
- Explain the uses of business research.
- List and explain the steps in problem solving.

Managers must be able to plan, organize, lead, and control. You have already learned about the activities involved in the first three management functions. In this chapter, we shall study the last function—controlling. Managers cannot do a good job of controlling if poor planning, poor organizing, or bad leadership is being practiced. To complete all four management functions effectively, managers must be able to make good decisions. An effective decision-making process used by business managers is also described in this chapter.

THE MANAGEMENT PROCESS

Planning involves setting goals for a business. Organizing deals with arranging the business so goals can be met. Leading involves guiding employees so the business operates according to plans. The controlling function involves determining whether the goals are being met and taking necessary action if goals are not being met. A manager must be able to determine why problems are developing and what can be done to solve the problems.

Each of the management functions is related to all of the other functions. Illus. 25–1 shows that management is a continuous process and that all functions are related.

ILLUS. 25–1

The four functions of management are directly related.

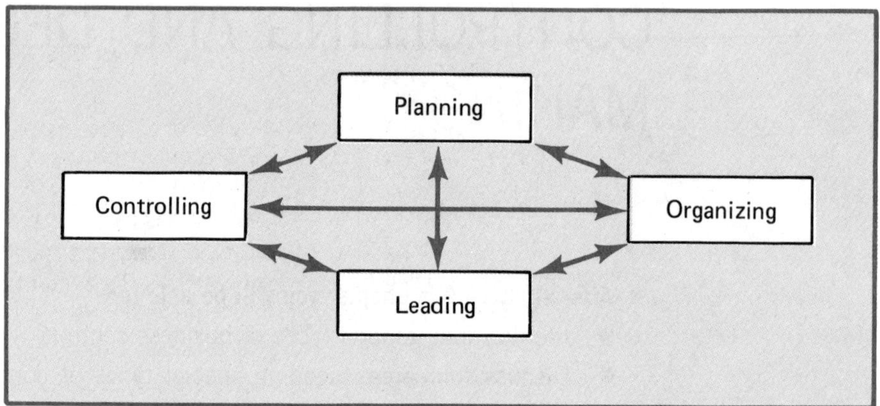

Without good planning to establish goals for the business, it is difficult to develop an organizational structure or assign authority and responsibility. Managers must have goals before they can decide on the best leadership style to use. In order to determine how well a company is performing, managers need to know what the company planned to do and who was responsible for completing all of the activities. When managers identify a problem, that information should be used in planning to correct the problem.

THE CONTROLLING FUNCTION

The process of controlling involves three basic activities:

1. Establishing standards for each of the company's goals.
2. Measuring and comparing current performance with the established standards to see if goals are being met.
3. Taking corrective action when problems are identified.

The important activities in controlling are shown in the following example. A business has a goal to manufacture and deliver to a customer 1,000 made-to-order blankets by a specific date. The standard is to produce 25 items each day for 40 consecutive days. During the first ten days, only 200 blankets are produced. Because production is 50 blankets below the standard—250 blankets in ten days—the manager must take action to increase production during the remaining 30 days. The corrective action may include scheduling overtime work or assigning more workers to the task.

As another example, the manager of a shoe store wants to make sure that new styles of shoes sell rapidly. The standard is that 30 percent of all shoes in a new style are sold within one month. If only 20 percent of a certain style are sold after one month, corrective action must be taken. The manager may choose to increase the advertising for the shoes, give salespeople a higher commission for selling that style, or mark down the price to sell more. The manager will also want to use this information when planning purchases in the future.

In each example, the manager had to set a standard based on the work to be accomplished. Then the standard was used to see if the company's goals would be met. Finally, if the standard was not being met, the manager had to determine what could be done to correct the problem.

Notice that in both examples the manager did not wait very long to begin measuring performance. Controlling activities should be completed before the problem is too big or too expensive to correct.

Types of Standards

Standards are determined by managers in the planning stage. The standards become the means for judging success and for applying controls. By setting fair standards, managers can identify employees working below standards as well as those working above.

Several types of standards are needed to control business operations. The standards used depend on the type of business, the size of the business, and the activities being controlled. The major types of standards used include quantity standards, quality standards, time standards, and cost standards.

Quantity Standards. Quantity standards are used frequently in business. Production managers specify the minimum number of units to be produced each hour, day, or month by individual workers or groups of workers. Sales managers establish the number of prospects that sales representatives must contact daily or weekly. Office supervisors may set an acceptable day's work for typists by the number of letters typed or indicate to data entry personnel the number of lines of information to be entered in one hour.

Quality Standards. Quantity standards alone are often not enough to judge an employee, a product, or a service. A fast worker, for example, can be very careless, or a slow worker can be extremely careful. Thus the quality of the work performed is often just as important as the quantity produced.

Perfection—no errors—may be the only acceptable standard for much of the work in a business. A light bulb that does not work will not sell; a letter with errors is not mailable. While perfection is a desirable standard, it

ILLUS. 25-2
There are numerous ways to visualize and present standards. Some managers find wall charts useful.

may not always be practical to hire hundreds of people to examine each finished product. Sampling a few bulbs every hour, however, may be enough of a spot check to catch faulty batches of bulbs.

If quality standards are carefully set, they should not have to be lowered. Numerous defective products reaching consumers will eventually decrease sales. When customer confidence is lost, the reputation of the business suffers. Management invites problems when quality standards are not given adequate attention.

Time Standards. Quantity and quality standards are tied closely to time standards. Most business activities can be measured by time. Time standards, however, are more important for some business firms, or for certain departments, than for others. Building contractors, bakers, or newspaper people normally have strict timetables to meet. For such people, delays may cause an immediate financial loss for the business.

There are various time control devices that managers use. Schedules, which are used for planning, also serve as time control aids. For example, a schedule may indicate a planned series of events and also show when events actually occur. The production goal for the week, for instance, may be planned and posted on Monday. On Friday the actual units produced are displayed. The difference between planned and actual figures, if any, aids in evaluating the production of the department and provides helpful information for planning future production goals. Therefore, schedules, like other planning devices, are also controlling devices.

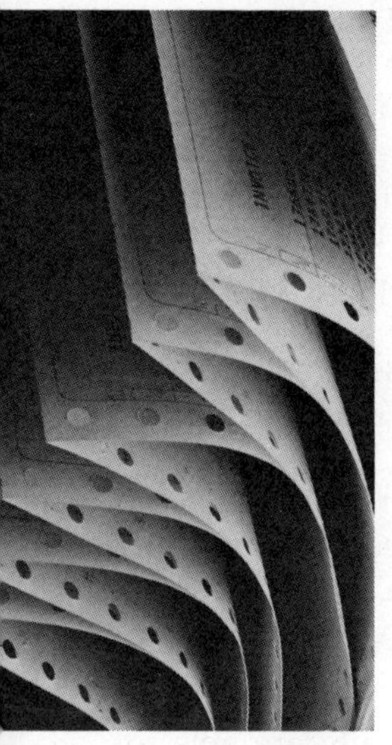

Cost Standards. The success or failure of a firm is measured in money—profit or loss. While trying to increase profits, managers are constantly aware of two specific objectives: (1) to increase sales and (2) to decrease costs. Not all managers or employees are directly connected with work that will increase sales. However, most employees and managers do influence costs. Wasting material or taking more time than necesssary to perform a task adds to the cost of doing business. Increased costs, without a proportionate increase in sales, will decrease profit. Business firms must be cost conscious at all times.

Generally more attention is given to cost controls than to any other type of control. The control devices used, as a result, are numerous. One of the main purposes of the accounting department is to provide detailed cost information. This is why the head of an accounting department is often called a controller. Most managers, however, act as cost controllers in some way.

The most widely used controlling device is the budget. Budgets, like schedules and standards, are also planning devices. When a budget is prepared, it is a planning device; after that it is a controlling device. Actual cost figures are collected and compared with estimated or planned figures. These comparisons permit judgments about the success of planning efforts and provide clues for making changes that will help assure that goals are reached.

Controlling Costs

All managers need to be constantly watching for areas where costs can be reduced. Excessive costs reduce the profit of a business. There are several areas in a business where managers can anticipate cost problems. They are inventory, credit, theft, and employee health and safety. Planning should be done in each area to prevent excessive costs from occurring.

Inventory. Businesses need to keep enough products in stock to be able to meet customer needs. If the inventory is too low, sales may be missed. However, if inventory is too high, the company is spending money for storage, and profits will be lower as a result. Also, there may be products in inventory that are never used or sold. If that happens, the company will lose all of the money invested in those products. Managers must keep close track of inventories so they do not get too large or too small. Purchasing must be done carefully to select products that can be sold at a profit. Products must be purchased at the right time and in the right quantities to reduce the inventory cost of a company. There are several statistical methods managers use to help them make these decisions.

Credit. Many businesses today must be able to extend credit to customers. Most businesses use credit when buying products from suppliers. If credit is extended to customers and they do not pay their bills, the company loses money. Also, businesses which use credit too often when making purchases spend a great deal of money for interest payments.

As discussed in Chapter 16, businesses must develop credit policies to reduce the amount of losses. Customers should be checked carefully before credit is given to them. Billing and collection procedures should be developed so that most accounts are collected on time. Managers need to watch the age of accounts because the longer an account is overdue, the greater the chance of loss to the company.

Managers responsible for purchasing must control the amount of money the company owes to other businesses. It is easy to make too many purchases on credit. When this happens, the interest charges are very high, and the company may not have enough money to pay all debts on time.

Credit should be used when the company will lose money if the purchase is not made. Credit may also be needed for the purchase of expensive equipment or large orders of merchandise.

Managers must be sure bills are paid on time to protect the credit reputation of the business. If a cash discount is offered, it should be checked to see if the company would benefit from the use of the discount. Before credit is used, the terms should be checked to see what it will cost. Credit can be a good business tool if used carefully.

Theft. By establishing theft controls, business firms usually are able to reduce losses. You learned in Chapter 12 that specific steps can be taken to safeguard cash from loss. Protection against losses from forged, stolen, or worthless checks was discussed in Chapter 15.

The theft of merchandise from warehouses and stores is a major concern of business. Retail stores are the hardest hit by such losses. One recent estimate showed that retailers lose between $30 and $40 billion annually due to crime, much of which is from theft of merchandise. Shoplifting by customers and employees equals about 6 percent of total sales each year. Much of the loss occurs during the Christmas shopping season when stores are crowded and part-time persons are employed. Some devices a company can use to reduce losses are shown in Illus. 25-3.

Many retail stores, warehouses, and trucks containing goods are burglarized during the night or on weekends. Security persons can be hired to lessen such thefts. A company can also install burglar alarms and purchase insurance.

Health and Safety. Even when employees are absent from work because of sickness or injury, the company must continue to operate. Other employees must be available to fill in for the absent employee. Usually the salary of both the absent employee and the substitute employee must be paid. Health insurance costs are often paid by the company as well. One study recently estimated that the annual costs to a business for employee absence and health costs amount to almost $3,000 for each employee.

ILLUS. 25-3
Stores must protect themselves against loss from theft.

Methods for Controlling Shoplifting

1. Hire security guards (in uniform).
2. Hire store detectives (not in uniform).
3. Install television cameras that scan entrances, exits, and check-out counters.
4. Place mirrors at key locations, which give views of various parts of the store.
5. Attach special inventory tags to products which give a signal when products are taken from the store. (When an article is sold, the salesperson will remove the tag.)
6. Station attendants at dressing rooms.
7. Keep unused checkout aisles closed.
8. Keep small expensive items in locked display cases.
9. Post signs warning customers of the consequences of shoplifting.
10. Train employees in what to do when they spot a shoplifter.

Costs that result from health and safety problems can be reduced. Companies should provide safety training for all employees. Work stations and equipment should be inspected regularly to be sure they operate correctly and safely.

MANAGEMENT INFORMATION SYSTEMS

To do a good job of planning, organizing, leading, and controlling, managers must have a great deal of information available. Records on production and sales, personnel, expenses, and profit or loss are needed before decisions can be made. Data must be collected, organized, and made available to managers so decisions can be made quickly and efficiently.

Even in very small businesses, the manager will be unable to remember all of the information needed to make decisions. In large companies with many managers and hundreds of employees, it would be impossible to operate without a systematic way to gather information for managers to use in decision making.

Management information systems were described in detail in Chapter 19. Every company needs such a system as an important management tool. The management information systems of large companies use a mainframe or minicomputer to process all of the information needed by management. Because of the development of time-sharing systems and microcomputers, and the low cost of those systems, small companies are also using computer technology for information management. Managers find computers to be very helpful in controlling business operations.

BUSINESS RESEARCH

Management information systems are designed to provide needed data to managers so decisions can be made and problems can be solved. However there are times when new problems arise or information is not available to answer questions or solve problems. When managers are unable to make decisions because of a lack of information, they may need to conduct research.

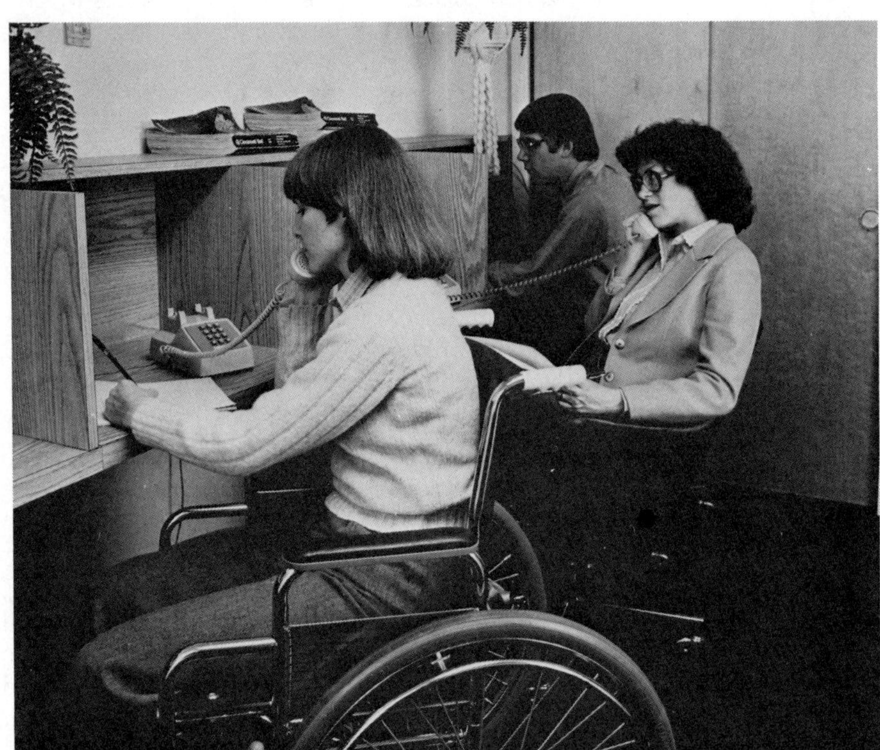

ILLUS. 25-4
Marketing surveys are an important type of business research.

Areas of Business Research

Business research is conducted in many areas to aid in decision making. Marketing research and product development research are two common areas. Personnel research studies are conducted on such topics as employee motivation and training techniques. Financial executives need the results of research that deal with decisions related to borrowing and investing. Research results are also needed regarding economic matters, such as those related to inflationary trends and forecasts of the level of economic activity for the country and for a particular type of business. These and other types of business research help executives make important decisions relative to the growth and development of their companies.

Resources for Conducting Business Research

Much needed business research is, of course, done by business itself. Most large companies have research departments or divisions which engage in research projects related to the specific problems of the company. Since research departments are expensive to maintain, small companies must depend to a considerable degree on professional research organizations.

Bureaus of business research and faculty members in universities conduct studies which are helpful to business. Extensive research is undertaken by various divisions of the federal government, and much of this research is available to and useful for business. Research studies which are useful to particular industries are made by trade associations. There are also many research organizations and individual consultants that may be used by a company to conduct a particular research study.

DECISION-MAKING

In the process of planning, organizing, leading, and controlling, managers are faced with problems that require making decisions. Some decisions are made at the top level of management—for example, by the president; some are made by middle management—for example, by vice-presidents; some are made at low levels of management—for example, by department heads and supervisors. It is important to the overall success of any business that the decisions be made as carefully as possible at every level of management.

Problems and Decision Making

Generally, a **problem** is a difficult situation requiring a solution. Problems usually do not have single solutions; instead, they have a series of possible solutions. There may be several good solutions, but there may also be several poor solutions. For example, the problem may be how to ship goods from Texas to Illinois. Possible solutions are to ship by airplane, boat, train, or truck. Depending on the circumstances, any one of the shipping methods could be the best or the worst solution. To find the best solution, managers should follow a systematic approach to solving problems.

Steps in Problem Solving

Every problem can be analyzed by following a series of steps. These steps include identifying the problem, listing possible solutions, analyzing the possible solutions, and selecting the best solution.

Identify the Problem. Before a manager can make a decision that may solve a problem, the problem must first be located and identified. Often a manager may not even be aware that a problem exists. For example, employees may be unhappy about another worker. The problem may not be known to a manager unless employees communicate this concern.

A manager must also be careful not to identify a symptom as the problem. A **symptom** is a sign or indication of something that appears to be the problem. When a patient complains of a headache, the headache may be a symptom. The problem could be high blood pressure, a cold, or other ailment. Falling sales in an appliance store may be a symptom. The problem could be ineffective advertising, a bad store location, low quality merchandise, poor service, and so on. Therefore, just treating the symptom may not solve the problem.

Why are customers not entering the appliance store? Why are customers entering the store but not buying? Managers can often identify the problem by asking such questions, thereby distinguishing between the problem and its symptoms.

ILLUS. 25-5
A truckload sale may be a sympton of several serious problems. Can you suggest some of those problems?

List Possible Solutions. Once a problem has been identifed, a manager should immediately begin to list all possible solutions. For example, if the problem is one of determining the best advertising medium to use, all possible ways to advertise should be listed. Every problem will have at least two or more possible solutions, and no solution should be overlooked at this point in the problem-solving process. For finding new solutions to old problems or for finding imaginative solutions to new problems, the brainstorming technique, as described in Chapter 18, can be helpful. No attempt should be made to evaluate the list of possible solutions at this time.

Analyze Possible Solutions. The third step in problem solving is to analyze the solutions. This is done by studying each possible solution separately, comparing the solutions, and reducing the number of solutions to the best two or three. To study each solution fairly, information may be needed from business records, trade associations, libraries, consultants, and government sources. The use of a management information system and business research of the type described earlier in this chapter is important.

When all of the necessary information has been collected, the strengths and weaknesses of each solution are examined one by one. Then the solutions are compared. An attempt is made to classify the solutions in some way, such as extremely desirable, somewhat desirable, and least desirable. Some solutions may be too costly or impractical, while others may be inexpensive or be very practical. For example, in a list of solutions containing advertising media being considered by a small appliance store, it may be found that television is far too costly while newspaper advertising is quite inexpensive. After all the analyses have been completed, there may be two or three solutions that will effectively solve the problem.

Select the Best Solution. The last step in problem solving is to make the final decision from among the remaining solutions. Some managers take several days or more before selecting the solution. Managers may discuss the best solutions with employees or close associates. Others may use past experiences with similar problems. Only after much thought and deliberation is the final decision made and put into action.

THE IMPORTANCE OF BUSINESS MANAGEMENT

Operating a business is a very complex process. Even managers of small businesses must make product, marketing, personnel, and finance decisions every day. If the manager does not have an organized method for operating the business, problems will soon develop. The manager who knows how to plan, organize, lead, and control will be well prepared to make the decisions needed to operate a business successfully.

NEW TERMS AND CONCEPTS

Define the following terms and concepts, which can be found in boldface type on the page shown in parentheses.

problem (495)

symptom (496)

CHAPTER REVIEW

1. What is a manager doing when involved in controlling activities?
2. How are the management functions related to each other?
3. Identify the three basic activities that are a part of the controlling process.
4. Describe how standards are used by managers involved in controlling.
5. What types of firms are most likely to use time standards?
6. List the type of control that usually is given the most attention in business.
7. What problems are likely to occur if inventory levels are too high in a business?
8. When should credit be used?
9. Approximately how much money is lost annually by retailers to crime of all types?
10. What records are needed by managers to make effective decisions?
11. How can small companies gain access to computer technology for information management?
12. Under what conditions should managers conduct business research?
13. List several resources available to help businesses conduct research.
14. Name the four steps in problem solving.
15. Describe a technique that will help to identify the real problem rather than to identify a symptom of the problem.

QUESTIONS FOR CLASS DISCUSSION

1. Justify the statement that effective management is not possible without good planning.
2. Why should controlling activities begin as soon as a new operation has been started?
3. How should a manager identify appropriate quantity standards for an activity?
4. Which types of standards should be used for a delivery person whose job is to take packages from a store to customers' homes by truck?
5. Why should a manager compare planned budget figures with the actual figures?
6. Identify several ways in which the credit costs of a business can be controlled.
7. Why does the amount of shoplifting in retail stores generally increase during the Christmas shopping season?
8. Why should health and safety programs be considered a part of cost controls?

9. Describe the value of a management information system to the manager of a small business.

10. What are some reasons why managers fail to use a systematic approach to solving problems?

PROBLEMS AND PROJECTS

1. Interview a manager and prepare a report to your class based on the answers you get to the following questions.
   a. What duties do you complete as a manager?
   b. What percentage of your time is spent on each of the management functions: planning, organizing, leading, and controlling?
   c. How do you use budgets and standards in your work?
   d. What are the most common types of problems that you must deal with as a manager?
2. In the following chart, several items from a budget of a business are shown. The categories for which budgets have been made are shown in column 1. The budgeted amounts are shown in column 2 and the actual amounts are shown in column 3. Complete the chart by calculating the difference between the budgeted and actual amounts (column 4) and the percentage increase or decrease (column 5).

	Budget	**Actual**	**Difference**	**% + or –**
Sales	$680,000	$720,000	______	______
Merchandise Returns	11,000	12,500	______	______
Cost of Goods	229,400	240,00	______	______
Operating Expenses	52,000	46,500	______	______
Administrative Costs	34,000	31,500	______	______
Marketing Expenses	306,000	350,500	______	______
Net Profit	47,600	39,000	______	______

3. Write a sample quantity standard, quality standard, and time standard for each of the following situations.
   a. a furniture factory building chairs.
   b. a salesperson calling on customers in a new territory.
   c. an assembly line manufacturing automobile tires.
   d. a cashier-checker at a supermarket.
4. Take the list of methods for controlling shoplifting, shown in Illus. 25–3, to a local store. Observe which methods are being used in the store. Then ask the store manager which other methods are being used.

5. A list of symptoms of business problems follows. For each symptom, write a question that could be used to help identify the actual problem.
   a. The rate of merchandise returns has increased greatly in the last six months.
   b. A new employee quit without giving notice.
   c. Advertising costs have increased by 10 percent this year.
   d. The number of customer accounts with debts over 60 days is increasing.
   e. There have been a number of times that the assembly line has had to be stopped due to defective materials.

CASE 25–1

Yvette and Eric are both considering careers as managers. One day they were discussing their views of a manager's work. The following conversation took place:

Eric: A manager's job is really very easy if the company hires good employees. All a manager has to do is be sure the work gets done.

Yvette: I think a manager has to be a good planner. If a manager can tell employees what to do, the employees will take it from there.

Eric: I wonder why companies have so many managers and spend too much time and money on management development.

Yvette: If you ask me, you are either a good manager or you are not. I do not think that taking classes in how to manage a company will do much good.

Eric: I agree. When you think about all of the different types of managers, there cannot be too many common things you could teach all managers.

Required:

1. Analyze the views of Yvette and Eric toward management. Do you agree or disagree?
2. Do you believe companies have too many managers and spend too much time and money on management training?
3. Can people be taught to be better managers?
4. What characteristics are common to all managers' jobs?

CASE 25–2

Jackson Blaine is the manager of the accounting department for the Overton Supply Company, an office supplies wholesaler. A standard had been established that invoices would be typed and mailed to customers within 24 hours after the order was received. Recently Jackson had learned that some invoices were not being mailed until three or four days after the order was received. Upon checking further, he discovered that his department did not always receive the necessary information from the shipping department on schedule.

Required:

1. What are some possible problems in this situation?
2. List the symptoms of the problems.
3. What are some alternative solutions?
4. How would you suggest that Jackson should proceed in this situation?

Have You Thought About Becoming . . .
. . . A CONTROLLER?

The use of resources in a business must be managed very carefully. The accounting department is responsible for controlling the use of financial resources. It is the responsibility of the accounting department to develop policies and procedures for the use of capital in the company and to develop and maintain financial records. Of course, many people are employed in the accounting departments of large companies, and many activities must be completed.

The person responsible for the operation of the accounting department is known as the controller. The controller is one of the top executives of the firm and works with other managers on information management, budgeting, and cost controls.

Within the controller's department there are people responsible for basic accounting, auditing, tax planning and preparation, and other financial activities. Reports are prepared for other departments in the business to help them control their resources.

A controller needs to be well prepared in finance and accounting. Many controllers have both a Master's degree in Business Administration and a CPA (Certified Public Accountant) license. They also have many years of experience in accounting before becoming a controller. Only a very few accountants become controllers, but those that do play an important role in the success of the businesses they help manage.

INDEX

A

B

C

D

E

F

G

H

I

J

K

L

Q

R

S

T

U

V

W

Y

Z